Series Editors

W. Hansmann
W. T. Hewitt
W. Purgathofer

M. D. Harrison and
J. C. Torres (eds.)

Design, Specification and Verification
of Interactive Systems '97

Proceedings of the Eurographics Workshop
in Granada, Spain,
June 4–6, 1997

Eurographics

SpringerWienNewYork

Prof. Dr. Michael Douglas Harrison
Human-Computer Interaction Group, Department of Computer Science,
University of York, York, U.K.

Dr. Juan Carlos Torres
Dpt. Lenguajes y Sistemas Informaticos,
ETS Informatica, Granada, Spain

© 1997 Springer-Verlag/Wien
Reprint of the original edition 1997

Typesetting: Camera-ready by authors

Graphic design: Ecke Bonk

Printed on acid-free and chlorine-free bleached paper

SPIN: 10635792

With 129 Figures

ISSN 0946-2767

ISBN-13: 978-3-211-83055-0   e-ISBN-13: 978-3-7091-6878-3
DOI: 10.1007/978-3-7091-6878-3

Preface

This book constitutes the proceedings of the Eurographics Workshop on Design, Specification and Verification of Interactive Systems. The meeting was held in Granada, Spain from June 4–6, 1997. It was the fourth of a series reviewing the state of the art of tools, notations and methodologies supporting the design of interactive systems. In previous years workshops have been held near Pisa, Italy, near Toulouse, France, and in Namur, Belgium.

The aim of the workshop series is to combine formal presentations with informal focused discussion in an informal setting. Attendees included researchers from many countries including the United States, Japan and New Zealand. Two invited papers were intended to provide a keynote for each day, one with an industrial perspective from Anthony Hall, the other with a university bias from Joelle Coutaz.

Seventeen of the papers included here were chosen from forty submitted and were presented formally at the meeting. These papers cover a range of topics including: the role of different representations in interactive systems design and how current notations need to be extended, how usability can be assessed, checking specifications against usability properties and tool support.

Poster sessions provided an additional vehicle for the dissemination of research material. The titles and abstracts of all the papers accepted are available on-line at http://www.info.fundp.ac.be/%7Ejvd/dsvis/dsvis97.html. The papers presented as posters will be published separately as a volume of the Eurographics Workshops series. The working groups focused on issues in the design, specification and verification of web browsers. These discussions have been summarised and presented as a paper in this book.

There is a permanent Web site, which can be contacted through the pointer at the EUROGRAPHICS Web page (http://www.eg.org/) to the special interest groups. This site contains information relating previous events, and a call for participation for the next edition.

We want to thank the following institutions and organisations, who helped to organize this meeting: Universidad de Granada, Escuela Técnica Superior de Ingeniería Informática de Granada, Junta de Andalucía, Ayuntamiento de Granada, La General, Telefónica, Eurographics Spanish Chapter, Comisión Interministerial de Ciencia y Tecnología and Valenzuela Informática.

Michael Harrison
Juan Carlos Torres

Contents

VIII

Do interactive systems need specifications?

Anthony Hall

Praxis Critical Systems,
Bath, UK

Abstract The obvious advantages of prototyping and incremental development for interactive systems lead some people to believe that specifications of such systems are unnecessary or even harmful. I question whether there really is a conflict between specifications and prototypes. In fact the two schools have more in common than is usually supposed. Both specifications and prototypes can be understood as theories about the system to be developed. Both have important and complementary roles in development.

1 Introduction

Interactive systems seem to be particularly fruitful subjects for prototyping and incremental development. Such approaches are increasingly popular and their attractiveness, compared with the known problems of traditional waterfall development methods, seems to throw into question the whole notion of specification and design. If we can build the system in small increments and validate each increment with its users, why write a specification at all? Why have a design, when it is only an approximation to the code?

I suggest that, valuable though these evolutionary approaches are, it is a mistake to think that they can replace specifications. On the contrary, I believe that the two approaches are complementary and it is only by using both that we can build interactive systems of any size. This paper tries to substantiate that claim.

First, I summarise the main benefits of prototyping and incremental development. Then I look at some of the problems that can arise if they are used to the exclusion of other methods. In contrast, I describe the main ways in which writing specifications can contribute to system development and assurance.

The central part of the paper proposes a unification of the two approaches: I propose that we can view each as a particular type of theory about the system under development. This suggests that, rather than being opposed, the two approaches are trying to solve different aspects of the same problem and indeed that their similarities are deeper than their differences. From that perspective, I show where the contributions of each approach are most valuable, and how they can complement each other.

We put this idea into practice on our projects, and have developed major operational systems using it. I describe how the idea works out in practice, and what problems we found in using it. This leads me to some research issues which I believe need to be addressed and which I hope will stimulate discussion at the workshop.

2   The case for evolutionary development

One of the fundamental difficulties of creating computer systems is the IKIWISI principle. I find it hard to envisage what it is I want, but I am sure that *I'll know it when I see it*. This principle describes the behaviour of users, who find it far easier to assess a working model than to review a technical document. It accounts for the frustrating experience of delivering a system only to have the user say "That's about right. There's just one small thing...." It suggests that document-based approaches, epitomised by the traditional waterfall lifecycle, are bound to fail.

The IKIWISI principle works just as well for developers, although this is less commonly acknowledged. Most developers are much more comfortable trying out a program to see what it does than thinking about whether a specification is right or not. We can be cynical and think this is just a preference for hacking over serious thought, but we have to recognise that there is a powerful psychological fact which we need to take into account if we want our development methods to be effective.

The best tool we have for overcoming the problems caused by IKIWISI is prototyping. Rather than tell the users what they are going to get, we show them. The hope is that what we show them is realistic enough, so they will explore its behaviour and tell us whether it is really what they want.

Prototypes are not only useful for showing users what they will get. They can also be used by developers to explore potential designs to see whether, for example, they are feasible and will perform adequately. It is important to realise that the kind of prototype that a designer needs is quite different from the kind a user needs. The designer may be interested in performance, for example, and will need a prototype which has a realistic processing load but does not need to have a usable interface. The user, on the other hand, will want the user interface to be as realistic as possible but is not concerned about how much processing is going on behind the scenes.

Fortunately, the need for prototyping is now accompanied by powerful means for achieving it. Technologies like user interface development kits, databases, languages like Visual Basic and the powerful hardware they run on mean that we can build complicated user interfaces with relatively little effort.

This combination of an obvious need and the technical means for meeting it has led to widespread interest in the evolutionary approach to development. The evolutionary process starts with a prototype: this is evaluated and improved, and a second prototype is built incorporating the lessons of the first. Eventually these prototypes will evolve into a full-blown system.

This process clearly works with, rather than against, the IKIWISI principle. It is also sometimes claimed that it is more responsive to change: that as requirements change, the prototypes will evolve to meet the new requirements. Indeed, so appealing is this approach that some people believe that it is a complete solution to the system development problem, and that there is no need for documents such as specifications or designs.

3 Is this enough?

Evolutionary development is clearly very attractive. It addresses some of the most difficult issues which arise when we try to satisfy user needs and deal with a changing world. Before we throw away all our previous ideas, however, we should look at the potential problems of adopting such an approach.

I am especially interested in operational systems—those which are used to support applications like railway signalling, air traffic control and fly by wire aircraft. All these are highly interactive and need to be prototyped and evaluated in the way I have described. However, there are many other issues to be addressed when building such systems.

3.1 Complexity

A key aspect of such systems is that they can be very complex. I am told that if you listen to cockpit voice recordings from fly by wire aircraft which have had difficulties, one of the most common things you hear is: *"Why did it do that?"* Indeed, how often have you asked just that question of your own word processor? Such a question arises when the user no longer has a clear mental model of what the system is doing. I think it is complexity which causes the difficulty in constructing such a mental model.

Complexity can arise from several sources. One of them is simply that the system may have a huge number of possible states. The tracks, points and signals for a reasonable railway junction probably have something like 10^{20} possible states—and that's before we consider the trains. No amount of prototyping is going to explore a significant fraction of that state space.

A more intractable source of complexity is, of course, concurrency. While it is fairly easy to expose the user to the main behaviours of, say, a single-user word processing system, it is literally orders of magnitude more difficult to explore a multi-user system (For an example, see [1]). It is even more difficult if the external environment is an unpredictable source of events. If the events and responses are time critical, the task gains yet another dimension of difficulty.

Of course we can—indeed we must—build prototypes of such systems. But we cannot expect these prototypes to tell the users everything about how the systems will behave in real life. Even if the prototype were the complete system, the evaluations carried out by the user could only explore a minuscule fraction of its behaviour. Faced with a new combination of circumstances, the system might do something quite unexpected.

3.2 Partiality

An evolutionary approach to system building has the attraction that it produces something looking like a real system early on in the development. However, it is important to remember that any such early version must necessarily be only a partial system. It will fail to display some of the characteristics of the final system. It may have only a limited set of functions available, or support only a single user, or differ in some other way from a full implementation. This may seem obvious, but it is easy to forget that it has important consequences. For example, a prototype may have only some of the functions available: it will then be impossible to detect harmful interactions involving other functions which are not included in the prototype.

In some applications such incompleteness may not be very important. I think it is annoying that different features of my word processor don't work together properly, but it is no worse than that. I may be prepared to pay that price for having the features in the first place. However, if we are building critical systems controlling trains or aeroplanes, such unexpected interactions could be disastrous.

Experience shows that errors in computer systems do frequently arise from incompleteness in the behaviour of the system. Such incompleteness, sometimes called "missing design", means that the system has simply not been programmed to cope with particular combinations of circumstances. As systems get more complex the scope for missing design increases.

There are, broadly, two styles of evolutionary development. Both are useful, but neither of them completely addresses the problem of missing design.

Throw-away prototypes

The first style is the "throw away" prototype, which is built to explore particular aspects of the system's behaviour. Once the prototype has been evaluated it forms part of the definition of what the real system is meant to do. For example, Sutcliffe [7] advocates a "requirements specification comprising the concept demonstrator, a set of analysed design rationale diagrams expressing the users' preferences for different design options, and specifications as text, graphics or more formal notations depending on the requirement engineer's choice."

Using the prototype as part of the definition of what the system is to do seems to me to be problematic. It begs the question of what it means to build something "like" the prototype. This is a problem even if the prototype is a fully functional system: I once talked to a hardware engineer who had been told to design a new disk drive. The new drive was to "exactly like the current drive, but faster". The trouble was, he had no idea what "exactly like the current drive" might mean.

There are two complementary difficulties: determining what behaviour the current drive has; then determining which parts of that behaviour are important, and which are just incidental. Failure to solve the first means that essential behaviour will be missed; failure to solve the second means that inessential behaviour will be preserved, constraining the designer and limiting the scope for improvement.

This is a problem not just for the designer, but for the customer too. Suppose the designer brings along a disk drive which, he claims, meets the requirement: how is it to be tested? Does it have to be indistinguishable from the current drive? Clearly not, for at the very least it is going to differ in speed. But does it, for example, have to behave in the same way when data are cached? Who knows?

My conclusion is that prototypes cannot be used as a *definition* of what the system is to do. They are an essential step on the way to arriving at such a definition, but they are not in themselves enough.

Incremental builds

The second kind of evolutionary development is incremental. Rather than being thrown away, each intermediate product is a version of the final system. The question of using it as a definition of the system does not arise: it *is* the system. However, this does not remove the problem of partiality. It is just as likely that, when new functions are added in later increments, they will interact in unexpected ways with the features of the earlier increments.

The incremental build approach may not even be feasible. If, for example, the final system is to be concurrent, distributed and have high reliability requirements then there needs to be a strong architecture in place before any functionality at all can be built. Such an architecture depends more on the non-functional requirements than on functionality seen directly by the user. Experiments like Sutcliffe's show that it is hard to gather non-functional requirements from users by working with prototypes.

3.3 Premature commitment

There is one other danger in prototyping solutions. That is precisely the fact that we are showing the user *solutions*, not talking about the *problem*. Some assumptions must already have been made about what the users' requirements are, and what kind of solution they are looking for. Prototyping on its own makes it difficult to question these assumptions. For example, air traffic controllers currently use flight progress strips to record details of flights. If we try to develop a system to replace flight progress strips, we will naturally start by prototyping different ways of presenting the information on the computer. But what we are unlikely to do is to rethink the whole question of what information is needed, when it is needed and how it might best be made available. To do that we need to do more than just present trial solutions: we need to think more deeply about the problem.

4 Requirements and specifications

Thinking about the problem is called Requirements Engineering. The outcome of a good requirements engineering exercise is a definition of the problem to be solved, and the constraints that must be met by its solution. This definition is a requirements specification. A requirements specification is much more than a sketch of the proposed system: it defines everything the implementer needs to know in order to produce a solution to the problem. Good specifications have some valuable characteristics:

- A good specification is *abstract*: it concentrates on the essence of the problem at the expense of detail. This helps to master complexity.
- It is, in a useful sense, *complete*: it covers all the important properties that the solution needs to have.
- It is, far more than a prototype can be, *free of bias* towards a particular solution.

4.1 The power of abstraction

One of the most powerful tools for writing specifications is abstraction: ignoring some of the details of the problem to concentrate on its essence. Abstraction is, of course, a different form of partiality: like a prototype, an abstract statement about a system misses things out. But it is partiality along a different dimension, and it has different benefits and costs.

Abstraction is most useful when we have the problem of managing complexity. If we have a system with a huge number of states, we don't enumerate them all: instead, we impose some structure which allows us to understand them. We build a model in which the concepts are at a higher level than the individual elements of the problem, and thus the model is small enough and regular enough to be comprehensible. Instead of thinking about individual track circuits and points, we think about routes; instead of thinking about individual train positions, we think about whether the route as a whole is free or occupied.

4.2 Completeness

To say that a specification is abstract is to say that it does not describe certain aspects of the problem. However, within the scope of what it does describe, a specification can be complete. That is, it can describe every possible behaviour of the system. For example, one can use quantifiers to say things like "*all* controlled signals on unset routes are red". This may not be as immediately appealing as seeing a prototype force signals to red when routes are unset, but it gives one much greater confidence that the system will *always* do the right thing. One reason is that the rationale for the signals being red is explicit in the rule, so the mental model of the system gives us an answer to "Why did it do that?". The second reason is that the rule clearly covers every case: it won't suddenly stop working if there are more than three routes, or if a new kind of route is implemented.

Another important property of specifications which is not shared by prototypes is that it is possible—indeed, quite easy—to say what the system will *not* do as well as what it will do. Important properties such as safety and security are often of exactly this form: "A route will *never* be set if conflicting routes are set". No amount of experimenting with a prototype can establish negative properties of this sort.

A third reason for writing specifications is to capture non-functional requirements for the system. Properties such as performance, capacity and reliability are not easily determined by experimenting with prototypes [7].

In contrast with a prototype, which is an example of what a system should do, a specification is a definition of what it must do. It is therefore a sound basis for a contract to implement the system. The relationship between an implementation and a specification is one of satisfaction: the implementation does or does not satisfy the specification. In contrast to the similarity relation, satisfaction can be determined unambiguously. If my hardware colleague had been given a specification of the current disk drive, he would have had no difficulty deciding what the new one should do. For that purpose, the specification is actually better than the real thing.

A good specification, therefore, serves everyone:

- Users can decide whether or not it defines what they want.
- Implementers can design and build a system which satisfies it.
- Verifiers can check whether or not the system does indeed satisfy it.

4.3 Describing requirements

It is possible, and indeed desirable, to avoid commitment to a particular solution when writing requirements. The key idea, described by Jackson [4], is to define the effects that are to be brought about in the real world. Some of these effects may be achievable directly by the system to be built, but others may not be. A requirement for a railway signalling system is to prevent collisions between trains; on its own, however, the signalling system cannot do that. It relies on a lot of real-world knowledge about the behaviour of train drivers and the braking distance of trains.

Jackson has shown how to relate the specification of a system to the requirements it is intended to meet. In order to do this one has to prove that the specification, taken together with relevant facts about the real world, entails the requirements. Such reasoning needs the specification to be written down explicitly. It also needs the relevant real-world properties to be made explicit. For example, the correct behaviour of an interactive system might well depend on its users behaving in particular ways. Making these assumptions explicit is one of the benefits of having specifications.

The "missing design" that is such a common cause of errors really means that the world is behaving in some way that the designer did not expect. This may be because the designer expected the world to behave in a different way; more often, it is because they never thought about the question at all. In either case, making the assumption explicit will go a long way to avoiding the problem and making the system behave consistently in all circumstances.

5 A Synthesis

Evolutionary development and specification-based development are frequently thought of as opposites. Proponents of one suppose that the other is wrong. I do not believe this at all. Both approaches emphasise the importance of the real world and the user. Both approaches try to establish, early on in the development, that it is going in the right direction. They have more in common with each other than either has with, say, so called structured or object-oriented approaches. One way of understanding more about them is to think of prototypes and specifications as being different kinds of theory about the system to be developed. We can then ask what each kind of theory is good for, and how we can best use them both.

5.1 Theories and Refutations

Popper [6] pointed out that the defining characteristic of a scientific theory is that it is refutable. If it is wrong, there is a way of showing that it is wrong. Furthermore, that is the best that can be done: there is no way of ever showing that a theory is right.

If we think of specifications, prototypes, designs and other artefacts of the development process as theories, then we can evaluate them by their degree of refutability. A powerful theory is one that says a lot: it could be refuted very easily. A weak theory does not say very much: most phenomena are consistent with it and it is hard to refute. Structured analysis typically gives rise to weak theories: it is very hard to argue with a data flow diagram, because it means so little.

Prototypes are often strong theories, because of the IKIWISI principle. If a prototype exhibits undesirable behaviour, it is easy to criticise it: that criticism is a refutation of the theory "the system should look like this".

Good specifications are also strong theories in this sense. If the specification says "A route can be set whenever its subroutes are clear", a signalling engineer will be able to tell you that it is wrong. Similarly, if you are relying on a description of the world which says "track circuits are activated whenever there is a train on the track", anyone who has experienced leaves on the track will be able to tell you how wrong you are.

5.2 Getting the best of both worlds

Clearly, specifications and prototypes are very different kinds of theory. I believe that both kinds are needed. That is because each is good at describing different aspects of the system. A prototype will quickly reveal defects in the user interface. On the other hand, even if it makes unwarranted assumptions about the real world it is unlikely to be falsified provided it behaves satisfactorily in the obvious cases. Conversely, a specification can often reveal inconsistencies but, provided it is consistent and complete it may be hard to find anything wrong with it, even if what it describes would be completely unusable.

The question for developers, therefore is not "Shall we write a specification or shall we build a prototype?". In my opinion specifications are always necessary, because it is only specifications that really define the system. The question is: "What kinds of specifications should we write, and how should we attempt to falsify them?" And, in particular, "What aspects of the specification should we prototype?"

These are open questions, and I do not offer a definitive answer. I will describe some of our experience and explain why I believe it may have some general validity.

Three-level model

Like others, [5], we find it useful to structure user interactions with a system into the usual lexical, syntactic and semantic levels. Lexical specifications describe the atoms of the interaction: keystrokes, mouse movements and so on. Syntactic specifications describe the dialogues between the system and the user: "select an object, then select an action", for example. Semantic specifications define the meaning of the interactions by describing their effects in the real world. They provide the users' conceptual model of what the system does.

This structure helps to manage the complexity of interaction specifications.

Use appropriate notations

Each of these levels is best described in its own notation. I think that one of the big mistakes that developers and theorists make is to try to use a single notation or a single development method for everything. I have seen attempts, for example, to describe the physical appearance of a screen using a Z model of the pixels. This is nonsense: the only sensible way to describe the appearance of a screen is to draw a picture or show the screen itself. Conversely, as I have discussed at length above, pictures or prototypes are quite inadequate for describing, say, safety properties of a signalling system.

Use appropriate verification methods

Just as different notations are appropriate for the different levels, so are different verification methods. In my opinion, prototyping is the only practical method for checking the lexical level. It is only by actually trying it out that you can tell whether, for example, it is easier to use a touch screen or a mouse to select particular trains on a track layout. Prototyping is also the best method of verifying the syntactic level, although here there are other methods that can be used to supplement it. For example, there are several different sequences of actions one might choose for a signaller to select a route through a junction, and the best way of finding which the signallers prefer is to let them try each one. In addition, though, once a method has been chosen then its syntax can be specified by a state-transition diagram. This allows it to be checked for completeness and unambiguity.

Prototyping at the semantic level is a necessary technique, but here it can only be one technique among others. It is the semantic level where the complexity of the state explosion, concurrent access and timing criticality prevents complete exploration. The number of states needed to verify the lexical representation is typically about 10^1. The syntax might generate 10^3. An exploration of the semantics might need 10^{20}. It is certainly necessary to check that the obvious things expected by signallers actually happen when they set routes. But since they can try out only a tiny number of cases, other techniques such as formal reasoning must be used to try and falsify the specification. For example, one can propose "challenge theorems"—properties that one believes should be ensured by the specification—and try to show that they are true. It is particularly important to use such techniques to establish negative properties such as the impossibility of setting conflicting routes.

6 The Synthesis in Practice

We have used these ideas in developing an air traffic information system. Our experience has been published [3], and has also been used as the source of case studies for the Amodeus project. [2]

6.1 Overall approach

The basis of our approach was that our biggest problem was to define the system at the conceptual level. Our central specification was therefore a formal model of the system state and behaviour, written in VDM. This specification was supported by user interface specifications for each of the types of user. In addition there were interface control documents defining the interface with other systems, and a concurrency definition defining the concurrent aspects of the system's behaviour.

We adopted the three-level model and the user interface specifications were confined to the syntactic and semantic levels. The semantics was defined by relating each dialogue to an operation specification in the VDM. The syntax was defined by state transition diagrams, and the lexis by pictures of the screens.

The granularity of this relationship was different for different interfaces. At one extreme, there was a page editing facility whose formal definition consisted of a single operation "Edit Page". At the other, there was one device (called a CERD) whose operation was so complex and critical that every keystroke was separately specified in VDM.

We built prototypes of each of the user interfaces. The purpose of these was primarily to evaluate the lexical and syntactic definitions. In the case of the CERD, these were so closely tied to the semantic definitions that we were necessarily verifying the semantics as well. The prototypes were strictly throw-away: the knowledge we gained from them was incorporated into the written specifications. We found many useful facts from these prototypes. For example, we discovered that the layout we had proposed simply did not work in the actual furniture of a controllers workstation, because it was physically too difficult to select the buttons accurately. We also found that the keystroke sequences we had proposed did not accord with the controllers' mental model: we had not recognised that they always thought of sequencing flights in terms of putting one flight behind another, rather than in front of another. However, we also needed a clean and complete specification to describe exactly which flights would be on the screen and where they would be: the combination of passage of time, flights landing, and controller actions simply presented too many possibilities to work through exhaustively with the prototype.

6.2 Effectiveness of the approach

Overall this approach was highly successful. The system is in use and has measurably better reliability than comparable systems. It is liked by its users. Perhaps most significant in this context is that an abnormally small proportion of its faults are specification errors—there is almost no "missing design". I believe this is because we did use an effective combination of methods to specify the system and to validate that specification.

We did have some problems using this approach. Some of these arose simply because we did not do our job well enough; others, however, were more fundamental and point to the need for further research and development.

One problem was that the specifications of the user interfaces were not always complete, because although we specified the user side of the dialogue completely, we omitted some of the system actions. The effect was that the implementers made wrong choices about, for example, what colours should be used for certain conditions.

A related problem is the difficulty of tying together the different specifications. Indeed this is probably the root cause of the first problem. If we had had a more formal relationship between semantic actions and user interface behaviour, we would have avoided some of the difficulties.

The third problem was more subtle, and was in fact discovered by the Amodeus investigations [2]. It turned out that the CERD specification allowed some undesirable behaviour: it could discard messages without the user being aware of it. The problem illustrates many of the points in this paper. First, it depended on a particularly unfortunate coincidence of concurrent events. Simple prototyping would never have found it. However, we failed to find it even though we also had a formal specification of the CERD interface. That is at least partly because we did not have a formal model of the environment and the users, so implicit assumptions about their behaviour went unchallenged.

In spite of these problems—indeed, because there were so few of them—I am convinced by this experience that the overall approach here is a practical and effective way to develop interactive systems for critical applications. I hope that the problems we did find can be addressed by better practice and more research.

7 Where should we go from here?

There are many areas of research where advances would help us to develop interactive systems in a more cost-effective way.

I suspect that we will always need different notations for different aspects of system behaviour. Research in multi-paradigm specifications [8] is relatively recent but promises to address this issue. We need to understand better how to divide the different aspects of the problem, how to specify each one and how to put the specifications back together again. Tool support for the combined notations would of course help enormously.

We need a closer integration between specifications and prototypes. A seamless generation of prototypes from comprehensible specifications is the ideal: there is a long way to go.

We also need to understand more about how to use prototypes. I have suggested that prototyping is most effective at the lexical and syntactic levels. It is also essential at the semantic level, but there it can never be a complete solution. We need to understand how to combine validation by prototyping with other aspects of validation such as proofs of consistency and completeness.

We need to understand more about the behaviour of users. It is only recently that the role of environment descriptions in requirements has really been understood, and of course users are a key part of the environment of any interactive system. I would like to see a synthesis between the user modelling work and some of the work in requirements engineering.

8 Summary

There has traditionally been a big difference of approach between those who believe in the importance of rigorous specification and those who believe in evolutionary development. I believe that this difference is founded on a mistaken belief that the two are antithetical. In fact, they are addressing different aspects of the same problem. That problem is to establish, before we go too far in building a system, just what system we really need to build. No one technique can solve that problem, and only by unifying the approaches can we make progress. That unification depends on understanding the roles and limitations of both techniques.

References

1. Abowd, G. D., Dix, A. J.: Integrating status and event phenomena in formal specifications of interactive systems. Proceedings of the 2nd ACM SIGSOFT Symposium on the Foundations of Software Engineering, Software Engineering Notes 19 (5), 44–52

2. Buckingham Shum, S., Blandford, A., Duke. D., Good, J., May, J., Paternó, F., Young, R. M.: Multidisciplinary modelling for User-centred system design: An air-traffic control case study. In: Sasse, A. Cunningham, J., Winder, R. (eds): People and Computers XI. Proceedings of HCI'96. London, Springer Verlag. pp. 201–219.

3. Hall, A.: Using formal methods to develop an ATC information system, IEEE Software 13 (2), March 1996, 66–76

4. Jackson, M. A.: Software Requirements and Specifications, ACM Press Addison Wesley, 1997

5. Knight, J. C. Brilliant, S. S.: Preliminary evaluation of a formal approach to user interface specification. In: Bowen, J. P., Hinchey, M. G. (eds): ZUM'97: The Z Formal Specification Notation. Springer 1997 (Lecture Notes in Computer Science, vol 1212, pp. 329–346)

6. Popper, K.: The Logic of Scientific Discovery.

7. Sutcliffe, A.: A technique combination approach to requirements engineering, Proceedings of the 3rd International Symposium on Requirements Engineering, January 1997, IEEE Computer Society Press, 65–74.

8. Zave, P., Jackson, M.: Where do operations come from? A multiparadigm specification technique, IEEE Transactions on Software Engineering, 22(7) July 1996, 508–528

PAC-ing the Architecture of Your User Interface

Joëlle Coutaz

Clips-IMAG, BP 53
38041 Grenoble Cedex 9, France
Joelle.Coutaz@imag.fr, http://outlet.imag.fr/coutaz

Abstract A number of architectural models, such as PAC, are available for the software design of interactive systems. These design abstractions, however, are not always clearly articulated nor do they explicitly exploit the foundational concepts developed recently in main-stream software architecture engineering. Similarly, technical solutions from main-stream software engineering may improve portability and reusability at the code level while hindering the quality of the resulting user interfaces. This article is an attempt to undertake an explicit bridging effort between software engineering and the specific domain of user interface software design using PAC as the running example. We present a brief evolution of the architectural models for single-user systems that motivated PAC. We then unfold PAC into PAC* for designing the conceptual architecture of multi-user systems.

Keywords : Software architecture modelling, multi-agent modelling, PAC, PAC-Amodeus, PAC*.

1 Introduction

Software architectural design is progressing from craft skill to engineering discipline. We observe an increasing interest in applying scientific knowledge to resolve conflicting constraints and requirements in a form suitable for software practitioners [28]. While architecture modelling as a recognized research field is a recent phenomenon in software engineering, it emerged explicitly in the early eighties in the specific domain of interactive systems. In this particular area, the iterative nature of the development process stimulated the design of conceptual tools that would minimize the effects of future changes: necessity triggered invention.

Today, a number of architectural models, such as PAC, are available for the software design of interactive systems. These design abstractions, however, are not always clearly articulated nor do they explicitly exploit the foundational concepts developed recently in main-stream software architecture engineering. The time is ripe to undertake an explicit bridging effort.

In this article, we analyze the PAC model in the light of the concepts devised in main-stream software engineering. These contributions are summarized in the following section. In Section 3, we present a brief evolution of architectural models such as

PAC for single-user systems. Section 4 unfolds PAC into PAC* and demonstrates the extension of PAC for designing the conceptual architecture of multi-user systems.

2 Foundational concepts and factors

Foundational concepts for software architecture modelling define an initial common ground for understanding the nature of an architecture. Factors make explicit requirements that a particular design solution should satisfy.

2.1 Concepts

Foundational concepts include the notions of component, connector, style, pattern, as well as the acknowledgment of the multiplicity of perspectives on a software architecture.

One perspective is the static structural decomposition of a system at the conceptual level. Another one is the dynamic behavioral description of the structure. A static structural decomposition is expressed in terms of primary computational and storage entities, called *components*, mediated by *connectors* such as procedure calls, client-server protocols, and event-based message passing. The structure may emerge from implicit hand-crafted knowledge or may be inspired from a style.

A *style* includes a vocabulary of design elements (e.g., pipes and filters), imposes configuration constraints on these elements (e.g., pipes are mono-directional connectors between two filter components), and determines a semantic interpretation that gives meaning to the system description [13, 28]. Within a style, patterns may emerge.

A *pattern* describes a particular recurring design problem, proposes a pre-defined scheme for its solution, and includes heuristic rules for how and when to use it [12]. Patterns solutions can be viewed as micro-architectures within a broad architectural picture.

Architectural static descriptions are primarily expressed using boxes to represent components, and arrows to denote connectors. Although box-and-arrow notations along with natural language are pervasive in the software community, they rely on common intuitions and past experience to make sense. Formal models and architecture definition languages [28] are intended to provide precise unambiguous descriptions as well as analytical techniques for sound design decisions. Although the benefits from such tools are unquestionable, their use, in practice, is still limited.

2.2 Factors

McCall has defined the foundational factors for software engineering [19]. Modifiability is one pervasive factor for the software design of user interfaces. In this section, we discuss two other prevalent factors: portability and reusability. We analyze how they are addressed by current tools and techniques and how they relate to user interface requirements.

Portability at the code level is claimed to be supported with general purpose abstract machines such as Java [2]. Actually, portability of user interfaces is more than platform-independent code execution. Typically, screen definition and processing power vary across workstations. As a result, the rendering and responsiveness of a Java applet may be satisfactory on the developer's workstation, while not usable for a remote Internet user. The developer must have access to some model of the characteristics of the unknown target site. Such information should not be hidden by layers of abstract machines. It should be clearly advertised to programmers.

Reusability is supported in various and complementary ways. It includes the subclassing mechanism as advocated by object-oriented languages, and the compositional approach. Reusability supported by object-oriented application frameworks and toolkits requires a thorough understanding of the environment in order to elicit what can be reused. If successful at discovering the right pieces, the next stage is to decide how to perform specializations and extensions while preserving the philosophy of the underlying conceptual architecture. Because this architecture is not self-explanatory, because it is not exoskeletal [18], reusability by specialization requires a time-consuming reverse engineering process.

The compositional approach to software is intended to make possible the creation of functionally powerful applications from existing systems. In general, system integration is hard to achieve due to conflicting architectural assumptions. As reported in [14], mismatches may occur both at the component and the connector levels:

- the control models used in the components may be incompatible (e.g., several of them may expect to own the main event loop),

- conflicts may arise between data models (e.g., one component is expecting a hierarchical representation while another one relies on a stream-like model),

- protocols implemented in the connectors may be inconsistent (e.g., connectors use different communication primitives or different kinds of data).

Techniques, such as Ole, for alleviating architectural mismatch are emerging. However, their conceptual applicability or their technical availability is of limited scope. For example, one general solution to the "event-loop problem" is to run the conflicting components as distinct processes and use event gateways to accommodate different control regimes. If, on the other hand, some design decision constrains the components to operate in the same process, then brute force modifications of the source code must be performed. CGI gateways are attractive solutions to the composition problem but they apply to Internet components only [15].

Actually, there is more to the compositional approach than technical conflicts: user interface inconsistencies may arise from components that implement their own user interface. Then, either conflicts occur at the lexical level and can be repaired by editing resource files, or the source of inconsistencies is deeper in the interaction model, and, again, brute force modification is unavoidable. Performing these modifications in a safe way requires reverse engineering the source code. This may be a tremendous task when the conceptual architecture of the user interface such as those presented next, is missing.

3 Evolution of software architecture models for interactive systems

Seminal Seeheim [25] and its revisited version, the Arch model [1], set the foundations for functional partitioning. Modifiability, motivated by the iterative design of user interfaces, was the driving principle. At that time, the slogan was "separate the functional core from the user interface". With the proliferation of toolkits, portability of the user interface at the widget level became a new concern: the Arch "Presentation Component" made explicit the notion of logical interaction object. By doing so, it defined a natural integration for virtual toolboxes such as XVT [29].

Direct manipulation introduced new functional requirements on software architectures including the notion of multi-threaded interaction and the concept of immediate semantic feedback. The PAC model (Presentation, Abstraction, Control), based on the notion of agent, was explicitly designed to support these new features while preserving the Seeheim principle [5]:

- an agent is intended to convey a thread of interaction,

- the three-fold functional partitioning of an agent makes provision for hosting domain-specific semantic in the Abstraction facet of the agent while immediate feedback is supported through its Presentation facet; the third facet, the Control, centralizes the expression of dependencies between the Abstraction and the Presentation as well as inter-agent communication.

Multimodal interaction, which supports multiple forms of interaction techniques such as speech and gesture, added yet another set of requirements. In particular, the CARE properties (Complementarity, Assignation, Redundancy, Equivalence) that characterize relationships between multiple modalities [6], made prevalent temporal constraints and style heterogeneity:

- the interpretation of deictic expressions such as "put that there", uses the notion of temporal window to combine partial information into meaningful expressions: gesture and speech expressions produced in the same temporal window can be considered for fusion. Alternatively, if they are not part of the same temporal window, then redundancy or parallel input of multiple independent commands may be planned;

- style heterogeneity comes from the integration of multiple sources of reusable code that each implements a modality interpreter. Typically, a speech recognition system that may adhere to a blackboard style, must be combined with an object-event-based style graphical toolkit such as Motif.

PAC-Amodeus has been devised to support the new requirements imposed by multimodality [20, 21]. It uses the Arch model as the foundation for the functional partitioning and populates the Dialogue Component of the arch with PAC agents. The two adapters of the Arch, the "Presentation Component" and the "Domain Adapter", are used to accommodate style mismatch. The PAC agents, which support concurrency, are augmented with processing capabilities, such as a fusion engine [22], to support the temporal aspects of the CARE properties.

So far, we have limited our historical analysis to single user systems. With the advent of groupware and Internet-based multimedia systems, complex functional requirements are emerging. Portability, reusability, interoperability, and efficiency are becoming crucial. In Section 2, we have discussed the limits of the current technical solutions. We now present PAC*, our conceptual architecture for groupware.

4 The PAC* conceptual model

PAC* is a combination of existing architectural models: 1) it instantiates Dewan's zipper model [9] with the five level functional decomposition of Arch, 2) like PAC-Amodeus, it populates Dialogue Control components with agents [20, 21], and 3) PAC agents are refined along the three functional dimensions of the Clover model [4].

This combination of Dewan's, Arch, and PAC models is motivated in the following way: the Arch functional decomposition is an appropriate framework for accommodating style heterogeneity and for anticipating changes and portability of the user interface portion of the system. Dewan's model provides the basis for reasoning about replication, coupling, and parallelism at the layers level. PAC-Amodeus explicitly models parallelism at a finer grain within Dialogue Control components of the architecture. It also brings in patterns and operational heuristics to devise agents in conformance to the external specifications of the user interface. The Clover model helps reasoning about the functional coverage of individual agents and provides the basis for additional refinements. The description of these models are briefly summarized in the following sections.

4.1 PAC* and Dewan's model

The "generic multi-user architecture" model proposed by Dewan [9] structures a groupware system into a variable number of levels of abstraction ranging from the domain specific level to the hardware level. Layers shared between users form the base of the system (e.g., layers S to L+1 in Figure 1a). At some point, the base gives rise to branches which are replicated for every user (see layers L to 0 in Figure 1a). Information flow between layers occurs vertically between adjacent layers along the input and output axis as well as horizontally for synchronizing states between peer and non peer replicated layers. Interestingly, Dewan makes a distinction between single-user events which are private to a personal workstation, and multi-user events which result in propagations to remote workstations.

The functional role and the number of layers in Dewan's model depend on the case at hand. A layer can be viewed as a level of abstraction or as a service that overlaps with other services as in SLICE[17]. Figure 1b) shows an instantiation of Dewan's model using the functional layers of Arch. ALV [16] is a three layer instantiation where the semantic level is mapped to the shared abstraction A and where branches are comprised of links L and views V.

Dewan's model offers a good basis for implementing various forms of coupling as well as for allocating functions to processes (e.g., reasoning about the granularity of parallelism, replication and distribution). For example, one can choose to execute the base and each branch within distinct processes. Similarly, without any automatic support from the underlying platform, the model helps reasoning about allocating processes to processors.

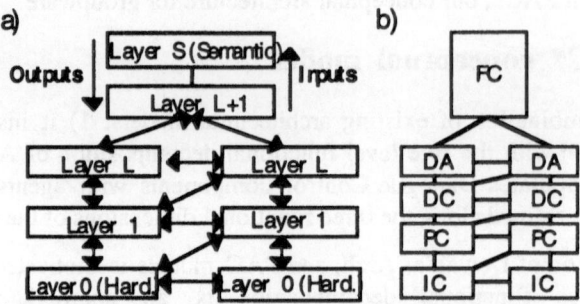

Fig. 1. a) Dewan's generic architecture for multi-user systems. Arrows denote information flow. b) An instantiation of Dewan's model using the functional layers of Arch. Here, the functional Core FC is shared while each branch is composed of a Domain Adapter DA, a Dialogue control Component DC, a logical Presentation Component PC, and a physical Interaction Component IC.

PAC* is a zipper-based architecture where the layers are instantiated using the five functional partitioning advocated by Arch: the Functional Core, the Domain Adapter, the Dialogue Component, the Presentation and Interaction Components. Although specified informally, the roles of these components are now well-understood by practitioners to cope with architectural mismatches, to reason about portability and to integrate multiple interaction techniques:

- Typically, the Domain Adapter is used as a wrapper for solving data models mismatch between the Functional Core and its user interface. For example, requests formulated from a Java user interface applet are transformed by the Domain Adapter into the SQL format expected by information retrieval engines [30].

- For interactionally rich user interfaces, such as MATIS [22] and CoMedi [7], the Presentation and Interaction Components correspond to the set of modality interpreters used in the user interface: speech recognition, computer vision-based gesture interpretation, and graphical abstract machines such as AWT [2] and Tk [23]. As shown in Figure 2, these machines sit side by side without any intercommunication and cover two levels of abstraction: the Interaction layer which provides the Presentation layer with device independence, and the Presentation layer which provides the Dialogue Component with interaction language independence. In addition, all of the interpreters of the Presentation layer can be encapsulated in a uniform way. For example, in CoMedi, two speech recognition systems, computer-vision trackers, and the continuous media provider are all encapsulated in Tcl for use from the Dialogue Component.

- The Dialogue Component is in charge of task level sequencing. In PAC*, we reuse the design rationale developed for PAC-Amodeus: whereas the Functional Core, the Presentation and the Interaction Components have their own architecture driven by domain (or subdomain) specific criteria, we recommend to structure the Dialogue Component using the PAC style in order to support multi-threading, modularity, and task conformance.

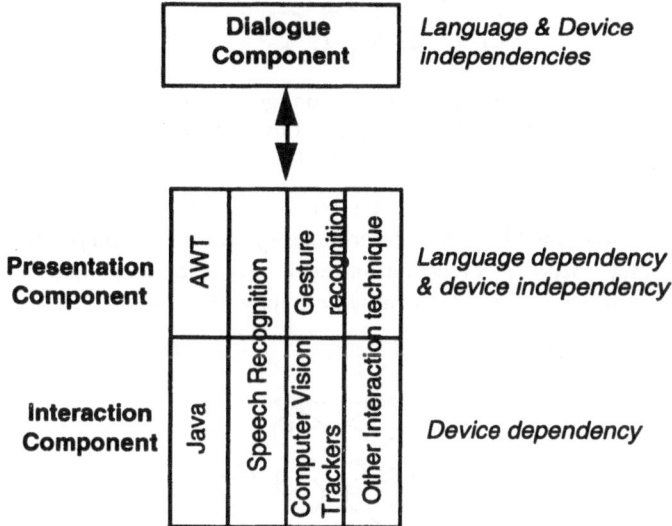

Fig. 2. Interaction Interpreters in the Presentation and Interaction Components.

4.2 PAC* and PAC

In the PAC style, the components are three facet agents interacting through event-based connectors. The facets (Presentation, Abstraction, Control) are used to express different but complementary and strongly coupled computational perspectives of the same functionality. As shown in Figure 3, no agent Abstraction is authorized to communicate directly with its corresponding Presentation and vice versa. Dependencies of any sort are conveyed via Controls. Controls serve as the glue mechanism to express coordination as well as data model transformations between the abstract and concrete perspectives. In addition, the flow of information between agents transits through Controls in a hierarchical way.

In PAC*, we reuse the heuristic rules developed for PAC-Amodeus to populate the Dialogue Component with PAC agents. Each of these rules proposes a configuration of agents, or pattern, that fits a particular situation. The complete set of PAC-Amodeus rules can be found in [20, 21]. Basically, these rules are driven by the external specifications of the user interface. Every interaction space such as a window, a drawing area, a menubar, etc., is modelled as an agent. Views opened in cascade are related by a hierarchical link. Consistency between multiple views of the same concept is maintained through a common parent agent. Distributed user's actions over multiple agents, such as a palette and a drawing area, are synthesized into a meaningful command using a cement agent.

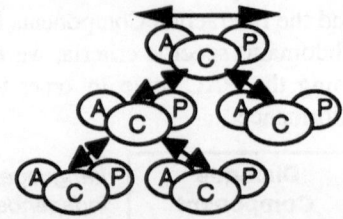

Fig. 3. In the PAC style, PAC components are configured hierarchically using event-based connectors. Arrows illustrate the information flow (vertical flow between agents, horizontal flow between the facets of an agent).

Agents, such as menus and buttons, that are implemented by the Presentation or Interaction levels are pruned from the hierarchical systematic decomposition: from first class agents, they become Presentation-level reusable code referenced in the Presentation facet of the parent agent from where they are pruned.

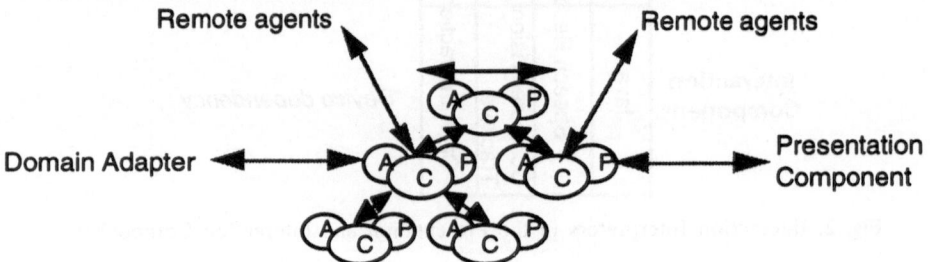

Fig. 4. A Dialogue Component in PAC* and its connectors. Dark arrows denote connectors within the Dialogue Component. Dimmed arrows represent connectors with other components.

In PAC*, just like for PAC-Amodeus, a Presentation facet maintains a data model for rendering the information maintained in its related Abstraction facet. This data model is used to feed into and receive information from the local Presentation Component. An Abstraction facet maintains a data model of domain-specific information exchanged with the Functional Core through the Domain Adapter.

Single-user events whose effects are private to a particular user are processed locally within the Interaction-Presentation-Dialogue components. Within the Dialogue Component, they are processed by local agents that may not have corresponding peers on remote workstations. Multi-user events, such as a user entering or leaving a conference, must be notified to remote sites. Dewans' model defines different forms of coupling between the layers. Within the Dialogue Component layer, coupling in PAC* is performed at the agent level. Figure 4 summarizes the possible connections within the Dialogue Component and with outside the Dialogue Component. CoMedi is used next to illustrate the architectural possibilities.

As shown in Figures 5 and 6, CoMedi uses a fisheye porthole to support communication and awareness in a mediaspace. A slot in the porthole corresponds either to a remote user or to a group of users. An individual slot displays personal information about the corresponding remote user (e.g., level of availability, absence/presence, video image published through a filter [8]). When opening a collective slot, the current porthole is replaced with the porthole of the corresponding group. In a dedicated area of the control panel (see bottom left of Figures 5 and 6), users can check the image they export about themselves (cf. the reflexivity principle [27]). When an audio/video connection is established with a remote user, a dedicated video image is opened dynamically.

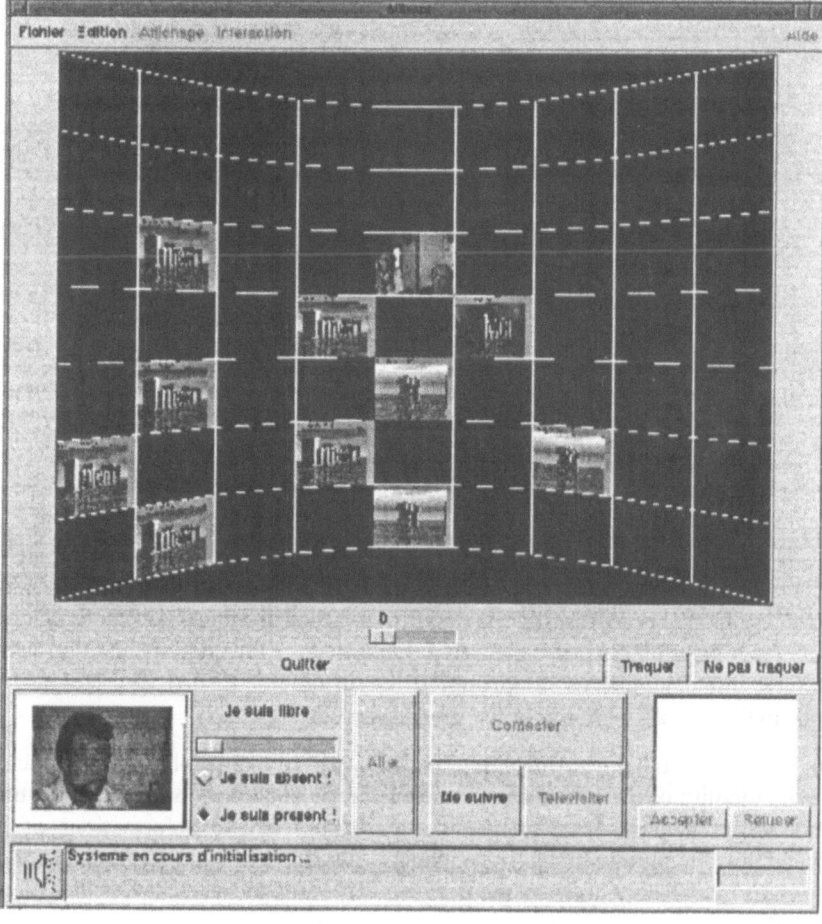

Fig. 5. Screen dump of CoMedi in neutral position: all of the slots of the porthole are of equal size.

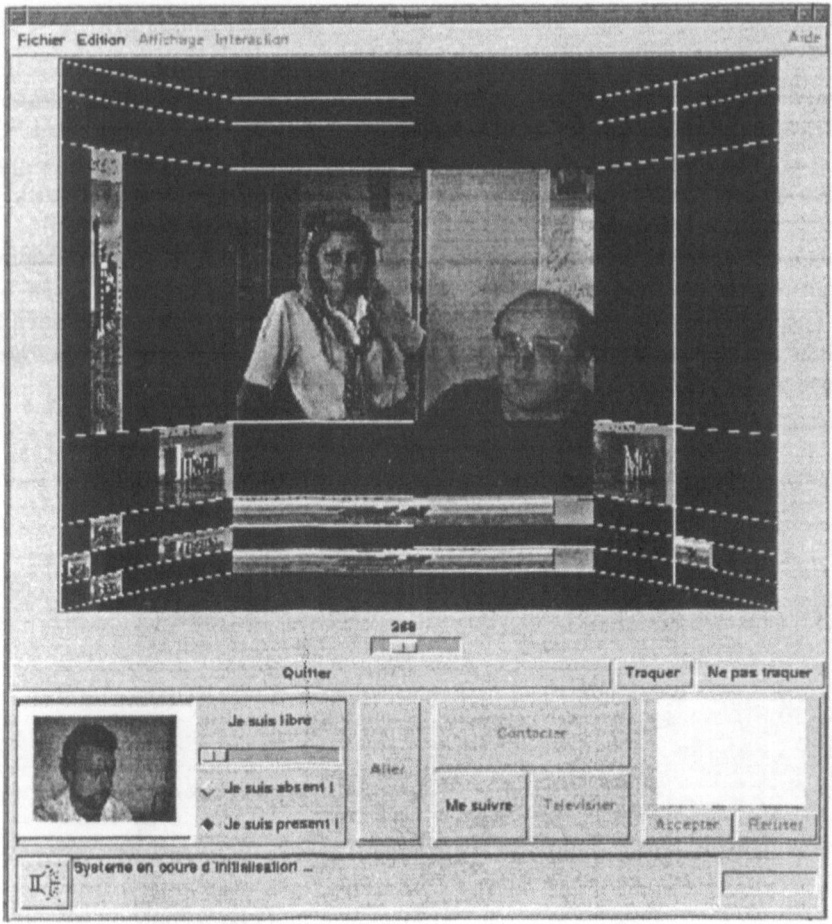

Fig. 6. Screen dump of CoMedi when focus is located on a particular slot

Figure 7 shows the refinement of the Dialogue Component of CoMedi. The Top-Level agent is in charge of the overall control of the dialogue. In particular, its Abstraction facet is in relation with the data base of users. (This data base is an active data structure implemented as a GroupKit environment [26].) Its Presentation corresponds to the overall menubar of the mediaspace.

The Porthole agent handles the local interaction with the porthole. Its Abstraction maintains the identity of the group in the current focus of attention of the local user. Its Presentation is a geometry manager that performs fisheye deformations of the porthole and maps the bitmap images provided by its siblings onto quadrilateral slots of varying sizes (the fisheye follows the mouse location as the user moves the mouse in the porthole).

Every remote user (or group of users) who belongs to the current porthole is represented by a Slot agent. Its Abstraction models the personal data of the remote user/group to be rendered in the slot while its Presentation produces a bitmap based on the knowledge of the surface available for rendering.

The Vphone agent models the dedicated open audio/video window for Vphone connections.

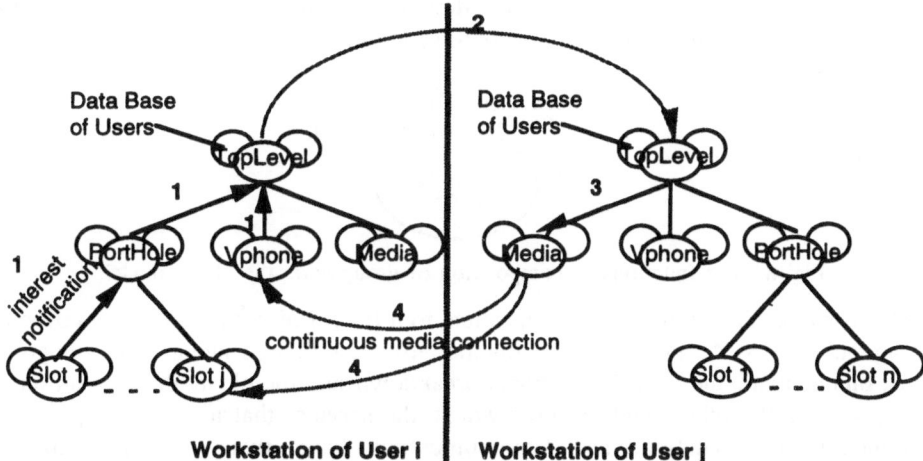

Fig. 7. The Dialogue Component of CoMedi.

The Media agent is in charge of acquiring and filtering the audio and video image of the local user. This filtered image is rendered locally in the Presentation facet of the Media agent; it is sent to every remote Slot agent that represents the local user currently rendered on remote sites; and finally, it is transmitted to the distant Vphone agent when the local user is Vphoning that distant user. For doing so, the remote slot agents and the remote Vphone agent express their interest to their local hierarchy in opening/closing an audio/video stream with that particular user (1). The remote TopLevel sends the request to the appropriate distant peer TopLevel agent (2) which, in turn, triggers the Media agent of the particular user (3). Direct audio/video connections are then established/suppressed between the Media agent and the remote subscribers (4).

4.3 PAC* and the Clover model

The Clover model, based on Ellis'model [11], provides a generic overview of the functional coverage of groupware. As shown in Figure 8, a groupware system covers three domain specific functions: production, coordination and communication [4]:

- The production space denotes the set of domain objects that model the multi-user elaboration of common artefacts such as documents, or that motivate a common undertaking such as flying an airplane between two places. Typically, shared editors support the production space.

24

- The coordination space covers activities dependencies including temporal relationships between the multi-user activities. Workflow systems are primarily concerned with coordination.

- The communication space supports person-to-person communication. Email and mediaspaces are examples of systems designed for supporting computer-mediated communication either asynchronously or synchronously.

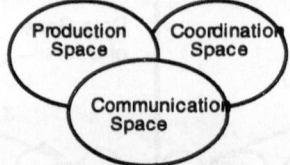

Fig. 8. The functional decomposition of groupware: the clover model.

PAC* uses the Clover model as a conceptual tool for refining the functional coverage of agents. In PAC*, agents can be functionally decomposed along two orthogonal axis: on one hand, the P, A, C functional breakdown and the clover decomposition of groupware on the other hand. In other words, the services that an agent supports for Production, Coordination, and Communication have their own Presentation, Abstraction and Control. This refinement of an agent functionality is shown in Figure 9 as a "Neapolitan PAC".

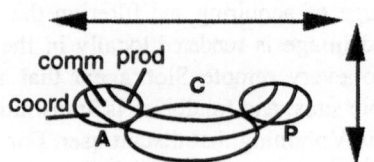

Fig. 9. A PAC* agent as a bundled "Neapolitan PAC". Arrows show horizontal communication between the A, P, C as well as vertical communication between the Production, Coordination, and Communication views.

In turn, a Neapolitan PAC* agent can be decomposed as a cluster of three PAC agents, each agent being dedicated to one class of the functional clover. One can refer to [4] for a detailed description of this refinement illustrated with an extended version of the SASSE multi-user editor [3].

.5 Conclusion

In this article we have demonstrated the motivation for PAC-ing the user interface of an interactive system ranging from single to multi-user systems. The PAC family conceptual models provide a sound basis for devising the right components of an interactive system with specific focus on Dialogue Components.

Although connectors within Dialogue Components are event-based, the nature of the connectors to be used between other components is underspecified. Experience shows that designing the connectors right is more difficult than getting the right components. We plan future work in this direction.

Another weakness of the PAC family models is the absence of formalization such as [10, 24]. Another missing element is a cookbook that would help practitioners to translate a PAC-based conceptual architecture into a motivated implemented architecture. This reflection is on our research agenda as well.

6 Acknowledgment

This work has been partly supported by project ESPRIT BR 7040 Amodeus II and by France Telecom CNET.

7 References

1. A Metamodel for the Runtime Architecture of an Interactive System, The UIMS Tool Developers Workshop, SIGCHI Bull., ACM, 24, 1, 1992, 32-37.

2. Arnold, K and Gosling, J.: The Java Programming Language, Addison Wesley, 1996.

3. Baecker, R.M., Nastos, D., Posner, L.R. and Mawlby, M.K.: The user-centered iterative design of collaborative writing software, in Proceedings of theWorkshop on Real Time Group Drawing and Writing Tools, CSCW' 92 (Toronto, 1992).

4. Calvary, G., Coutaz, J., and Nigay, L: From Single-User Architectural Design to PAC*: a Generic Software Architecture Model for CSCW, Proceedings of CHI 97, ACM publ., pp. 242-249.

5. Coutaz, J.: PAC, an Object Oriented Model for Dialog Design, in Proceedings Interact'87 (North Holland, 1987), 431-436.

6. Coutaz, J., Nigay, L., Salber, D., Blandford, A., May, J. and Young, R.: Four Easy Pieces for Assessing the Usability of Multimodal Interaction: The CARE properties, Proceedings of the INTERACT'95 conference, S. A. Arnesen & D. Gilmore Eds., Chapman&Hall Publ., Lillehammer, Norway, June 1995, pp. 115-120.

7. Coutaz, J., Bérard, F. and Crowley, J.: Coordination of Perceptual Processes for Computer Mediated Communication. in Proc. Second International Conference on Automatic Face and Gesture Recognition, IEEE Computer Society Press Publ. Oct. 1996, pp. 106-111.

8. Coutaz, J., Crowley, J. and Bérard, F. Eigen space Coding as a Means to Support Privacy in Computer Mediated Communication. Proceedings of INTERACT'97, Sydney, to appear.

9. Dewan, P.: Multiuser Architectures, in Proceedings EHCI'95, Working Conference on Engineering Computer Human Interaction.

10. Duke, D. and Harrison, M.: Folding Human Factors into Rigourous Development, in Proceedings of Eurographics Workshop "Design, Specification, Verification of Interactive Systems", Paterno', F. ed., 1994, 335-352.

11. Ellis, C. and Wainer, J.: A Conceptual Model of Groupware, in Proceedings CSCW'94, ACM Conference on Computer Supported Cooperative Work, Furuta, R., Neuwirth, C. eds., 1994, 79-88.

12. Gamma, E., Helm, R., Johnson, R. and Vlissides, J.: Design Patterns: Elements of Reusable Object-Oriented Software, Addison-Wesley, Reading, MA. 1995.

13. Garlan, D. and Shaw, M.: An Introduction to Software Architecture, Advances in Software Engineering and Knowledge Engineering, Ambriola, V. and Tortora, G. eds., Vol. 1, World Scientific Publ., 1993, 1-39.

14. Garlan, D., Allen, R., and Ockerbloom, J.: Architectural Mismatch or Why it's hard to build systems out of existing parts, ICSE'95, ACM, 1995, pp. 179-185.

15. Gundavaram, S.: CGI Programming on the World Wide Web, O'Reilly & Associates, Inc., 1996.

16. Hill, R.: The Abstraction-Link-View Paradigm: Using Constraints to Connect User Interfaces to Applications, in proceedings CHI'92 (NewYork, 1992), ACM, 335-342.

17. Karsenty, A. and Beaudoin-Lafon, M.: SLICE: a Logical Model for Shared Editors, in Real Time Group Drawing and Writing Tools, Greenberg, S., Haynes, S., Rada, R. Eds, McGraw-Hill.

18. Kramer, J.: Exoskeletal Software-Making Structure Explicit. Software Architectures, Schloss Dagstuhl Seminar, Garlan, D. Paulish, F. and Tichy, W. eds., Dagstuhl Seminar Report 106, 1995, pp.23-23.

19. McCall, J.: Factors in Software Quality, General Electric Ed., 1977.

20. Nigay, L. and Coutaz, J.: Building User Interfaces: Organizing Software Agents. In Proceedings ESPRIT'91 Conference, 1991, 707-719.

21. Nigay, L.: Conception et modélisation logicielles des systèmes interactifs: application aux interfaces multimodales, Thèse de doctorat de l'UJF, 1994.

22. Nigay, L. and Coutaz, J.: A Generic Platform for Addressing the Multimodal Challenge, CHI'95, ACM New York, Denver, May 1995, pp. 98-105.

23. Ousterhout, J.,K.: Tcl and the Tk Toolkit. Addison Wesley Professional Computing Series, 1994.

24. Paterno', F., Leonardi, A. and Pangoli, S.: A Tool Supported Approach to the Refinement of Interactive Systems, in the Proceedings of Eurographics Workshop "Design, Specification, Verification of Interactive Systems", Paterno', F. ed., 1994, 85-96.

25. Pfaff G.E. et al.: User Interface Management Systems, Pfaff, G.E. ed., Eurographics Seminars, Springer Verlag, 1985.

26. Roseman, M. and Greenberg, S.: GROUPKIT: A groupware Toolkit for Building Real-Time Conferencing Applications, in Proc. CSCW'92 (Toronto, Canada, 1992), ACM Conference on CSCW, 43-50

27. Salber, D.: De l'interaction individuelle aux systèmes multi-utilisateurs. L'exemple de la Communication Homme-Homme-Médiatisée, Thèse de doctorat de l'Université Joseph Fourier, September, 1995.

28. Shaw, M. and Garlan, G.: Software Architecture, Perspectives on an Emerging Discipline, Prentice Hall, 1996.

29. Valdez, J.: XVT, a Virtual Toolkit, Byte ,14(3), 1989.

30. VITESSE, Visualization and Interaction Techniques to Enhance Superscalar Search Engines. http://iihm.imag.fr/vernier/Vitesse.html.

DMVIS: Design, Modelling and Validation of Interactive Systems

Bob Fields,* Nick Merriam** and Andy Dearden***

Human-Computer Interaction Group,
Department of Computer Science,
University of York, York, YO1 5DD, U.K.
Email: { bob nam andyd } @cs.york.ac.uk

Abstract. Much of the work reported in the first three DSVIS conferences has concentrated on techniques and languages for specifying and developing interactive systems. In this paper, we argue that a change of emphasis may be necessary as the field matures. We argue that real projects with specific objectives for formal methods are more likely to employ a range of diverse, lightweight modelling techniques. We explore this view by showing how, on one example, several quite different kinds of analysis can be performed using different models.

1 Introduction

In much of the work reported at previous Design, Specification and Verification of Interactive Systems (DSVIS) workshops, there is the tacit assumption that interactive systems can be developed using a single, unambiguous, formal notation to specify the desired behaviour of the system. This approach is intended to allow designers to *verify* that software conforms to its specification. An additional benefit of using unambiguous formal notations is that it may be possible to analyse whether the design actually meets the original requirements of the customer, i.e. to *validate* the design. However, there are two major problems facing this approach. Firstly, none of the techniques so far reported at DSVIS can claim to capture all aspects of a realistic system. Secondly, any specification that achieved this aim would be unwieldy for tackling any particular design question.

We feel that, as the field matures, approaches will be expected to deliver an increasing validation benefit instead of just supporting verification. We aim to show that one way to answer the diverse questions that arise during validation, is by selectively using a diverse set of narrowly focused models. It is our contention that the activities of specification and modelling to support validation are distinct. We shall demonstrate that models, both formal and informal, can be used to support validation, without requiring a formal definition of the semantic connections between them, or between the models and the emerging design.

* Dependable Computing Systems Centre
** Employed on EPSRC grant GR/K09205
*** Employed on EPSRC grant GR/J07686

In Section 2, we discuss the different roles that formal methods can play in a development process. In Section 3, we show how multiple, different models of the same design can provide complimentary insights. Note that this section is not intended as a review of formal methods for interactive systems, the models have been selected because they serve to illustrate our argument, and because the modelling notations are relatively familiar to us. In Section 4, we examine the pragmatic issues and possible theoretic objections to the use of multiple models. Finally, in Section 5, we conclude our arguments, urging that DSVIS should place as much emphasis on modelling for validation as on specification and verification.

2   Different roles for formal notation

A brief look at the proceedings of the previous three DSVIS workshops reveals that the majority of papers are concerned with the presentation of a single formal language to support interface development. Our own broad categorisation shows that over half explore existing and new notations by demonstrating their ability to specify the state, behaviour or presentation of a system or part of a system, and many of these go further by describing how such a specification can be reified towards an implementation. Within these papers, authors often refer to the possibility of conducting some reasoning over the specification, but few papers actually provide sufficient information about the reasoning process to allow a reader to apply the reasoning to their own specifications. For example, (Palanque et al. 1996) indicate a number of properties that can be checked using either TLIM or MICO, and indicate the formalisms that permit the analysis (ACTL and Petri Nets), but provide only an outline of how the analysis can be conducted. A similar criticism can be applied to work by the current authors, e.g. (Fields et al. 1995).

In contrast, a few papers present models of interactive systems that seem quite limited in their ability to support reification towards a system. For instance, the models of Faconti and Duke (1996) support a comparison of the cognitive work involved in using different interaction devices, but can be seen as an adjunct to a specification process (based on interactors) rather than a part of the specification itself.

We can summarise this distinction in the literature by saying that when a formal notation is used to say something about a system, it can be used either to *describe* what the system does or to *prescribe* what it should do. Descriptive models of systems are used primarily for analysis, perhaps to help in making a choice between possible designs. A prescriptive specification is used to say how a system should be built, to express choices that have already been made. Of course, the design of specification languages and modelling notations reflects the primary intention of providing support for either refinement and verification, or for validation and analysis. Although both specification and modelling notations may be used in roles for which they were not intended, doing so may well prove difficult or inconvenient.

An alternative perspective on the difference between descriptive and prescriptive use of models is to consider their role as communicative artefacts in the design process. Recalling the waterfall model of software development, specifications are used to drive the process forwards, informing future stages of design. On the other hand, modelling can reflect the current design back to the original requirements, thus exploring the consequences of previous design decisions. Models must be convenient for the analysis to which they are subjected. The requirements for notations to support specification and verification may be very different to those for models to support validation.

In the next section, we explore this view by showing how several quite different kinds of analysis can be performed by applying different modelling techniques to different issues connected to the design of the same artefact.

3 Multiple views on a single artifact

In this section, we explore the possibility that a number of techniques may be applied to the design of an artefact (actually to an existing design), each providing a distinct perspective on the artefact in question, and each capable of highlighting particular types of design issue. The techniques we apply are not new: they have all been reported in previous DSVIS conferences or similar fora. We demonstrate that applying techniques in this way yields useful insights about an emerging or extant design, even when the languages do not fit into anything recognisable as a common semantic framework.

A number of modelling approaches (none of which properly constitutes a specification technique or a formal method in the way that it's used) will be applied to a simple example. This will be the spelling checker component of a popular word processor, shown in Fig. 1. This example was used by Fields et al. (1995).

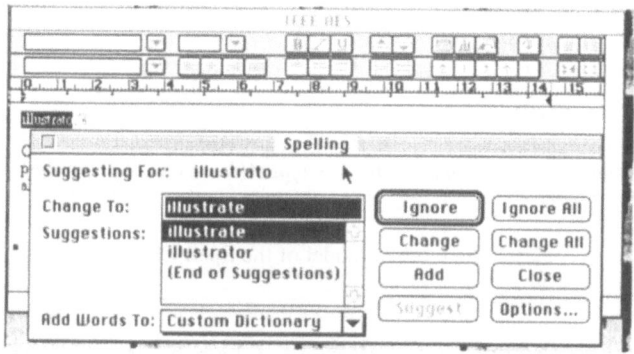

Fig. 1. Microsoft Word's Spelling Checker

We emphasise again that this section is *not* intended as a catalogue nor a review of formal methods in HCI. Rather, we present a selection of models that provide complementary insights into the design of the spelling checker.

3.1 Properties of interactive systems

Historically, some of the earliest work on formal models to support reasoning about usability-related properties was carried out in a state-based framework. A number of authors have formalised properties that capture issues concerned with the relationship between the internal parts of a system's state and parts that are perceivable. As an example, possibly the simplest such property is referred to as *predictability* (see, for example (Dix et al. 1993) or (Dix 1991) for discussions of this and other properties). This property states, basically, that the state of the system can be determined from the perceivable state. It is acknowledged that few systems actually satisfy this property. Harrison et al. (1989) use the concept of *template* to qualify properties such as predictability by considering only those parts of the state that are relevant to a particular task.

To reason about whether a property like predictability holds for some system or some part of a system, requires a model that describes the internal state, that indicates which parts of the state are presented to the user, and that shows how actions on the model change the state and the presentation. One model that satisfies these requirements is the notation described by Bramwell (1995) and Bramwell et al. (1995), based on the structuring concept of interactor, and the Action Systems formalism.

---

interactor *SpellCheck*

var   *misSpelt* : seq *Word*
          dict : *Dictionary*
     suggestions : seq *Word*

pres *head*(*misSpelt*); *suggestions*

action *ignore* $\hat{=}$ *misSpelt* $\neq \langle \rangle \rightarrow$
        misSpelt, $\cdot \left[\begin{array}{c} misSpelt = tail(misSpelt_0) \land \\ suggestions = suggest(head(misSpelt), dict) \end{array} \right]$
        suggestions

Fig. 2. State-based model of the Spell Checker

The interactor shown in Fig. 2 describes part of the behaviour of the spelling checker. The vars section lists the state variables of the interactor: *misSpelt* is a list of misspellings in the word processor document, *dict* is the dictionary used to check spellings and make suggestions for corrections, and *suggestions* is the list of suggestions for the current misspelling. The pres clause lists those properties that will be made available to the user in the interactor's presentation: in this case, the first misspelling and the list of suggestions. Only one action is shown here, corresponding to the Ignore button. Its definition states that it can be invoked whenever the list of spelling mistakes is non empty, and that its effect is update the *misSpelt* and *suggestions* variables appropriately.

For the spelling checker, the predictability property, i.e. that the presentation function is injective, could be stated as:

$$\forall s, s' : (\text{seq } Word \times Dictionary \times \text{seq } Word) \bullet pres(s) = pres(s') \Rightarrow s = s'$$

where the presentation function *pres* is is derived from the interactor specification:

$$pres : (\text{seq } Word \times Dictionary \times \text{seq } Word) \rightarrow (Word \times \text{seq } Word)$$
$$pres(misSpelt, dict, suggestions) = ((head(misSpelt), suggestions)).$$

This property is clearly not respected by the spelling checker: information exists in the internal state that is not presented in the display (specifically the dictionary and the tail of the *misSpelt* list).

Using the template concept of (Harrison et al. 1989) we might ask instead whether the spelling checker's response to the ignore action is predictable to the user, if we exclude the dictionary and *misSpelt* list from the task template. This weaker property is respected by the spelling checker.

3.2 Checking a design against an expectation

In much the same way as Action Systems can be used to model and reason about the behaviour of interactive systems, a simpler formalism based on Propositional Production Systems (PPS) has been used. Using the Action Simulator software developed by Monk and Curry (1994) it is possible to model a system as a collection of state variables together with "if–then" style production rules describing the transformations to state variables that occur as a result of user actions. This approach has been used as a specification technique by Szwillus and Kespohl (1996).

The Action Simulator style of description can be used to construct a model of the interaction between the spelling checker window and the main word processor. The model in Fig. 3 covers slightly different ground from the Action Systems interactor above, and concentrates on what happens when the user switches between spell checking and word processing functions. The model represents three state attributes: whether or not any text is selected in the word processor, whether the spell checker is checking just the selected text or the entire document, and whether the spell checker window is currently active and checking is in progress.

The user interacts with the system by means of a number of actions, of which only two are modelled here. The *spell* action activates the spell checker when the word processor is active, and the *edit* action re-activates the word processor. Each of the user actions is represented in the model by one or more *production rules*, expressed as a *pre-condition* on when the rule can be "fired" and a *post-condition* on what the effect will be if the rule is fired. The pre- and post-conditions are recorded in a table showing the values of state variables under which each condition is satisfied. For instance, the first rule for the spell action is:

	text selected	checking selection	spell checking	
spell	false	—	false	Pre-condition
	true	false	true	Post-condition

The first line of the rule is the pre-condition which states that the rule fires when both 'test selected' and 'spell checking' are false (and 'checking selection' may have any value). The post-condition on the last line indicates that when spell is applied in a situation satisfying the pre-condition, 'test selected' and 'spell checking' are both set to be true and 'checking selection' is set to false. The complete model, containing an additional rule for *spell* and a rule for *edit* is shown in Fig. 3.

	text selected	checking selection	spell checking
spell	false	—	false
	true	false	true
spell	true	—	false
	true	true	true
edit	—	—	true
	—	—	false

Fig. 3. Action Simulator style model of the Spelling Checker

Even a very simple model like this can highlight some interesting facts about the interface. It might seem natural for the actions *spell* and *edit* to simply toggle between a state where the document may be edited and one where the spelling of the document is being checked. However, the model reveals that this is not the case, as the action of invoking the spelling checker changes the selected text in the editor. For users of the word processor, this is often revealed in an interaction beginning in a state where no text is selected, so the spelling of the entire document is being checked. If the actions "*spell; edit; spell*" are carried out, the result is a state where a single word is selected and its spelling is being checked – probably not what the user was expecting!

Models constructed in this way can be analysed in several ways. The simplest is that using the Action Simulator, models may be executed "by hand". This allows designers and users to obtain fairly rapid feedback about whether the model describes a system that satisfies the original requirements. Others have suggested a more automated approach to the analysis of PPS descriptions. Olsen et al. (1995), define algorthims that check a number of "standard" usability-related properties with respect to a PPS model. Wang and others (1994, 1995) describe a way of checking similar properties expressed in temporal logic using a general temporal logic model checker.

3.3 Investigating liveness properties

In contrast to the models of the previous section, a number of formal software engineering approaches can be applied so as to emphasise temporal aspects of an interactive system, e.g. using notations based on state transitions such as Petri nets or process algebras. In these approaches, the emphasis is on constructing representations of the temporal ordering of actions supported or enforced by an interface. Although both Petri net derivatives such as ICO (Palanque and Bastide 1995b) and developments of the LO-TOS process algebra (e.g., Paternò et al. 1995) do allow the definition and manipulation of data, it is the temporal ordering aspects of interfaces that are made most evident by these models.

Figure 4 shows a Petri net representation of the process of skipping through words which are not in the dictionary using the mouse and the "Ignore" button. Inputs from the environment cause tokens to be added in the appropriate places at the top. The other places in the net are used to record the state. The model shows, for example, that the spell checker must be Ready for input and the mouse key be pressed Down while the pointer is In the "Ignore" button in order to make the button Active. Then the mouse may either Leave the button, or the mouse key may be moved Up, causing the button to become Inactive and the checker to be Searching for the next misspelt word.

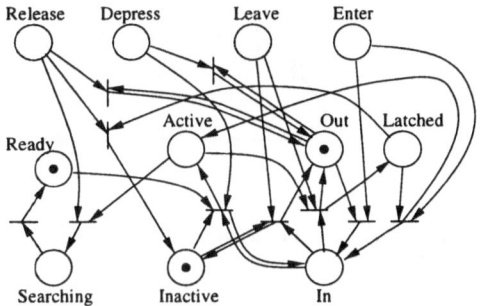

Fig. 4. Petri net model of the Spelling Checker

The model highlights the order in which actions may be performed and the fact that certain actions are available only at certain times. Also it may be subject to analysis for certain conditions. Palanque and Bastide (1995b) list a number of kinds of such checking, which Petri net descriptions support, including detection of the presence of deadlock, checking the predictability of commands (i.e., does a command always have the same effect in the same context), and reinitiability.

3.4 Sequencing of user and system events

An approach that focuses on the sequencing of events, but is firmly rooted in a philosophy of modelling for validation, rather than specification and refinement is Interaction Framework (Harrison et al. 1995; Blandford et al. 1995). Interaction framework provides a language for discussing interaction that aims to be 'agent neutral', i.e. to treat events within the computer system, interaction events, and events that only involve humans, e.g. cognitive events or human-human communication events, equally.

Interaction Framework models an interaction trajectory as a partial order of events. For instance, during the evolution of the spelling checker's design, we might consider an interaction trajectory consisting of the following events:

e_1 the user releases the mouse button over the ignore button;
e_2 the system finds and displays the next misspelt word;

e_3 the user moves to the second button (change / delete)[1] and depresses the mouse button;

e_4 the user releases the button;

e_5 the system finds a list of suggestions within the dictionary;

e_6 the system displays the list of suggestions.

It is clear that event e_1 must precede all the other events. Assuming that event e_2 precedes event e_3 and e_5, that e_3 precedes e_4, and e_5 precedes e_6, Fig. 5 shows the partial order that is generated from these constraints.

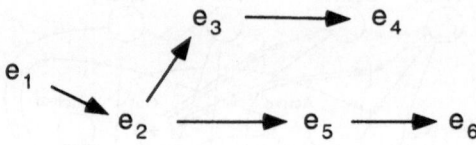

Fig. 5. A partial order of interaction events

Figure 5 does not specify any constraints on the ordering of events e_2 and e_3 or e_6 and e_4. However, if the actual order of events is $\langle e_3, e_6, e_4 \rangle$ then the user may inadvertently replace the misspelt word when their intention was to delete it. The contribution of Interaction Framework, in this case, is to provide a language in which this design problem can be described. The solution adopted by Microsoft Word is to ensure that if e_3 occurs before e_6, then no alternative suggestions are displayed, unless the user releases the mouse button whilst outside of the 'delete' button area.

3.5 The structure of displays

The models described so far have used abstract descriptions of the *behaviour* of interactive devices to support analysis. This form of abstraction means that many features of the resulting user interface, such as *where* things will be located on the screen and *how* they will appear, are outside the scope of the models. In order to answer questions about the accessibility of information on the screen, a collection of modelling techniques has been developed. For example, May et al. (1995) use *structure diagrams* to model the visual structure of the interface. Figure 6 shows a structure diagram for the Spelling checker dialogue box. By focusing their attention on an object, the user makes this the "psychological subject". The white-on-black objects form the "pragmatic subjects", the dominant parts of the display to which a user's attention will first be attracted.

While the structure diagram shows the objects present in an interface and the relationships between them, May et al. (1995) use a second type of diagram to indicate some of the perceptual and cognitive work involved in *using* the display. A *transition path diagram* records the changes over time of psychological subject and "predicate", or surrounding context, for the subject as the user scans for relevant information.

---

[1] The button is labelled delete when the 'Change To:' slot of the display is empty.

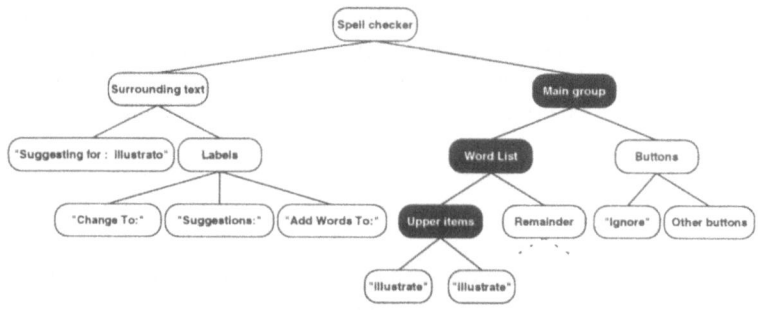

Fig. 6. Structure diagram representing the spelling checker interface

For example, Fig. 7 shows the transitions between objects that occur as a user of the Spelling Checker searches for the unrecognised word, navigating through the perceptual field of objects. The transitions follow the attentional shifts, starting with the most prominent subject, i.e. Upper items, then rejecting this and moving eventually toward the misspelt word. This analysis shows that it takes a relatively long time to find the

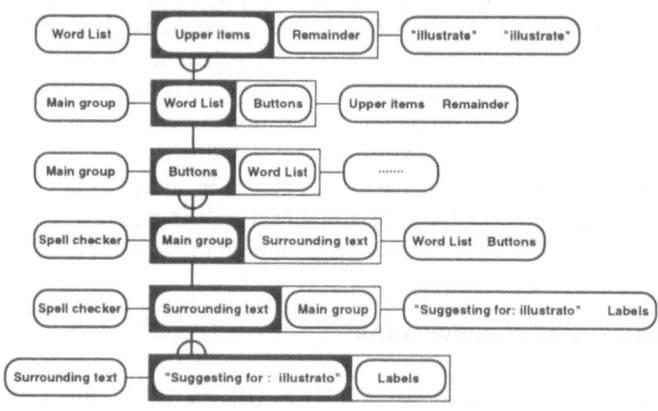

Fig. 7. Transition diagram for the spelling checker interface

misspelt word in the dialogue box, probably an undesirable characteristic. In addition, the structure diagram shows why this is the case and gives clues about how to modify the display to make this feature easier to locate. The misspelt word might be given more emphasis and be aligned with the word list, causing it to become part of that group in the structure. The structure diagram also shows that the word list is more closely linked with the buttons than with the word list labels, also probably undesirable.

Clearly, the transition path taken in a given situation is very dependent on the task that is being carried out. In order to be able to construct a transition diagram for a task and to understand the cognitive work involved, an additional theoretical tool might be employed to gain an understanding of how perceptual aspects of the interfaces interact with the user's knowledge. One such tool is the framework of Interacting Cognitive Subsystems which has been described at a previous DSVIS conference (Barnard and May 1995).

3.6 Ensuring that interaction is adequately resourced

Hutchins (1995) points out that individual episodes of interaction with a device always take place in the context of a network of cognitive activities that are distributed in both time and space. From this viewpoint, an important question to ask is how the resources that are needed to perform a particular task are going to be made available to the user at the time they are needed. The distributed information resources model (Wright et al. 1996) aims to support analysis of this question. Rather than focusing on sequences of user behaviour that a system is required to support, the resources model takes as its unit of analysis a distributed cognitive system, consisting of computer artefacts and users. The model looks at the information that is required in order to decide how to act, and where in the distributed system this information is located.

Using this model, we may consider the stage in the interaction that is shown in Fig. 1. In order to interact with the system, the user needs various resources. Some of those resources may be available from the display, some may need to be recalled from the user's memory, others may be located in manuals. Some relevant resources are the knowledge about the functions supported by the buttons, the knowledge that the interaction will involve reviewing a sequence of misspelt words, knowledge about the fact that the dictionary may not contain proper nouns, etc. Another resource that will affect the user's choice between two suggestions ("illustrate" or "illustrator") offered, is the context in which the misspelt word appears. In the current design of the spell checker, this resource is sometimes unavailable from the display, as in Fig. 1. Various alternative designs for the spell checker might attempt to correct this problem.

4   Discussion and observations

In the previous section, we demonstrated how different issues that might arise during the design of one artefact, could be tackled by analysing different types of model. None of the models that we presented is suitable to derive all the insights that we mentioned. Thus, these different models should be seen as complementing each other, rather than competing. In practice, the decision to use any particular tool or method in a design project will not be taken in a vacuum, but will be driven by particular project goals. This suggests that the creation of different models of the artefact should also be driven by the analytic tasks that we hope to perform.

An important point about the models that we applied was that the models varied in their scope. Fig. 8 shows one way in which the scope of the models might be compared. State-based models, such as our interactor and propositional production systems models, allow properties that relate the display to the internal state to be investigated, and can be used to explore the effects of particular sequences of action. Behavioural or temporal models, such as our Petri-net and Interaction Framework models, allow analysis of the way in which actions can combine into legal sequences of behaviour over time. Questions of layout and presentation can be addressed by constructing models of structural aspects of the interface as it will be perceived by users, e.g. our display structure model. Task models (of which we have not presented an example) can provide insight into the appropriateness of dialogue structures to the users task. The scope for analysis is enlarged further in models which encompass not only the interactive system, but also its user and the distributed cognitive system of which both are a part, as with our discussion of interaction resources.

Fig. 8. Scope of HCI models

The second point to note about the models is that the focus of each is partial, i.e. we modelled only those aspects of the system that were relevant to the particular analysis we were conducting. An important question in learning to use diverse models will be how to construct the right model for the right job.

Our contention is that, all of these models, with their varying scope and varying focus, can provide valuable perspectives on a designed (or yet to be designed) artefact. For the models to be useful, it is not necessary for them to be complete in either scope or focus, nor for any single model to be privileged or identified as the definitive specification.

Using multiple heterogeneous representations in a design process does raise some methodological issues. In particular, we may need to consider the twin problems of *consistency* and *veracity*. Briefly, the consistency problem, closely allied to the concept of "viscosity" (Green 1989), is one of managing change and propagating the effects of change throughout a representation or collection of representations. The veracity problem is that of making sure that all the different models are veracious representations of the same reality.

In dealing with consistency, it may be possible to construct multiple models that have a precisely defined semantic connection with each other. However, we do not wish to exclude those models that do not enjoy such status, as we can often obtain insights into our designs with methods that do not have a common, complete mathematical foundation. Indeed divergence and disagreement between models from different viewpoints can be exploited to actually enhance our understanding of design issues. For example, Arnold et al. (1995) describe how an informal comparison of two formal models allowed them to detect ambiguities in a requirements document and to correct mistakes in each of the models. Nuseibeh (1996) advocates collecting disparate, partial, requirements specifications into a single logical framework that can tolerate and even exploit inconsistency. Finally, we would argue that the problem of managing consistency does not disappear if a single unified notational framework is used. Requirements documents written in such frameworks may still contain multiple references to the same part of the state or behaviour of a system, giving rise to a high degree of viscosity.

It is in dealing with veracity issue that the use of a single unified notation appears to find its strongest support. When an abstract specification is refined to produce a concrete one, the rules of refinement guarantee that the former is necessarily a veracious abstraction of the latter. In departing such well-founded territory, as suggested in this paper, it seems that we must forego some of the certainty afforded by refinement that our models are accurate abstractions of reality. However, the certainty afforded by refinement may be, to some degree, illusory. As Dix (1991) points out, the fact that the various steps of refinement are correct still leaves the question of the mapping from the interactive system and the requirements of its users into the formalism, the so called "formality gap". Thus, whether we choose a single unified formalism and use refinement to develop our design, or we use a range of modelling techniques to support validation, in the end we must rely on the professionalism of the modelling or specification practitioner to ensure that the models and analyses are veracious.

Finally, it is interesting to compare our more diverse, less rigorous use of models with the approach applied in other engineering disciplines. In common with other authors (eg. (Hooper 1986)), we can draw an analogy between HCI and designing and erecting a building, where several different kinds of model will be used. It will be described as a set of lines and masses for the structural analysis. Plans and elevations will show the layout of the building. A functional description will show the interconnecting roles of the interconnecting parts. Perspective drawings, sketches, physical scale models and computer simulations are used to get an impression of the building's ultimate appearance. Different models and levels of rigour afford different kinds of analysis and prediction. Ultimately, the confidence one can have in the building rests largely on trust in the professionalism of the architects, engineers and builders engaged in its construction.

5   Conclusions for design methodology

To summarise, this paper has suggested that research in the DSVIS community could benefit from a stronger orientation towards modelling and analysis for validation. The way such an approach can gain power, is by applying formal modelling and analysis to selected aspects of an artefact, rather that by attempting to specify all aspects of a system's function using a single notational framework. Although the argument for using diverse models has not previously been made in the DSVIS forum, it reflects current practice in many other engineering disciplines. Such a change in emphasis would demonstrate that formal approaches have more to offer HCI than simply specification and refinement. On the other hand, we may need to recognise that, in HCI, the correctness of an implementation with respect to a specification may provide even fewer guarantees of a "good" system, than in other areas of software engineering.

To make this conclusion more concrete, we can suggest a number of changes of orientation and focus for future work in this area, stressing the importance of modelling, analysis, and validation, in addition to specification, verification, and refinement. We look forward to future DSVIS papers that attempt to combine techniques at a methodological, rather than a semantic, level and which adopt a more problem driven, rather than a notation driven, approach. These focus shifts can be summarised as follows.

From prescription to description: To think more seriously about *models* and *modelling languages* and their use as descriptive and analytic tools than about prescriptive specifications.

From verification to validation: Instead of concentrating on the representation of requirements, designs, specifications, and the transformations between them at the core of the formal development process, we can look at other roles for models. In particular, the way that models and representations of the artefact under development function as analytic tools or mediate communication between participants in the development process.

From broad to narrow models: Rather than describe all parts of a system, or propose techniques that rely on all parts of a system being covered, a more piecemeal approach allows progress to be made and useful results determined, when the focus of the modelling activity is narrowly directed at only certain parts of a system.

From single to multiple representations: Rather than aiming to construct a single unified model of an artefact or phenomenon, consider instead using a number of models reflecting different perspectives on the artefact.

From general to specific notations: Many existing modelling or specification languages reflect a desire to capture all properties of an artefact. When a notation is unable to express some class of properties, it can be seen as deficient — a situation that can lead to unwieldy, hybrid notations. Rather than setting our sights on a universal language capable of specifying all aspects of a system, we can profitably apply a number of loosely coupled modelling notations, constrained by the analysis they seek to support.

This focus shift is summarised by Fig. 9: from (a) concentrating on specifications and the process of transforming them (with analysis taking a back seat) to (b) models and analytic tools being in the foreground and given greater prominence than the development route. In the former situation, the mechanics of constructing specifications and implementations are emphasised, whereas in the latter, the focus is more on the contributions that models can make to design. This decoupling of validation from refinement allows alternative views of how reification takes place while still getting some of the benefits of formal analysis, suggesting an approach where lightweight, narrowly focused models with fewer dependencies mean more opportunities for gaining insight.

42

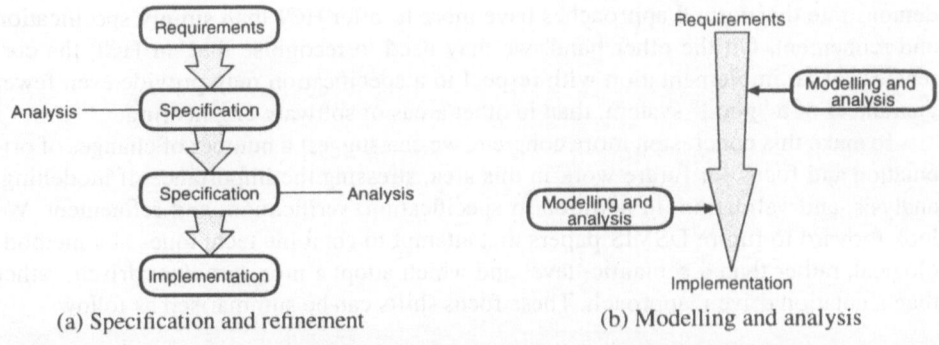

(a) Specification and refinement   (b) Modelling and analysis

Fig. 9. Two views of the status of models

We conclude with a quotation from David Lorge Parnas which, from a more general software engineering standpoint, echoes the sentiment of this paper.

> *The distinction between model, description, and specification is missed in most books and examples. People often use the word "specification" when they mean "model".*
>
> ...
>
> *There is an unreasonable focus on proof of correctness. In other areas, engineers rarely prove theorems; instead they use mathematics to derive important properties of their designs. They also use mathematics to describe their designs in a way that makes mathematical analysis possible.*   **(Parnas 1996)**

References

Abowd, G., H.-M. Wang, and A. Monk (1995, August). A formal technique for automated dialogue developments. In *Proceedings, First Symposium on Designing Interactive Systems — DIS'95, Ann Arbor, MI.*

Arnold, A., M.-C. Gaudel, and B. Marre (1995, September). An experiment on the validation of a specification by heterogeneous formal means: The transit node. In *5th IFIP Working Conference on Dependable Computing for Critical Applications (DCCA-5)*, Urbana-Champaign, USA, pp. 24–34.

Barnard, P. and J. May (1995). Interactions with advanced graphical interfaces and the deployment of latent human knowledge. See Paternò (1995), pp. 15–48.

Blandford, A., M. Harrison, and P. Barnard (1995). Using interaction framework to guide the design of interactive systems. *International Journal of Human-Computer Studies 43*, 101–130.

Bodart, F. and J. Vanderdonckt (Eds.) (1996). *Design, Specification, Verification of Interactive Systems '96*, Springer Computer Science. Springer Wien New York.

Bramwell, C. (1995). *Formal aspects of the Design Rationale of Interactive Systems*. Ph. D. thesis, Dept. of Computer Science, University of York.

Bramwell, C., B. Fields, and M. Harrison (1995). Exploring design options rationally. See Palanque and Bastide (1995a), pp. 134–148.

Dix, A. (1991). *Formal Methods for Interactive Systems*. Computers and People Series. Academic Press.

Dix, A., J. Finlay, G. Abowd, and R. Beale (1993). *Human-Computer Interaction*. Prentice-Hall International.

Faconti, G. P. and D. J. Duke (1996). Device models. See Bodart and Vanderdonckt (1996), pp. 73–91.

Fields, B., M. Harrison, and P. Wright (1995). Modelling interactive systems and providing task relevant information. See Paternò (1995), pp. 253–266.

Green, T. R. G. (1989). Cognitive dimensions of notations. In A. Sutcliffe and L. Macaulay (Eds.), *Proceedings of the Fifth Conference of the BCS HCI Special Interest Group*, pp. 443–460. Cambridge University Press.

Harrison, M., A. Blandford, and P. Barnard (1995). The requirements engineering of user freedom. See Paternò (1995), pp. 181–194.

Harrison, M., C. Roast, and P. Wright (1989). Complementary methods for the iterative design of interactive systems. In G. Salvendy and M. Smith (Eds.), *Designing and Using Human-Computer Interfaces and Knowledge-Based Systems*, pp. 651–658. Elsevier.

Hooper, K. (1986). Archtectural Design: An analogy. In D. Norman and S. Draper (Eds.), *User-Centered System Design: New Perspectives on Human Computer Interaction*, Chapter 1, pp. 9–23. Lawrence Erlbaum Associates Inc.

Hutchins, E. (1995). *Cognition in the Wild*. MIT Press.

May, J., S. Scott, and P. Barnard (1995). *Structuring Displays: A Psychological Guide*. Eurographics Tutorial Notes Series. EACG: Geneva. Appeared as Amodeus report B04.

Monk, A. and M. Curry (1994). Discount dialogue modelling with Action Simulator. In G. Cockton, S. Draper, and G. Weir (Eds.), *Proceedings, HCI'94*, Number IX in People and Computers, pp. 327–338. BCS HCI Specialist Group: Cambridge University Press.

Nuseibeh, B. (1996). To be *And* not to be: On managing inconsistency in software development. In *Proceedings of 8th International Workshop on Software Specification and Design (IWSSD-8)*, pp. 164–169. IEEE CS Press.

Olsen, D., A. Monk, and M. Curry (1995). Algorithms for automatic dialogue analysis using propositional production systems. *Human Computer Interaction 10*, 39–78.

Palanque, P. and R. Bastide (Eds.) (1995a). *Design, Specification, Verification of Interactive Systems '95*, Springer Computer Science. Springer Wien New York.

Palanque, P. and R. Bastide (1995b). Petri net-based design of user-driven interfaces using the interactive cooperative objects formalism. See Paternò (1995), pp. 383–400.

Palanque, P., F. Paternò, R. Bastide, and M. Mezzanote (1996). Towards and integrated proposal for interactive systems design based in TLIM and ICO. See Bodart and Vanderdonckt (1996), pp. 162–187.

Parnas, D. L. (1996, April). Mathematical methods: What we need and don't need. *IEEE Computer*, 28–29.

Paternò, F. (Ed.) (1995). *Interactive Systems: Design, Specification and Verification*, Focus on Computer Graphics Series. Springer-Verlag.

Paternò, F., M. Sciacchitano, and J. Löwgren (1995). A user interface evaluation mapping physical user actions to task-driven formal specifications. See Palanque and Bastide (1995a), pp. 35–53.

Szwillus, G. and K. Kespohl (1996). Prototyping device interfaces with DSN/2. See Bodart and Vanderdonckt (1996), pp. 123–140.

Wang, H.-M. and G. Abowd (1994, July). A tabular interface for automated verification of event-based dialogues. Technical Report CMU-CS-94-189, School of Computer Science, Carnegie Mellon University.

Wright, P., B. Fields, and M. Harrison (1996). Distributed information resources: A new approach to interaction modelling. In T. Green, J. Cañas, and C. Warren (Eds.), *Proceedings of ECCE8: European Conference on Cognitive Ergonomics*, pp. 5–10. EACE. URL: *http://www.cs.york.ac.uk/~bob/papers.html*.

Users as rational interacting agents: formalising assumptions about cognition and interaction

Ann Blandford, Richard Butterworth & Jason Good

School of Computing Science, Middlesex University, Bounds Green Road, London, N11 2NQ, U.K.

A.Blandford@mdx.ac.uk   *http://www.cs.mdx.ac.uk/puma/*

Abstract: One way of assessing the usability of a computer system is to make reasonable assumptions about users' cognition and to analyse how they can be expected to work with the system, using their knowledge and information from the display to achieve their goals. This is the approach taken in Programmable User Modelling Analysis, a technique for predictive usability evaluation of interactive systems. The technique is based on the premise that an analyst can gain insights into the usability of a computer system by specifying the knowledge that a user needs to be able to use it and drawing inferences on how that knowledge will guide the user's behaviour. This may be done by observing how a cognitive architecture, "programmed" with that knowledge, behaves. An alternative approach is to develop a formal description of the essential features of the cognitive architecture and to use that description to reason about likely user behaviour. In this paper, we present the approach and an outline formal description of the cognitive architecture. This initial description is derived from an existing implementation. We illustrate how the description can be used in reasoning by applying it to the task of setting up call diverting on a mobile phone. Successful performance of this task involves a combination of planned and responsive behaviour. The process of doing this analysis highlights what assumptions have been made by the designers about the user's knowledge. We discuss limitations of the current formalisation and identify directions for future work.

Keywords: User modelling, formal description, cognitive architecture, interactive systems.

1. Introduction

One approach to predictive usability evaluation of an interactive computer system is to model how a user is likely to work with it. Traditionally (e.g. Kieras & Polson, 1985; Polson & Lewis, 1990; John & Kieras, 1996), such user modelling techniques have given analytic leverage largely by providing a constrained language with which the analyst can lay out assumptions about the user and system, and occasionally by allowing the analyst to construct running simulation models of interactive behaviour. Programmable User Modelling Analysis (PUMA) is such a user modelling technique. It involves considering the design of a computer system in terms of the tasks which the system is designed to support, and what the user is expected to do to achieve those tasks. At the heart of the approach is the idea that a PUMA analyst should have access to a Programmable User Model (PUM) which can be programmed with domain and device specific knowledge and run to simulate interactive behaviour. However, rather than always aiming towards producing a running model of interactive behaviour, there are potential advantages of developing a formal description of the underlying architecture as a basis for reasoning without simulation.

One advantage of formal description is that the developer of any simulation model needs to make assumptions which are not a part of the core theory just to get the simulation 'ticking over', and it can be difficult to be sure whether a particular modelled behaviour is a logical consequence of the core theory or of incidental features of a particular implementation. It can also become unclear, over time, which aspects of an implementation are theoretically motivated, as opposed to being local utilitarian decisions to get something running.

A second advantage is that a formal description is less open to multiple interpretations, and that the core assumptions that lead the analyst to make particular usability predictions can be stated unambiguously. We are heading towards a point where it should be possible to prove that a particular behavioural prediction is a logical consequence of particular axioms about cognition and particular user knowledge. As discussed below, in many cases a PUM Analysis involves hand simulation of behaviour without constructing a running model; a formal description expresses clearly the basis on which such a hand simulation is done.

A third motivation for this approach is that it may be possible, in future, to integrate such a description of user properties with the formal specifications of computer systems that are generated (comparatively) routinely within the design process (Bowen & Hinchey, 1995) in order to infer properties of interactive systems.

The work reported in this paper is a step in the process of developing and testing a set of axioms about user cognition that can be used for reasoning about user behaviour.

2. Background

The original vision for this work (Young, Green and Simon, 1989) was that the analyst should gain insight into the usability of an interactive system both through the process of specifying the knowledge the user needs (in the PUM Instruction Language) and by observing the behaviour of the running model. The knowledge analysis is guided by the requirements of the Instruction Language, which in turn is designed as a programming language for the PUM.

The PUM is a constrained problem solver whose design is based on established theories of rationality and human problem solving (Newell & Simon, 1972; Card, Moran & Newell, 1983). The core of the PUM is a problem-solving mechanism based on means-ends reasoning, one of the less powerful approaches to problem solving that people employ. If this problem-solver can solve problems in a domain, there is a good chance that people will be able to too; conversely, if the problem-solver makes mistakes, or if the analyst has difficulty specifying what knowledge the problem solver needs to work with, then this simple tool can give the analyst insights into aspects of the problem-domain that people might have difficulty with (Young, Green & Simon, 1989).

PUM analysis generally proceeds through several stages (Blandford & Young, 1996), and may also involve iteration between stages. The first three stages take place for all analyses; these involve identifying domain tasks to be analysed (usually either the most frequently performed tasks, or critical ones), identifying conceptual operations (the things that the user must do, in a way that "makes sense" in the domain) for achieving the tasks, and expressing the user's knowledge in terms of the Instruction Language. If doing this highlights major difficulties with the design of the device, then analysis may stop at this stage. Otherwise, the next stage is to do hand-simulation of the interactive behaviour, giving an account of how the user's knowledge of the state of the system changes, and how the user adopts goals and commitments in the course of the interaction; the description presented below lays out a simple set of axioms for rigorous hand simulation. The final stage has traditionally been the construction of a running model.

Several alternative implementations of a PUM, using a variety of approaches, have been produced. The description presented below is based on one particular implementation, a simple prototype problem solver called the Programmable Interactive Problem Solver (PIPS; figure 1). PIPS is a model of a user, implemented in Lisp, that interacts with a modelled device to simulate plausible interactive behaviours. It omits many aspects of cognitive processing that are the focus of ongoing research. However, it provides a basis for developing a formal description of a cognitive architecture. This formal description has been produced retrospectively, to make explicit the important abstract properties of the implemented system, to enable more abstract reasoning, and as a basis for further work.

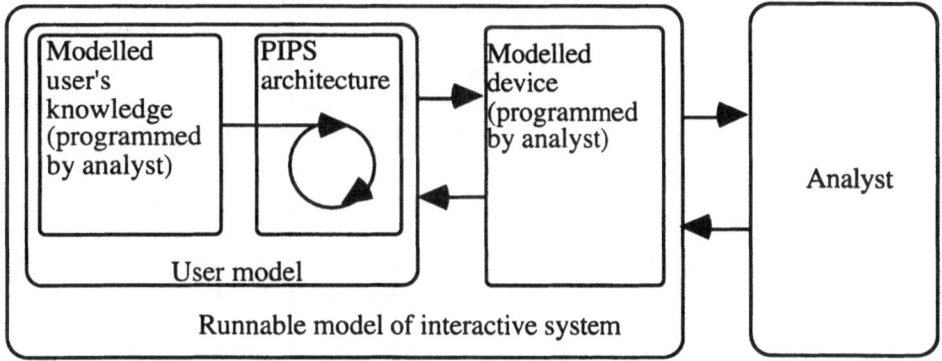

Fig. 1: the overall system configuration for the PIPS interactive system

The description language used is based on Modal Action Logic (MAL; Ryan, Fiadeiro & Maibaum, 1991). We use standard predicate logic with the addition of deontic operators ("per" and "obl") to describe when the agent is permitted or obliged to perform an internal action, and "[action]" which can be read as "after action is performed...". An agent may have obligations to perform several actions at the same time; if so, then the ordering on those actions is undefined. Also, an action that becomes obliged while not permitted cancels the non-permission, and vice versa. This allows us to express the essential features of the agent architecture at an appropriate level of abstraction.

The PIPS architecture implements simple means-ends reasoning with precondition subgoaling. That is, the model selects actions to achieve goals, and if the currently selected action cannot be done because preconditions are not satisfied, then those preconditions are adopted as goals and the model selects further actions to achieve those goals. In Newell's (1982) terms, the system satisfies the principle of rationality (selecting actions to achieve goals); it does not model any more sophisticated reasoning, or non-rational behaviour.

3. Formal description of the architecture

An outline description for this system, capturing the essential properties of the architecture, is as follows. In this description, an "operator" links together what the user model, or agent, knows about how to achieve effects in the world. In brief, an operator defines what external action might be applied for what purpose, and under what circumstances. The same action might address different goals in different circumstances; conversely, the same goal might be achieved by different actions under different circumstances; these are specified as different operators.

state:

committed:	Poperator	the agent becomes committed to applying operators
adopted:	Ppredicate	adopted goals, beliefs and the task are all expressed in terms of predicates on the state.
beliefs:	Ppredicate	external actions, which are executed when a committed operator becomes doable, are not explicitly components on the state.
task:	Ppredicate	

relations:

precond _:	operator → Ppredicate	goals (predicates) must be achieved before operator can be applied.
purpose _:	operator → predicate	the purpose of the operator is to achieve a goal.
performs _:	operator → action	there is an external action that performs the operator.
filter _:	operator → Ppredicate	filters must be true for operator to be considered as a candidate (be "acceptable").

tracked-effect-of _:	operator → $\mathbb{P}$predicate	the agent knows that when the operator is applied, the predicates become true on the state.
visible-effect-of _:	action → $\mathbb{P}$predicate	the agent can see that when an external action is performed, the predicates become true on the state.

The internal actions (which cause the agent's state to be updated) are:

internal actions:

adopt:	$\mathbb{P}$predicate	adopt goals.
note-achieved:	$\mathbb{P}$predicate	note when goals have been achieved.
commit-to-preferred:	$\mathbb{P}$operator	select between alternative candidate operators.
commit:	operator	commit to applying an operator.
execute:	action	execute an external action.

Then the core behaviour of the agent can be defined in terms of the following axioms.

Initialisation and termination:

The first internal action is to initialise the task goal. Any differences between the task goal state and the beliefs about the current state are adopted as goals.

$$\text{task} \setminus (\text{beliefs} \cup \text{adopted}) \neq \varnothing \Rightarrow \text{obl(adopt(task} \setminus (\text{beliefs} \cup \text{adopted})))} \qquad \text{[Axiom 1]}$$

The agent ceases to behave when the task goals have been achieved; if Act is the set of all possible internal actions then

$$A \in \text{Act} \wedge \text{per}(A) \Rightarrow \neg \text{ task} \subseteq \text{beliefs} \qquad \text{[Axiom 2]}$$

commit to an operator:

For each adopted goal there is a set of operators the purpose of which is to achieve that goal. The function acceptable_ops returns such a set of operators (the filters of which are satisfied) for a given goal.

$$\text{acceptable\_ops : predicate} \rightarrow \mathbb{P}\text{operator}$$
$$\text{acceptable\_ops}(g) \equiv \{ \text{ o : operator} \mid g = \text{purpose}(o) \wedge \text{filter}(o) \subseteq \text{beliefs} \}$$

The agent architecture implements means-ends reasoning; if no operator has been committed to for addressing a goal, then select one (whose filters are satisfied). Then the result of doing a selection is that one operator will be identified as preferred:

$g \in$ adopted $\land$ acceptable_ops(g) $\cap$ committed $= \emptyset$

$\Rightarrow$ obl(commit-to-preferred(acceptable_ops(g)))   [Axiom 3]

If there is more than one possible operator that might be selected, each possibility is investigated (currently manually) so that the space of possible behaviours can be explored.

Once a unique preferred operator has been identified, the agent becomes committed to applying it, and the preference is removed. The system implements precondition subgoaling; on committing to o, if o has preconditions that are not currently satisfied then they are adopted as goals too:

committed $= C \Rightarrow$ [commit-to-preferred(O)] $\exists$ o : operator $\bullet$ o $\in$ O $\land$ committed $= C \cup \{o\} \land$

obl(adopt(precond(o) \ beliefs)) $\land \neg$per(commit-to-preferred(O))

[Axiom 4]

adopted $= A \Rightarrow$ [adopt(G)] adopted $= A \cup G \land \neg$per(adopt(G))   [Axiom 5]

drop goals and commitments when appropriate

Once a goal has been achieved or a commitment fulfilled, it should no longer be retained as a goal or commitment. In the case of a goal, this means that the current state of the system satisfies the goal (i.e. it is a state-based evaluation). In the case of a commitment, this means that the corresponding external action is executed (regardless of the outcome).

adopted $\cap$ beliefs $\neq \emptyset \Rightarrow$ obl(note-achieved(adopted $\cap$ beliefs))   [Axiom 6]

adopted $= A \Rightarrow$ [note-achieved(G)] adopted $= A \setminus G \land \neg$per(note-achieved(G))   [Axiom 7]

o $\in$ committed $\land$ precond(o) $\subseteq$ beliefs $\Rightarrow$ obl(apply(o))   [Axiom 8]

committed $= C \Rightarrow$ [apply(o)] committed $= C \setminus \{o\} \land \neg$per(apply(o)) $\land$

obl(execute(performs(o)))

[Axiom 9]

interaction:

The agent maintains its knowledge of the state of the world through two separate mechanisms. The first is through mentally tracking the effects of operators ("I know that doing this causes that, so when I do this, that becomes true"). The second is through observing visible changes to the state of the world.

beliefs = B ⇒ [apply(o)] beliefs = B ⊔ tracked-effects-of(o) [Axiom 10]

beliefs = B ⇒ [execute(a)] beliefs = B ⊔ visible-effects-of(a) ∧ ¬per(execute(a))

[Axiom 11]

We use B ⊔ C here to mean B ∪ C excluding any {b, ¬b} subsets. Essentially, any predicates on the state that become visible as a consequence of a user action (or tracked as a consequence of the user applying an operator) are added and any that have gone away are deleted.

As shown, the essential properties of this architecture are as follows:

- the system implements means-ends reasoning. The reasoning is intentionally simple, to model plausible human problem solving (in the tradition of Newell & Simon (1972)).

- goals and external actions are related to other relevant knowledge through *operators*, which provide a structure for relating goals and actions with their preconditions and predictable effects.

- only one level of goals and actions have to be specified, to make expressing users' knowledge a tractable proposition for the analyst (Young, Green and Simon, 1989). Goals are predicates on the state of the world, so the agent can explicitly check whether or not a goal has been achieved (subject to the information being knowable by that agent).

- the agent maintains its knowledge about the state of the device partly through tracking the effects of operations (see Blandford and Young, 1995) and partly through observing visible changes to the state of the device display. This maintenance is implemented as an explicit part of the description, not indirectly through actions.

We now proceed to illustrate the behaviour of this architecture when primed with knowledge about a particular device and task.

4. Example

We take as our example for analysis one task on a mobile 'phone, that of setting up call-divert to divert incoming calls to another 'phone number. This analysis is based on a 'phone that we will refer to as the Tango 'phone (Figure 2). In common with many mobile 'phones currently in use, and a variety of other interactive devices, the settings of this 'phone are defined or modified by navigating a nested menu structure (Figure 3). Once the menu system is entered, the display shows one menu option at a time. No indication is provided of the level within the menu structure of the current item, or whether there are other items at this level.

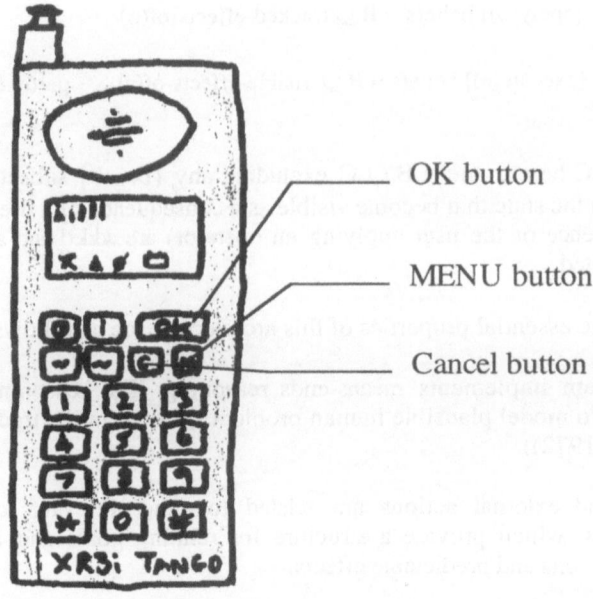

OK button

MENU button

Cancel button

Fig. 2: a mobile phone interface

The menu system is entered initially by pressing the "Menu" button. From that point on "Menu" is used to switch between different options at the same level, whilst "OK" is used to descend further into the menu structure. For the purposes of this analysis, we ignore backing up through the menu hierarchy; in practice, pressing "Cancel" takes the user back up one level in the menu structure, whilst pressing and holding "Cancel" takes the user out of the menu structure altogether.

4.1 Specification of user knowledge and device behaviour

To be able to conduct the analysis, we need to identify candidate tasks then specify what the user knows about the available operators. The following specification of user knowledge is only one of many possible representations, but we can lay out this knowledge, check it for plausibility ("telling a story" about how likely it is that a particular user would know these things) and drawing inferences from this knowledge and the description of the architecture (presented above) about possible user behaviour.

We have chosen to analyse the task of setting up call diversion, mainly because our own experience of mobile 'phones leads us to believe that this is one of the more frequently performed tasks that involve the menu hierarchy. We start by stating that the user knows that there will be a point in the menu hierarchy where they can specify under what conditions calls are to be diverted. [The conditions under which calls can be diverted include "all calls", "if 'phone is engaged", etc.. In practice, a novice user may not know that there are alternative modes that have to be specified at the start of the interaction, and only become aware of it when asked by the device to give this information.] In detail, we specify that the operator select-divert-mode has the purpose of being in the state where the mode is set, that it is doable when the 'phone is in "menus" mode and the current menu display ("M") is the one that allows the user to achieve the goal, that the user has to mentally track what divert mode has been set because the display does not show it, and that it is achieved through the user pressing "OK":

> purpose(select-divert-mode(D))=divert-mode-set(D)
>
> precond(select-divert-mode(D))={ in-mode(menus), is-displayed(M) }
>
> filter(select-divert-mode(D))={ allows-achievement(M, divert-mode-set(D)) }
>
> tracked-effect-of(select-divert-mode(D))={ divert-mode-set(D) }
>
> performs(select-divert-mode(D))=press " OK"

Similarly, we state that the user can identify the relevant menu item instructing them to enter a number, and can enter it.

> purpose(enter-number(N))=number-entered(N)
>
> precond(enter-number(N))={ in-mode(menus), is-displayed(M)}
>
> filter(enter-number(N))={ allows-achievement(M, number-entered(N)) }
>
> performs(enter-number(N))= <type in number N>

The user can navigate the menu structure by identifying relevant menu items. If the user has a goal ("G"), and menu item M is currently displayed, and the user knows that it is relevant to G, then the user should press "OK":

> purpose(choose-menu(M))=G
>
> filter(choose-menu(M))={ in-mode(menus), is-relevant(M, G), is-displayed(M) }
>
> performs(choose-menu(M))= press "OK"

The user can navigate within one level of the menu structure for two possible reasons; one is because the currently displayed item is known not to be relevant; the other is to find out *which* of the items at the current level is the most relevant. For the purpose of this analysis, we ignore the second possibility (although it is very important), and state that the user must know whether or not a particular menu item is relevant to their current goal(s):

> purpose(skip-menu(M))=is-displayed(P)
>
> filter(skip-menu(M))={ in-mode(menus), ¬is-relevant(M,G • G∈ adopted),
>
>   is-relevant(P,G), is-displayed(M)}
>
> performs(skip-menu(M))= press "MENU"

The user knows that the 'phone has two "modes": number mode (in which the user can simply make and accept calls) and menu mode (in which the user can alter the phone settings), and that the way to enter menu mode is to press the MENU button:

> purpose(enter-menus)=in-mode(menus)
>
> filter(enter-menus)= { in-mode(number) }
>
> performs(enter-menus)= press "MENU"

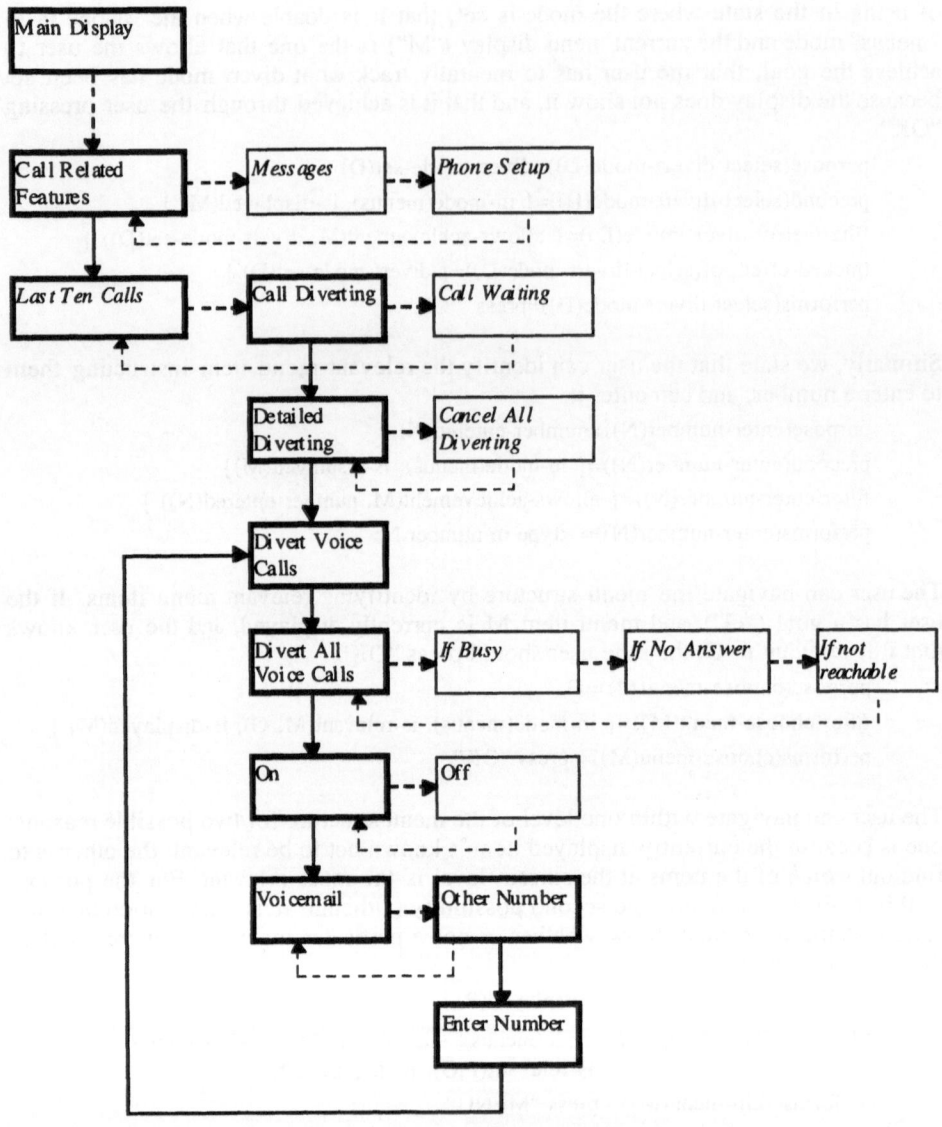

Fig. 3: extract from the phone menu structure

Finally, we assert that once the user has specified the divert mode and the number to divert to, they will recognise the need to confirm the settings:

purpose(set-divert(D, N))=diverted-to(D, N)

precond(set-divert(D, N))={ divert-mode-set(D), number-entered(N)}

performs(set-divert(D, N))= press "OK"

So far, we have specified what the user knows; in addition, we need to specify how the device state changes, and what the user can see of the device state. Such specification includes:

> visible-effect-of(enter-menus)={ in-mode(menus), ¬in-mode(number) }
>
> visible-effect-of(enter-number(N))={ number-entered(N) }
>
> visible-effect-of(choose-menu(M))={ is-displayed(P), ¬is-displayed(M) }
>> -- where P is the first item at the level below M as shown in Figure 3
>>> ...etc.

Much of the device specification is summarised informally in Figure 3, so for the sake of brevity we omit the full formal specification.

4.2 Reasoning about interactive behaviour

We are now in a position to reason about the interactive behaviour, starting from the state where the user knows that the 'phone is switched on and in number mode. We can express the user's initial knowledge as follows:

task={diverted-to (all, 01811234567)}	- the goal of the task is to be in a state where all calls are diverted to 01811234567
beliefs={in-mode(number)}	- the user knows that the telephone is on and in number mode.
adopted=∅	- initially, the user has no adopted goals...
committed=∅	-...or commitments

Applying axioms 1 and 5, the modelled user adopts the goal of the task:

adopted={diverted-to (all, 01811234567)}	- adopt the goal to be in a state where all calls are diverted to 01811234567

Since there is only one valid operator that addresses this goal, and this operator has two unsatisfied preconditions, axioms 3, 4 & 5 are applied, and the user becomes committed to set-divert and adopts additional goals:

committed={set-divert(all, 01811234567)}
adopted={divert-mode-set(all), number-entered(01811234567),
       diverted-to(all, 01811234567)}

Again, there is only one valid operator that addresses each of these goals, but each has unsatisfied preconditions so axioms 3,4 & 5 are applied:

committed={select-divert-mode(all), enter-number(01811234567),
                  set-divert(all, 01811234567)}
adopted={in-mode(menus), is-displayed(M), is-displayed(N),
           divert-mode-set(all), number-entered(01811234567),
           diverted-to(all, 01811234567)}

                          — M and N are menu-items such that
                          allows-achievement(M,divert-mode-set(all)) and
                          allows-achievement (N,number-entered(01811234567))

There is only one valid operator that addresses the first goal, and none that addresses the second or third, and the preconditions for that operator are satisfied so axioms 3, 4 & 5 are applied:

committed={enter-menus, select-divert-mode(all), enter-number(01811234567),
                                             set-divert(all, 01811234567)}

Now we are in a position where the agent can actually do something! Axioms 8, 9 & 11 are applied to the operator enter-menus (action: press "MENU" button):

committed={select-divert-mode(all), enter-number(01811234567),
                  set-divert(all, 01811234567)}
beliefs={in-mode(menus), is-displayed("Call related features")}

Axioms 6 & 7 are applied, and the user drops a goal:

adopted={is-displayed(M), is-displayed(N), divert-mode-set(all),
                  number-entered(01811234567), diverted-to(all, 01811234567)}

Now that we are in menus mode, the two operators that might be committed to are choose-menu and skip-menu. According to axioms 3,4 & 5, the user will become committed to one or the other, depending on which is known (or judged or guessed) to be relevant to any adopted goal. Then according to axioms 8, 9 & 11,the user will press "MENU" or "OK" as appropriate, and update beliefs about the current display. For example, the very first selection is made assuming that the user recognises that "call related features" is relevant to the current goals. Axioms 3-6 lead us to infer:

committed={choose-menu("call related features"), select-divert-mode(all),
                  enter-number(01811234567), set-divert(all, 01811234567)}

Then according to axioms 8, 9 & 11, the user executes the corresponding device action, drops the commitment, and updates her knowledge of the state of the device:

committed={select-divert-mode(all), enter-number(01811234567),
                  set-divert(all, 01811234567)}
beliefs={in-mode(menus), is-displayed("last ten calls")}

Since none of the adopted goals are satisfied, selection of "MENU" and "OK" (as relevant) continues until "Divert all voice calls" is displayed. At this point, two possible operators are candidates for axiom 3: select-divert-mode(all) and choose-menu("Divert all voice calls"), and the user has to select the preferred operator. A general heuristic, not included in the description above, is that the user should prefer the operator that addresses the more specific goal. If this heuristic is applied, then the user will become committed to select-divert-mode(all), and when she applies this operator (by pressing "OK"), she will track the fact that she has achieved the goals is-displayed(M) and divert-mode-set(all) [where M is defined as being the menu that enables the user to set divert-mode-set(all)]. However, if this heuristic is not applied then, according to this analysis, the user might select "OK" to choose-menu("divert all voice calls"), and then fail to recognise that these goals have been reached. In this particular case, this is unlikely to be problematic, but it highlights a cause of possible confusion.

Assuming that this preference heuristic is applied, the state after pressing "OK" at "Divert all voice calls" is:

adopted={is-displayed(N), number-entered(01811234567),
                 diverted-to(all, 01811234567)}
committed={enter-number(01811234567), set-divert(all, 01811234567)}
beliefs={in-mode(menus), is-displayed("on"), divert-mode-set(all)}

Again, the user has to select from menus until asked to enter a number for diverting calls, at which point the user has to recognise that pressing "OK" is not relevant, but that pressing the number digits is. After executing the action of entering the required number, the state becomes:

adopted={diverted-to(all, 01811234567)}
committed={set-divert(all, 01811234567)}
beliefs={in-mode(menus), is-displayed("01811234567"), divert-mode-set(all),
                 number-entered(01811234567)}

Now, the preconditions on set-divert are satisfied and the user can press that final "OK":

adopted=∅

committed=∅

beliefs={in-mode(menus), is-displayed("01811234567"), divert-mode-set(all),
            number-entered(01811234567), diverted-to(all, 01811234567)}

The task goal is now satisfied, so the agent is no longer permitted to act.

4.3 Use and usability issues for the mobile 'phone

The overall story from this analysis is that the user starts the interaction knowing (or being expected to recognise) that two pieces of information are going to have to be communicated to the device: what circumstances calls are to be diverted under (the "divert mode"), and what number they are to be diverted to. Initially, the modelled behaviour is based on means-ends planning, involving precondition subgoaling. If the user does not know at the outset of the interaction that both these items of information will have to be communicated then she must be able to infer that they are needed "at the time" from the display. For example, the user may not be aware that there are different divert modes.

Once the user has got the device into "menus" mode, the user's behaviour becomes reactive, as she navigates through the menu hierarchy to the point where she can communicate the necessary information and confirm the diversion. This analysis shows how important it is that the menu items should be easily discriminable, and identifiable as being relevant or not relevant to the user's goals. As shown in figure 3, both of these requirements are violated by the Tango 'phone. For example, "Divert voice calls" and "Divert all voice calls" are likely to be confusable, while any of the top-level options ("Call related features", "Messages" and "Phone setup") could be construed as being relevant to the task of setting up the 'phone to divert all incoming messages or calls to another number.

There is a sense in which this detailed analysis has revealed nothing surprising about the usability of this device. For example, the fact that "MENU" is used for two contrasting purposes (to enter the menu hierarchy and to navigate within one level of that hierarchy) could have been easily recognised by doing a TAG (Payne & Green, 1986) or similar analysis. It also does not take this level of analysis to determine that the wording of menu items should make it easy for users to recognise their functions, and that in this particular case there are many confusable menu items. However, this analysis gives an account of the way in which a user must integrate means-ends planning and responsive behaviour when interacting with this device. It also highlights the fact that successful use of this device demands that the user engage in extended interactions with the device that have no domain significance.

The analysis above is incomplete in many respects. Most obviously, we have said nothing about error recovery (e.g. how does the user become aware that she is in the wrong part of the menu hierarchy, and decide how to correct that?), how this task structure relates to that of other tasks that also involve navigating the menu hierarchy, where exactly the user's knowledge can come from, or how the user learns about the device through interacting with it. Our aim has not been to present a full usability analysis of the 'phone, but to use it as an example to demonstrate how one can construct an axiomatic basis for reasoning about planned and reactive behaviour, and how the two different styles of interactive behaviour can be integrated within one coherent framework.

5. Discussion

The architecture description presented here is based on means-ends reasoning, which has its roots in the literature on human problem solving, realised through two main principles: selection by purpose and precondition subgoaling. It is concerned with capturing aspects of human problem solving, and therefore with representing a few aspects of cognition in a way that enables analysts to reason about the demands being made on users, and about likely patterns of interactive behaviour. The description is based on a scoped model of the user that ignores aspects such as peripheral input/output mechanisms and their role in cognition (Barnard & May, 1995; Kieras & Meyer, 1995; Duke, 1995). In particular, as discussed by Blandford and Duke (1997), it contrasts with the syndetics approach of Duke and others (Duke, 1995; Faconti & Duke, 1996), which also develops complementary axiomatic representations of user and system, but which conducts the analysis in terms of the resources of user and system and the channels of communication between them. The approach presented here also ignores other important determinants of behaviour traditionally considered to be outside the scope of rationality, such as emotion, fatigue, and interpersonal differences.

In most applications, there are alternative possible ways of achieving a goal, and a choice has to be made between them. One aspect of the model that is currently under-specified is that of selection between alternatives; axioms 3-5 refer to selecting the preferred operation without giving any basis for such a selection. Consequently, there may be multiple possible behaviours that are consistent with the specified architecture. The addition of further axioms (e.g. to constrain the preference of operations) will limit the space of possible behaviours over which the analyst is reasoning.

Conversely, the addition of other axioms may open up the space of possible behaviours. For example, we have not specified how a user might acquire new knowledge. We referred briefly to the idea that a user of the mobile 'phone who was not familiar with the menu structure might explore all the menu items at one level to judge which was most relevant to their current goals. The operators of finding out more information might lead to a wider space of possible behaviours. The specified architecture does not accommodate acquisition of such knowledge. It is, however, possible to reason about users with different expertise by priming the agent with different knowledge (e.g. Blandford and Young, 1996).

The formal description presented here allows the analyst to reason about interactive behaviour. The generic axioms about user cognition are supplemented with a specification of the device and of the device-specific knowledge of the user. The user agent tracks predictable effects of applying operators and also notes changes to the device state through visible effects.

The approach presented here is a "proof of concept" to illustrate that it is possible to reason formally about interactive behaviour that involves both means-ends planning and responsive behaviour (that depends on local knowledge of the state of the device). We have already highlighted some areas for further work. Other areas that we propose to investigate include the proof of properties of the interactive system, and the application of such an approach at different levels of abstraction.

Acknowledgements

We are grateful to David Duke and Richard Young for helpful discussions. This work is funded by EPSRC, grant number GR/L00391.

References

BARNARD, P. & MAY, J. (1995) Interactions with Advanced Graphical Interfaces and the Deployment of Latent Human Knowledge. In F. Paterno'(ed.) *Eurographics Workshop on the Design, Specification and Verification of Interactive Systems,* Berlin: Springer Verlag.

BLANDFORD, A. E. & DUKE, D. J. (1997). Integrating user and computer system concerns in the design of interactive systems. *International Journal of Human-Computer Studies,* pp. 653-679.

BLANDFORD, A. E. & YOUNG, R. M. (1995) Separating User And Device Descriptions for Modelling Interactive Problem Solving. In K. Nordby, P. Helmersen, D J Gilmore, and S Arnesen (eds.): *Human-Computer Interaction: Interact'95.* Chapman and Hall, 1995. pp. 91-96.

BLANDFORD, A. E. & YOUNG, R. M. (1996) Specifying user knowledge for the design of interactive systems. *Software Engineering Journal.* **11.6**, 323-333.

BOWEN, J.P. & HINCHEY, M.G. (1995) Ten Commandments of Formal Methods. *IEEE Computer.* Vol 28 (4), pp. 56-63.

CARD, S. K., MORAN, T. P. AND NEWELL, A. (1983). *The Psychology of Human Computer Interaction,* Hillsdale : Lawrence Erlbaum.

DUKE, D.J. (1995) Reasoning About Gestural Interaction. *Computer Graphics Forum,* Vol 14(3). Proceedings of Eurographics'95. pp. 55-66. NCC/Blackwell,

FACONTI, G.P. & DUKE, D.J. (1996) Device Models. In F. Bodart & J. Vanderdonckt (Eds.) *Design, Specification and Verification of Interactive Systems '96.* pp.73-91. Vienna : Springer-Verlag.

JOHN, B. & KIERAS, D. (1996) The GOMS family of user interface analysis techniques: comparison and contrast. *ACM Transactions on CHI. ,* **3**, 320-351.

KIERAS, D. & MEYER, D.E. (1995) *An overview of the EPIC architecture for cognition and performance with application to human-computer interaction.* (EPIC Tech. Rep. No. 5 (TR-95/ONR-EPIC-5). Ann Arbor, University of Michigan, Electrical Engineering and Computer Science Department.

KIERAS, D.E. & POLSON, P.G. (1985) An approach to the formal analysis of user complexity. *International Journal of Man Machine Studies,* **22**, 365-394.

NEWELL, A. (1982) 'The knowledge level' *Artificial Intelligence,* **18**, 87-127.

NEWELL, A. AND SIMON, H. (1972). *Human Problem Solving,* Englewood Cliffs, NJ: Prentice Hall.

PAYNE, S. J. AND GREEN, T.R.G. (1986). Task-Action Grammars: a model of mental representation of task languages. *Human-Computer Interaction,* **2**, 93-133.

POLSON, P. & LEWIS, C. (1990) Theory based design for easily learned interfaces. *Human Computer Interaction,* **5**, 191-220.

RYAN, M., FIADEIRO, J. & MAIBAUM, T. (1991) 'Sharing Actions and Attributes in Modal Action Logic' in T. Ito and A. Meyer (Eds.) *Theoretical Aspects of Computer Software.* Springer Verlag.

YOUNG, R.M., GREEN, T.R.G. & SIMON, T. (1989) 'Programmable user models for predictive evaluation of interface designs' in Bice, K. and Lewis, C. (eds.) *Proceedings of CHI '89*, 15-19, New York : ACM.

Establishing a link between usability and utility: validation of task-based dialogue using a semantic prototype

Marcos F. Sanz, Enrique J. Gómez*

Andersen Consulting, Torre Picasso, 28020 Madrid, Spain
Marcos.Francisco.Sanz.Verdu@ac.com
*Grupo de Bioingeniería y Telemedicina, E.T.S.I. Telecomunicación, 28040 Madrid, Spain
egomez@teb.upm.es

Abstract. Usability is not sufficient condition to procure utility. The tasks performed by the system user, as a member of the organisation, must contribute to reach the business goals, establishing the basis for the system utility; and besides, the system usability depends, among other context variables, on the features of the user's tasks supported by the system. The use of 'semantic prototypes' can enable the identification of the work domain to be supported by the system and can also aid the determination of opportunities for change in this work domain and, consequently, in the business process in which it is immersed. After their validation, this prototypes could also aid the definition of specific usability goals that can be attained through the subsequent correct designs of user interface syntax and articulation.

As a result of our experience we claim that the use of 'semantic prototypes' for the design and evaluation of the user interface dialogue at the semantic level provides means to assess the utility of an interactive system in advance as well as to establish the starting point for usability.

1. Introduction

The European Telecommunication Standards Institute (ETSI) considers usability as an ergonomic concept which is not dependant on the costs of providing the interactive system; usability together with the balance between the benefit for the user (or for the organisation) and the financial costs form the concept of utility (ETSI, 1993). One of the most useful ways to view usability is that it is a dimension of quality dealing with human-computer interaction; in order for a system to be accepted, the system must meet all quality standards set for it, i.e., usefulness, cost, compatibility, reliability, etc.; usability and utility can be considered independent factors that address usefulness (Nielsen, 1992).

Although usability can contribute significantly to increase the economic performance of an interactive system (and consequently its usefulness), and although the lack of usability can greatly reduce (or even eliminate) a previously expected benefit, usability is not sufficient condition to procure utility. This means that an ergonomical highly usable system may have low utility for a particular user who considers the cost to be too high in respect of his or her need for using the system.

Even when stating that the usability concept, including the effective and efficient support of user's tasks, is responsible for the main benefit produced by the interactive system, we should note that those user's tasks should relate to the work objectives in which the user operates, and these objectives must be aligned with business objectives.

Possibly, this is one of the main differences between the scope of the scientific perspective and the practitioners perspective: designs must also cater for whatever business goals are set by the organisation for each particular user; information systems are no longer viewed as isolated entities, but as enablers of new business processes that go hand in hand with organisational restructuring and new human resource structures (Cabrera, Rincón and González, 1996). Besides, the cost-benefit analysis of the system-user performance, which allows verification of the system utility, must be fulfilled in a business context instead of a system-user context. This analysis should also allow identification and differentiation of the usability contribution to the system benefits, guaranteeing the acceptance of user interface design as a valuable activity (Cabrera, Rincón and González, 1996).

2. Usability, Utility And Business Process

In Figure 1 we summarise the relationships between business processes, usability, utility and user-system performance, described in the introduction.

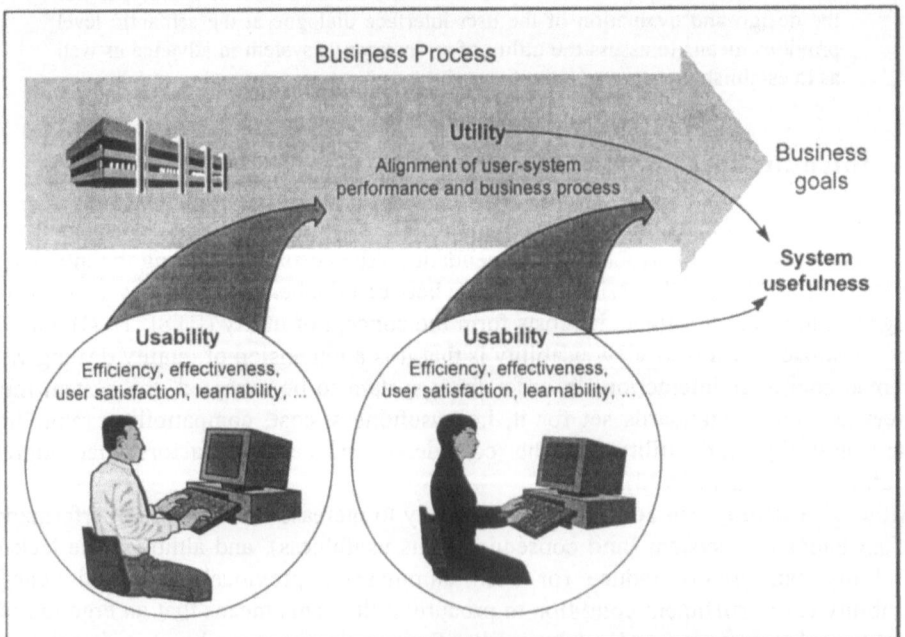

Fig. 1 Alignment between user's tasks and business process

We know that a user-centred design increases the usability of a new interactive system by assuring at least the effective and efficient support of user's tasks; however, taking into account the above considerations, this development paradigm should also increase the system's utility by ensuring a cost-effective achievement of the business goals. The responsibility of the user-centred design is much higher when it is the interactive system which drives a change in the business process.

The user-centred design and verification of interactive systems supporting the current or a new business process is a complex task which is carried out by a team of process analysts, human resource experts, usability evaluators, user interface designers, and software developers. They all build different models that concentrate on a particular aspect of the design and take a general look at the rest; however they all share, although with different techniques and 'languages', the consideration of user's tasks; sometimes they even share techniques; this is the case with task analysis, which is used during the initial stages of user interface and systems design (Diaper and Addison, 1992), and also in the analysis of workers behaviour (Annett and Duncan, 1967).

The selection, modelling and validation of the worker tasks to be supported by a new interactive system is an earlier and critical activity in a user-centred design; this is because the tasks performed by the system user, as a member of the organisation, must contribute to reach the business goals, establishing the basis for the system utility; and besides, the system usability depends, among other context variables, on the features of the user's tasks supported by the system (for instance, the dialogue with the system depends strongly on the tasks temporal relationships). This selection, modelling and validation of user's tasks is usually immersed in a task-artifact cycle (Carroll and Rosson, 1992): an interactive system designed to support a set of tasks ends up inducing a change in the initial set of tasks, and consequently, in the business process. Consequently it is necessary to define the user's tasks supported by the system, and the dialogue to accomplish them, with the minimum effort and as early as possible in the system's life cycle; at the same time, the definition process must allow to explore all the possibilities of improving the business process (producing a task-artifact cycle).

The development and evaluation of low fidelity prototypes or abstract dialogue models of the system user interface is the most appropriate way of defining the user's tasks supported by the system. These prototypes provide a simulation of what the interface permits, without specifying how it is to be achieved, and are therefore a useful expression of the design at a conceptual level. One example of an abstract dialogue model, based on a propositional production system, is the Action Simulator developed by Monk and Curry (1994); an abstract dialogue model like this determines how well the system supports the users in doing their work; however, a specification of the low level system behaviour would describe how the user achieves these settings e.g., what happens when the user clicks or types with the mouse cursor on a particular field; this level of design is equally important but has been made easier with the advent of style guides and their associated tool kits.

In a user-centred design aimed to increase both the usability and utility of a system that supports a business process, such low fidelity prototypes or abstract dialogue models must allow a clear identification of the features of user's tasks that will determine the system's usability as well as the contribution of these user's tasks to the business process. In addition, these models must be easy to understand and use for all the professionals mentioned above and also for the future users of the system, and the tools used to develop them must be as useful and usable as the systems they help to develop.

But, what is the adequate level of abstraction that best meets the above requirements?, and, which tools are most appropriate to develop these models?

In order to define and justify the level of abstraction we need to link the usability and the utility through an abstract dialogue model, we will describe a widely agreed cognitive model of human-computer interaction, which will allow us to define the concept of 'semantic prototype', and allocate it within the interactive system life cycle.

In this paper we also present two software tools (integrated in a User Interface Management System) that are designed to reduce the cost of developing semantic prototypes, allowing to reuse them when the development of the user interface begins. These tools are: an editor for task models that includes a graphical representation of temporal relationships (mainly based on hierarchical task analysis); and an automatic generator of semantic prototypes, which are based on a previously defined task model.

Finally, we show the use of the aforementioned tools during the designing of the user interface for a Multimedia Conversational Service.

All the software developments were accomplished during the first author's stay in the 'Grupo de Bioingeniería y Telemedicina' of 'Universidad Politécnica de Madrid', within the framework of the 'Multimedia Terminal (TEMA)' project funded by the Spanish National Broad-band Research Program.

3. A Cognitive Model Of Human-Computer Interaction

Since GOMS model (Card, Moran, and Newell, 1983), many user cognitive models have been produced (John and Kieras, 1994). However, they all share Norman's basic model of interaction (Norman, 1988), which describes the phases of execution and evaluation.

This understanding of human-computer interaction was complemented by Abowd and Beale (1991), who included performance and presentation phases in the system; in this model the user observes the system output during the evaluation phase, and articulates the formulation of the desired task in the system input language.

Shneiderman (1982) defined the concept of direct manipulation, and he proposed the 'Semantic-syntactic object-action' (SSOA) model (Shneiderman, 1987) specifically for this kind of user interface. This model describes the knowledge the user needs firstly to formulate the desired task, and secondly, to understand the system's output. This knowledge can be classified as task semantic knowledge, system semantic knowledge and syntactic knowledge.

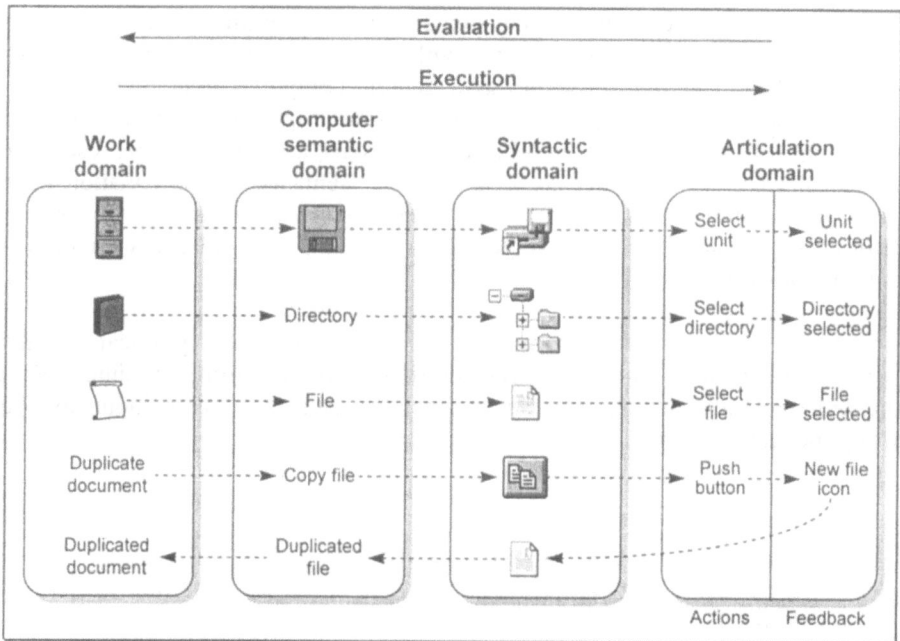

Fig. 2 Graphical representation of a Task Mapping Model

Mayo and Hartson (1993) described another similar model to represent the use of an interactive system: the 'Task Mapping Model' (TMM) (see Figure 2).
We use this model to show the relationship between the interaction and business processes and we do not need too much detail. It provides a task decomposition and description framework at some abstraction levels, which is a combination of the SSOA model and the work on articulation specification by Hartson et al (1990). These levels or domains are: the work domain (at semantic abstraction level), the system semantic domain, the syntactic domain, and the articulation domain.

In the TMM (see Figure 2), the execution phase of Norman's model consists in a mapping from tasks and objects in the work domain, through tasks and objects in the system semantic domain and syntactic domain, to an articulation (in the articulation domain). Consequently, the evaluation phase consists of the reverse of these mappings.

In this cognitive model the work domain contains items (objects, operations, and sub-tasks) directly related to user task performance described in specific real-world terminology. Thus, the scope of this domain is defined by the users' tasks or job (Mayo and Hartson, 1993). Domain items are the physical and conceptual real-world entities that comprise the users tasks, and are often not related to computer systems. The work domain does not contain anything defined outside this scope; there are no items concerned with computer hardware or software in this domain.

The system semantic domain contains items (objects, operations, and sub-tasks) that build a representation of the users' tasks with abstract computer concepts (Mayo and Hartson, 1993). This domain serves as a generic computer 'middle-ground' in the users' translation of tasks between the real world and a specific computer system.

Computer syntactic domain items (objects, operations, and sub-tasks) represent actual syntactical components related to both computer semantic and articulation domain items (Mayo and Hartson, 1993). These items represent user interface software entities and actions which are employed during task performance with particular computer or software packages.

The articulation domain contains the specification of the users' physical interaction while communicating computer syntactic items to and from the interface; the articulation domain contains both system feedback to users and users inputs to system (Mayo and Hartson, 1993).

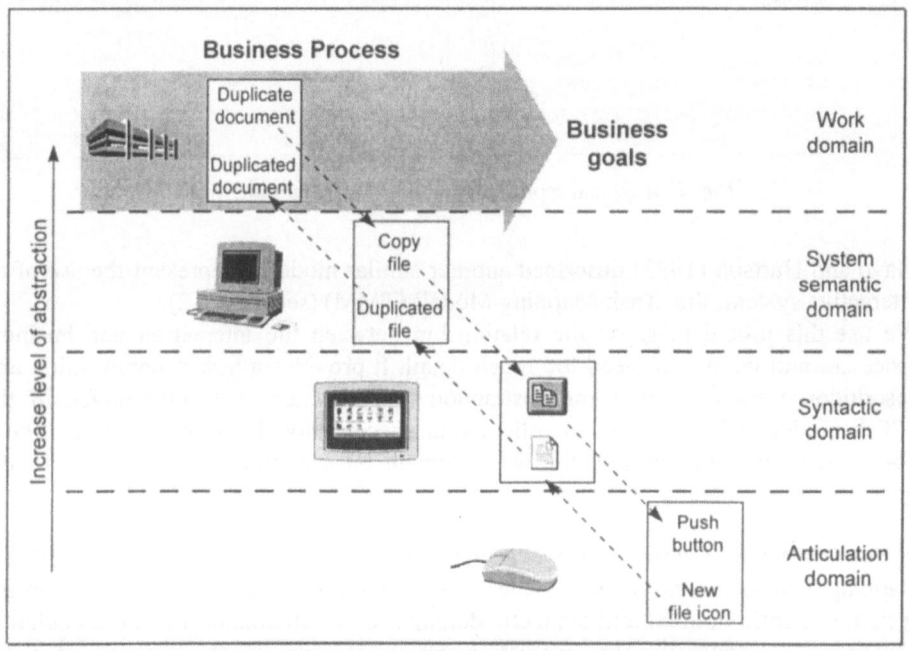

Fig. 3 Alignment of user's tasks with the business process.

It is important to observe that it is precisely the work domain of the TMM that represents the output performance from the user and the interactive system as a whole, to the business context, and that this domain is completely independent of the hardware and software concepts and the specific user interface syntax and articulation which enable such performance. In other words, the work domain is completely independent of the items that are usually handled by user interface designers and software developers.

As depicted in Figure 3, the work domain of each interactive system user is at the same abstraction level as the business process, the basis for the interactive systems utility will be established if we manage to 'align' each user work domain with the business process, during a task-artifact cycle of design and evaluation that could provoke a change in business processes. At the same time, defining and describing the users' tasks at this level of abstraction an essential part of the information needed to design and develop a user interface with high usability is provided.

4. The Semantic Prototype

Taking into account the above considerations we define the 'semantic prototype' as a low fidelity prototype that shows items exclusively at the semantic levels of abstraction of the TMM cognitive model. Consequently, with a semantic prototype we could show and evaluate the work domain selected (or designed) provided that this prototype exclusively contains items (objects, operations, and sub-tasks) that are directly related to user task performance described in specific real-world terminology. Furthermore, if the semantic prototype were to contain only items that build a representation of the users' tasks with abstract computer concepts, we could show and evaluate the system semantic domain designed.

In any case, the semantic prototype does not represent neither syntax nor articulation of the future user interface (which describes how user's tasks can be performed by physically using the system). Consequently, this semantic prototype, expresses without 'technological noise' the relationship between the interaction with the system and the business process through the description of the dialogue employed to perform those user's tasks that contribute to the business goals.

However, a prototype cannot be 'visible' at semantic domains of the cognitive model, so we need an auxiliary syntax and articulation to represent semantic items; consequently a semantic prototype can be seen as an extremely simple user interface that shows exclusively real world objects or abstract objects, and tasks directly related to user performance at the work domain (or at the computer semantic domain).
We can use also abstract interaction objects to show abstract objects for which a clear graphical representation does not exist; sooner or later we must choose an abstract graphical representation of these objects (at the computer semantic domain) if we are designing a graphical user interface.

It is important to note that this auxiliary syntax and articulation must not be more than the minimum required to show semantic objects and an abstract dialogue with them; they are never intended to advance the syntax and articulation that will physically allow performance of those tasks in the final user interface.

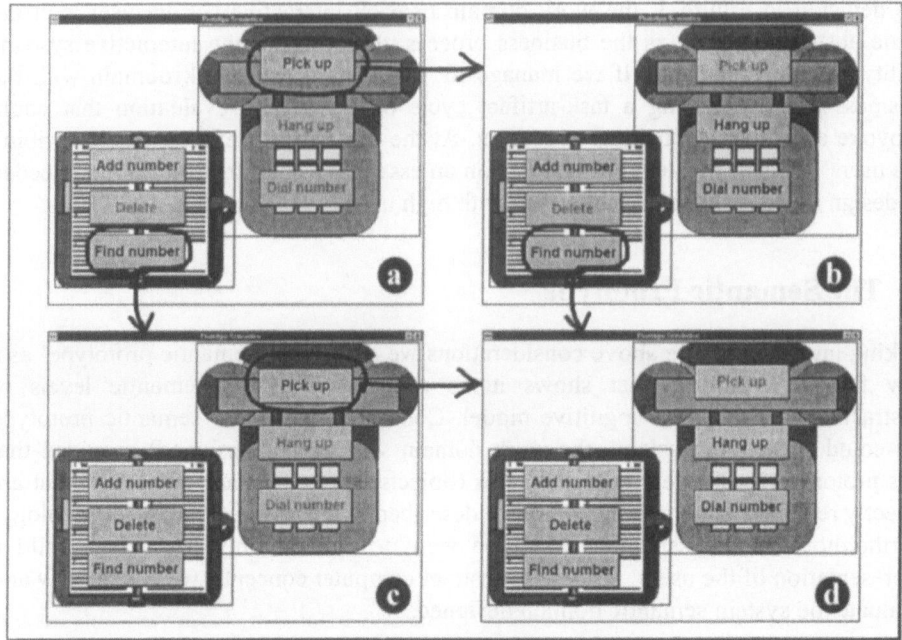

Fig. 4 An example of semantic prototype.

In Figure 4 we show an example of dialogue with a semantic prototype that represents a very simple work domain: the use of a telephone and an agenda to make telephone calls; it was developed with Microsoft® Visual Basic™, and shows two real world objects (an agenda and a telephone) with some buttons simulating the tasks that can be performed with them. During the execution of this semantic prototype the dialogue with these objects was simulated allowing concurrent performance of temporal independent tasks (in Figure 4 some arrows point to the following screen where a task is simulated by pushing a button).

5. The System Life Cycle Using The Semantic Prototype

The use of semantic prototypes can enable the identification of the work domain to be supported by the system and can also aid the determination of opportunities for change in this work domain and, consequently, in the business process in which it is immersed. In both cases we should use the semantic prototype as an aid to qualitative assessment of the system's contribution to the cost-effective achievement of business goals.

Having defined this work domain, a conceptual user interface at the computer semantic domain can be designed. At this abstraction level another semantic prototype can help to increase the users' and developers' understanding of the proposed system without involving any decision in respect of the design of syntactic and articulation domains.

The use of semantic prototypes to validate a conceptual user interface, before the implementation begins, again propitiates the identification of opportunities for change in the business process, allowing a cost-effective task-artifact cycle.

After their validation, this prototypes could also aid the definition of specific usability goals that can be attained through the subsequent correct designs of user interface syntax and articulation.

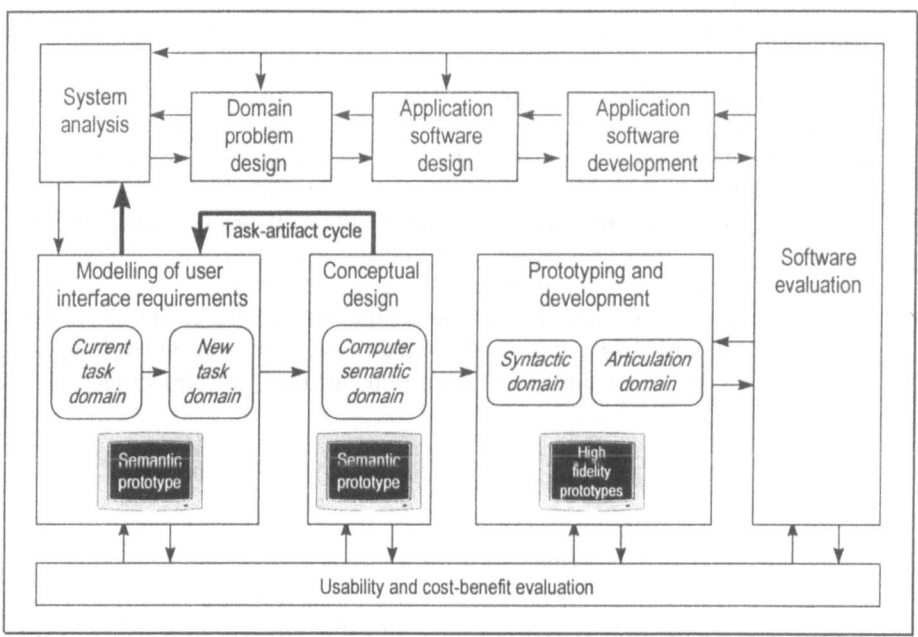

Fig. 5 Design and development process for interactive information systems.

To represent the role of semantic prototypes, in Figure 5 we have set out the design and development process for interactive information systems, which results from the sequential design of the interaction cognitive domains proposed above.

This was an adaptation of the process described by Hix and Hartson (1993); the general activities for user interface design were replaced with the design of cognitive domains in three phases: Modelling of User Interface Requirements (new work domain design), Conceptual Design (computer semantic domain design), and Prototyping and Development (syntax and articulation design and development). Each one of these phases includes its corresponding usability evaluation, according to an evaluation-centred process, as described theoretically by Hix and Hartson (1993).

It is important to note the influence of the user-centred design (assisted by semantic prototypes) on the initial system specification included in the traditional systems analysis: 1) during the Modelling of User Interface Requirements, the initial system specification could be changed in order to support a new work domain; 2) during the user interface Conceptual Design, (and perhaps more specifically, during the evaluation of a conceptual design that represents the computer semantic domain) another new work domain could be suggested (task-artifact cycle).

I order to finish this section, and as the evaluation of the semantic prototype is a key issue in the systems life cycle depicted above, we have listed some criteria that should be met if the evaluation is to be considered successful (which would mean that the work domain represented by the semantic prototype is aligned with the business process, and that it is ready to be implemented as an interactive system with high usability):

1. The users are familiar with the greater part of the system semantic objects included in the semantic prototype, and they also know the tasks that can be done with them. However, if it were otherwise, the cost of learning to use new conceptual objects should be acceptable for the users and the managers.
2. The users, managers and process designers agree on the task plan (or abstract dialogue design); they specifically agree on the existence and usefulness of task scenarios which require the fulfilment of concurrent tasks.
3. The users, managers, process designers and user interface designers do not suggest the definition of a new work domain or a new conceptual design of the user interface, and the benefits of the current 'artifact' are clearly identified and assessed.

6. Software Tools

In this section we briefly describe two software tools that are designed to reduce the cost of developing semantic prototypes and also to illustrate how these prototypes can be developed and used; besides, the integration of these tools in a User Interface Management System (UIMS) allows to reuse the semantic prototypes when the development of the user interface begins. The UIMS selected was MASAI, from ILOG company, because it included two integrated components that allowed us to quickly develop both tools.

These components are: the Grapher, a tool that allows management of graphical structures composed of nodes and links between nodes (which was useful to store and represent tasks and temporal relationships), and the Dialog Manager, a tool that allows the development of a user interface model which is similar to a theatre play; the Dialog Manager includes also an engine to 'perform' the play in a similar way as a runtime execution of a model based user interface (Sukaviriya et al, 1993).

6.1 Task Models Editor

This tool is essentially a graphical editor that allows tasks to be represented as nodes, and their temporal relationships as links between nodes. This is based on Hierarchical Task Analysis: nodes (tasks) are decomposed in graphs that contain more nodes (more tasks); however, its main purpose is to permit the analysis and visualisation of the temporal relationships among the simplest tasks at the work domain, as a stage prior to the generation of the dialogue.

Considering the fact that we wanted this tool to be usable for non technical users, a very simple graphical notation was developed to represent all the temporal relationships that are needed to represent work domains (Sanz and Gómez, 1995).

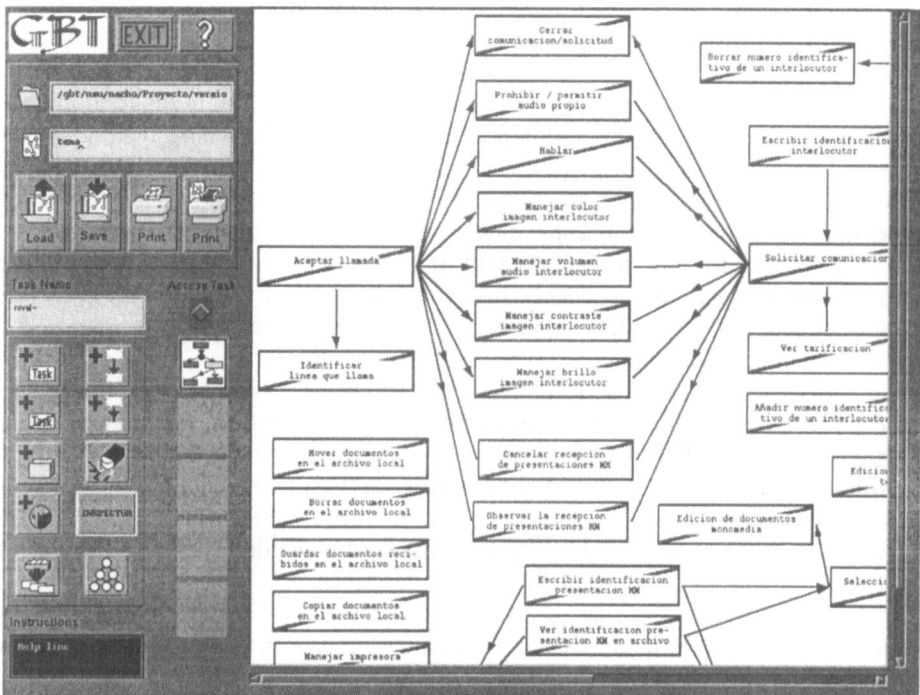

Fig. 6 Task Models Editor

In Figure 6 we show the use of the Task Models Editor with the task model developed to design the user interface for a Multimedia Conversational Service; the nodes and links displayed in this screen represent tasks and temporal relationships between tasks: sequence (arrow between two tasks), conditional sequence (link with an arrow in the middle), discretionary (two or more links from a single task to some tasks), optional tasks (two paths through different links from one task to another), and the sum of tasks (two or more links from some tasks to another task through an auxiliary AND node).

To fulfil the task model, the nodes include a specification of the tasks they represent, which include: name, description, agent, action, object, instrument, frequency and importance.

It is important to note if we have a task model of the work domain which is supported by the system, we only need to substitute the real world or abstract objects included in the tasks specification with computer semantic objects to achieve a task model of the interactive system; what is more, we can maintain the real world objects and try a real world metaphor at the computer semantic domain. However, some times, as we mentioned above, we have to design abstract or conceptual objects at the computer semantic domain to allow the interaction with abstract objects at the work domain for which a clear graphical representation does not exist. In other cases, the system will allow performance of some new tasks with new conceptual objects; in this case the interactive system induces a new work domain that can be modelled in the same way.

6.2 Semantic Prototype Generator

First, in order to visualise the semantic prototype all the objects referred to in the task model must be created in the editor panel of the UIMS, including their graphical hierarchy and their graphical appearance.

Using these interaction objects the Semantic Prototype Generator translates the task model developed previously to a specification for the Dialog Manager of MASAI.

This specification includes a dialogue with the objects referred to in the task model that preserves temporal independence between tasks; that is to say that the user can dialogue concurrently with those objects to perform tasks; the main rules observed to generate the dialogue with the prototype are the following:

1. All the objects needed to perform available tasks must be visible and accessible.
2. If a new task is available after the fulfilment of another task, the related objects must become visible and accessible.
3. An object must not be accessible (it could be visible) when the tasks related with this object are not available.
4. A whole graphical hierarchy of objects must not be visible when the tasks related with all the objects of the hierarchy are not available.

We have to comment at this point, that at this early stage in which we use semantic prototypes, we are not interested in the development of a full dialogue specification that allow to analyse some of its properties (i.e.: completeness, determinism, consistency, reachability, reversibility, etc.) in order to identify potential usability problems. Moreover, at this stage of design, at the semantic level of abstraction, what we want is to establish as early as possible the tasks to be supported by the system that will be useful for the business process. This requires identification and stimulation of the opportunities offered by the technology to improve the business process and the system benefit, regardless of the contribution of usability to these benefits. Consequently, we do not need to waste effort on developing a complete dialogue, but merely to simulate tasks scenarios at the semantic level. As we said above, the integration of this semantic prototype generator in a UIMS will allow a continuation of the dialogue specification (with the syntactic level) after the validation of the semantic level.

7. Case Study: The Multimedia Conversational Service

This service, developed in the framework of the Multimedia Terminal (TEMA) Project (Martínez et al, 1993) funded by the Spanish National Broad-band Research Program, includes high quality video conference between two remote terminals and allows creation, visualisation and transfer of multimedia documents.

The Grupo de Bioingeniería y Telemedicina of Universidad Politécnica de Madrid was responsible for the design and development of the service user interface.

It must be stressed that the functionality provided by this user interface, and supported by a generic hardware and software platform, had to be useful in various different business environments, like information exchange between hospitals or travel agencies. Of course, the user interface also had to be usable in all those contexts.

The modelling of a generic work domain for all the business contexts considered, and the visualisation of the semantic prototype that showed the computer semantic domain were essential activities, firstly to identify and assess the utility of the interactive system, and secondly, to provide the starting point for the development high usability user interface.

In this case, the work domain modelled was a completely new one, due the new tasks that were made possible by the service (such as the creation and transfer of multimedia documents).

On considering the prior knowledge of a generic service user it was decided that a real world metaphor at the semantic level of description should be designed, and consequently, that the real world objects selected would be the same for both, the task model and the semantic prototype.

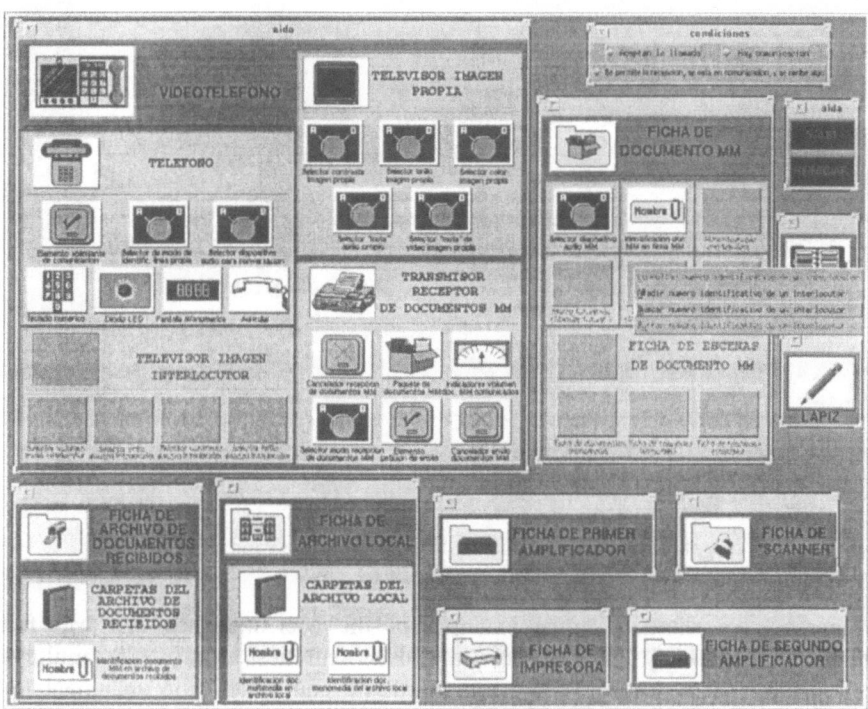

Fig. 7 Semantic prototype of the Multimedia Conversational Service

In Figure 7 we show the first tasks scenario of the semantic prototype generated for this service.

We can observe that only the objects that allow performance of tasks are presented at the beginning; they all show a menu with the tasks allowed when they are clicked with the mouse. Amongst this objects are: a video-telephone (that includes a television monitor to visualise the user's own image, some controls to manage the colour, brightness, etc., and a telephone to call another terminal), an agenda to manage terminal numbers, cards that contain information, and cards that allow management of the printer, amplifiers, etc.

After validation of this semantic prototype with some users and managers from the different business contexts, we started the development of the user interface syntax and articulation.
During this stage it was decided that the real world metaphor should be extended to the syntax and articulation domains.

Fig. 8 Final design of the Multimedia Conversational Service

In Figure 8 we show a screen example of the user interface that was finally developed; specifically we see how the user searches a particular multimedia document during the conversation; afterwards he could send the document to the other user or he could visualise the document.

8. Conclusions

As a result of our experience we claim that a semantic prototype helps to increase the users' and developers' understanding of the proposed system without involving any decision in respect of the design of syntactic and articulation domains. Consequently, the use of semantic prototypes to validate a conceptual user interface propitiates the identification of opportunities for change in the business process, allowing a cost-effective task-artifact cycle, before the implementation begins.

Furthermore, we think that semantic prototypes provides means to assess the utility of an interactive system in advance, as well as to establish the starting point for usability. First, the 'alignment' of user tasks with the business process can be qualitatively evaluated, and second, specific usability goals (that can be attained through the subsequent correct designs of user interface syntax and articulation) can be settled for the user's tasks at the semantic level.

This analysis should also allow identification and differentiation of the usability contribution to the system benefits, guaranteeing the acceptance of user interface design as a valuable activity.

However, integrated tools and methodologies are necessary to achieve a cost-effective development and evaluation of semantic prototypes. Besides, these tools must be useful and usable for a wide range of professionals.

The fact that we need to make a huge effort to develop useful and usable interactive systems that will help us to develop the useful and usable interactive systems of the next century is an unquestionable paradox.

Acknowledgements

This work is supported in part by grants CYCIT TIC92 1288 PB, CICYT Telemedicina Lab TIC 95-0145 and CAM I+D 7694. The authors are grateful to all researchers of 'Grupo de Bioingenieria y Telemedicina', in particular to Francisco del Pozo, Antonio Alcolea and Pilar Cano for their support during TEMA Project development, and very specially to José I. del Río and Elena Cordero for their implementation of the software tools integrated in the User Interface Management System. We give special thanks to Telefónica I+D, main project contractor.

References

Abowd, G., Beale, R. (1991) 'Users, systems and interfaces: A unifying framework for interaction'. In D. Diaper and N. Hammond, editors, HCI'91: People and Computers VI, Cambridge University Press, 73-87.

Annett, J., Duncan, K.D. (1967) 'Task analysis and training design'. Occupational Psychology, 41, 211-221.

Cabrera, A., Rincón, M., González, J. (1996) 'Ergonomics in the Wild: The Practitioner's Perspective'. Proceedings of Eighth European Conference on Cognitive Ergonomics: Cognition and the Worksystem, Granada (Spain), 83-87.

Card, S.K., Moran, T.P., Newell, A. (1983) 'The psychology of human-computer interaction'. Lawrence Erlbaum Associates, New Jersey.

Carroll, J., Rosson, B. (1992) 'Getting Around the Task-Artifact Cycle: How to Make Claims and Design by Scenario'. ACM Transactions On Information Systems, April, vol. 20, no. 2, 181-212.

Diaper, D., Addison, M. (1992) 'Task analysis and systems analysis for software development'. Interacting with Computers, vol. 4, no. 1, 124-139.

ETSI, European Telecommunication Standard Institute (1993) 'Guide for Usability Evaluations of Telecommunications Systems and Services'. ETSI DTR/HF 3001.

Hartson, H.R., Siochi, A.C., Hix, D. (1990) 'The UAN: A User-Oriented Representation for Direct Manipulation Interface Designs'. ACM Transactions on Information Systems, 8(3), 181-203.

Hix, D., Hartson, R. (1993) 'Developing user interfaces. Ensuring usability through product & processes'. John Wiley & Sons.

John, B.E., Kieras, D.E. (1994) 'The GOMS family of analysis techniques: tools for design and evaluation'. Technical Report CMU-CS-94-181, School of Computer Science, Carnegie Mellon University, Pittsburgh, USA.

Martínez, F., Fernández-Amigo, J. (1993) 'Servicios Multimedia: TEMA/PLANBA'. Comunicaciones de Telefónica I+D, vol. 4, no. 42 (in Spanish).

Mayo, K.A., Hartson, H.R. (1993) 'Synthesis-Oriented Situational Analysis in User Interface Design'. Proceedings 1993 East-West International Conference on Human-Computer Interaction, Moscow, Russia, ACM.

Monk, A., Curry, M. (1994). 'Discount dialogue modelling with Action Simulator'. Cockton, Draper and Weir (Eds.), People and Computers 9 - Proceedings of HCI'94, Cambridge University Press.

Nielsen, J. (1992). 'Usability Engineering'. Academic Press, New York.

Norman, D.A. (1988) 'The Psychology of Everyday Things'. Basic Books.

Sanz, M., Gómez, E.J. (1995) 'Task Model for Graphical User Interface Development'. Technical Report gbt-hf-95-1, http://www.teb.upm.es.

Shneiderman, B. (1982) 'The future of interactive systems and the emergence of direct manipulation'. Behaviour and Information Technology, vol. 1, no. 3, 237-256.

Shneiderman, B. (1987) 'Designing the User Interface: Strategies for Effective Human-Computer Interaction'. Addison-Wesley, New York.

Sukaviriya, P., Foley, J., Griffith, T. (1993) 'A Second Generation User Interface Design Environment: the Model and the Runtime Architecture'. Proceedings INTERCHI 1993, ACM New York, 375-382.

Evaluating Narrative in Multimedia

Bride Mallon
Brian Webb

School of Management,
Queen's University of Belfast, Northern Ireland.
e-mail:
B.Mallon@fujin.qub.ac.uk
B.Webb@fujin.qub.ac.uk

A need exists within multimedia for a method which evaluates a holistic design as opposed to aspects of a design such as structure or interface style.

Narrative is an entity which incorporates structure, content, process and context; a method based on this construct has the potential to evaluate a complete media design. Literature describes good narrative as crucial for good media design and as pivotal in determining the quality of a user's experience. The evaluation method described here employs a working assumption of these premises and then tests them empirically.

This paper defines narrative, its origins, dimensions, essential components, and uses. It describes criteria for evaluating narrative within multimedia, identified through a literature survey, an inductive content analysis of specific texts and empirical analysis of commercial multimedia titles. These are broad evaluation criteria, identified as four narrative constructs visible within and directly relevant in interpreting commercial multimedia titles.

1   Introduction

The quantity of multimedia titles has increased but quality is often poor. There is little evaluation of multimedia titles, save for product reviews. The interface component can be evaluated using traditional usability metrics and Software Engineering offers some methods to evaluate multimedia based on data structure, but the authors are not aware of any method to evaluate multimedia based on a unique combination of structure, content and context and process. Given the scope and influence of narrative within traditional media - in terms of structure, content, context and process, published research suggests that a method based on this construct has the potential to evaluate a complete design. No such evaluation model has been uncovered during our research.

Given the high costs of multimedia, a mechanism which evaluates a complete design and particularly the experiential nature of the design would have a high market as well as a high research value.

The influence of narrative on the experiential nature of design is suggested within film theory, drama, literature, media, communication theory, semiotics and narratology. Theorists within these fields link good narrative with good quality in media design. [Brannigan, 1992] [Stratford, 1994] [Cinema and Television 673, 1995]. Research concludes that narrative is a specific structure, a cultural universal that presents an 'ideal' at the top of a hierarchy of non-narrative data types [Brannigan, 1992] and that the closer other data types are to narrative within the hierarchy, the more media appeal the product engenders.

The paper reports on the empirical study which uncovered manifestations of the criteria within the commercial titles. The first evaluation category defines narrative and non-narrative data types, the other three categories evaluate dimensions which are essential to the articulation of the narrative form. The paper evaluates the method in terms of its features and benefits, problems and weaknesses; and outlines further research required.

A method based on narrative is expected to [a] provide a holistic evaluation method, [b] be of practical value for consumer reviews as a method for qualitatively evaluating the experiential nature of a design and [c] be of practical value to developers for product evaluation and process improvement.

2   Background theory: Narrative

> "Narrative is present in every age, in every place, in every society; it begins with the very history of mankind and there nowhere is nor has been a people without narrative. All classes, all human groups, have their narratives, enjoyment of which is very often shared by men with different, even opposing cultural backgrounds. Caring nothing for the division between good and bad literature, narrative is international, transhistorical, transcultural; it is simply there like life itself" Roland Barthes in the Introduction to the Structural Analysis of Narratives.

Within the field of multimedia there is a dearth of evaluation methods. Some methods do exist but they are limited to product reviews, Human Computer Interaction or Software Engineering approaches. Product reviews concentrate on evaluating the presence and quantity of physical features with some metrics adapted from Human Computer Interaction and Software Engineering. The psychological or behaviourist based methods are useful but concentrate on the interface and are too specific to provide developers with a tool for evaluating a complete design. Software Engineering approaches begin with consideration of the data structure and only then proceed to the interface. While attractive from an engineering point of view, this approach relegates graphic and representational design to a supporting role and again cannot evaluate the whole design.

The important insights obtained by investigating theatre as a paradigm for human computer interaction [Laurel, 1993] suggested that research into a similar area, film (one with many parallels with multimedia) might also be valuable - that the underlying conceptual framework might be extremely appropriate for multimedia. (An apparent problem exist here because Brenda Laurel states that narrative is unsuitable as a metaphor and compares it unfavourably with drama as an interface agent. However she essentially is speaking of narrative in its written mode). The underlying construct within film is narrative - the film production process translates an oral or written narrative into an enacted multi-media narrative.

A new field of study, narratology, or narrative theory, which has its roots in the Soviet Union of the late 1920's, specifically in the work of the Russian Formalists and Vladimir Propp and has since been fed by the studies of a diverse, international group of linguists, semiologists, anthropologists, folklorists, literary critics, and film theorists [Kozloff, 1992], defines narrative as "a representation, considering the story's world, its portrayal of some reality, or its broader meanings...."; "as a structure, a particular way of combining parts to make a whole"; and "as a process, the activity of selecting, arranging, and rendering story material in order to achieve specific time-bound effects on a perceiver" [Bordwell, 1985]

In its usual usage, the term narrative connotes a communication mode which expresses fact or fiction. This is one of its definitions - but it is its narrowest. In a scientific sense, as defined by narratology, narrative is an entity which integrates structure, content, context and process. Narrative includes 'both the story being told (content) and the conditions of its telling (structure and context)" [Don 1990]

It does this by employing a global and local cause and effect framework, by using a unified non-discrete structural organisation; as opposed to a discrete framework where content units merely extend the content base - to remove one of the units lessens the volume but does not leave a missing link in the overall theme or purpose or development. A narrative structure conversely affects the content selection process in that all information units serve some function in relation to an overall theme, with the removal of one affecting the overall logical structure. The global purpose provides logical purpose and context for smaller content units

Narrative also refers to a particular way of developing, ordering and rendering events. It does not simply reflect or transmit reality, it constructs it. We notice the adequacy of the construction intuitively when we assess the media appeal of something. A good example of this might be old television advertisements versus newer ones. Older advertisements might have a static picture on the screen with a voice over describing its features or suggesting its purchase; newer ones may use narrative to dynamically paint a scene or story with the product either filling a gap in the story or proving a centre for it.
It is the multidimensional nature, the cause and effect unity, the ubiquity and dominance of the narrative form within traditional media and the link with good

design which suggests that a method based on this construct has the potential for holistically evaluating a design.

Masterman [1985] cites three reasons for interpreting media texts as narrative: (1) familiarity with narrative strategies and the issues raised by different narrative forms will be transferable to a wide range of media genres, and to any new media text; (2) because the differences between many media forms are largely explicable in terms of their different narrative structures, students need to grapple with issues of narrative if they are to make important basic distinctions between dominant media forms and (3) narrative study raises in an unforced way, the central concern of media education: the 'constructedness' of what are frequently portrayed as natural ways of representing experience.

Many CD-ROM titles are not narrative structurally i.e. dictionaries, or encyclopaedias. Though an 'ideal' structure is narrative, if this is not compatible with the purpose of the product then the structure closest to narrative [described within Brannigan's spectrum of data types in the Data Organisation discussion section below] presents the next most favourable option.

There are many, many narratives but no one narrative. Narrative is in a sense an abstraction. It reaches concrete form by being articulated within concrete dimensions within a medium: within space, through visual elements or sound. Narrative is articulated in a particular way through these dimensions. Non-narrative data types are also manifested within these dimensions. If the data type is non-narrative structurally, it still can manifest itself in the same way as a narrative would within some dimensions of a medium: within the space, the interface, the development style or the navigational design.

The first category, (1) data organisation type evaluates the data type. The next 3 categories explore the dimensions within which narrative is articulated. These categories are (2) the interface and navigational systems with 'hiddenness' of the computer as an artefact as the evaluation criterion (3) the nature of the development of the content material with 'constructedness' as the evaluation criterion and (4) the spatial dimension with purpose as the evaluation criterion.

Given the skeumorphism of new media (the adoption of techniques and strategies from an existing medium to a new medium) which occurred, for example, with the transition from orality to literacy or from manuscript to print; and with the development of film, it might be expected that narrative be inherited and modified within a new media [Warner, 1997]. The process of deconstructing narrative into practical evaluation metrics and testing their validity in relation to multimedia titles furthers a current research area within multimedia, Interactive Narrative Theory. [Cinema and Television 673 on Interactive Narrative Theory, 1995] [MENO project, 1995]

3 Empirical Work

3.1 Methodology:

Stage 1

Phase 1 of the study involved a literature survey and a search for an external interpretative framework to assist in comparative media analysis. During a literature survey of media theory, film theory, semiotics, structuralism and multimedia; and through discussions with a number of experts in film theory, multimedia and media studies, narrative was identified as the key entity underlying media communication. Good narrative was defined as a key determinant for good media design and as an construct actualised in many media. The search for an 'outside' interpretative framework ended.

Stage 2

A content analysis of three texts composed stage two. Bordwell's *Narrative in the Fiction Film*, 1985; Brannigan's *Narrative Comprehension and Film*, 1992; Chatman's *Story and Discourse: Narrative Structure in Fiction and Film*, 1978; were isolated as each text deconstructs narrative in a different way offering a spectrum of interpretative approaches. A range of narrative constructs, approaches, and design techniques were identified.

Stage 3

Ten CD-ROM titles chosen for [a] their similarity of purpose for education or information dissemination, and [b] availability, were previewed. These were five interactive encyclopaedias, one Virtual Reality museum title, two film guides, one tourist information package and an interactive Almanac.

- *Haliwell's Interactive Film Guide* [FIT Vision Ltd. for Beckett Fiennes Enterprises, 1993];
- The *Virtual Museum* [Apple Computer, Inc., 1992];
- *How Computer Work*, [Warner New Media, 1993];
- *America Alive* [CD Technology, Inc., 1992]

were chosen for indepth analysis as they represent a wide spectrum of design styles.

The four 'non-narrative' multimedia titles illustrate that narrative at a local level can be contained within a non-narrative global structure and that the original material need not be a story (for example a film documentary where the material is not initially a narrative but is constructed into narrative form).

Fig. 1

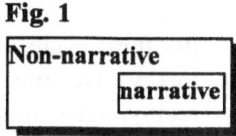

The designs of the four titles were deconstructed in terms of global design, navigational structure, access mechanisms, metaphors, the representation of individual content components, the logical and thematic relation between independent components and the relation between components and the global design. Specification of what constituted individual components, the global level and amount of levels followed evident subject divisions within the titles.

While the theoretical base acquired during phase two formed a mental background to phase three, the four titles were initially analysed without specific reference to the collated constructs. The purpose of this was an attempt to allow criteria to emerge heuristically from the analysis rather then impose them on the titles and to see if the empirical study might independently validate theoretical constructs collated within stage two.

Stage 1 confirmed narrative as a key entity underlying media production. Stage 2 took a range of interpretative approaches and identified a range of narrative constructs. Stage 3 confirmed and strengthened four constructs as visible within and directly relevant in defining, interpreting and influencing commercial multimedia design. These had previously been described by their proponent theorists as underpinning narrative constructs. Stage 3 therefore validated Stage 1 and Stage 2.

3.2   Results Summary

The evaluation categories are:
1. Data Organisation, separated into six types (a heap, a catalogue, an episode, an unfocused chain, a focused chain, a simple narrative/a narrative); each structure differing according to the organisation or relationship between elements. There is a hierarchy of integration and cohesiveness ranging from one to another. A narrative provides an 'ideal', it integrates units linked at a micro level within a global cause and effect framework. A hierarchy in increasing order in interest, in terms of media appeal, is engendered by each data type.
2. The interface and navigational system were the subjects for evaluation with 'hiddenness' of the media artefact as the evaluation criterion. 'Hiddenness' refers to the extent to which the techniques and processes of production, access and use are hidden within the designs. Traditional media such as a film, a documentary or a news story hide the sense of being a constructed artefact; empirical work suggests that this aspect of traditional media production would translate well to multimedia, as illustrated in the effectiveness of a virtual reality interface, where the 'computer' is relatively well hidden.
3. 'Constructedness', the extent and nature of the presentation of the content base is the third evaluation criterion. This relates to an early argument within film theory. The initial supposition was that film simply reflected or transmitted reality, later theorists defined film as a production, a constructed artefact, independent of the 'reality' it transmits. Constructedness is a defining feature in distinguishing between good or poor quality within presentational design. It also is an element which divides Brannigan's six data types into two groups - those that simply list content material (heap, list or catalogue structures) and those that develop it (episodes, unfocused chains, focused chains and narrative).

4. Space is the fourth category and the criterion for evaluation is purpose.   As mentioned above, narrative is not a concrete entity, it must be embodied within different dimensions and one of these is space.   An interesting aspect of space within multimedia, uncovered during the empirical work, is the amount of purposes it can serve and that the more purposes it has the more effective the design.   Space can be analysed by whether it is simply a background to further access points or display components; provides context for content units as, for example, in a map, or is a dynamic navigational environment as in a Virtual Reality design.

Each criterion will now be discussed in detail under the headings of description, theory, empirical analysis and "towards an evaluation metric". The purpose at present is not to evaluate the titles; examples selected from the CD-ROM products are not meant to compare them but to illustrate the criteria.

3.3   Discussion of Results

3.3.1   Criterion 1, Data Organisation Type

Description
Data organisation type was the first evaluation criterion.   As this is the most important criterion Brannigan's six classifications are described below.   These are based on Applebee's [1978] work on how children develop a sense of story and Applebee's work is based on Vygotsky's [1962] stages in concept development. While narrative is just one of the six types specified, it presents an 'ideal' which is contrasted with non-narrative data organisation types.

Theory
1. A heap is a virtually random collection of data or objects assembled largely by chance. Objects are linked to one another only through an immediacy of perception, a free-association of the moment.
2. A catalogue is created by collecting objects each of which is similarly related to a 'centre' or core. For example, a list of objects that belong in a particular room; or are used by a particular person or are recorded in a particular time span (which yields a chronology)..
3. An episode is created by collecting together the consequences of a central situation: for example, collecting everything that happens to a particular character in a particular setting as well as everything that the character does in that setting.   Unlike a heap or a catalogue, an episode does not simply grow longer, it shows change; it develops and progresses. Because the parts of an episode are defined through cause and effect, it is easier to remember an episode than to remember the miscellaneous parts of a heap or a catalogue.
4. An unfocused chain is a series of cause and effects without a continuing centre. For example, character A is followed for a time, then character B, then character C.

84

5. A focused chain is a series of cause and effects with a continuing centre. For example, the continuing adventures of a character, the events surrounding an object or place, or the elaboration of a theme.
6. A simple narrative organisation is a series of episodes collected as a focused chain. The structure on a global level is linked by cause and effect, the parts within each episode are linked by cause and effect and there is "a continuing centre which develops, progresses and interacts from episode to episode". Each component serves some purpose in relation to the development of the continuing centre' or plot. The structure is therefore highly integrated at multiple levels. A narrative ends when its cause and effect chains are totally delineated.

Figure 2, Data Structures

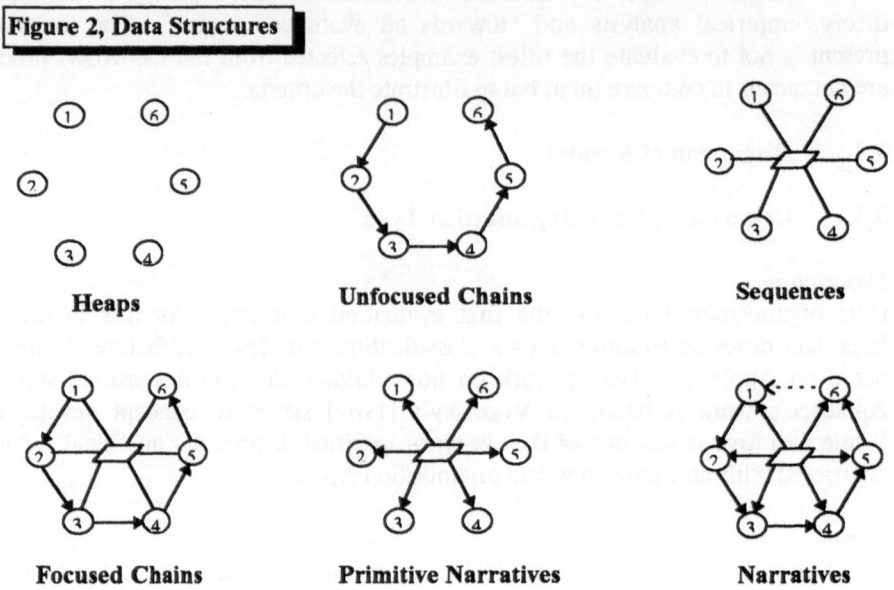

Depicted by Applebee, [1978] to describe the structure of children's stories. Arrows indicate complementary attributes; straight lines, shared attributes; parallelograms, centres; circles, incidents or elements.

Empirical analysis

As the content base of each of the four titles was organised into discreet components, without a holistic cause and effect logical unity, none were structured globally as narrative. While narrative presents an 'ideal' there are five other data structures being evaluated within the method; their rating being determined by their position within the heap...narrative hierarchy. Some examples from each product are presented to illustrate how and where Brannigan's classifications can apply.

The *Interactive Film Guide* has a catalogue structure at global level (information is organised by director, year, screenwriter, actor/actress, chronologically by film title) and a list structure at subject level [films by a particular actor, films by a screenwriter are listed). The results of a search (excluding the search by year) appeared unconnected to a time dimension. Elements are displayed simultaneously, the content does not develop over time, there isn't a time dimension to its display [aside of access and retrieval] and the time one spent was not connected to any unfolding of material but rather to ones own purpose. An analysis of time helps define its catalogue or list structure.

It is a good reference guide but in terms of media appeal it is very limited.

The catalogue or list structure of the Film guide, is a valid organisational type but it is one which the authors think a film producer would avoid as unsuitable for a media product. Certainly examples of such an organisation as the primary structure for a film or television product have not been seen, though a list structure as a small component of a media product is sometimes dramatic when placed in context with other media displays, for instance the lists of 'accidental deaths' at the end of *Cry Freedom.*

The *Interactive Film Guide* can be contrasted with the *How Computer Work* title. In this product topics are discussed, processes are explained and animation's are provided to illustrate the processes. There is a temporal nature to the display i.e. one sat there while events happen (display time), while content unfolded (content development time).

The *How Computer Work* CD might be described as a focused chain - the parts within each topic are defined through cause and effect, the topics within develop and progress; collected within topical units are "the consequences of a central situation", what happens and is acted upon within a particular setting. Each section explains one aspect of a computer which serves the global purpose of explaining how computers work.

The overall structure of the *Virtual Museum* seems to fit the definition for an unfocused chain - "a series of cause and effects but with no continuing centre". For example, the plants within the planet room are explored for a time, then the anatomy room is investigated, then planets are visited through the astronomy room.

The data structure of the Virtual Museum is more difficult to define because while the content units are discrete, the 3-D spatial design unifies them spatially. Also while the graphics which display each content unit have a time dimension, there isn't a lot of other information presented ·i.e. one sees a plant unfolding, or a dynamic illustration of the workings of the heart, but no other information is provided on these content units. It therefore has a narrative style spatially, but might be defined as an under-developed collection of episodes.

While a subjective judgement, I found the appeal of each CD-ROM closely linked to its place within the Brannigan's 'heap to narrative' hierarchy; the *Interactive Film*

Guide, America Alive, Virtual Museum and How Computer Work titles being preferred in ascending order. This may be a product of the differing levels of cohesion and integration associated with each data structure.

Towards an evaluation metric

The placement of each data structure along Brannigan's 'heap to narrative' data organisation spectrum presents a hierarchy in terms of media appeal. A rating system can be attached to the data types with a heap structure scoring lowest and a narrative highest. Categorisation of multimedia titles into data structure type will be somewhat more complex, but a number of aids present themselves. Brannigan's descriptions may be used. Causality and time vary within the data structures producing a system of differences which may help to define data type - causality because causal relations amongst content elements and between content elements and the global organisation differ in relation to each structure; and time because within the spectrum of data types, from a heap to a narrative, time becomes increasingly consequential and directional.

3.3.2 'Hiddenness' of the computer artefact. Criterion 2

Description

'Hiddenness' of the computer as an artefact refers to the visibility or obtrusiveness of the mechanisms of production and access, to the relative visibility of the medium itself. Winograd and Flores, [1987] hold 'hiddenness' of the computer as an artefact as an essential 'good' for design. They suggest that a computer should resemble a tool, like Heidegger's hammer - when in use the focus is on the task in hand, such as nailing a board. The hammer only becomes visible when it hits one's thumb. They suggest that the computer should also be such a tool - the medium which transmits its content should be hidden, the 'constructedness', the techniques and processes for production, access and use should where possible be concealed. The Trilobyte design company, in their design of very successful computer games, *7th Guest* and *11th Hour,* support this idea.

Theory

There are a number of levels at work within any media production. There are (1) the initial content events or 'reality'; (2) the construction of the content (3) the display of the content. Hiding the 'artefactness' of the media product means that the transitions amongst the levels are hidden; that the medium delivers but does not intrude upon the content.

Empirical analysis

The interface and navigational structure of the *How Computer Work* product is obviously a computer specific interface rather then a subject oriented 'environment'. The linkage mechanisms are buttons, which are not shaped around the picture they contain but are square boxes. The interface screens, though beautifully designed (they contain faded out pictures and appealing textures) are 2 dimensional screens. The computer as an artefact is very visible.

Though association links, information depth, 'constructedness' of subject material; graphical design and presentation are good, the interface and navigational design of *How Computer Work* does not have the same spatial appeal as that within the *Virtual Museum* title.

Within the *Virtual Museum*, the Atrium, the entry area, corresponds to an introductory screen which displays global subject choices, but the effect is different. There is a feeling of being drawn into the product - in terms of peeping objects within rooms, 3-D space depth and visual layers and the forward moving action of 'walking' around.

With navigating through levels within a 'normal' product, clicking on a button produces a requested screen, but the process of getting there is something hidden, something magical, that 'happens within the computer'. With the Virtual Reality design one simply walks into a room - the computer as an artefact is hidden, no 'mysterious process' appears to be happening through the operation though they are both, theoretically - button clicking for a subject area and walking into a room - the same action. As a result of this there is a greater sense of control. Also, there is no feeling of disorientation as can sometimes happen when context is lost as screens suddenly replace one another.

'Erasing' the medium makes the content appear more real, lends it a sense of veritude, hides the fact that it is constructed and allows the user to concentrate on one level, the content, rather then on the medium and mechanisms which transmit it.

The 'artefactness' of the computer is hidden, instead of thinking of computer buttons or retrieving information - one visits it. This type of visual metaphor which moves away from the sense of being a computer design and closer to the idea of a 3-D natural world is clear, intuitive and very appealing.

Towards an evaluation metric
With 'hiddenness' of the artefact" as a media quality benchmark, design components can be specified and compared - an icon shaped like an object as an access mechanism is preferable to a button showing the object's picture; a map is preferable to a blank screen with access points; an 3-D immersive environment is preferable to a static interface .... and so on.

3.2.3 'Constructedness', Criterion three

> *"Television, newspapers, films, radio, advertisements and*
> *magazines are produced. The media that is, are actively involved*
> *in processes of constructing or representing 'reality' rather than*
> *simply transmitting or reflecting it."* [Masterman, 1985]

Description
'Constructedness" or design for display is the fourth criterion. 'Constructedness' refers to the extent and nature of the development of content units for display.

Theory
This links closely with the Data Organisation categories. Data types closest to narrative within Brannigan's heap to narrative schema construct their material more than those at the lower end of the spectrum.

A narrative selects one topic or theme from reality; develops this theme by mapping out conflicts and dramas; looks for the most visual illustrations of its theme within a visual medium [though the most visual are not necessarily the most important]; organises local items into a global cause and effect framework; and orders and renders this material dramatically.

Empirical analysis
Within *How Computers Work* the information is extremely well constructed. Non-visual technical information is given life and visual form through concrete example and analogy.

For instance, to explain the operations of an operating system, a controller program, an input/output program, a file manager, a memory manager and a central processing unit are presented as animated robots working in a large room. The memory manager works with memory containers in the wall, the input/output manager receives task boxes through an assembly line style chute, the controller apparently controls the activities within the operating system and all of the robots work with blue task boxes prepared by it.

This product uses the possibilities within multimedia to visualise technical information. In a sense *How Computer Work* is designed as a good film would be: information is 'constructed', made visual and dynamic rather then just displayed, where the material isn't naturally visual (as a lot of it isn't), then the information is portrayed through a metaphor or analogy with visual potential. In other words, other forms of expression are sought to give technical material life and so *How Computers Work* is a good example of 'constructedness'.

Towards an evaluation metric
A static versus dynamic dichotomy can also be used for describing content and

content display. Static refers to something still, such as a personality attribute or still object. Dynamic refers to something active, something which has a temporal nature or happens over time. Video, animation, a screen where visual units develop or change over time are visually dynamic; sound, music and voice are also dynamic. Static media are still media such as text and still graphics like photographs, maps and diagrams (though these can be translated into dynamic format within a video or animation). This static versus dynamic dichotomy may be used as a measure to compare content with the nature of its presentation. A dynamic construction seems particularly important for the design of dynamic, process information [process information is described by Chatman, 1978]. For instance, an operating system described above is conveyed very effectively by an animation - the textual description of such a system or even a diagram (stasis media) would take much longer to visualise.

'Lower level' data types such as a heap and a catalogue do not construct their material - they simply list it whereas higher levels develop the material. So data type presents a second mechanism for helping to describe constructedness.

3.3.4   Purpose of spatial design, Criterion 4

Description
Purpose was identified as a criterion in relation to spatial design.

Theory
Within a film or book spatial representation or description is often more then simply a platform for action. It is used to reinforce or accompany development, atmosphere, theme, point of view (a particular perspective, how much information one agent/character has) to stress disparities in information, to disseminate information, to stress aspects of a content base or to suggest hypothesis.

Within multimedia spatial design can be used to convey structure, context, geography or concept [Dieverger and Bolter, 1995].

Empirical analysis
A criterion for spatial analysis is therefore purpose. Within the four CD-ROM titles the greater the function of the spatial dimension, the more effective the impact.

Within *Haliwell's Film Guide* and *How Computers Work* information is accessed through buttons on a screen. There isn't a visual metaphor and the background is simply that - a background. In the *America Alive* title the spatial design is geographic - the interface is a map of the United States and the information on each state is accessed through its representation on the map. The spatial design therefore organises content into context. This also happens within the *Virtual Museum*. The interface is a museum which houses logically discreet subjects thus providing a metaphor for unifying them spatially. An atrium provides a central access mechanism, subject areas are 'rooms' of the museum; the trips around the planets within the astronomy section create a story space and engender a feeling of undertaking a journey. The museum is a navigable environment and a visual metaphor.

Towards an evaluation metric

Space can be classified by purpose, by whether it is simply (1) a background or (2) a static platform for content as in a non-interactive map, or (3) by whether it itself constitutes the navigation system, either statically (an interactive map) or (4) dynamically (as in a Virtual Reality environment). Value ratings may be attached to these classifications in ascending order.

4 Future Work

1. The criteria at present are broad criteria rather then metrics. The classification and rating systems will be developed.
2. The method must be balanced against the product's purpose. Titles will be classified by genre, demarcated by product purpose, and each criterion within benchmarked according to narrative possibilities for that purpose.
3. Additional criteria need to be incorporated from both Software Engineering and Human Computer Interaction: examples are robustness, ease of use or graphical quality. These criteria are also essential to the construction of a good media product but they are not focused on within the investigation as they are well researched elsewhere. All criteria will be rated and described individually. So the user instead of being given one overall 'score' is aware of which dimension is being rated against what criterion.
4. Designers will be asked to try out the method to provide further verification as to its validity, utility, and ease of use. Feedback will be used to iteratively redesign the method.

5 Conclusion

This paper is not saying that narrative data type is the best organizational structure for all designs. The most suitable structure is primarily determined by the purpose of the product, for example a catalogue list/structure may be the best choice for a reference guide.

It is saying that narrative is the best choice in terms of media appeal - but media appeal may not be the purpose of the product. It is also saying that the further a product moves along the described heap...narrative spectrum, the more media appeal the product begins to engender.

Therefore while the method is an evaluation method and is not meant to be used prescriptively for design, the criteria do illustrate a hierarchy of least to most favourable options in producing media appeal. Most data types can be developed from heap to at least focused chain form by developing the material, visualising it, introducing a time dimension, providing a centre, chaining content units, linking the material (if not globally then locally) within a course and effect framework. To move past the fifth data type, the unfocused chain, there may be a barrier depending on the nature of the content material (i.e. if this is discreet as with material for an interactive encyclopaedia, the global structure cannot be narrative, but each subject area could be developed locally as a narrative).

The empirical work did validate four narrative criteria as visible within and directly relevant in defining, interpreting and influencing a multimedia design. The criteria had previously been described by their proponent theorists as underpinning narrative constructs.

A range of data structures ranging from non-narrative to narrative were specified by Brannigan. An increasing hierarchy in terms of interest engendered accompanied movement towards and use of narrative structures within the multimedia titles. Such an empirical result is supported by previous research within traditional media and sustains the premise that narrative is a unique selling proposition and a means to discriminate between commercial titles.

The method directly addresses the more abstract quality of engagement engendered by a particular multimedia product - a quality which in itself is otherwise difficult to measure yet is heavily influential in terms of a product's success.

References:

1. Aristotle. *Poetics* Translation by Else, Gerald F. The University of Michigan Press, 1969.
2. Applebee, Arthur N. *The Child's Concept op Story*, University of Chicago Press, 1978.
3. Barthes, Roland. *Introduction to the Structural Analysis of Narratives*, 1975.
4. Bordwell, David. *Narrative in the Fiction Film*, Routledge, 1985.
5. Brannigan, Edward. *Narrative Comprehension and Film*, Edward Brannigan, Routledge, 1992.
6. Brannigan, Edward. Virginia Broods Film, Perception and Cognitive Psychology *Millennium Film Journal* No 14/15 Fall/Winter 84-85.
7. Chatman, Seymour. *Story and Discourse: Narrative Structure in Fiction and Film*, Cornell University Press, 1978.
8. Cinema and Television 673, *Interactive Narrative Theory*, South California, 1995.
9. Heidegger, Martin. Cited within *Understanding Computer's and Cognition*, Winograd and Flores, Wesley, 1986, 1987.
10. Kozloff, Sahra. "Narrative Theory and Television" within *Channels of Discourse Reassembled*, Routledge, 1992.
11. Laurel, Brenda. *Computers as Theatre*, Addison-Wesley, 1993.
12. Masterman, Len. *Teaching the Media*, Routledge, 1985.
13. *MENO* project. ESRC Cognitive Engineering Programme, Institute of Educational Technology, Open University, 1995. [focuses on understanding the form and function of narrative in educational and interactive multimedia programmes]
14. Ricoeur, Paul. *Time and Narrative*, translated by Kathleen McLaughlin and David Pellauer, University of Chicago Press, 1985.
15. Stratford, Michael. *Investigation Into the Design of Educational Multimedia: Video, Interactivity and Narrative*, PhD thesis, Open University, 1994.
16. Vygotsky, L.S. *Thought and Language*, M.I.T. Press, 1962.
17. Vygotsky, L.S. *The Psychology of Art*, M.I.T. Press, 1971.
18. Winograd and Flores. *Understanding Computer's and Cognition*, Wesley, 1987.

Multimedia titles

- *America Alive*, MediAlive, CD Technology, Inc., 1992
- *How Computer Work*, Warner New Media copyright 1993 based on How Things Work and Understanding Computers series copyright 1990, 1992
- Haliwell's *Interactive Film Guide*, produced by FIT Vision Ltd for Beckett Fiennes Enterprises, 1993;
- The *Virtual Museum* copyright Apple Computer, Inc., 1992.

Interactors and Haggis:
Executable specifications for interactive systems

Meurig Sage and Chris Johnson,

GIST,
Department of Computing Science,
University of Glasgow, Glasgow,
Scotland, United Kingdom, G12 8QQ.
E-mail: {meurig, johnson}@dcs.glasgow.ac.uk

Abstract Executable formal specifications, of interactive systems, allow programmers to both reason about their systems, and test them on users. The feedback provided allows an iterative approach to interface design. We argue that new developments in concurrent functional languages make them ideal for executing specifications. To show this, we make use of Haggis, a concurrent functional graphical toolkit. We describe the development of a highly interactive game, from specification to execution. We start with an agent based specification, making use of the CNUCE LOTOS interactor model. This model provides for both modularity and reasoning power. We, however, make use of a VDM like specification language to describe the internal state of our interactors, and so overcome some of the problems with CNUCE interactors. We then show how this specification can be easily and quickly transformed into executable code, using the Haggis system. This application typifies the dynamic, real-time interfaces that many previous prototyping environments do not support.

1 Introduction

Formal specifications allow designers to demonstrate the functional correctness of their systems. When applied to interactive systems, these techniques can be used to reason about interaction problems[22]. Many different formalisms have been suggested to achieve this, including temporal logics[16], state-based CSP[1], and LOTOS[18]. Multi-agent models, which treat systems as a group of interactors or "communicating interactive processes"[1, 4], have been used to build systems in a modular manner. To allow proper user testing of interfaces, techniques for executing these specifications still need to be properly developed[12].

1.1 Why executable specifications?

It has been argued that making specifications executable may reduce clarity and expressiveness[13]. Fuchs[10], however, has shown that this is not necessarily so. Alexander[2], has demonstrated the usefulness of executable specification for rapid prototyping, as they allow interfaces to be tested early on. This allows designers to develop systems iteratively, to meet user's needs. For instance,

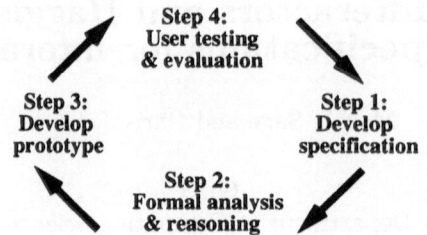

Fig. 1. Iterative Development of Interactive Systems

a partial implementation of a system could be evaluated in a user's working environment.

1.2 Functional programming

In this paper, we argue that new developments in functional programming should be used to bring Alexander's work up to date. We demonstrate how Haggis[9], a Graphical User Interface system for the lazy functional language Haskell[19], can be used to bridge the specification-execution gap. It provides a compositional, concurrent programming language which can be used to build interactive systems in a high level, modular manner. This makes it easy to produce a prototype from a high level specification, and so perform user testing and evaluation.

To show how this can be done, we use a highly interactive game, as an example. We specify it in LOTOS (Figure 1, step 1), and convert this into Haggis code (Figure 1, step 3). Our example shows the power of the Haggis framework: the Haggis representation is at almost the same level of abstraction as the specification. We, however, still need the LOTOS specification as it allows high level reasoning about the concurrent interaction in the system (Figure 1, step 2). This reasoning power is important as studies have shown that programmers often have problems making proper use of concurrent languages[14]. This example is relevant as it demonstrates that Haggis can deal with the kind of highly interactive systems that declarative languages are frequently bad at handling.

2 Functional Programming & Executable Specifications

To bring Alexander's work into the 1990s, we use 'leading edge' techniques from functional programming and formal specifications. Alexander used eventCSP, a subset of the concurrent specification language CSP, to specify human-computer interaction[2]. For instance, consider a Quit button, that may appear to be pressed or unpressed, with an updateable label. We could specify it as follows:

```
quitB =  (mouse-down-in-button-> pressedButton ->
            (  (mouse-up-in-button -> quit -> exit)
            [] (mouse-up-outside-button -> quitB)))
        [] (setLabel -> upDateLabel -> quitB)
```

Alexander argued that it is easy to understand and reason about the interaction in this specification. Possible sequences can be built using the prefix (->) operator. Different paths are shown using the choice ([]) operator.

Alexander used an executable subset of VDM (Vienna Development Model) to describe the data, and operations used in eventCSP. This language, called "me too", used pre and post conditions to describe the events[3]. She used a functional language to execute these specifications. We develop her approach, by using newer developments in functional languages, which make executing specifications easier.

3 Interactors

Newer specification approaches have made better use of concurrency than Alexander. The interactor model, developed under the Amodeus project, treats systems as a number of interacting components, each with a state, and behaviour. These "interactors" can communicate with each other, with users and with the underlying application. This approach allows for more modular and readable specifications. By relating tasks to interactors, user centred design becomes possible. The York interactor model exploits the Z specification language, along with a variety of different logics. This approach is concerned with states and displays, and the relationships between them[4]. In contrast, the CNUCE interactor approach uses LOTOS to specify interactors. It is more event based, making the communication structure clearer[4]. The lack of a proper representation of state can, however, be a problem.

The CNUCE model views an interactor as an object that can:

- "receive (and accumulate) output from the application side (oc),

- receive an output trigger (ot), the interactor then sends output to the user side (os),

- receive (and accumulate) input from the user side (im), and provide feedback toward the user (os)

- receive an input trigger (it) that causes the interactor to send the accumulated input to the application side (is)."[4]

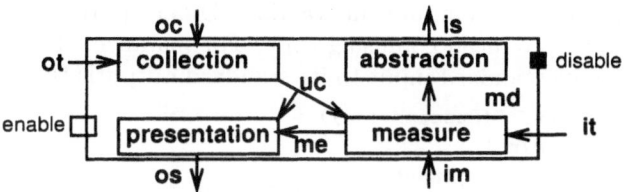

Fig. 2. CNUCE interactor

Internally an interactor has four components (see Figure 2). The *collection* maintains a representation of the model of the interactor. When triggered by the event ot, it passes output (using the event uc) to the *presentation*, which performs the actual rendering. Input from the user side is received by the *measure* which, when triggered, passes it (using the event md) to the *abstraction*. The abstraction alters the input into the form that the application requires; for instance, turning a button click on a menu, into a message saying which menu element had been chosen. The measure may provide feedback on user input, using the event me, for example, to make a button look pressed. The measure may also tell the presentation to modify any new output data. For instance, if a button interactor were told to change its label (by the event oc), the measure would be informed (by the event uc) and could tell the presentation (using the event me) whether the button should be drawn in the pressed state.

We could define a button interactor (see Figure 3) as follows:

```
Button[mousedown,mouseup,getButtonClick,setLabel,ot,os]
      (pic:Picture, n:Any)
```

This receives input which is either a mouse press (mousedown), or a successful click (mouseup). Each will cause feedback: the button will appear to be pressed and then unpressed. A successful mouse click is the input trigger, which causes the value n to be sent to the application side. The interactor can also receive output (setLabel) that gives a picture to display on the button. The button can also be enabled, so that it accepts input, or disabled so that it does not.

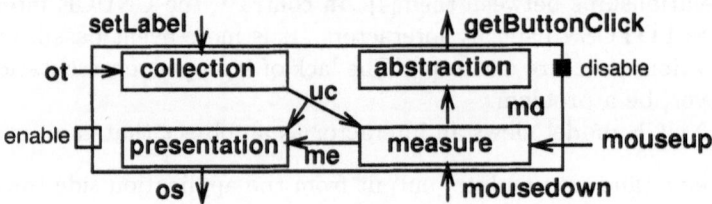

Fig. 3. Button interactor

4   Functional Programming & Specifications in the 1990s

4.1   Imperative Functional Programming

Despite having a number of demonstrated advantages, functional languages have suffered from severe problems in the past. One of the main difficulties has been supporting human-computer interaction. Older approaches, based around *stream based I/O*, produced confusing code. For instance, the following simple program, copies its standard input to its standard output[11]:

```
main ~(Str input: ~(Success : _)) =
  [ ReadChan stdin,
    AppendChan stdout input
  ]
```

How input, is transferred between ReadChan and AppendChan is unclear. The resulting confusion caused serious problems for programmers learning to exploit functional programming.

Newer approaches based around *monadic I/O* provide a more imperative programming style, familiar to most programmers[11, 20]. The same program, with monadic I/O, would be:

```
main = do
        ch <- getChar
        putChar ch
        main
```

The sequencing of actions is more explicit here; the input from `getChar` (ch) is used by `putChar`.

4.2   Concurrency

Previous techniques for executing interface specifications, have not used concurrent programming languages to implement concurrent specifications. In contrast, we make use of *Concurrent Haskell*[21], which provides lightweight processes, and makes use of monadic I/O. Programmers can create new child processes with the `forkIO` function. Communication occurs asynchronously, through shared variables (`MVars`) which operate like semaphores. We argue that being able to turn our concurrent specification into concurrent code, makes the transformation to executability easier.

To keep this transformation simple, we have developed an extended concurrency library. This provides programmers with synchronous communication, through a library of LOTOS like operators. We also include asynchronous communication along channels. This provides a more efficient and, arguably, a more elegant way of implementing any asynchronous communication in a LOTOS specification. Asynchronous and synchronous communication can be combined freely within this system.

4.3   Virtual I/O device

Haggis, the graphical framework, is built on top of Concurrent Haskell[9]. This approach provides for modular design. A common problem with many graphical user interface systems is their reliance on an event loop, and call backs. This style has well known problems[17]. Haggis, instead, treats the user interface as a virtual device, allowing the application to maintain control. The concurrent features of Haggis allow several virtual I/O devices to operate at once. For instance, one process could block waiting for a mouse click while others got on with necessary work.

4.4   Declarative structured graphics

A further problem with the development of graphical interfaces is that conventional languages tend to be highly imperative. This means that rather than considering how a picture should look, programmers must describe the sequence of actions that must be used to render it. This added complexity makes mistakes more likely. In contrast, in Haggis all graphical output is specified declaratively through a `Picture` type[8]. Haggis provides operations to transform and combine objects, along with an extensive list of graphical primitives. For instance,

98

we could specify one of the enemy ships (Figure 4), used in our example game, as:

```
enemy = fillSolid $ withColour grey $
        beside (ellipse (5,12))
               (above thruster thruster)
where thruster = coverlay cross (ellipse (15,6))
          -- centre one image over another
        cross = withColour black $
               beside (rectangle (12,2)) (rectangle (2,8))
```

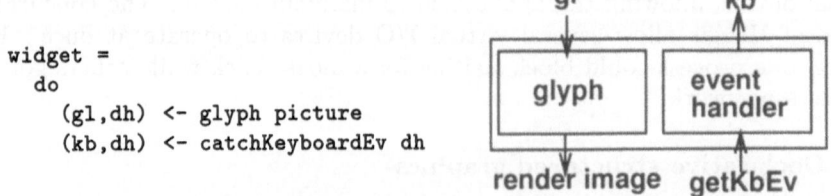

Fig. 4. A simple picture

Haggis takes care of converting pictures into calls to the window system, with the Glyph output abstraction. This declarative approach makes it easy to build, and manipulate complex images.

4.5 User interface, application separation

Application-interface separation is allowed for, as user interface components are represented by two different parts. For instance, the glyph output abstraction returns a Glyph handle which the application can use, for instance, to update the image. It also returns a Display Handle, which is a reference to the interactive graphical surface.

```
glyph :: Picture -> Component (Glyph, DisplayHandle)
```

This application interface separation allows programmers to build more modular systems.

4.6 Compositional structure

Haggis provides layout combinators and other functions to combine the Display Handles mentioned above. For instance, we could make an interactive widget by combining an input event controller with the Glyph described above.

```
widget =
  do
    (gl,dh) <- glyph picture
    (kb,dh) <- catchKeyboardEv dh
```

gl   kb

| glyph | event handler |

render image   getKbEv

Fig. 5. A Haggis widget

The resulting widget (see Figure 5) has much in common with an interactor. The glyph is like a combination of the presentation and collection components: it is updateable via the gl handle. The event handler is like the measure. It receives input which is passed on via the kb handle.

5   The Example

In the past, Haggis has been used to build only very simple systems[9].   As
a more complex example, we describe the development of a highly interactive,
real-time user interface. It is a space ship game, as shown in Figure 6. The
user inputs commands via the keyboard. A number of enemy ships fly in waves
across the screen. These destroy the player's ship if they collide with it. The
player must avoid hitting the hills at the bottom, and the enemy ships. The
aim is for the player to destroy the enemy base when it is finally reached, while
shooting as many enemy ships as possible. There are buttons to allow the user
to pause the game, restart it, or quit from it. The current score will be displayed
on the screen. Though the graphics are only simple, the game requires real-time
animation. This example therefore provides a highly concurrent system, with a
number of different interactors: the game and all the buttons. The specification
concentrates on this concurrency.

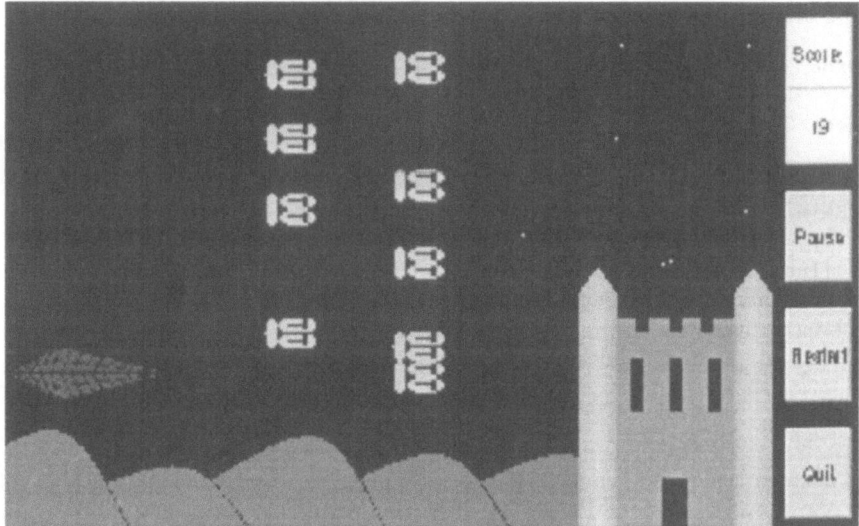

Fig. 6. Game Display

6   LOTOS Specification

In common with the CNUCE approach to interactors[18], we specify our system
in LOTOS.

6.1   The Structure of the Game

The game can be modelled as six interacting processes:

- an interactor for the Quit Button (`Quit`)

- an interactor for the Restart Button (`Restart`)

- an interactor for the Pause Button (Pause)

- an interactor for the Game Input and Output (GameIO)

- an output interactor to display the score (Score)

- an application process for the Game itself (App)

```
process Main[nscore,sendpause,
              display,input,
              restart]:noexit:=
  hide oc,is,it,iw in
    ((GameIO[oc,display,sendpause,
             input,is,it,iw]
       |[oc,is,it,iw]|
      App[it,iw,is,oc,nscore])
    [> (Restart[restart] >>
        Main[nscore,sendpause,
             display,input,restart]))
endproc

process Game[display,input,restart,
             pause,quit]:exit:=
  hide nscore,sendpause in
    ((Main[nscore,sendpause,display,
           input,restart]
       |[nscore,sendpause]|
      (Score[nscore] ||| Pause[sendpause,pause]))
    [> Quit[quit]
endProc
```

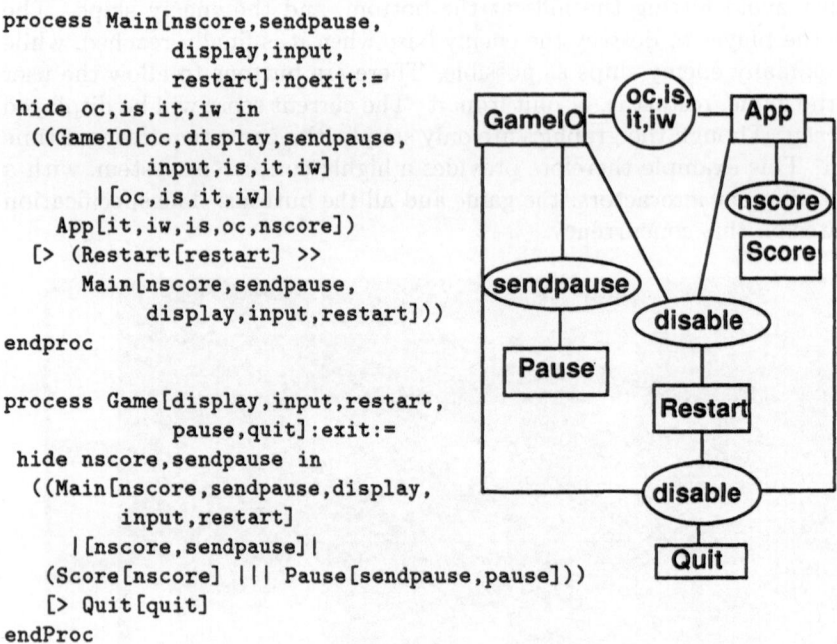

Fig. 7. The Communication

These can then be synchronised over a number of events to allow the necessary communication (see Figure 7). The two processes Main and Game are used to compose the components above, and define how they interact.

In LOTOS, a |[c]| b means run process a in parallel with process b, synchronising over gate (event) c; a ||| b means run processes a and b in parallel without any synchronising; and a [> b means run process a until b starts. A process definition P[a], means process P with gate a; hide a in P means that event a is visible only in process P.

Our specification can be described informally as follows. The Game continues to run, with input being passed from GameIO to App and output from App to GameIO and Score, until the Restart interactor fires (ie the Restart button is pressed). At this point Main starts all over again. When the Pause interactor is fired, the game will be paused, and will remain so until unpaused. This all continues until the Quit interactor is fired.

In Figure 7 we can see a graphical representation of the communication in the system. In this *Process Interaction Network*, processes are represented by named boxes, communication gates by circles, and communication by lines[7]. From this diagram and LOTOS specification we therefore have a clear understanding of how the system fits together.

6.2 Handling Input and Output - GameIO

We will now show how one of the above interactors, the GameIO process can be defined. The GameIO process (Figure 8) performs two purposes. It receives input from the user and passes it to App. It also receives pictures from App and displays them to the user. This is, therefore, a simplified version of a CNUCE interactor. The *Collection* and *Presentation* have been combined into one component GameOutput. The *Measure* and *Abstraction* remain in modified form as GameInput and Buffer. As there is no immediate feedback from user input, the GameInput and GameOutput processes are unconnected. Output sent to the interactor should be immediately displayed, so we assume that an output collect action is also an output trigger.

The GameInput process can be specified as follows:

```
process GameInput [putBuffer,getInp,pause]
                     (kb:Keyboard):noexit :=
   (pause;putBuffer!Pause;
    pause;putBuffer!Unpause;
    GameInput [putBuffer,getInp,pause] (kb))
  []
   (getInp!kb?inp:KeyboardEv;
    ([valid inp] -> putBuffer!(interpret inp);
                  GameInput [putBuffer,getInp,pause] (kb)
    []
    [not (valid inp)] ->
                  GameInput [putBuffer,getInp,pause] (kb)))
endproc
```

It either collects input events and places valid ones in a buffer, or is blocked by a pause event until another pause event occurs. Pause and unpause events, are also placed as input into the buffer.

The Buffer process can be specified as follows:

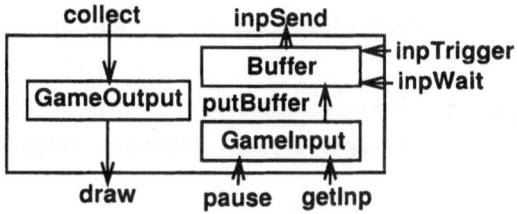

Fig. 8. The GameIO interactor

```
process Buffer [putBuffer,inpTrigger,inpWait,inpSend]
               (ns:seq InputEvent):noexit:=
    inpTrigger;inpSend!(first ns);Buffer [...] (rest ns)
[] putBuffer?inp:Input;Buffer [...] (add inp ns)
[] inpWait;
        [null ns] -> putBuffer?inp:Input;
                     inpSend!inp;
                     Buffer [...] ns
    [] [not (null ns)] -> inpSend!(first ns);
                          Buffer [...] (rest ns)
endProc
```

It allows the Application to acquire input in one of two ways. The `inpTrigger`
event may fire. This means that the application asks for the next piece of input.
If there is none, it merely gets back the value `Nothing`, otherwise it gets back the
first input event. Alternatively, the application may use `inpWait`. This causes
it to wait until some piece of input is actually available. The `inpTrigger` and
`inpWait` actions are both used by `App`. The Game should continue whether the
user sends input or not, therefore usually `App` will use `inpTrigger`. However,
when `App` receives a `Pause` event, it should block until an unpause event. This
is done by using `inpWait`.

The `Buffer` process is an example of asynchronous communication in LO-
TOS. If two processes communicate via it, the sender need not wait for the
receiver before it can continue. We shall exploit this fact in the conversion to
Haggis code.

The `GameOutput` process is much simpler, it collects pictures from the application and draws them on the screen.

```
process GameOutput[collect,draw] (screen:Screen):noexit :=
    collect?pic:Picture;
    draw!pic;
    GameOutput[collect,draw] screen
endproc
```

The complete interactor is therefore formed, by running in parallel the three
components:

```
process GameIO[collect,draw,pause,getInp,inpSend,inpTrigger,inpWait] :=
  hide putBuffer in
    (GameInput[putBuffer,getInp,pause] kb
        |[putBuffer]|
    Buffer[putBuffer,inpTrigger,inpWait,inpSend] (emptyBuffer))
    |||
    GameOutput[collect,draw] screen
endproc
```

From this specification, we can clearly see, and reason about, how the `GameIO`
process operates, and interacts with other processes.

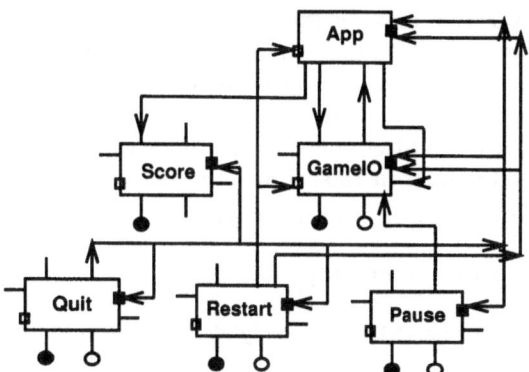

Fig. 9. Combining the interactors

6.3 The Rest of the System

The Pause, Restart and Quit interactors are simply instances of the button interactor defined earlier (see section 3). The Score interactor is simply a label that behaves identically to GameOutput.

The interactors can be represented in an interactor diagram (see Figure 9). This demonstrates how the interactors can be combined together, by linking their inputs and outputs. Black circles represent an interactor being connected to the user output, white circles to user input[18]. This provides another way of understanding how the system fits together.

We therefore have a clear, high level specification which designers may use to reason about a proposed system. They could, for instance, use a tool such as LITE[6], to prove that their specification preserved certain predefined properties. Design errors could therefore be found prior to implementation. There are further benefits to the use of interactors. The modularity of the specification makes it easy to replace individual agents. For instance, we could easily reuse the interface components with a different application. To do this we could replace the application process (App), and then with only minimal modification, of the GameIO interactor (to respond to any change of input keys), we could produce an entirely different game.

6.4 Specifying the data types and operations

In common with Alexander[3], we use an executable subset of VDM to define the data and operations in our specification. This allows a more easily programmable notion of state with invariants and operations. This approach proves particularly useful when specifying the application (App) process, which maintains data about the lasers, enemies, ship and background. We have, for instance, access to sequences to maintain the data about collections of lasers and enemies.

As an example, we will show how the ship data can be specified. Its position, width and height are maintained using a rectangle data type. The ship also has an image pic which will be displayed at its current position, using the shipPic function. There is an invariant (inv). The ship must remain on screen at all times, that is its x position must be greater than 0 and less than the width of the screen (minus its own width, so that all of the ship is displayed). The equivalent is true for its y position with respect to screen height and its own height. The ship's data is all packaged up within a Haskell record. The invariant will be applied to any attempt to alter the record, for instance, when we try to move the ship. This would appear in Haskell as follows:

```
data Ship = Ship {rect :: Rectangle,pic :: Picture}
inv ship =
 let (Rect x y w h) = rect ship
 in
 x >= 0 && x <= screenWidth - w && y < screenHeight - h && y >= 0

shipPic ship = let (Rect x y w h) = rect ship in placeAt (x,y) pic
```

In Haskell record fields, such as rect, are applied to a record as functions, using the syntax `rect ship` rather than with the more common `ship.rect` syntax.

We therefore abandon the ACT ONE algebraic data specification language, normally used with LOTOS, as it lacks modularity. The new LOTOS standard, E-LOTOS, itself replaces ACT ONE with a more functional style because of the difficulty programmers had with it[15]. Our approach overcomes some of the problems with LOTOS interactors, as they now have both a behaviour and internal state, but with the behaviour still clearly visible on top.

7   Conversion to Haggis

We can convert LOTOS specifications into Haggis code as follows:

- events become Haggis I/O actions (section 4.1); these IO actions need to be defined. They can be presentation layer events, defined using structured graphics, and Haggis interaction objects. They can perform communication between interactors, or can alter the system state (application layer);

- LOTOS communication is converted into Haskell code using our extended concurrency library. Synchronous LOTOS communication becomes synchronous Haskell communication, and asynchronous communication, simulated in LOTOS, becomes asynchronous Haskell communication;

- the data manipulation operations are already executable.

Haggis provides a number of abstractions that make this conversion easier. This is important if specifications and prototypes are to be cost effective. We make use of the button abstraction, to allow an implementation of the button interactors. This abstraction is equivalent to the interactor described earlier (see section 3). It takes a picture to display (pic), and a value (n) to return on any successful button click; it provides setLabel, and getButtonClick operations, and provides equivalent feedback on user actions. The Pause interactor can be seen in Figure 10. Input is sent from the interactor via the pauseBtn channel. Another process can receive this data by using the getButtonClick pauseBtn operation. The trigger that causes input to be sent, is a button click.

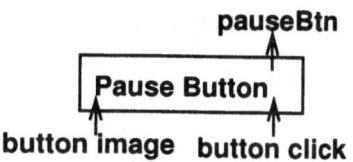

Fig. 10. The Haggis Pause Button

We can translate the GameIO process fairly simply. The Buffer process can be replaced by an asynchronous channel, as it is an example of a LOTOS specification, of asynchronous communication. Specifically, consider a channel with three operations sendChannel, which sends a value along the channel, waitChannel, which blocks until a value is received, and getChannel, which either returns the next value from the channel, or Nothing if the channel is empty. Placing values into the buffer (putBuffer) can be done with sendChannel. The Buffer will be triggered by waitChannel or getChannel, either of which will cause input to be sent out from the buffer. waitChannel is equivalent to the inpWait branch of the Buffer process; getChannel to the inpTrigger part of the Buffer process.

The GameIO interactor would therefore function as shown in Figure 11. The GameInput process sends input via the inpSendChan channel. Input is taken from this channel by either a waitChannel or a getChannel operation. These operations use the inpSendChan. Input is received from both the Pause button (via the pauseBtn channel) and the Keyboard (via the kb channel). The GameInput process can therefore be defined in Haggis as follows:

```
gameInput :: Button ()
          -> Keyboard
          -> Channel InputEvent
          -> EventIO ()
gameInput pauseBtn kb inpSendChan =
 choose
   (event (getButtonClick pauseBtn) -=> do
     sendChannel inpSendChan Pause
     receive (getButtonClick pauseBtn)
     sendChannel inpSendChan Unpause
     gameInput pauseBtn kb inpSendChan)
 .|.
   (event (getKeyboardEv kb) ==> \inp ->
     if valid inp then do
       sendChannel chan (interpret inp)
       gameInput pauseBtn inpSendChan kb
     else
       gameInput pauseBtn inpSendChan kb)
```

The .|. symbol is our choice operator. The expression event e ==> \x -> a, means perform event e, and then let x equal the result of e in action a. Choice can take place between event guarded expressions. The syntax is similar to that used in Microsoft's Functional Reactive Animation[5].

We can implement the GameOutput process very simply as a Glyph. It receives pictures to display via setPicture, and renders them on the screen.

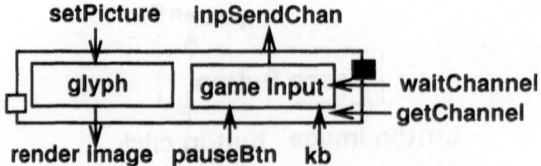

Fig. 11. The Haggis GameIO process

The above translation has shown that we can easily convert the interactors specification into executable code. We have therefore dealt with the behaviour of the system. As a final step, we will show how to describe what the system looks like, and so build the full screen shown in Figure 6. Again, we are concerned with supporting full graphical interaction as easily as possible.

We build the screen with six types of operation. The mkDC operation creates a Display Context dc, which contains information about style values and the window that will be created. The button operation creates a button as described earlier. The label operation creates a label displaying the given string, which may be updated (using the lbl handle). The glyph operation creates a simple output area containing the specified picture. The catchKeyboardEv operation makes the glyph interactive and able to receive keyboard events (via the kb channel). Finally the realiseDH operation renders the components on to a window using the vbox combinator to place Display Handles above one another, and using hbox to place Display Handles next to one other.

```
screen = do
            dc <- mkDC [];
            (rbutton,rdh) <- button (text "Restart") True dc;
            (pbutton,pdh) <- button (text "Pause") True dc;
            (qbutton,qdh) <- button (text "Quit") True dc;
            (_,ldh) <- label "Score:" dc;
            (lbl,ldh2) <- label "0" dc;
            (gl,screendh) <- glyph screenImage dc;
            (kb,sdh) <- catchKeyboardEv screendh
            realiseDH (hbox [sdh,vbox[ldh,ldh2,pdh,rdh,qdh]])
```

The system can now be run, and tested on users. At this stage, problems with the interface can be discovered and used to reshape the initial specification. For example, early prototypes of the system did not provide a pause button. This was clearly necessary to allow users to abandon the game temporarily.

8 Conclusions and Further Work

Through our short example, we have shown that functional languages make good tools for transforming high-level concurrent specifications into executable code. In particular, the Haggis system provides a high level compositional concurrent interface that makes this easy. We start with a high level, modular, LOTOS specification that can be used to reason about possible interaction problems in a system, using tools such as LITE. We can then easily transform this into executable Haggis code. The resulting executable system, supports user testing.

The high level specification can be used to target resulting evaluations. This all provides for an iterative, user centred approach to design.

We have shown, through our example, that Haggis is capable of implementing highly interactive, real-time interfaces, something many prototyping tools are incapable of. We, however, need to build more complex systems, with more interaction objects, to test our specification and prototyping system to the full. Finally, we need to fully automate the translation between specification and executable Haggis code.

9   Acknowledgements

Thanks go to Simon Peyton Jones, and Sigbjorn Finne for providing Haggis for us to work with. Thanks also to Phil Gray and other members of the Glasgow Interactive Systems Group (GIST). David Duke, Andy Dearden and members of the York HCI group also provided valuable feedback on our use of interactors. This work was supported by UK EPSRC Grant No GR/K69148.

References

[1] Gregory D. Abowd (1990), Agents: Communicating Interactive Processes. In D. Diaper et al (eds.) *Human Computer Interaction - INTERACT '90.*

[2] Heather Alexander (1990), Structuring dialogues using CSP, in MD Harrison and H Thimbleby *Formal methods in Human computer interaction*, Cambridge University Press.

[3] Heather Alexander, Val Jones (1990), *Software design and prototyping using me too*, Prentice Hall.

[4] David Duke, Giorgio Faconti, Michael Harrison, Fabio Paterno (1994), Unifying View of Interactors, Amodeus Project Document: SM/WP18.

[5] Conal Elliott and Paul Hudak, Functional Reactive Animation, in *Proceedings of the Second ACM SIGPLAN Internation Conference on Functional Programming, June 9-11 1997.*

[6] P.van Eijk (1991), The Lotosphere Integrated Tool Environment LITE, in *Proceedings 4th International Conference on Formal Description Techniques*, Sydney, North-Holland, pp.473-476.

[7] G.P. Faconti et al (1993), Graphical Process Interaction Networks for Lotos Parallel Expressions, Amodeus Project Document: SM/WP25.

[8] Sigbjorn Finne, Simon Peyton Jones (1995a), Pictures: A simple structured graphics model. In *Glasgow Functional Programming Workshop*, Ullapool, July 1995.

[9] Sigbjorn Finne, Simon Peyton Jones (1995b), Composing Haggis. In *Proceedings of the fifth Eurographics workshop on Programming Paradigms in Graphics*, Maastricht, Sept 2-3 1995.

[10] N.E. Fuchs (1992), Specifications are (preferably) executable. In *Software Engineering Journal*, 1992, 7, (5), pp. 323-334

[11] Andrew D. Gordon and Kevin Hammond (1995), Monadic I/O in Haskell 1.3. In Paul Hudak, editor, *Proceedings of the haskell Workshop*, pp 50-69. La Jolla, California, June 25 1995.

[12] M.D. Harrison and D.J. Duke (1995), The Specification of User Requirements in Interactive Systems, Amodeus Project Document: SM/WP60.

[13] I.J. Hayes and C.B. Jones (1989), Specifications are not (necessarily) executable, Software Engineering Journal, 1989, 4, (6), pp. 330-338

[14] J.M. Hoc, T.R.G. Green, R. Samurcay and D.J. Gilmore (eds) (1990), *Psychology of Programming*, Computers and People Series, Academic Press Ltd.

[15] A. Jeffrey and G.Leduc (1996), E-LOTOS core language. Output of the Kansas City meeting, version 1996/09/20, (ISO-IEC/JTC1/SC21/WG7).

[16] C.W. Johnson and M.D. Harrison (1992), Using temporal logic to support the specification of interactive control systems. *International Journal of Man-Machine Studies*, 37:357-385.

[17] Brad A. Myers (1991) Separating application code from toolkits: Eliminating the spaghetti of callbacks. In *Proceedings of the ACM SIGCHI'91 Conference on User Interface Software Technology*. ACM Press, November 11-13 1991.

[18] Fabio Paterno et al (1994), A Tool-supported Approach to the Refinement of Interactive Systems, Amodeus Project Document: SM/WP39.

[19] John Peterson et al (1996), Haskell 1.3: A non-strict, purely functional language. Technical Report YALEU/DCS/RR-1106: Department of Computing Science. Yale University. May 1996.

[20] Simon Peyton Jones and Philip Wadler (1993), Imperative functional programming. In *ACM Conference on the Principles of Programming Languages*, pp 71-84. ACM Press, January 1993.

[21] Simon Peyton Jones, Andrew Gordon, and Sigbjorn Finne (1996), Concurrent Haskell. In *ACM Symposium on the Principles of Programming Languages*, St. Petersburg Beach, Florida, January 1996.

[22] Simon Buckingham Shum, Ann Blandford, David Duke, Jason Good, Jon May, Fabio Paterno, and Richard Young (1996), Multidisciplinary Modelling for User-Centred System Design: An Airtraffic Control Case Study. In *People and Computers XI: Proceedings of HCI '96*.

Formally Verifying Interactive Systems: A Review

José C. Campos & Michael D. Harrison

Human-Computer Interaction Group
Department of Computer Science, University of York
Heslington, York YO1 5DD, U.K.
e-mail: {jfc,mdh}@cs.york.ac.uk

Abstract. Although some progress has been made in the development of principles to guide the designers of interactive systems, ultimately the only proven method of checking how usable a particular system is must be based on experiment. However, it is also the case that changes that occur at this late stage are very expensive. The need for early design checking increases as software becomes more complex and is designed to serve volume international markets and also as interactions between operators and automation in safety-critical environments becomes more complex. This paper reviews progress in the area of formal verification of interactive systems and proposes a short agenda for further work.

1 Introduction

Although some progress has been made in the development of principles to guide the designers of interactive systems (see for example principles suggested in [25,8]), ultimately the only proven method of checking how usable a particular system is must be based on experiment. Successful systems have evolved over time, using experiments with prototypes through trial and error [17]. Part of the reason for this is, of course, that systems must be judged in work context. The effect of a particular design using particular interaction principles can in the end only be judged when the system is used in a typical work environment.

However, it is also the case that changes that occur at this late stage are very expensive and any early testing of a design through verification against design principles may have the effect of reducing the cost of changes late in the design process. In practice it is very difficult to check that a system captures properties that correspond to the design principles. This paper reviews progress in this area and proposes a short agenda for further work. The need for early design checking increases as software becomes more complex and is designed to serve volume international markets and also as interactions between operators and automation in safety-critical environments becomes more complex. The challenge then is to build interactive systems that are "correct by design".

Proving that the design of a software system is correct is not possible in abstract since correctness is a relative concept. What we can do is formally verify that the specification has some required properties. Work in formal verification of software has been traditionally concerned with two issues: the verification of implementations against their specifications and, particularly in the context of concurrent systems, that certain properties of the specification hold — that the system is free from deadlock, that the axioms of the specification are consistent and so on. Two main techniques for proving these properties are supported by automation: Model Checking and Theorem Proving. Interactive Systems have interesting characteristics that mean that both general system specification techniques and specific techniques relevant to dealing with concurrency properties are appropriate, but they pose a set of new and specific problems. We can think of an Interactive System as a heterogeneous system. On one side of the interface we have software with a fixed and predetermined behaviour while on the other we have humans, with flexible, adaptable and ultimately non-deterministic behaviour. It is the coupling of these two distinct entities that give Interactive Systems their special nature.

In this paper we start by analysing (section 2) what type of properties are of interest in Interactive Systems and establish a framework for the classification of such properties. Having done so, we go on to analyse the available approaches to the formal verification of Interactive Systems' specifications. In all, we have identified four approaches that use automated techniques: three using Model Checking (section 3) and one using Theorem Proving (section 4). We compare and relate these different approaches and establish an agenda for further work with particular emphasis on the role of hybrid specification techniques such as those developed at York [10] (section 5).

2   A Framework for the Classification of User Interface Properties

Formal verification techniques have been used in program verification, as well as in specification verification. While the tools used are basically the same, the two approaches tackle different aspects of the formal development of software. Program verification starts with a program and its specification and, given a formally defined semantics for the programming language, tries to prove that the program satisfies the specification. Specification verification has to do with proving that the specification itself has desired properties. The research on the formal verification of Interactive Systems builds on results from these fields, our particular interest being focused on the latter issue. Interactive Systems, however, raise a set of new problems and questions. The fundamental factor that differentiates Interactive Systems from other software systems is the human factor. An Interactive System is usually a mediator between humans and an underlying physical system (or some logical representation of it). Typically the humans (the users) will want to influence the underlying system, and will do it through the Interactive System. In order to enable this, the Interactive System must: support users in the execution of their tasks, present users with accurate representations of the underlying system and of the interface state (for example, mode), and minimize the interference of the interface on the performance of tasks.

These general requisites may be refined to more concrete properties that can be verified of an Interactive System. In the end, however, some properties will be more appropriate for some systems, while other properties will be more appropriate for other systems. So, what we really should look for is a framework identifying the entities involved and the classes of general properties that will make them more usable or less human error prone.

We have already seen that we have *users* interacting with an *underlying system* through a *user interface*. These will be our three entities of concern. In order to analyse the interaction between them, we must identify the mechanisms used in the interaction.

Two basic mechanisms of interaction are *events* and *status phenomena* [7]. They are used by the interface to provide information to the user, and by the user to manipulate the interface. Typically the user will invoke specific combinations of events and/or status phenomena in order to achieve its goals. The set of strategies available to achieve a given goal is called a *task*. The way the User Interface reacts to events or status phenomena might change depending on its state, and in some cases one Interactive System will provide access to more than one underlying system. When this happens, we say the User Interface has different *modes* of interaction. We can now identify four interaction mechanisms: Events, Status Phenomena, Tasks and Modes.

Finally, what properties should we consider when analysing an Interactive System specification? We want to keep a high level of abstraction, not going into too much detailed analysis, in order to be able think about Interactive Systems in general. We will identify three different classes of properties. The first class we call *visibility*. Visibility concerns what is shown at the user interface, how it is shown, and how the users perceive it. Visibility includes questions like: *"do events have appropriate feedback?"*, or *"will the user correctly perceive the displayed information?"*.

The second class of properties we call *reachability*. Reachability properties deal with what can be done at the user interface, how it can be done, and how the way it can be done relates to the users' way of doing it. Reachability includes questions like: *"can the effects of actions be undone?"* or *"how does the way a task is modelled at the user interface match the users' mental model of the same task?"*.

These two classes of properties have to do with what can be seen, and what can be done (and how). We are also interested in the behaviour of the Interactive System and in properties of its state like: *"does the same event always have the same effect in a given mode?"* or *"does some predicate on the state of the system always hold?"*. This type of questions does not directly analyses the interaction between users and user interface, but how the user interface and the underlying system work. We will call these the *reliability* properties.

In figure 1 we summarize the framework. Basically its shows what classes of properties we want to prove of the interaction between the different entities of a given Interactive System specification.

Entities	User	User Interface	Underlying System	
Interaction Mechanisms	Events	Status phenomena	Tasks	Mode
Properties	Visibility	Reachability	Reliability	

Fig. 1. The framework

3 Model Checking

The first approaches to formal verification of Interactive Systems, where based on Model Checking technology (see [1] and [23]).

Model checking was originally proposed as an alternative to the use of theorem provers in concurrent program verification [5]. The basic premise was that a finite state machine specification of a system can be subject to exhaustive analysis of its entire state space to determine what properties hold of the system's behaviour. By using an algorithm to perform exhaustive state space analysis, the two main drawbacks of theorem provers were avoided:

- the analysis is fully automated (as opposed to a theorem provers' high reliance on the skills of its users);
- the validity of a property is always decidable (as opposed to theorem provers' undecidability problems).

A main drawback of Model Checking has to do with the size of the finite state machine needed to specify a given system: useful specifications may generate state spaces, so large, that it becomes impractical to analyse the entire state space. Hence, theoretically decidable systems may become undecidable in practice. The use of Symbolic Model Checking somewhat diminishes this problem. Avoiding the explicit representation of states and exploiting state space structural regularity, enables the analysis of state spaces that might be as big as 10^{20} states [4]. Unfortunately software specifications are usually not as regular as hardware ones. Furthermore, the problem remains that some systems might not be specifiable by a finite state machine at all.

We will now briefly describe and compare the two above mentioned approaches: Abowd, Wang & Monk's approach [26,1] and Paternó's approach [23]. In order to describe, and afterwards compare, the two approaches, we will be focusing on three main aspects: how the user interface is specified, how that specification translates into some kind of finite state machine, and finally how the resulting finite state machine description can be analysed.

3.1 Using SMV

In this approach, Abowd, Wang and Monk [1] combine the simplicity of Action Simulator (AS) with the power of the Symbolic Model Verifier tool (SMV). The user interface is specified using AS and then translated into the SMV input language, then the specification is analysed in SMV using Computational Tree Logic (CTL) formulae [5].

The Dialogue Specification As we said above, the user interface is specified using Action Simulator. AS is a spreadsheet package that allows for the PPS[1] specification of dialogues in a tabular fashion. The tool additionally has dialogue simulation capabilities: the specification can be executed allowing the designer to observe its behaviour.

To specify a dialogue in PPS, we must identify the user actions (the events) and a set of fields (or conditions). Each field represents some information on the system state and at each state a field can only have one value. Thus, input is event based, while output is status based.

In figure 2 (adapted from [20]) we can see the specification of a very simple photocopier: rows correspond to events and columns to fields, the first row is the state of the system.

The dialogue is specified by associating with each event pre- and post-condition pairs. Pre-conditions are written on the top side of the rows, and post-conditions on the bottom side. The pre-condition of an event defines the combination of fields' values that makes the event enabled (events marked with "$********$" in the example

---

[1] Propositional Production System.

	Conditions		No. rules = 6 No. conds = 3
	A4	*Black*	*Single copy*
State	TRUE	TRUE	TRUE
Request A3 ********	TRUE FALSE		
Request A4	FALSE TRUE		
Request Red ********		TRUE FALSE	
Request Black		FALSE TRUE	
Req. >1 copies ********			TRUE FALSE
Reset Copies			FALSE TRUE

Fig. 2. PPS specification using Action Simulator

are enabled). The post-condition of an event defines which will be the values of the fields after the event takes place. Blank fields in pre-/post-conditions mean, respectively, don't care/don't change values. In our example, event *RequestA3* is enabled, as its pre-condition is verified by the present state. If the user chooses to generate this event, the field *A4* will be set to *false* and the other fields will be left unchanged (see post-condition of *RequestA3*).

We can view a PPS specification as a tuple $PPS = (A, \Sigma, T, P)$ where:

- A is a finite set of event labels;
- Σ is a finite set of dialogue states;
- T is a binary relation where $T \subseteq A \times (\Sigma \rightarrow \Sigma)$, in which each member specifies a rule;
- $P : \Sigma \rightarrow \mathcal{V}^F$ assigns to each state a partial function mapping fields (F) to their values in that state ($\mathcal{V}$ is the set of all possible field values)

It is clear from T that the events are labels on the transitions from state to state.

The Finite State Machine In order to be analysed, the PPS specification must first be translated into the SMV input language. This input language describes the transition relation of a finite state machine, which can then be analysed in SMV using CTL formulae. In the context of SMV, the finite state machine is called a CTL machine. A CTL machine can be described by the triple $CTL = (S, R, P)$ where:

- S is a finite set of states;
- $R \subseteq S \times S$ gives the possible relations between states, and must be a total relation;
- $P : S \rightarrow 2^{AP}$ assigns to each state the set of atomic propositions (AP) true in that state.

From this definition it follows that in the translation process from PPS to SMV, the transitions' labels are lost: the transitions in the CTL machine are not labeled. This would mean losing the information on which event caused which state change. The problem is overcome by including the events as state information. This way each CTL state represents the state of the system and a possible next event in the dialogue. This means that each state in the PPS specification will be represented by n states in the CTL machine, one for each of the n possible events in the original PPS state (see figure 3). This means the notion of state in the PPS is different from the same notion in CTL, so we must be careful when talking about PPS states during verification in SMV.

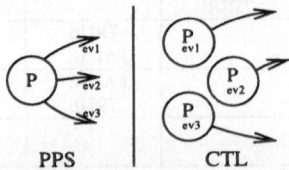

PPS   CTL

Fig. 3. From one PPS state to n CTL states

Additionally, as R must be total, dialogues with deadlocks cannot be represented in CTL machines. This problem is solved by including in the PPS specification a special event *stuck* that will be enabled when no other event is, and that will be associated with the identity transition.

In [26] Wang & Abowd present an algorithm for the automatic translation from PPS to CTL, they also say that they have developed a tool to make this translation an automatic process.

Checking the Specification Once the PPS specification is translated into a CTL machine, the SMV tool can be used to verify (or not) the validity of CTL formulae in the machine. Basically the CTL machine is a finite state transition machine and the CTL formulae allow us to ask questions over the execution paths of that machine. For the syntax of CTL see [26], besides the usual propositional logic connectives, CTL allows for operators over paths that enable us to write formulae of the type:

- a property is universal, inevitable, possible or impossible;
- a property must/may hold at the next step;
- property $p1$ will/may hold until property $p2$ holds.

As the CTL specification is state based, dialogue properties will be expressed in terms of the atomic propositions that describe states. It must be noted that any given combination of properties does not necessarily identify, uniquely, one and only one state, but a set of states that satisfy these properties.

The authors propose a set of templates for testing properties with this approach. The questions that are proposed are of the type: *"can a rule somehow be enabled?"* or *"is it true that the dialogue is deadlock free?"* or *"can the user find a way to accomplish a task from initialisation?"*.

Looking at the approach in the light of our framework, we start by noticing that there is no distinction made between user interface state and underlying system state. The system is looked at as a whole and the fields that define the state information are supposed to represent the interface of the system as well as its underlying state. Although this can be so for small simple systems, in complex systems it will not be feasible (or even desirable) to show every thing at every time. If we were to think of the fields as representing only the interface, then we would have no explicit connection with the underlying system. But even then, because the user interface must reflect the underlying system in some way, and because only events manipulate the interface state, the PPS specification would be implicitly enforcing the behaviour of the underlying system. Because of this *unification* between interface and underlying state, and also the lack of a mechanism for structuring the specification, there is no way of thinking about visibility properties (everything is visible), or making distinctions between actions that affect the underlying state as against actions that affect the interface.

The main properties dealt with are reachability properties and tasks are only vaguely defined as some target state or action. Reliability conditions can also be analysed, although the level of specification and SMV do not allow for very detailed analysis.

Finally, no user model is included in the specification, neither is the notion of mode of interaction.

3.2 Using The Lite Tool Set

PPS supports very simple state transition descriptions, we will now look at how a more powerful notion can be used. In [23] Paternó proposes the use of the Lite tool set to translate Interactor based specifications written in LOTOS into a finite state machine, and then analyse the finite state machine using Action-based Temporal Logic (ACTL) formulae (for an introduction to ACTL see [21]).

The Dialogue Specification In this approach the specification of the user interface is based on the interactor architecture presented in figure 4.

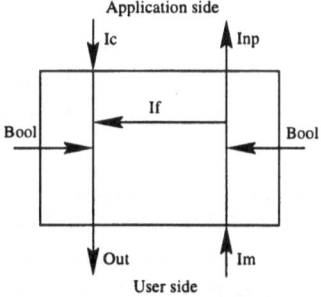

Fig. 4. LOTOS Interactor Architecture

An Interactor conveys information from the user side to the application side through channels *Im* and *Inp* (internal dialogue), and from the application side to the user side through channels *Ic* and *Out* (external dialogue). The boolean gates are triggers that determine when information is conveyed. To allow for feedback, there is also a flow of information from the internal dialogue to the external dialogue (*If*). The interactors can be composed to construct a hierarchy, allowing for a modular specification of the interface.

After defining the architecture of the user interface using interactors, each interactor is specified in LOTOS. Because of the non deterministic way in which channels might behave, a control process may have to be introduced, at this stage, in order to constrain the dynamic behaviour of the specification.

This specification notation has clearly more expressive power than the PPS above. It allows for a modular style of specification and supports the distinction between user, user interface, and application. An example of a complex system analysed using this approach is MATIS, the Multi-model Air Travel Information System [9].

The Finite State Machine So that it can be analysed, the LOTOS specification must be translated into a Finite State Machine (FSM). This translation is done by the Auto tool [18], but with some limitations.

In order for the translation to be possible, the LOTOS specification must first be translated from Full LOTOS to Basic LOTOS. This translation process implies that data type information will be lost, as well as the boolean guards used to constrain behaviour. Suppose we have an OK button in a dialogue box that should only be enabled after all the entries in the dialogue box have been edited. We could model this behaviour putting a boolean guard in the button's specification. However, when translating from Full to Basic LOTOS, the guard is lost and the button becomes available at all times.

The loss of data type information does not seem to be a serious problem. Different gates can be automatically created for each data type thus creating necessary distinction, and the approach is not concerned with the system response to particular data values, but with overall behaviour.

The loss of conditional guards, on the other hand, will cause the Basic LOTOS version of the specification to be a superset of the Full LOTOS version. This means the FSM will have traces of behaviour that are not present in the initial specification, so at least the reachability properties of the specification will be affected. In [23] it is suggested that boolean guards should be avoided and that process synchronisation should be used whenever possible. This, however, means that the natural way to describe the system is no longer possible. In [22] it is shown that a manual translation from Full to Basic LOTOS might further obviate this problem, but at the cost of loosing some automation.

Checking the Specification Once the specification has been translated into a FSM, we can use the Logic Checker tool [18] to analyse it. Logic Checker uses Action-based Temporal Logic (ACTL). ACTL is a branching time temporal logic that allows reasoning about the actions that a system can take. ACTL formulae can be interpreted over a Labelled Transition System - $LTS = (Q, Ac \cup \{\tau\}, \rightarrow, Q_0)$ - where:

- Q is a set of states;
- Ac is a finite, non-empty set of visible actions;
- τ represents the internal, not visible, actions;
- $\rightarrow \subseteq Q \times (Ac \cup \{\tau\}) \times Q$ is the transition relation;
- Q_0 is the initial state.

Looking at the definition of the $\rightarrow$ relation we can see that the transitions are labeled by the actions. It should also be noticed that, as there is no explicit state information, we can only refer to dialogue properties that involve state implicitly. For instance, in ACTL we do not ask *"is it possible, in the future, to have the copier in single copy mode?"* but *"is it possible, in the future, to perform the Reset Copies action?"*

A number of property templates are proposed for checking the specification. These are divided into interactor, system integrity and user interface properties.

The interactor properties are general properties of the Basic LOTOS specification of the Interactors. The system integrity properties have to do with the system architecture. These properties are more directly connected with technical aspects of the specification and its consistency, than they are with properties of the user interface that is being specified, so we will discuss them no further.

Regarding user interface properties, templates are proposed for a number of properties. The properties fall into three broad classes: Reachability, Visibility, and those that are Task related. Reachability is defined in [23] as: "... given a user action, (...) it is possible to reach an effect which is described by a specific action.".

Visibility is defined in the same way, the action associated with the desired visible effect being an action in the output port of the Interactor.

Relative to tasks, three formulae that classify various types of error are presented. These formulae allow the analysis of the impact of a given user action on a predetermined task, where a task is some target action. Minimal errors are those actions after which "it is possible to get to the next state by performing one action useful for the current task" [23]. Recoverable errors are those after which several actions must be performed before a useful action for the task is possible. Unrecoverable errors are those after which it is not possible to perform the task anymore. The concept of 'task useful action', however, is not defined. This kind of information must be obtained elsewhere, possibly in the task specification.

A notion of task reversibility is also defined. The property expresses that once a task is initiated, an action can be performed that cancels the previous effects so that the task can be performed again. The notion of 'cancelling previous effects' is not defined and is not clear whether it refers to the whole Interactive System, or just to the fact that the task can be initiated again. This seems to be a consequence of the impossibility to characterise states: as we cannot characterise states, we cannot express that the system returns to the previous state, this in turn means we have to rely on the notion of action that cancels effects without really formalising it.

Referring to our framework, we see that users are still not considered in the specification. The approach, however, separates the user interface from the underlying system, this enables the verification of visibility properties. However, this separation is done in such a way that there is no way to reason about the underlying system's state and its reliability properties: the underlying system's specification is not part of the Interactive System specification.

The approach is heavily based on the notion of event, and as such has no way to handle status phenomena. Even tasks are defined only as a target event to be executed. So, achieving a task is performing the target event, independently of the strategy that leads to it. This does not correspond to our understanding of what task is, a set of strategies available to achieve a desired goal. It is easy to see that we could have two sequences of actions with the same final action but corresponding to different tasks, for example: `<select_landing_mode, engage_auto_pilot>` or `<select_goaround-_mode, engage_auto_pilot>`. Finally, and as in Abowd's et al. approach, mode is not explicitly represented.

3.3 Comparison

The main difference between both approaches comes from the specification notations used. Abowd et al. adopted a simple and easy to use approach with the advantage of having tool support (Action Simulator). The approach might be too simple, however. In fact, for the verification to be useful it must be done at an appropriate level of detail, whereas Action Simulator was designed for very high level abstract specifications [20]. At this level some of the useful properties that we want to investigate might even be not yet present. It is doubtful that we should give up so much for ease of use when the verification process, in itself, might be a complex task.

Paternó avoids this problem by using a more powerful specification notation. By using Interactors, that are composed to build a complete specification of the user interface, he separates user interface information from the underlying system's information and is able to talk about properties specific to the user interface, like visibility. Unfortunately, information about the state of the underlying system is only available indirectly through events. Despite the use of a better specification notation, the verification has still to be done at the model checking level, and the translation of the Interactors specification to a finite state machine might mean the version of the specification being analysed has more behaviour (allows more traces of events) than the original one. This seems to be a problem that will affect all the attempts of using powerful specification notations, as the specification will always have to be translated into a finite state machine in order to be model checked, and the expressive power of those is limited. In the next section we will see how Bumbulis uses an approach that avoids this problem.

At the verification level, the main difference to be noted between both approaches has to do with the temporal logics that each approach uses. While CTL focuses on the states and the transition between states, ACTL focuses on events and the sequences of events that can be generated.

These different foci allow for different styles of analysis. ACTL formulae have to do with analysing the future to determine if some event will or will not happen under certain conditions (related to other events happening or not). CTL formulae, on the other hand, have to do with analysing the future to see if a system state will or will not be reached under certain conditions (this time related to other states being reached or not); however, as Abowd et al. encode events as state information, the former analysis can also be done.

Different foci also raise different problems. ACTL has problems when we want to express properties that have to do with the state the dialogue is in (undo for example). On the other hand, CTL has some problems when we wish to express that "*something is possible from a state*": as every state in the original PPS generates a set of similar states (one for each event that can come next), what we can actually express is that "*something is possible from a state whatever action is taken*" (which is stronger). This problem can be overcome by explicit elimination of undesired actions.

Although Paternó's approach is more expressive, in the sense that the separation of the user interface from the underlying system allows for a better reasoning about properties specific of the former, the separation seems to be excessive. In fact, as the underlying system is not made explicit in the specification, it is impossible to reason about it directly and how it relates to the user interface.

As a final note on the use of model checking techniques for the formal verification of interactive systems, a last approach should be mentioned. It has been proposed by d'Ausbourg et al. in [6] and uses the data flow language Lustre. This approach is similar to that of Paternó in that it uses the notion of interactor to model the user interface. In this case, however, interactors are derived from UIL descriptions, and modelled in Lustre. Verification is achieved by augmenting the interface with Lustre nodes modelling the intended properties, and using the tool Lesar to traverse the automaton generated from this new system. Generating an automaton for the conjunction of system and property specifications means that only that part of the system relevant for the property being verified is actually considered. This allows for the analysis of bigger systems than if a complete automaton was required.

While the use of the same language to model both the system and its properties seems to solve some of the problem of translation between LOTOS and FSM in Paternó's approach, nothing is said about how data types are handled (in [6] only boolean values are considered). Thus, some problems remain. However, the data flow nature of Lustre means status phenomena are better dealt with than in Paternó's approach. Lustre makes no mention of user related issues like tasks or mode, so it doesn't seem possible to deal with properties relating to those.

4 Theorem Proving

Having seen how Model Checking is being used in the formal verification of User Interfaces, let us now turn to the alternative approach to system verification: Theorem Proving.

Theorem Proving is a deductive approach to the verification of systems. Available systems can differ considerably regarding the way they can be used and the facilities they provide. Theorem provers range from fully interactive systems to systems that, given a proof, check if the proof is correct with no further interaction from the user. While some systems provide only a basic set of methods for manipulating the logic, giving the user full control over the proof strategy, others include complex tactics and strategies, meaning the user might not know exactly what has been done. Another commonly made distinction is that between first order and higher order logic deduction systems.

Due to this *mechanical* nature, we can trust a proof done in a theorem prover to be correct, as opposed to the recognisedly error prone manual process. While this is an advantage, it also means that doing a proof in a theorem prover can be more hard, as *every little bit* must be proved.

4.1 Using HOL

In [3] Bumbulis et al. show how they are using HOL (a Higher Order Logic Theorem Prover) in the verification of User Interface specifications.

They use a language - IL (the Interconnection Language) - to specify User Interfaces as sets of connected interface components. These specifications can then be implemented in some toolkit as well as modelled in the higher order logic of the HOL system for formal verification.

An immediately obvious advantage of this approach is that the formalism used to perform the analysis, Higher Order Logic, is (at least) at the same level of expressiveness of the formalism used to write the specification. So, we can anticipate we will not have the translation problems of Paternó's approach.

The Dialogue Specification As said above, User Interfaces are specified as sets of connected components using IL. The notion of component in IL is similar to that of interactor (especially the Lotos version) although is has been developed to more closely resemble that of widget in a toolkit, in order to allow for an easy implementation of the specification. A component is defined as having a set of ports (input, output or observer), and different components can be connected through their input and output ports, much in the same way as widget's methods and callbacks are connected. Input ports are also the mechanisms by which users manipulate the components. The authors do not show how output to the user can be specified.

A IL description (taken from [3]) of a window with a dial and a slider is shown on figure 5. The Main component defines the global User Interface.

```
component Window(width,height)
component Dial(parent,x,y,width,height) set< changed>
component Slider(parent,x,y,width,height) set< changed>
component Main {
    f:Window(170,220)
    d:Dial(f,5,5,160,160)
    s:Slider(f,5,165,160,160)
    s.changed-->d.set
    d.changed-->s.set
}
```

Fig. 5. A IL description

The behaviour of a single component is described by a collection of code fragments defining the behaviour of its ports, and the overall behaviour of the instances of the component. The semantics of the language used to write the code fragments is defined by HOL predicates for each of the constructs of the language.

After having the User Interface specified by a set of components, a HOL model of the specification can be generated. This is done by modelling each component with a predicate. These predicates will consist of a series of conjuncts specifying the behaviour of each of the input ports and observers and also of the instances of the component. Next we show the predicate modeling the Slider component:

$$Slider\ i\ c\ s\ q\ e\ parent\ x\ y\ width\ height\ set\ changed =$$
$$(set = (\lambda\,v.\text{if}(q(\lambda\,n.\neg\,(n = v)))(\text{assign}(s(\lambda\,n.v))\,\S\,changed\,v)))$$
$$\wedge\ (i = 0)$$
$$\wedge\ (c = \exists\,v.\text{atomic}(\text{numEv}\,ev)(set\,v)))$$

For a full explanation of this predicate see [3], here it is enough to say that i is the initial state, and c the behaviour of an instance of Slider.

Verifying the Specification Given the definition of all the components we can then think of verifying properties. Properties to be verified are expressed as predicates over sets of runs. A run being a sequence of event/resulting state pairs. Verifying that a model has a given property P amounts to proving the following theorem:

$$\forall i\ c.\ \mathsf{Main}\ i\ c\ (\lambda f.f)\ (\lambda P.P)\ [] \Rightarrow P((\lambda s.s = i) \to \mathsf{do\_od}\ c)$$

where Main is a predicate modelling the component with the same name. What the formula expresses is that for every possible initial state (i), and for every possible behaviour (c), P is a valid property of the execution of the behaviour from the initial state. That is, P is a universal property of the dialogue. It should be noticed that this is a safety property [19], and as such can, in general, be proved by a Model Checker if there are a finite number of states.

In this approach, if we are to be able to perform proofs, a logic that allows us to reason about the properties of interest must be mechanised. In the cited paper, a logic is presented to reason about this type of property of the overall behaviour of the specification. The authors then show how it can be proved that the slider and the dial will always be synchronised. This proof takes 20 steps and relies on the previous proof of a lemma. Although it is a fact that by doing the proof a greater insight is acquired about the specification, such a level of effort seems somewhat exaggerated given the system that is being analysed, and the fact that this type of property could be proved automatically in a Model Checker.

Besides this problem with complexity of use, the approach also seems limited in the type of analysis it provides. This seems to spring from two main factors. At the specification level, only the interface is considered, there is no mention of the underlying system's state or of a user model. Although we can imagine that some special component could be developed to model the underlying system, this is not shown. Further, what is specified is not so much the interaction between the users and the interface, but the interface architecture and how the different components communicate with each other. Output to the user seems to be defined implicitly by the states of the components, so this approach suffers from the same problems as Abowd's et al. and visibility properties do not seem to be verifiable.

At the verification level, not using a logic that can capture temporal properties limits the scope of analysis to invariants of the user interface. So, reachability is also a problem.

In conclusion, although the approach uses a powerful verification environment, it has two main drawbacks. The specification style and the logic used do not allow reasoning about some of the important aspects of interaction, and the verification process is complex.

5 Moving On...

Until now we have been looking at how the formal verification of Interactive Systems is currently approached. In figure 6 we summarize the results of our analysis.

We will now look at what can be done in order to increase our capabilities of reasoning about specifications of Interactive Systems. We will first consider what one such

		Abowd et al.	Paternó	d'Ausbourg et al.	Bumbulis et al.
Entities	Users	×	×	×	×
	User Interface	$\sim^a$	✓	✓	✓
	Underlying System	$\sim^a$	×	×	×
Interaction Mechanisms	Events	$\sim^b$	✓	✓	$\sim^b$
	Status phenomena	$\sim^c$	×	✓	$\sim^c$
	Task	$\sim^d$	$\sim^d$	×	×
	Mode	×	×	×	×
Properties	Visibility	×	✓	✓	×
	Reachability	✓	✓	✓	×
	Reliability	✓	$\sim^e$	$\sim^e$	$\sim^e$

[a] Specified together. [b] Just input. [c] Just output. [d] Just as a target action or state. [e] Just of the user interface.

Fig. 6. Summary of the comparison

specification should deliver, and then what type of tools we should use in order to analyse it.

A first conclusion to draw from Abowd's et al. work is that a clear distinction must be drawn between the user interface and the underlying system. The acknowledgment of the need for this separation is not new, going back to the Seeheim Model [14]. From the other approaches we can see that, although necessary, this separation must not be done in such a way that we loose information about the underlying systems. It is also self evident that, if we want to reason about interesting aspects of an Interactive System, a sufficiently expressive notation must be used. Aspects that have not yet deserved necessary attention are task, mode and visibility issues. Also, the interaction mechanisms by which communication between the user interface and the users is achieved have not been addressed thoroughly. In fact, all the approaches are heavily based on the notions of event or status phenomena, little or no attention being payed to task or mode. Further, it is important that some sort of user model be included in the specification in order to enable the analysis of the interactive system against the users' needs and capabilities.

It is our belief that York Interactors [10] are capable of delivering the expressiveness that will enable us to address these problems. York Interactors enable the homogeneous specification of both the user interface and the underlying system, and some work has been done to include models of the user in the specification [13,11].

From a technological viewpoint, we can expect to have problems if we intend to use model checking, as we have seen in Paternó's approach. On the other hand, the traditional first- and higher-order logics used by most theorem provers, do not seem to have the expressiveness that we need, namely when dealing with dynamic aspects of the dialogue between users and user interface. We intend, then, to study the use of Temporal Logic theorem provers and how they can be used in the analysis of York Interactor based specifications. At the moment we are considering the use of TLP [12] (an extension of the Larch Prover [15] to include TLA, the Temporal Logic of Actions [16]), PVS [24], and STeP (the companion system of the book by Manna and Pnueli [19]). These two last systems, in particular, by combining the power of theorem proving with the automated analysis of model checking, seem promising.

In short, we hope that by using a expressive specification formalism (York Interactors) to specify an Interactive System as a whole, modeling system and interface behaviour, and the users' needs and capabilities, and by using the analytic power of theorem proving coupled with the expressiveness of temporal logic, we will be able to improve our ability to reason about Interactive Systems in order to correctly predict/verify how they will be integrated in a real work situation.

6 Conclusions

In this paper, we started by introducing a framework for Interactive Systems properties. This framework allows us to look at techniques for the formal verification of Interactive Systems and see how they handle the different aspects that must be considered.

Four approaches were identified. Three use Model Checking (one by Abowd et al. [1], one by Paternó [23], and one by d'Ausbourg et al. [6]), the latter uses automated Theorem Proving (by Bumbulis et al. [3]).

Using our framework we were able to identify the strengths and weaknesses of the different approaches. These could be found either at the level of the specification notations, which affect what type of properties can be expressed, as well as at the level of the verification techniques, which affect what type of properties can be verified.

At the first level we identified a need to express how the user interface relates to the underlying system, users, and to better address the interaction mechanisms of the user interface. At the second we identified the need to combine the expressive capabilities of model checking and theorem proving.

We hope that, by using York Interactors based specifications, and the combined power of theorem proving and temporal logic reasoning, we will be able to achieve these objectives. This is ongoing work.

Acknowledgements

José Creissac Campos is supported by grant PRAXIS XXI/BD/9562/96. We are grateful to Gavin Doherty who made comments on earlier drafts of this paper. We also wish to thank the anonymous reviewers for their comments, and HCM network on Interactionally Rich Systems for financial support under contract ERBCHRXCT930099.

References

1. Gregory D. Abowd, Hung-Ming Wang, and Andrew F. Monk. A formal technique for automated dialogue development. In *Proceedings of the First Symposium of Designing Interactive Systems - DIS'95*, pages 219–226. ACM Press, August 1995.
2. F. Bodart and J. Vanderdonckt, editors. *Design, Specification and Verification of Interactive Systems '96*, Springer Computer Science. Springer-Verlag/Vien, June 1996.
3. Peter Bumbulis, P. S. C. Alencar, D. D. Cowan, and C. J. P. Lucena. Validating properties of component-based graphical user interfaces. In Bodart and Vanderdonckt [2], pages 347–365.
4. J. R. Burch, E. M. Clarke, and K. L. McMillan. Symbolic model checking: 10^{20} states and beyond. In *LICS*, 1990.
5. E. M. Clarke, E. A. Emerson, and A. P. Sistla. Automatic verification of finite-state concurrent systems using temporal logic specifications. *ACM Transactions on Programming Languages and Systems*, 8(2):244–263, April 1986.
6. Bruno d'Ausbourg, Guy Durrieu, and Pierre Roche. Deriving a formal model of an interactive system from its uil description in order to verify and to test its behaviour. In Bodart and Vanderdonckt [2], pages 105–122.

7. Alan Dix and Gregory Abowd. Modelling status and event behaviour of interactive systems. *Software Engeneering Journal*, 11(6):324–346, November 1996.

8. Alan Dix, Janet Finlay, Gregory Abowd, and Russell Beale. *Human-Computer Interaction*. Prentice Hall, 1993.

9. David Duke, Michael Harrison, Jöelle Coutaz, Laurence Nigay, Daniel Salber, Giorgio Faconti, Menica Mezzanotte, Fabio Paternó, and David Duce. The Amodeus system reference model. Technical Report System Modelling/D9, Amodeus Project, June 1995.

10. David J. Duke and Michael D. Harrison. Abstract interaction objects. *Computer Graphics Forum*, 12(3):25–36, 1993.

11. D.J. Duke, P.J. Barnard, J. May, and D.A. Duce. Systematic development of the human interface. In *Asia Pacific Software Engeneering Conference*, pages 313–321. IEEE Computer Society Press, December 1995.

12. Urban Engberg, Peter Grønning, and Leslie Lamport. Mechanical verification of concurrent systems with TLA. In *Computer Aided Verification, Proceedings of the Fourth International Workshop, CAV'92*, volume 663 of *Lecture Notes in Computer Science*. Springer-Verlag, 1992.

13. Bob Fields, Peter Wright, and Michael Harrison. A method for user interface development in safety-critical applications. Human-Computer Interaction Group, University of York (unpublished), 1996.

14. Mark Green. A survey of three dialogue models. *ACM Transactions on Graphics*, 5(3):243–275, July 1986.

15. John V. Guttag, James J. Horning, et al. *Larch: Languages and Tools for Formal Specification*. Texts and Monographs in Computer Science. Springer-Verlag, 1993.

16. Leslie Lamport. The temporal logic of actions. *ACM Transactions on Programming Languages and Systems*, 16(3):872–923, May 1994.

17. Nancy Leveson. *Safeware: System Safety and Computers*. Addison-Wesley Publishing Company, Inc., 1995.

18. José A. Mañas et al. *Lite User Manual*. LOTOSPHERE consortium, March 1992. Ref. Lo/WP2/N0034/V08.

19. Zohar Manna and Amir Pnueli. *Temporal Verification of Reactive Systems: Safety*. Springer, 1995.

20. Andrew F. Monk and Martin B. Curry. Discount dialogue modelling with Action Simulator. In G. Cockton, S. W. Draper, and G. R. S. Weir, editors, *People and Computer IX - Proceedings of HCI'94*, pages 327–338. Cambridge University Press, 1994.

21. R. De Nicola, A. Fantechi, S. Gnesi, and G. Ristori. An action-based framework for verifying logical and behavioural properties of concurrent systems. *Computer Networks and ISDN Systems*, 25(7):761–778, February 1993.

22. Philippe Palanque, Fabio Paternó, Rémi Bastide, and Menica Mezzanote. Towards an integrated proposal for interactive systems design based on TLIM and ICO. In Bodart and Vanderdonckt [2], pages 162–187.

23. Fabio Paternó. *A Method for Formal Specification and Verification of Interactive Systems*. PhD thesis, Department of Computer Science, University of York, 1995.

24. S. Rajan, N. Shankar, and M.K. Srivas. An integration of model-checking with automated proof checking. In *Computer-Aided Verification, CAV '95*, volume 939 of *Lecture Notes in Computer Science*, pages 84–97. Springer Verlag, July 1995.

25. Harold Thimbleby. *User Interface Design*. Frontier Series. ACM Press, 1990.

26. Hung-Ming Wang and Gregory D. Abowd. A tabular interface for automated verification of event-based dialogs. Technical Report CMU-CS-94-189, Department of Computer Science, Carnegie Mellon University, July 1994.

Investigating the Behaviour of PREMO Synchronizable Objects *

G. P. Faconti and M. Massink

CNR - Istituto CNUCE, Via S.Maria 36, 56126 PISA, Italy
Tel: +39 50 593 241 - Fax: +39 50 904 052
e-mail: Faconti@cnuce.cnr.it, M.Massink@guest.cnuce.cnr.it

Abstract. PREMO stands for Presentation Environment for Multimedia Objects and is a major new standard under development within ISO/IEC. It addresses the creation of, presentation of and interaction with all forms of information using single or multiple media. The standard (u.d.) is currently developed using an Object Oriented approach. Such a state based specification, however, does not support conveniently the analysis of the temporal relationships occurring among operations. In this paper we model PREMO synchronizable objects defined in the standard as processes in the standardized process algebra Lotos. The approach we follow is a new way to obtain a specification in a constraint oriented style and is inspired by the Object Oriented approach. We let methods correspond to actions and values of control variables with processes. Each process consists of actions that are enabled for the value of the control variable that is modelled by the process. This style leads to Basic Lotos specifications that are directly suitable for computer assisted analysis such as model checking and simulation.

1 Introduction

Technology has evolved to the point that many interactive applications are enriched by the simultaneous use of multiple presentation media. While on the input side, the widespread use of sophisticated techniques, such as those employed within virtual reality systems, is limited to research laboratory prototypes, multimedia technology offers the capability of developing commercial products where the presentation becomes extremely complex in terms of the system architecture. We can think of systems as diverse as medical systems, real-time command control systems and geographical information systems. In each of these systems different presentation techniques may be used, such as the simultaneous use of 3D graphics, video animation, and sound. The presentation of data has become

---

* This work has been carried out within the ERCIM Computer Graphics Network - Contract No. CHRX-CT92-0085, the Interactionally Rich Systems Network - Contract No. CHRX-CT93-0099 and as part of the Community Training Project Interactionally Rich Immersive Systems - Contract No. CHBG-CT94-0674 funded by the European Union under the Human Capital and Mobility Programme.

a complex task in which a large number of diverse requirements have to be taken into account.

In order to deal with this complexity in a way that allows for extension and adaptability to specific needs in a uniform way a standardization project is currently developing a standard that addresses the creation of, presentation of and interaction with all forms of information using single or multiple media. This standard (u.d.) is called PREMO, Presentation Environment for Multimedia Objects and is a cooperation between ISO (International Organization for Standardization) and IEC (International Electronical Committee). In particular PREMO addresses the issues of configuration, extension, and interoperation of and between PREMO implementations. This highlights the main difference between PREMO and two other major ISO/IEC multimedia standards HyTime and MHEG. These standards are concerned with multimedia and hypermedia *documents* and do not cover application areas where *interactive* applications allow an operator to create or modify information. The MHEG and HyTime standards could be viewed as complementary to PREMO in the sense that their implementations could benefit from the use of services provided by PREMO implementations.

The approach taken within PREMO is an *object oriented* one [8]. It defines complex object-oriented systems that are to be used in a distributed environment. Objects defined in PREMO are supposed to function largely independent and to cooperate and synchronize with other objects by means of communication. This aspect of PREMO requires a thorough investigation of the *behavioural aspects* of the combination of those objects. Many theories and tools for such an analysis have been developed in the context of concurrency theory and for protocol analysis. The aim of this paper is to investigate the use of Lotos (Language of Temporal Ordering Specification) for this purpose. It is has been standardized within ISO [5,13], and there exist many verification tools for this process algebra and automatic transformations to other formats that allow the use of additional tools based for example on automata.

In this paper we specify the behavioural aspects of one of the central objects in the standard; the Synchronizable Object. We based our work on the English version of the standard (u.d) [14] and a preliminary but rather detailed Object-Z specification [10]. However, it may not reflect in all detail the current description of the standard because the development of the standard is still continued. This is no problem for this paper since our main aim is to report on our experiences in using Lotos for the specification and analysis in the context of this standard.

We experimented also with a new way to obtain a constraint oriented, modular Basic Lotos specification that can be directly used for computer assisted verification such as simulation and model checking. In this paper we report on our experience with this approach and show some of the results obtained by the use of the verification environments Lite (Lotos Integrated Tools Environment) [19] and JACK [7,2,4]. The first provides tools for checking the syntax and some semantic properties of Lotos specifications and allows for simulation of the specification and a translation of it into a common format for automata.

The latter can be used on this common format and gives an integrated set of tools which comprises (M)AUTO and Autograph [17,15] and the (X)AMC [6] model checker for action based temporal logic formulas [9]. In a later stage we want to use UPPAAL [1], that is a tool for the verification of properties of timed automata which are essentially the automata generated by Autograph with additional annotations regarding time.

The long term aim of this research is to gain insight in the particular requirements to formalisms and tools for the analysis of specifications in the area of multimedia. The specification of PREMO Objects serves as a representative case study.

Section 2 describes the specification of PREMO Synchronizable Objects and gives an intermediate analysis of the components. In Section 3 we give an example of how Synchronizable Objects can be used to describe the synchronization of two media; a video and an audio presentation. In Section 4 we give an analysis of the behaviour of the composed processes. For the analysis we used a branching time temporal logics model checker. The transition diagrams have been automatically generated using Autograph. In Section 5 we describe our main conclusions of this investigation and we give an outline of future research.

2 Synchronizable Objects

The PREMO synchronization model is based on the fact that objects can be active elements. Different continuous media (e.g. a video sequence and corresponding sound track) are modelled as concurrent activities that may have to reach specific milestones at distinct and possibly user definable synchronization points. This is the *event based* synchronization approach, which forms the basic layer of synchronization in PREMO. Although a large number of synchronization tasks are, in practice, related to synchronization in time, the choice of an essential timeless synchronization scheme as basis offers greater flexibility. While time-related synchronization schemes can be built on top of an event-based synchronization model, it is sometimes necessary to support purely event-based synchronization to achieve special effects required by some application. Examples of how the various synchronization objects may be used can be found in [14].

In line with the object-oriented approach of PREMO, the synchronization model defines abstract object types that capture the essential features of synchronization. For the event-based synchronization scheme two major object types are defined. *Synchronizable objects*, which form the super types of, e.g., various media object types and *synchronization points*, which may be used to manage complex synchronization patterns amongst synchronizable objects.

2.1 Supporting synchronization in PREMO

A synchronizable object is a finite state machine modelling various operations that control the presentation of a medium within a possibly complex multi-media presentation environment.

A synchronizable object can be in one of four states or modes (namely STOPPED, PLAYING, PAUSED and WAITING). It has a number of operations to perform state transitions, and to modify or inquire several parameters controlling the progression along an internal one dimensional co-ordinate space. No particular interpretation is placed on these states, except that certain operations can only be performed in certain states. Similarly, the internal co-ordinate space is introduced as an abstract concept. The intention is that object types representing different kinds of media will inherit from this class and specialise the co-ordinate space and state machine in an appropriate way by giving different semantic meaning (i.e. media objects, such as audio, may represent time while others, such as video, may address frame numbers along this space).

On the internal co-ordinate space reference points can be defined where synchronization elements can be attached. Synchronization elements contain information on an event instance, a reference to a PREMO object, a reference to one of the operations of this object, and, finally, a Wait flag. When a reference point is reached during the progression through the coordinate space, the synchronizable object uses the stored information to call, by means of messaging, the indicated operation on the referenced object using the event instance as an argument to the call. Finally it may suspend itself if the Wait flag is set to true. This mechanism allows for the definition of complex synchronization patterns amongst objects so that one synchronizable object can stop other objects, restart them, suspend them, etc. Operations are defined on synchronizable objects also to add and delete reference points, and to add and delete synchronization elements associated with reference points. A graphical presentation of the coordinate space, and its relevant attributes and reference points is given in Figure 1.

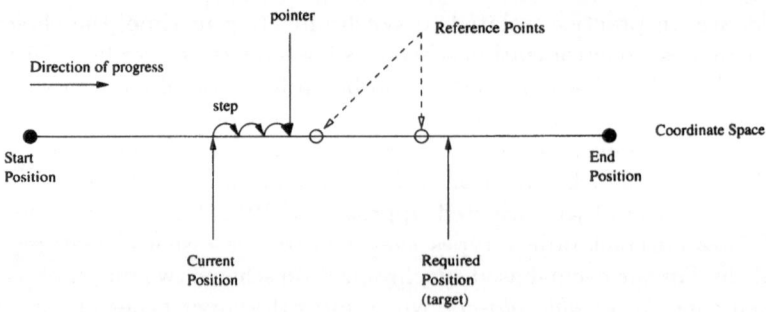

Fig. 1. Simplified representation of coordinate space of Synchronizable Object

2.2 The behaviour of Synchronizable Objects

In this paper we are interested in investigating the behaviour of synchronizable objects in greater details than it is possible with state based specification. The

Object Z specification of PREMO objects, accompanying the standard, explains and explores the state space of objects by defining the variables that make up this state, and the operations that result in changing the value of one or more of such variables. However, Object Z, as any other state based specification such as for example Z [18] and VDM [3], doesn't fully exploit the temporal order relations between operations. A process algebraic approach is better suited for this and gives a complementary view on the system under specification. Here, Lotos has been chosen out of other available notations, such as CSP [12] and CCS [16], mainly because it is the only formal specification language that has been standardised so far and because for LOTOS many tools have been developed. Moreover there are automatic transformations available to translate LOTOS specifications into automata. This way also the tools developed for automata can be used for the analysis.

Since we are concerned with the relationship of operations within synchronizable objects, only *basic* Lotos is used. A more complete analysis can be performed by extending the basic specification with the definition of the abstract data types that make up the state space of synchronizable objects in the ACTONE language. This will allow to specify the full set of operations of synchronizable objects. In this paper we will only define those operations that result in a mode transition and in progressing the position within the co-ordinate space. In [11] we describe and analyse different ways to add a "jump" operator to the set of operations.

2.3 Basic mode transitions

The synchronizable object types define operations for making transitions between four different synchronization modes: STOPPED, PLAYING, PAUSED and WAITING. The initial mode is STOPPED. For each mode, operations are defined that result in a transition to a different mode of the synchronizable object.

Following the informal specification of the standard and the formal definition of the variables making up the state space given in the Object-Z specification, we define the Lotos actions that direct the mode transition of synchronizable objects, distinguished as observable external actions and non-observable internally performed ones. The external actions are doSTOP, doPLAY, doPAUSE and doRESUME.

- doSTOP directs a transition to STOPPED mode from every mode except STOPPED,
- doPLAY directs a transition to PLAYING mode when in STOPPED,
- doPAUSE directs a transition to PAUSED mode when in PLAYING or WAITING,
- doRESUME directs a transition to PLAYING mode from PAUSED mode or WAITING,
- exc models the raise of an exception in case an operation is invoked that is not allowed in this mode

The internal actions are doWAIT and donePlay

- doWAIT enters the WAITING mode from PLAYING mode (it is an abstraction for the Wait flag set at a reference point during progression)
- donePlay enters the STOPPED mode on completion of a playing cycle.

With the above definitions, a process describing the behaviour of the synchronizable object is one specifying its basic mode transition mechanism. This mechanism is in the Object-Z specification controlled by one control variable that can assume values corresponding to the four different modes. Pre- and post conditions for each mode transition operation make use of this variable. We describe the mode transition behaviour by means of one Lotos process for each of the possible values of this control variable. Each process is defined as a non-deterministic choice between behaviour expressions that model a mode transition operation that can occur in the state represented by the name of the process. This approach allows for the development of the specification per control variable. The different parts of the specification can be combined by using a constraint oriented [20] style of specification in the sense that the parts are combined by means of a synchronization operator. We show this in more detail while developing the specification step by step.

```
process SynchronizableObject[doSTOP,doPLAY,doPAUSE,doRESUME,exc] :
noexit :=
    hide doWAIT,donePlay in
    modeTransitions[doSTOP,doPLAY,doPAUSE,doRESUME,doWAIT,donePlay,exc]
endproc
```

The basic mode transition mechanism itself is specified by a process that behaves as in STOPPED mode, which is the initial mode of each synchronizable object:

```
process modeTransitions[doSTOP,doPLAY,doPAUSE,doRESUME,doWAIT,
                        donePlay,exc] : noexit :=
    STOPPED[doSTOP,doPLAY,doPAUSE,doRESUME,doWAIT,donePlay,exc]
endproc
```

When in STOPPED mode, only a play operation can be invoked, while any other request results in an exception. Consequently, the corresponding process offers the choice of performing a doPLAY action and creating an instance of the PLAYING process, or to raise an exception. The creation of a PLAYING process models the fact that the process goes into PLAYING mode. If an exception is raised, the mode does not change, so the process remains in STOPPED mode.

```
process STOPPED[doSTOP,doPLAY,doPAUSE,doRESUME,doWAIT,donePlay,exc] :
noexit :=
    doPLAY; PLAYING[doSTOP,doPLAY,doPAUSE,doRESUME,doWAIT,donePlay,exc]
[] exc;  STOPPED[doSTOP,doPLAY,doPAUSE,doRESUME,doWAIT,donePlay,exc]
endproc
```

When playing, synchronizable objects may respond to external as well as to internal operation invocations. The current play process can be explicitly stopped by entering the STOPPED mode or it can be paused by entering the PAUSED mode. Any other invocation of externally observable actions results in an exception. However, a synchronizable object can perform mode transitions as a consequence of internal actions. When the playing cycle is completed, it enters the STOPPED mode and we model this by the donePlay action. Furthermore, it enters the WAITING mode when a reference point is encountered during progression with the Wait flag set. This behaviour is captured by the following process:

```
process PLAYING[doSTOP,doPLAY,doPAUSE,doRESUME,doWAIT,donePlay,exc] :
noexit  :=
    doSTOP; STOPPED[doSTOP,doPLAY,doPAUSE,doRESUME,doWAIT,donePlay,exc]
[] doPAUSE; PAUSED[doSTOP,doPLAY,doPAUSE,doRESUME,doWAIT,donePlay,exc]
[] exc; PLAYING[doSTOP,doPLAY,doPAUSE,doRESUME,doWAIT,donePlay,exc]
[] donePlay ; STOPPED[doSTOP,doPLAY,doPAUSE,doRESUME,doWAIT,donePlay,exc]
[] doWAIT; WAITING[doSTOP,doPLAY,doPAUSE,doRESUME,doWAIT,donePlay,exc]
endproc
```

Similar reasoning applies to the specification of the processes defining the behaviour of synchronizable objects when in PAUSED and WAITING modes. In the former, it is possible either to resume playing by invoking the doRE-SUME action, or to enter the STOPPED mode. In the latter, it is possible to choose between resuming the play process, stopping, or pausing. In both modes an exception is raised in the case an operation is invoked other than those specified. The corresponding Lotos processes are very similar in structure as process PLAYING and omitted here.

By simulating the specification with the simulation tool available within Lite an Extended Finite State Machine (EFSM) is generated consisting of four states, each one representing a mode, and fourteen transitions as shown in Figure 2. This figure has been generated by writing the EFSM in a common representation format by means of Lite, and then again by using Lite, in a format (FC2 transformation) that can be used as input into the Autograph tool developed at INRIA [17,15]. With the autograph tool the transition graph can be obtained and modified in a convenient way.

2.4 Analysis of mode transition behaviour

The automata, generated with the verification toolset of Lite, that corresponds to the process that models the mode transitions can be shown automatically to satisfy safety properties expressed as ACTL formulas. We give a few examples. For reasons of lack of space we refer to [6] for an explanation of the details of the ACTL formulas and give here an informal description of some of the properties that we verified. Of course such an informal description may not be completely unambiguous. This shows at the same time why a formal notation is useful as a basis for the discussion of properties.

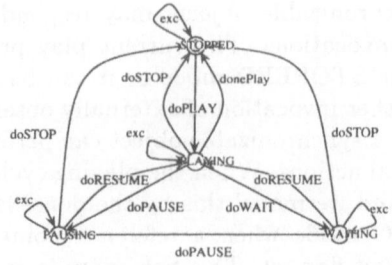

Fig. 2. Mode transition diagram

In order to address internal actions in the temporal logic formulas we made these actions observable in the specification before model checking.

1. In all states it is always possible to raise an exception $AG < exc > true$;
2. Whenever a doPLAY occurs, then whenever a doPAUSE or doWAIT occurs, eventually a doRESUME is enabled.

$$AG\,[doPLAY]\,AG\,[doPAUSE\,|\,doWAIT]\,AF\, < doRESUME > \,true$$

Note that if we replace the F (indicating eventually) by a G (indicating in all future states) the formula does not hold. This shows that not in every state that can be reached after a doPAUSE or doWAIT the doRESUME action is enabled! The model checker gives an example of such a trace:

$$\rightarrow doPLAY \rightarrow target \rightarrow doneStage \rightarrow doPAUSE \rightarrow doSTOP$$

2.5   Specification refinement

Having described the basic transitions of modes, the next step is to get more insights into the system behaviour by introducing more details. An interesting refinement is the specification of the meaning of progression through the co-ordinate space when the object is playing. To extend the specification two approaches are possible. Since the refinement is addressing operations that occur in PLAYING mode, a natural choice will be to redefine the behaviour of the PLAYING process by adding further expressions that model the progression. Alternatively, a new process can be specified describing only the behaviour of progressing the position. This process is subsequently composed with the modeTransitions process following a constraint oriented style of specification. This second alternative presents a number of advantages including modularity and incremental refinement of the specialization by cumulating locally defined constraints. Consequently, we adopt a constraint oriented style of specification and define a new process to describe the actions performed by synchronizable objects when progressing the position in their respective co-ordinate space.

When directed to start a playing cycle, synchronizable objects enter a loop in which the next required position is computed that is reached by performing a sequence of steps. Such a sequence is called a stage. While stepping, the signalling of an event occurs when a reference point is encountered. Stepping is terminated when the object reaches the required position or because it completes playing. New actions are defined to express the above behaviour as in the following:

- external actions:
  - doSignal models the encountering and signalling of a reference point;
- internal actions:
  - target models the computation of the next required position;
  - doStep models the progression of the position during a stage;
  - doneStage models the termination of progression because the target has been reached.

Because the execution of each stage is to be considered as an atomic operation, the progression process must be informed about the invocation of operations on the object performed by the environment. Therefore, the gates at which mode transition actions occur must be part of the process definition.

The process describing the progression of the position initially creates an instance of a process offering the choice of possible behaviour when the object is not stepping.

```
process progressPosition[doSTOP,doPLAY,doPAUSE,doRESUME,doWAIT,donePlay,
                         doSignal] : noexit :=
  hide doStep, doneStage in
  NOTSTEPPING[doSTOP,doPLAY,doPAUSE,doRESUME,doWAIT,donePlay,
              doSignal, doStep,doneStage]
endproc
```

Progress through the co-ordinate space is controlled by a Boolean variable called "stepping" in the Object-Z specification. During execution of a stage the variable is set to true. When a stage is ended the value is set back to false. The processes NOTSTEPPING and STEPPING reflect the two values that the stepping variable can have.

The NOTSTEPPING process either reacts to a doPLAY or a doRESUME because the stepping stage is performed only when the synchronizable object is in PLAYING mode. It computes a new required position with the NEW-TARGET process, or performs a simple recursion in the case of doSTOP or doPAUSE. Since the doStep and doneStage actions are hidden actions in the process definition, they are not observable from the environment. Eventually, their refinement will require the reworking of this process definition to take into account the special needs of different media types. To avoid some repetitions in the next process we define "gate list" as the list of actions of NOTSTEPPING, i.e. doSTOP,doPLAY,doPAUSE,doRESUME,doWAIT,donePlay,doSignal, doStep,doneStage.

```
process NOTSTEPPING[doSTOP,doPLAY,doPAUSE,doRESUME,doWAIT,donePlay,
                    doSignal, doStep,doneStage] : noexit :=
   doPLAY; NEWTARGET[gate list]    [] doRESUME; NEWTARGET[gate list]
[] doSTOP; NOTSTEPPING[gate list] [] doPAUSE; NOTSTEPPING[gate list]
endproc
```

The computation of a new required position is modelled by the action "target" in the NEWTARGET process. A more concrete specification will require the reworking of this process to match the characteristics of specific media types. After the target has been computed the STEPPING stage is entered.

```
process NEWTARGET[doSTOP,doPLAY,doPAUSE,doRESUME,doWAIT,donePlay,
doSignal,doStep,doneStage] : noexit :=
hide target in
    target; STEPPING [gate list]
endproc
```

The STEPPING process defines at a high level of abstraction the possible actions that may take place during one stage progression. The behaviour initially offered in a choice by stepping is either to perform a step progression, or to notify the completion of a stage or of a play cycle. When a stage is completed a new one can be entered by computing a new target, or the progression can be terminated. The completion of a a play cycle is always possible.

In the specification of the STEPPING and NOTSTEPPING processes we have been using non-determinism to abstract from the Object-Z specification. Instead of modelling all the variables that describe the precise movement of a pointer in the coordinate space, we modelled only the events that trigger a change in the behaviour, such as the fact that the pointer reaches the end position of a playing cycle that generates a donePlay. In the specification we abstract from *when* exactly such events occur and model only *that* such an event can occur by means of a non-deterministic choice of the possible events. This way we capture everything that *may* happen and we can investigate all possibilities.

When the object is progressing its position by stepping, it can encounter a reference point. In this case it signals the event and may enter the WAITING mode if the Wait flag is set. According to the specification of mode transition, after the WAITING mode is entered the object can be either stopped or paused or resumed. It should be noted however that this is not equivalent to re-instantiate the NOTSTEPPING process. In fact, the doRESUME action continues the playing cycle with exactly the same stage that was active before waiting, when performed in the WAITING mode. Conversely, the same action initializes a new stage by computing a new target when performed in the PAUSED mode. In the following process "gate list" denotes the same list of actions as defined before.

```
process STEPPING [doSTOP,doPLAY,doPAUSE,doRESUME,doWAIT,donePlay,
doSignal,doStep,doneStage] : noexit :=
  doStep;(    STEPPING[gate list]
          [] doSignal; (    STEPPING[gate list]
                        [] doWAIT;(   doRESUME; STEPPING[gate list]
                                   [] doSTOP; NOTSTEPPING[gate list]
                                   [] doPAUSE; NOTSTEPPING[gate list] )))
[] doneStage;(   NEWTARGET[gate list]
              [] NOTSTEPPING[gate list])
[] donePlay; NOTSTEPPING[gate list]
endproc
```

By combining the definition of modeTransitions and progressPosition processes, the refined version of synchronizable objects can be defined as:

```
process SynchronizableObject[doSTOP,doPLAY,doPAUSE,doRESUME,doWAIT,
donePlay,exc,doSignal,doStep,doneStage] : noexit :=
    modeTransitions[doSTOP,doPLAY,doPAUSE,doRESUME,doWAIT,donePlay,exc]
    |[doSTOP,doPLAY,doPAUSE,doRESUME,doWAIT,donePlay]|
    progressPosition[doSTOP,doPLAY,doPAUSE,doRESUME,doWAIT,donePlay,
                     doSignal]
endproc
```

The two processes are composed in parallel with synchronization on the gates doSTOP, doPLAY, doPAUSE, doRESUME, doWAIT, donePlay. Consequently, the processes constrain each other so that progressPosition cannot force a mode transition that would violate the transition mechanism specified by modeTransitions and, conversely, modeTransitions can let the object make a mode transition only at those points where also progressPosition is enabled to perform the same action.

The simulation of the specification shows, as expected, a more complicated transition system with 8 states and 30 transitions in which it is obviously much harder to check properties manually.

2.6 Analysis of mode transition and progression

The properties expressed for the mode transition part in Section 2.4 hold also for the refined specification. In addition the following properties hold that are specific for the extended specification and were formulated in the Foundation Component document of the PREMO standard [14] on section "7.9 Synchronization".

1. After a doRESUME from the PAUSING state always a new target is computed before stepping is continued.

    $AG \, [doPAUSE][doRESUME]$
    $\sim E[true \, \{\sim target\} \, U \, \{doStep \mid donePlay \mid doneStage\} \, true]$

2. After a doRESUME from the WAITING state it is not the case that first a new target is computed before stepping is continued.

    $AG \, [doWAIT][doRESUME]$
    $\sim E[true\{\sim (donePlay \mid doStep \mid doneStage)\}U\{target\}true]$

3 An example of media synchronization

The specification in the previous section is sufficient to develop an example showing how two media can be synchronized. The example is a typical situation where a video and an audio are played together while their synchronization is established by means of synchronization points. The fragment of the multimedia presentation under examination consists of three sections. Initially the video starts playing its first stage and gives a signal that is used to start the audio. The audio plays its first stage at the end of which it waits for the next signal from the video to resume playing. Finally the video continues playing while the audio stops.

3.1 Structure of media content

In order to model the above example both the video and the audio are described as Lotos processes. The structure of the video is modelled by four stages: the first three stages are defined as step or step and signal sequences followed by the termination of the stage, the last one is defined as a step sequence followed by the termination of playing. Signaling will direct the playing of the audio and its resuming after waiting. Similarly the audio structure is modelled as a first stage consisting of a step and signal followed by the entering of the WAITING mode. After resuming to play it plays one more stage and stops. Under these assumptions we define the following processes:

```
process Video[donePlay,doSignal,doStep,doneStage] : exit :=
      doStep; doSignal; doneStage; doStep; doneStage;
            doStep; doSignal; doneStage; doStep; donePlay; exit
endproc

process Audio[doWAIT,donePlay,doSignal,doStep] : exit :=
      doStep; doSignal; doWAIT; doStep; donePlay; exit
endproc
```

Clearly, the specification of the media content is defined at a very high level of abstraction. The doneStage and donePlay actions, for example, model that the position pointer in the coordinate space of the Synchronizable Object reaches the requiredPosition and the endPosition respectively. However, it captures the essential features of the media that enable to conduct qualitative analysis on the underlying synchronization mechanism. In order to perform a more detailed analysis, an exact description of the structure of the media would be required by extending the specification with state information.

3.2 Synchronizable media

Having described the structure of media with reference points modelled by signals, both video and audio need to be made synchronizable. This is a straightforward definition: two distinguished instances of the Synchronizable-Object process defined in the previous section are composed in parallel with synchronization respectively with the Video and Audio processes. The set of synchronization gates in the parallel composition operators equals the set of the gates of the media processes. In this way their behaviour is fully constrained to follow that of synchronizable objects as defined by the modeTransitions and the progress-Position processes.

```
process SynchVideo[doSTOP,doPLAY,doPAUSE,doRESUME,exc,doSignal] : exit :=
    hide doWAIT, donePlay, doStep, doneStage in
        Video[donePlay,doSignal,doStep,doneStage]
        |[donePlay,doSignal,doStep,doneStage]|
        SynchronizableObject[doSTOP,doPLAY,doPAUSE,doRESUME,doWAIT,donePlay,
                             exc,doSignal,doStep,doneStage]
endproc
```

The process SynchAudio is identical, except that the process Video is replaced by the process Audio.

The specified synchronizable video and audio offer to the environment the set of gates doSTOP, doPLAY, doPAUSE and doRESUME, at which corresponding mode transitions may occur, the exc gate for the environment to be able to recover the raise of exceptions, and the doSignal gate used to communicate to the environment that a reference point has been reached during progression.

3.3 A synchronization director

EventHandler object types are defined in PREMO to provide basic support for allowing objects to register interest in particular events, and for those objects to be notified when such events occur. For example the SychAudio and the SynchVideo processes both raise events at the doSignal gate. In order to co-operate for the purposes of the intented multimedia presentation, each of the processes needs to know when the other one is signalling and the nature of the raised event.

The specification of event handlers is out of the scope of this paper. However, a special process that is specific to our example is defined here for completeness of the example. It is a handler that synchronizes with the SychAudio and the SynchVideo processes at distinct sets of gates so that a gate-renaming operation takes place. The handler is the parallel composition of three behaviour expressions. The first one is responsible for starting the video, the second one starts the audio when the video signals that it has reached the appropriate reference point, and the third keeps the audio and the video playing synchronized.

Although at first sight the Director seems to be a reasonable specification we will show in the analysis of this example two problems with it that need careful attention when specifying synchronization handlers. One problem can be solved by improving the Lotos specification, the other illustrates a shortcoming of the expressiveness of Lotos to model behaviour that requires further assumptions about time aspects of actions.

```
process Director[VdoSTOP,VdoPLAY,VdoPAUSE,VdoRESUME,Vexc,VdoSignal,
AdoSTOP,AdoPLAY,AdoPAUSE,AdoRESUME,Aexc,AdoSignal] : exit :=
    (VdoPLAY; exit ||| VdoSignal; AdoPLAY; exit)
    |||
    MIXER[AdoSignal,AdoRESUME,VdoSignal]
where
```

```
    process MIXER[AdoSignal,AdoRESUME,VdoSignal] : exit :=
        AdoSignal; VdoSignal;
        ( AdoRESUME; MIXER[AdoSignal,AdoRESUME,VdoSignal]
        [] VdoSignal; exit )
    endproc
endproc
```

3.4   Completing the example

The final step in the specification of the example is to compose together all the processes defined in the previous sections. The Director must synchronize on the gates of synchronizable objects distinguishing video from audio. The synchronization is necessary to be aware of the signalling of the objects and to enforce their safety properties with respect to mode transitions. The video and the audio objects are composed in parallel with no synchronization since they may exist, and consequently play, independently. Their coordination when playing together is guaranteed by the Director. Consequently, the overall behaviour of the system implementing the worked example is:

```
behaviour
Director[VdoSTOP,VdoPLAY,VdoPAUSE,VdoRESUME,Vexc,VdoSignal,
          AdoSTOP,AdoPLAY, AdoPAUSE,AdoRESUME,Aexc,AdoSignal]
|[VdoSTOP,VdoPLAY,VdoPAUSE,VdoRESUME,Vexc,VdoSignal,
AdoSTOP,AdoPLAY, AdoPAUSE,AdoRESUME,Aexc,AdoSignal]|
(SynchVideo[VdoSTOP,VdoPLAY,VdoPAUSE,VdoRESUME,Vexc,VdoSignal]
||| SynchAudio[AdoSTOP,AdoPLAY,AdoPAUSE,AdoRESUME,Aexc,AdoSignal])
```

4   Analysis of the example

From the simulation of the complete example by means of the Lite simulator a number of interesting observations can be made.

First of all, the Director process forces, by means of parallel composition with synchronisation, the Audio to start playing and to give a signal *before* the second doSignal of the video can take place. At first sight this seems exactly what we want, but note carefully that this way the video presentation gets *implicitly* suspended if for some reason the Audio did *not* produce the signal (yet)! Implicitly suspended means that it is suspended due to the underlying synchronization principle of Lotos and not due to the encountering of a reference point that indicated the Video to go to WAITING mode. This means that in this specification the 'output' of a signal by the video has been constrained so that it cannot take place freely! This is a delicate point in the use of Lotos because Lotos allows restrictions on all kind of actions, so both on those that model *input* actions and those that model *output* actions. The imposed restriction on the signal output can be released by changing the behaviour of the Director in such a way that a signal can always be accepted and a proper exception is generated in case the signal appears in the wrong moment.

Another observation is that even when the Audio gives a signal, this does not necessarily mean that it performs immediately the internal doWAIT action. This has the consequence that the video can just continue to play and signal but that the Audio does not accept a doRESUME from the Director because it did not perform (yet) the internal doWAIT action. In general in Lotos there is no way to express that internal actions, when they are enabled, *have* to be performed with highest priority or urgency.

In this example we can therefore check some safety properties such as "the Audio does not start before a signal is issued by the Video" and "the Audio does not resume to play before it receives a doRESUME issued after a signal of the Video". We can however not check properties like "the Audio starts as soon as a signal is issued by the Video". In order to answer that kind of questions some additional assumptions have to be made on the occurrence of actions. In the near future we will investigate additional tools, such as for example the tool UPPAAL [1], for these aspects. UPPAAL is a verification tool that accepts automata produced with Autograph and allows to enrich these automata with assumptions about temporal aspects of the actions.

5   Conclusion

In this article we have investigated the use of the standardized process algebra Lotos for the specification of PREMO Synchronizable Objects. We presented a specification of the behavioural aspects of the mode transition and progression aspects of these objects. To this purpose we experimented with a new approach of specification of behavioural aspects of Objects that were already specified in an Object Oriented style in a state based language which lead to an encouraging result that motivates further research.

We showed that starting from a Lotos specification we can use existing verification tools that allow for graphical representation of the specification, model checking and several transformations of the specification that are useful for checking properties that have been formulated in the PREMO standard.

Finally we have been pointing out two intricate problems that can be encountered when using Lotos for the specification of media synchronization. One problem is the fact that Lotos allows synchronization also on actions that are interpreted as output actions. This may lead to unintended suspension of a media object that is presenting output. The other problem is the fact that internal actions cannot be required to happen urgently, or with high priority. In fact modelling this kind of aspects requires a formalism in which timed behaviour can be expressed. In future research we will investigate specification languages and tools in which these properties *can* be specified preferably while keeping a clear relation with Lotos specifications without these additional requirements.

We showed the use of a new approach of specification of behavioural aspects of Objects that were already specified in an Object Oriented style in a state based language.

References

1. J. Bengtsson and K. G. Larsen and F. Larson and P. Petterson and Wang Yi. *UPPAAL— A Tool Suite for Automatic Verification of Real-Time Systems.* In Proceedings of the 4th DIMACS Workshop on Verification and Control of Hybrid Systems, LNCS, October 1995.
2. C. Bernardeschi and G. Ferro. A Sample Study Exemplifying the Use of JACK. In: Proceedings Workshop on Automated Formal Methods, ENTCS, vol. 5, University of Oxford, 1996.
3. J.C. Bicarregui et al. Proof in VDM: A Practitioner's Guide. Springer-Verlag, 1994.
4. A. Bouali and S. Gnesi and S. Larosa. The Integration Project for the JACK Environment. Bulletin of the EATCS, 54, October 1994, pp. 207-223.
5. T. Bolognesi and E. Brinksma. Introduction to the ISO specification language LOTOS. *Computer Networks and ISDN Systems*, 14:25–59, 1987.
6. R. De Nicola and A. Fantechi and S. Gnesi and G. Ristori. *An action based framework for verifying logical and behavioural properties of concurrent systems.* In: Proceedings 3rd International Workshop CAV'91, K. G. Larsen and A. Skou (Eds.), LNCS 575, Springer-Verlag, 1991
7. R. De Nicola and A. Fantechi and S. Gnesi and G. Ristori. Verifying Hardware Components within JACK. In: Proceedings of CHARME'95, LNCS 987, Springer-Verlag, 1995, pp. 246-260.
8. R. Duke and G. Rose and G. Smith. *Object-Z: A Specification Language Advocated for the Description of Standards* Technical Report, No. 94-45, Software Verification Research Center, Department of Computer Science, University of Queensland, 1994.
9. R. De Nicola and F. Vaandrager. *Action versus State based Logics for Transition Systems.* In: Semantics of Systems of Concurrent Processes, I. Guessarian (Ed.), LNCS 469, Springer-Verlag, 1990.
10. D. J. Duke and D. A. Duce and I. Herman and G. Faconti. *Specifying the PREMO Synchronization Objects* ERCIM Computer Graphics Network Technical Report, 02/97-R048, February , 1997. (submitted for publication)
11. G. P. Faconti and M. Massink. *Using LOTOS for the evaluation of Design Options in the PREMO Standard* In proceedings of the BCS-FACS Northern Formal Methods Workshop, Ilkley, July 1997, Springer-Verlag. (submitted for publication)
12. C.A.R. Hoare. Communicating Sequential Processes. In *Communications of ACM*, 21(8), 1978.
13. International Standards Organization ISO. Information processing systems - open systems interconnection - LOTOS - a formal description technique based on the temporal ordering of observational behaviour, 1989. ISO 8807.
14. International Standards Organization ISO. Information processing systems, computer graphics, presentation environment for multimedia objects (PREMO). ISO/IEC 14478, 1996.
15. E. Madeleine and A. Pnueli. *AUTO: A Verification tool for Distributed Systems using reduction of Finite Automata Networks.* Formal Description Techniques, II (S. T. Vuong, ed.), 1990, pp. 61-66.
16. R. Milner. *Communication and Concurrency.* Series in Computer Science. Prentice Hall, 1989.
17. V. Roy and R. De Simone. *AUTO and Autograph.* In Proceedings Workshop on Computer Aided Verification, LNCS 531, Springer-Verlag, 1990, pp. 65-75.

18. J.M. Spivey. The $\mathcal{Z}$ Notation: A Reference Manual. Prentice Hall, 1989.
19. P. van Eijk. The Lotosphere Integrated Tool Environment LITE. In *Proceedings of 4th International Conference on Formal Description Techniques*. North Holland, 1991.
20. C. A. Vissers and G. Scollo and M .van Sinderen and E. Brinksma. *Specification Styles in Distributed Systems Design and Verification*. Theoretical Computer Science, vol. 89, 1989.

Formal Transducers:
Models of Devices and Building Bricks for the Design
of Highly Interactive Systems

Johnny Accot[1], Stéphane Chatty[1], Sébastien Maury[1], Philippe Palanque[1,2]

[1]	[2]
CENA	LIS - FROGIS
7 av. Edouard Belin	Université Toulouse I
31055 Toulouse cedex, France	31042 Toulouse cedex, France
{accot,chatty,maury}@cena.dgac.fr	palanque@cict.fr

Abstract. Producing formal descriptions of low level interaction is necessary to completely capture the behaviour of user interfaces and avoid unexpected behaviour of higher level software layers. We propose a structured approach to formalising low level interaction and scaling up to higher layers, based on the composition of transducers. Every transducer encapsulates the behaviour of a device or software component, consumes and produces events. We describe transducers using a formalism based on Petri nets, and show how this transducer-based model can be used to describe simple but realistic applications and analyse unexpected defects in their design. We also identify properties that are meaningful to the application designer and users, and show how they can be formally checked on a transducer-based model of the application.

1. Introduction

The problem of applying formalisms to user interface construction has been an open issue for several years now. The goals are clear to all: interactive software is complex, and formalisms would help mastering that complexity by providing HCI designers and programmers with a common and precise language, and by allowing formal verifications of the behaviour of their software. However, no formal approach has been fully successful yet, and some even wonder whether a unique formalism will ever permit a full description of an interactive system [32] which leads to a wide variety of partial approaches. Some focus on the early stages of the design process such as requirements elicitation and analysis or early specification [15, 28, 25, 26] other on the elicitation of domain related properties [14]. Others describe the dialogue component of applications, making the reasonable assumption that low level interaction components have been taken care of by some error-free industry developer such as all the work done on the formal design of WIMP interfaces relying on the set of predefined interaction objects [5, 34, 35].

In any case, we believe that low level interaction cannot be ignored by formalisms and left to programmers and their craftsmanship. If a unified formalism ever exists, it will have to describe actions to their finest level of detail. And if several formalisms have to be used, one will have to be devoted to sequences of low-level events and the way they propagate to higher layers of software. We see several reasons to that opinion. First, as mentioned in [1], we observe that direct manipulation styles such as those used in the Macintosh Finder do not rely on widespread reusable widgets. Actually, they use supposedly simple programming techniques, which are undocumented and misunderstood by many programmers and even by some HCI software researchers. Furthermore, most new direct manipulation styles that are currently being devised are not obtained by combining existing styles: they involve new handling schemes for low level events such as button presses and moves, time-outs, or key presses. We thus consider that languages and methods are necessary to design and reason about those new interaction styles.

Our second reason is more disturbing to software engineering researchers. Many programmers have been confronted to evidence that minor and unspecified behaviours of low level software or hardware components can dramatically affect the behaviour of their software system as perceived by users. For instance, we all think we know what a keyboard is and what is behaviour is: every key can be pressed then released. Then how comes that on some workstations, the key "3" is ignored when the keys "1" and "2" are held down[1]? What happens if those keys are mapped to actions that are supposed to be performed simultaneously, such as playing notes on a synthesiser, firing multiple guns in a video game, or showing different representations of data on an air traffic control workstation? We argue that one cannot predict the behaviour of an interactive application without a precise specification of all its hardware and software components.

Finally, we take the point of view that formalisms are the most useful when integrated with production tools such as UIMSs, toolkits or user interface description languages. Therefore, it is important that formalisms manipulate the same notions as toolkits. As of today and as far as highly interactive interfaces are concerned, those notions are limited to graphical objects, events, and event handling schemes such as callbacks or interactors.

Those reasons have led us to work on formal models for low level interaction, with the goal of producing a UI toolkit that manipulates formal notions. This brought to us a number of problems that can be generalised to other approaches: how can a formal description be structured in readable and reusable modules? what are the meaningful properties to be checked over a model?

In this paper, we outline a formal model that allows a modular description of applications while taking low-level interaction into account, down to the behaviour of models. Formal transducers encapsulate the basic behaviours involved in an interface: devices (mouse, keyboard, etc.), behaviours of graphical objects (click, drag, etc.), and behaviours of the functional part of the application, when applicable. Transducers consume and produce events. They can be combined in a client-server fashion. Each transducer exports a formal description of its behaviour; in this paper, we use a dialect of Petri nets for those descriptions: timed Petri nets. Such a formal declaration of behaviour allows consistency checks when connecting two transducers. It also makes it possible to observe how the actions of the user are successively translated, and to detect wrong assumptions that are made when using lower level components.

A lot of work has been devoted to devices and can be mainly classified in the following categories:

---

[1] This precise behaviour can be easily observed on SUN Sparc 10 workstations

- classifying devices [10]
- understanding of devices [21]
- building of transducers for managing low level events produced by physical devices [1, 11]
- assessing usability of devices according to task [8] and more generally tasks and to users' cognitive capabilities [22]
- evaluating the performance of input devices [2], [19].

This paper belongs the third category as its aims are:

- to propose a formalism allowing designers to describe the behaviour of physical devices,
- to propose a formalism allowing designers to describe the behaviour of high level modules (called transducers) extending the set of events offered by the device,
- to propose a model and tools for building application from transducers,
- to define a set of properties that characterise transducers.

This is significantly different from the work of [11] as it fits in a more generic framework based on object oriented concepts, properties of transducers and has been directly implemented. However, due to space reasons the implementation is not presented in this paper.

The paper is organised as follows. The next section gives a outline of formal transducers, that are exemplified in section 3. We then analyse a simple but realistic application, which highlights how bad assumptions on low level transducers may lead to unexpected software failures. We also show how transducers may exhibit undesirable properties for certain purposes. We identify some of those properties, and show how they can be checked.

2. Formal Transducers

Most computer interfaces today are event-driven, and part of the job of designers is to manage the event flow produced by the user's interaction with physical devices. But managing all the possible combinations of event occurrence is hardly thinkable, especially considering the increasing complexity of systems (e.g. multimodal interaction). One possible solution to solve this issue is to supply designers with a formalism and an associated methodology, that would assist them in describing unambiguously the behaviour of the interface. However it is possible to model such complex behaviours using formal specifications, they unfortunately quickly get incredibly complex, and some research has still to be done on software engineering for formal models in order to supply designers with tools and methods to organise their work. Among the methodologies still to be explored, we believe that an object-oriented approach to formal specification of user interfaces is among the most promising ones. The difficulty in such a design approach is not only to define formally the behaviour of the objects but also to define the system modules and the rules to connect them. Even though this problem has been identified for a long time and description techniques are available such as Pre and Post conditions [29], statecharts [6] or using object-oriented Petri nets [30], work has still to be done to build a convenient software architecture (to favour reusability through encapsulation) and a methodology to help designers to organise their work.

As this research work is directed towards air traffic control (which is a critical domain regarding system security) we are very concerned with the validation of interactive systems. This validation mainly consists in the proof of some pertinent properties on the system. Splitting an application in a set of cooperating transducers makes easier the analysis of properties as they can be checked separately on each model.

Besides, it is important to characterise transducers according to the way they process events. We give hereafter three properties for transducers: *chatty*, *sly* and *regular*. In the next section we will show that a *chatty* transducer may introduce malfunctions in some applications and not in other ones, depending on the set of events used by the application. However, no such malfunction can occur with a *regular* one.

The Accepted Stream (AS_T) of a transducer $T = (I_T, O_T, PN)$ is defined by:

> Let L(PN; M) be the language defined by all the possible firing sequences of transitions of PN
>
> Let T_r be the set of transition of PN and T_e be the subset of transitions of T_r that feature an event place (grey circle in the Petri net)
>
> $AS_T = L(PN; M) \mid T_e$ (| means the mathematical restriction)

AS_T defines all the possible sequences of input events that can be processed by the transducer T.

The Produced Stream (PS_T) of a transducer $T = (I_T, O_T, PN)$ is defined by:

> Let L(PN; M) be the language defined by all the possible firing sequences of transitions of PN
>
> Let T_r be the set of transition of PN and T_p be the subset of transitions of T_r that feature an action part producing events (transition with the Post(event) actions)
>
> $PS_T = L(PN; M) \mid T_p$ (| means the mathematical restriction)

PS_T defines all the possible sequences of output events that can be produced by the transducer T.

A transducer T is said *chatty* (there is production of information during the filtering) if and only if:

> $$\exists event \in I_T \Rightarrow PS_T(event) > AS_T(event)$$
>
> This means that the transducer T is producing more events of the type of input event than it has received.

A transducer T is said *sly* (there is loss of information during the filtering) if and only if:

> $$\exists event \in I_T \Rightarrow PS_T(event) < AS_T(event)$$
>
> This means that the transducer T is producing less events of the type of input event than it has received. In that case, information is lost

A transducer T is said *regular* (there is no production and no loss of information during the filtering) if and only if:

> $$\forall event \in I_T \Rightarrow PS_T(event) = AS_T(event)$$
>
> This means that the transducer T is producing exactly as many events of any type it has received. However, it is possible for it to produce events of a different type as the transducer of Fig. 2 produces *repeat* events.

3. Formal Transducers and the Keyboard

This section aims at describing the actual behaviour of a physical device keyboard. The behaviour of this device is quite simple as it only consists in translating user's actions on the keys into low level events. In order to provide more interesting events the keyboard is coupled with a software transducer that interprets and enriches these low level events. The next section describes the formal model of the keyboard. Section 3.2 presents a formal specification of a transducer describing precisely how low level events are consumed and which higher level events are produced according to software designers' needs. The last two sections describes how these formal specifications can be used to prove properties on the models.

3.1 The Formal Model of the Device Keyboard

Fig. 1 describes the behaviour of a key using high level Petri nets [24]. When modelling with Petri nets, a system is described in terms of state variables (called *places*, depicted as ellipses) and by state-changing operators (called *transitions*, depicted as rectangles), connected by annotated *arcs*. The state of the system is given by the *marking* of the net, which is a distribution of *tokens* in the net's places. In coloured Petri nets, the tokens assume values from predefined types, or *colours*. State changes result from the *firing* of transitions, yielding a new distribution of tokens. Transition firing involves two steps: (1) tokens are removed from *input* places and their values *bound* to variables specified on the input arcs, and (2) new tokens are deposited in the *output* places with values determined by *emission rules* attached to output arcs. A transition is *enabled* to fire when (1) all of its input places contain tokens, and (2) the value of those tokens satisfy the (optional) Boolean constraints attached to the input arcs.

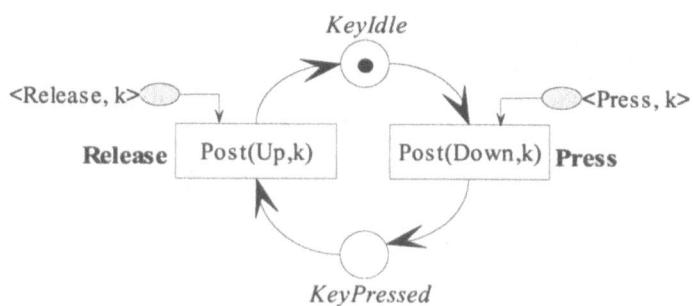

Fig. 1: Formal model of a key

The model of Fig. 1 is made up of two places modelling the two possible states of a key (pressed or released). The actual state of the key is fully stated by the token in the place *KeyIdle* stating that the key is not in use. From that state the user can press the key, that will trigger the transition Press thus removing the token from the place *KeyIdle* and setting it into the place *KeyPressed*. The connection between the transition and the user's action on the device is represented by the broken incoming arrow with the tiny grey circle.

As all the keys (except the modifiers such as ALT, CTRL and SHIFT) are

148

independent, the behaviour of the keyboard is exactly the sum of the behaviours of all its keys. Thus the modelling of the behaviour of the keyboard can be done by adding one token for each key. However, it is important to differentiate the keys as rendering actions associated to keys might differ (this is the case for example in text editors). This is modelled using coloured tokens in the Petri net. In the following of the paper we shall represent all the keys of a keyboard using coloured tokens. In order to be exhaustive we should have represented as many coloured tokens as there are keys on the keyboard but for readability reasons only few tokens are displayed.

Each time a key is pressed, the device emits an event *down* along with the identification number of the key that has been pressed. Each time a key is released the device emits an event *up*. This is represented in the model of Fig. 1 by the action part of the transitions where the function Post is invoked with the corresponding parameters.

A transducer $T = (I_T, O_T, PN)$ is defined by:

1. I_T be the set of input events received by the transducer
2. O_T be the set of input events produced by the transducer
3. PN the high level Petri net describing the behaviour of the transducer

The keyboard LL is a transducer between user's actions and low level events produced. It corresponds to a filtering function (F_0) and can be defined as follow:

Let Key be the set of keys of the keyboard.

1. $\forall k \in Key$, $I_{LL} = \{(Release, k), (Press, k)\}$
2. $\forall k \in Key$, $O_{LL} = \{(Up, k), (Down, k)\}$
3. PN = the high level Petri net of Fig. 1

3.2 The Formal Model of a Transducer

The low level events produced by the keyboard are aimed at being used by software systems. However, most of the applications are interested in a set of richer events. For example the fact that the user is holding a key is usually relevant to the semantics of the application.

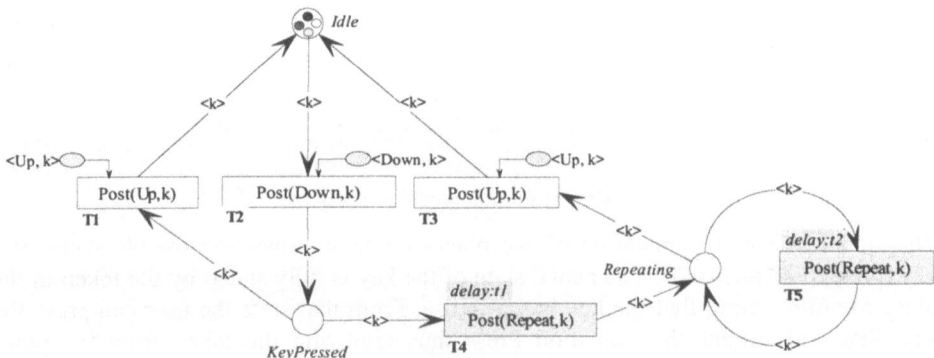

Fig. 2: Formal model of the high level events transducer

The Petri net in Fig. 2 describes such a transducer. In addition to the low level events, a higher level event named *repeat* is produced by the transducer in order to represent the holding of a key by the user. The *repeat* event is related to temporal manipulation of keys. Two different temporal aspects can be taken into account:

- white transitions (as previously) that fire as soon as they are enabled (i.e. there is at least a token in each of their input places), they are called immediate transitions.
- greyed out transitions are associated with a delay. The semantic of these transitions is of Generalised Stochastic Petri Nets [3]. When a token is set in the place *KeyPressed* a timer associated to the token is started by the transition T4. If the token is still there after t1 seconds (the delay associated to transition T4) then T4 is fired. If within these t1 seconds an event *up* occurs then the transition T1 is fired and the timer associated to the token is destroyed[2].
- a first delay (t1) is used to differentiate between briefly pressing a key and holding it. The transducer waits during t1 seconds before a *repeat* event is emitted.
- a second delay (t2) corresponds to the delay between the production of two *repeat* events.

With respect to the keyboard model of Fig. 1 the transducer above models another state for a key represented by the place *Repeating*. The two delays t1 and t2 are associated to the timed transitions. If the user quickly releases the key (before t1 seconds) then the key returns to its initial state (Idle) before the first timed transition has been fired. The loop including the second timed transition represents the repetitive production of repeat events when the user holds down a key.

The filter HL is a transducer between low level events produced by the keyboard and higher level events. It corresponds to a filtering function (F_1) and can be defined as follow:

> Let Key be the set of keys of the keyboard.
> 1. $\forall k \in Key$, $I_{HL} = O_{LL} = \{(Up, k), (Down, k)\}$
> 2. $\forall k \in Key$, $O_{HL} = \{(Up, k), (Down, k), (Repeat, k)\}$
> 3. PN = the high level Petri net of Fig. 2

3.3 Formal Analysis of Models

The use of a formal notation for describing transducers and input devices allows us to perform formal analysis on these models. Using analysis techniques it is possible to check generic properties of good allowing to assume the good functioning of the models but also to verify properties specific to the considered application.

This section concentrates on the generic properties such as liveness, reinitilisability, boundedness. Specific properties will be explicited and proved on the application described in section 4. As the transducers are supposed to be used repetitively it is important to be sure that they are reinitialisable, i.e. it is always possible to find a sequence of actions that put the transducer back to its initial state. As transducers are used very often it is also important to be sure that they are not over producing

---

[2] This semantics is quite different from classical timed Petri nets as there is no duration associated to transitions i.e. a token is not held by a transition but always remain in a place. However, if there is no immediate transition the semantic is the same as the one of T-Timed Petri nets [31]

information and that they do not feature dead branches i.e. part of the specification that can become unreachable. Using Petri nets this can be proved by checking conservative and repetitive components [27].

Analysis of the transducer. The transducer of Fig. 2 is live (there are no dead branches in the specification), bounded (they consume as many resources as they produce, and vice-versa), and reinitialisable as there is always a sequence of actions that can lead the model back to the initial state. We detail hereafter the calculus of the these properties.

Conservative components are sets of places for which the number of tokens remains the same as the one of the initial state whatever sequence of transition is fired. In the model of the transducer there is only one conservative component which includes all the places of the model. Thus the sum of tokens in all the places of the nets remains constant and equal to the number of tokens in the initial state. As all the places of the Petri net belong to a conservative component then the net is bounded.

Repetitive components are set of transitions such that the firing of this state does not change the marking of the Petri net. In the generic transducer model there are six repetitive components namely: T5, T1+T2, T2+T3+T4. All the transitions belong to a repetitive component, and this is a necessary condition for the Petri net to be live [27]. The model of the keyboard presented in Fig. 1 features the same properties as the transducer, but as the model is very simple their proofs are not detailed here.

Verification of specific properties. Given a model, it is usually interesting to prove specific properties that depend only on the actual meaning of the model. Without referring to general properties on the class of system that is considered (such as predictability for example [14]) more precise ones are of interest for the designer.

Using Petri nets it is easy to model undetermined behaviours either by having conflicting transitions or multiple tokens. This happens when several transitions are available at the same time, but this is most of the time avoided by using events as triggers for a transition. However, the event might not be selective enough. In Fig. 2 for instance, if there is a token of type (k) in place *Repeating* and another token of the same type in place *KeyPressed*, and if the event (Up,k) occurs, then it is undetermined which of the transition T1 or T3 will be fired. In order to avoid this kind of undesirable behaviour, it is important to be sure that the token(s) representing a given key cannot be in several places of the net at the same time. This can easily be proved on the transducer as:

- all the places belong to the same conservative component (*Idle+ Keypressed +Repeating*)
- the value of this conservative component is equal to one

This means that there is no production of tokens by the model, and as at the initial state there is only one token for each key, then for a given event all the transitions of the net are mutually exclusive.

3.4 Conformance of Models

The models we have presented above function as a pipeline of events as it is represented on Fig. 3. Users are the sources of the pipeline as they produce the initial events. The pipeline architecture of events introduces specific requirements for the behaviour of the components. Indeed, the consumption of events by a given transducer has to be compatible with its preceding transducer and its production has to be compatible with its following transducer.

This can be formally proven by the analysis of the language underlying to each model, i.e. the study of all the possible sequences of transitions as we have shown it in [1] for the mouse and a transducer handling Click, Drag, Drop and Double_Click events.

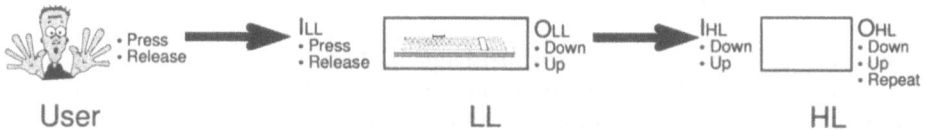

Fig. 3: The pipeline of events

Using regular expressions to represent the languages, the language accepted by the Petri net in Fig. 1 is: (Press, Release)* and the language generated is (Down, Up)*. According to the pipeline of Fig. 3, conformance has to be check between the generated language of this model and the accepted on of the high level event model of Fig. 2. The language accepted by this high level event model is (Down, Up)* and the one generated is [(Down, UP)* | (Down, Repeat, Up)* | (Down, Repeat, Repeat*, Up)]*

These sequences of transitions can directly extracted from the marking graph of the Petri net which can be automatically calculated due to the boundedness of the models.

The temporal transitions have not been taken into account in the calculation of acceptance language because they are not related to incoming events. However, they are taken into account for the production of events as their internal actions consist in posting events. In all the cases the temporal value of these transitions are never taken into account as we only consider here what actions are available and not when they are available.

We can deduce from that analysis that the models are compatible i.e. the transducer will never wait for sequences of events that cannot be produced by the model of the keyboard device. However, as temporal aspects are not taken into account it is not sure on one hand that a model will not be waiting for events and on the other hand that the events produced will be immediately consumed.

4. Analysing defects in an application

This section aims at presenting an application in order to illustrate the effective use of formal transducers for understanding, analysing and then building reliable applications.

In order to demonstrate the importance of the transducer choice and transducer understanding, we will describe here a simple application which uses extensively the keyboard. This application allows users to use the keyboard as a piano. Beyond the toy aspect of this application, the problems highlighted by this example are widely

152

encountered as soon as a keyboard is used for other purposes than entering text. More precisely, our examples represents all applications where the keyboard is used as a continuous source of information. For example when arrow keys are used in order to move objects on the screen (such as in games), the information that the key is held by the player has to be considered as a stream of input events. Widgets for handling time related objects such as the buttons 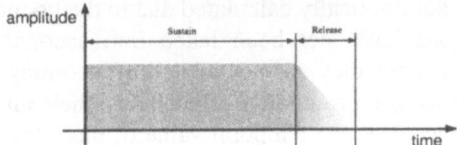 in VCR like interface need interpret users' continuous actions on the widgets as continuous stream of application events.

Besides this specific use of the keyboard this section will demonstrate that formal specification of transducers are necessary in order to understand failures in the functioning of applications and to build new versions. Another aspect will be to raise relevant properties.

4.1 Informal Presentation of the Piano Application

This application simulates a musical keyboard with the computer keyboard. Each musical sound note is associated with a specific key on the computer keyboard.

The sound of a note (called the envelop) is here simplified and consists of two parts: the *sustain* and the *release* (Fig. 4). Each time the user presses a key, a note is played. The sustain part is played until the key is released. When it is released the sound continues for few milliseconds, and this corresponds to the release part of the sound. Like using classical pianos the performer can play numerous notes simultaneously by pressing multiple keys. All the other musical aspects of the application are not considered here.

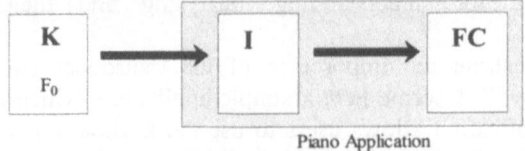

Fig. 4: The envelop of a sound note

4.2 Formal Model of the Application

As shown in Fig. 5 the keyboard is the source of the event stream for the application.

The formal specification of the application is split in two models: the sound generator of the notes (considered as the functional core FC) and the user interface (I) to this rendering engine. These two subsystems cooperate according to a client-server protocol defined itself in a formal way in terms of Petri nets [31]. The sound generator is only a server while the interface is only a client of this server.

Fig. 5: The pipeline communications between components

The behaviour of the sound generator is described in Fig. 6. The Idle state corresponds to no sound (the associated key is released). To play a note, the T_2 transition has to be fired. The T_2 transition features an internal function called Play which starts the emission of the sustain part when the transition is fired. The sound hardware will maintain the emission of the frequency until an explicit stop. This stop corresponds to the firing of the transition T_1. At that time, the Stop internal function requires the sound hardware to stop the emission of the sustain sound, and to play a sound corresponding to the release part of the note.

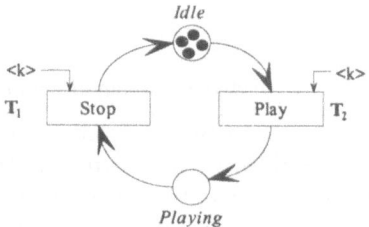

Fig. 6: The model of the note generator engine (FC)

It is important to notice that the model in Fig. 6 describes the behaviour of a note generator. The number of tokens in the place *Idle* correspond to the ability of the note generator to play several notes simultaneously (according to the implementation this could correspond to the number of different channel available). The exact number depends on the hardware characteristics.

Indeed, the sound hardware may still be playing a note "n" while the model of "n" is in the Idle state. This behaviour allows the performer to hit again the same note-key even if the previous release sound is not finished.

4.3 The formal model of the interface of the Piano Application

Fig. 7 presents a formal model of the piano application. This model highlights the communication with the sound engine as each transition of the model includes an action part describing a request to the sound generator. In Fig. 7 the place Idle features a set of coloured tokens modelling the fact that more than one note can be played simultaneously. As for the keyboard colours are used in order to differentiate the notes being played. The application is monitored by the user through events produced by the keyboard transducer. This is represented on the model by the input events of the transitions.

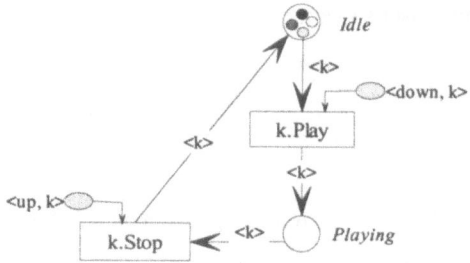

Fig. 7: The formal model of the interface part of the Piano application

This model has been directly implemented on the X Window system ™. The result of this implementation was quite different from what we expected at first as shown in Fig. 8.

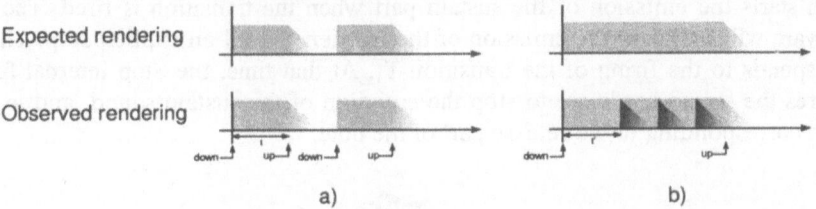

Fig. 8: Expected and effective rendering of the Piano application

The upper part of the Fig. 8 represents the expected continuous sound from he sound generator between the events emitted by the keyboard. The lower part of the figure describes the effective behaviour observed by the user. As we can see in the left hand part of the figure if the user releases the key after a short period of time t then the expected sound is exactly the one perceived by the user. However, if the key is held for a longer period of time t', then the sound produced is different. The sound is not stable but presents variations both in amplitude and in pitch. This is represented on the right hand part of Fig. 8.

Introspection of the code of the application has not provided any information about the origin of this problem. So we decided to trace the stream of events. Fig. 9 presents the results of this investigation for the long down-up sequence that has led to the unexpected behaviour described earlier. We have analysed the events received by the application at run time. This has highlighted the existence of a X Window' transducer (named F_1') responsible having produced these events.

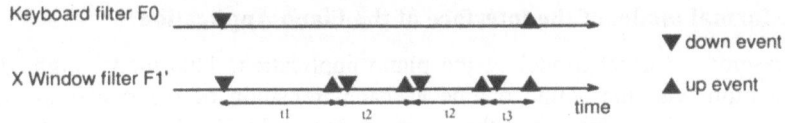

Fig. 9: The stream of events produced by the transducers

The first line of Fig. 9 represents the events produced by the keyboard. The total amount of time during which the key has been pressed is represented at the bottom of the figure and is equal to t1+2t2+t3. The second line represents the stream of events received by the application. We can see that several up-down sequences have been inserted between the two user's events.

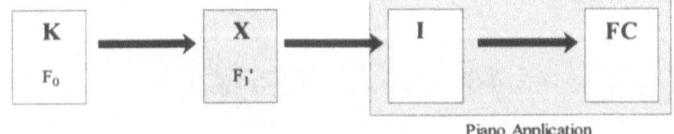

Fig. 10 : There was a ghost in the machine

This explains the observed rendering of the application: it made a wrong assumption on the sequences of events it would receive. This mistake is caused by a bad understanding of X Window, which had its own transducer to emulate repeat events (Fig. 10).

The model presented in Fig. 11 describes, using the same formalism as before the behaviour of this transducer. This model differs from the one presented in Fig. 2 only by the events produced by the transducer in the timed transitions. Indeed, instead of producing repeat events it produces the same events as the one received by the low level keyboard transducer i.e. up and down.

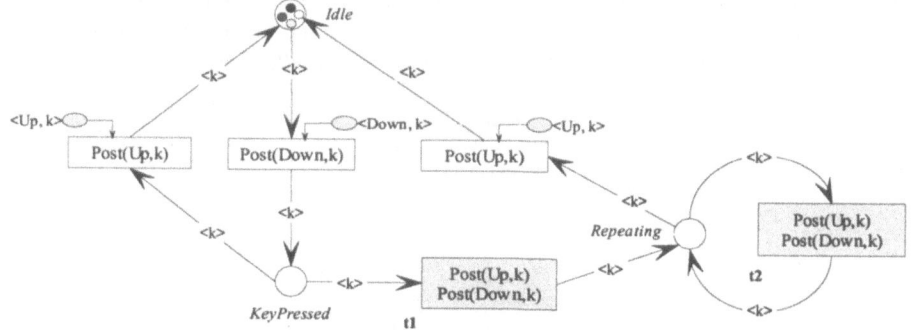

Fig. 11: The behaviour of the keyboard transducer F_1' of the X Window system

The filter XL is a transducer between low level events produced by the keyboard and a different sequence of the same low level events. It corresponds to a filtering function (F'_1) and can be defined as follow:

> Let Key be the set of keys of the keyboard.
> 1. $\forall k \in Key$, $I_{xL} = O_{LL} = \{(Up, k), (Down, k)\}$
> 2. $\forall k \in Key$, $O_{xL} = \{(Up, k), (Down, k)\}$
> 3. PN = the high level Petri net of Fig. 11

This transducer is used by all the applications running over the X Window system but no specification of it was available. Its understanding by programmers that have to deal with it could only occur through empirical testing and experience.

4.4 The piano application adapted to the X Window Transducer

In order to use the piano application despite the X Window transducer, we have written a new transducer F_1^{r-1} (Fig. 12). This transducer aims at hiding the X Window transducer by featuring the opposite effect on both the production and the consumption of events.

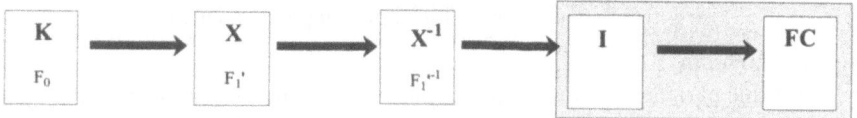

Fig. 12: The new transducer X^{-1} to adapt our application to X

The model of the new transducer (Fig. 13) is based on this characteristic and differentiates user's from synthetic events using a temporal transition. The model must

156

be read as follows. After a down event has been received the token corresponding to the key that has been pressed is set in the place *KeyPressed* and a Down event is produced. Then only an up event can be received which removes the token from place *KeyPressed* and sets it into the place *Repeating*. This up event may be either a synthetic event or a real one. In the case of a synthetic one, a synthetic down event should be received right after and thus the transition T3 will be triggered and the token set back to the place *KeyPressed*. If after t seconds (this quantitative time is expressed aside the transition T4) no down event has be received, the application assumes that the up event was a real one, hence transition T4 is fired requesting the sound generator to play the release sound and the token is set back to the *Idle* place.

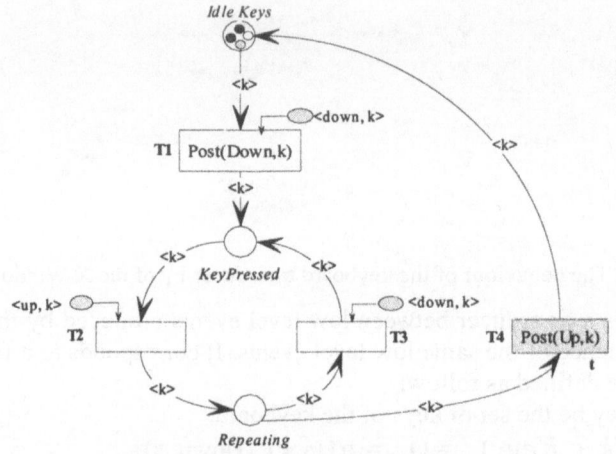

Fig. 13: The model of the F_1^{r-1} transducer

However, usability testing of the new piano application has shown the critical aspect of the temporal parameter t.
The consequences in our Piano application is that it is waiting t seconds before playing the release of the sound (as shown in
Fig. 14.a). If the delay is more than few milliseconds then it becomes perceivable by the user.

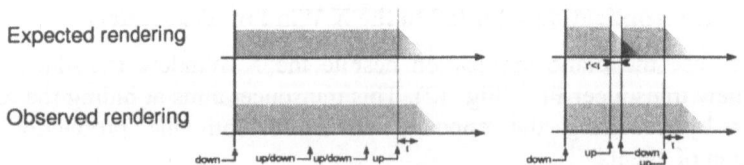

Fig. 14: Two problems with a long temporal parameter t

Indeed, as shown in
Fig. 14.b if this parameter is too long it is possible for the user to press and release the key in a shorter delay. This means that the application will interpret user's real actions as synthetic events. The observed rendering (described on the second line of the figure) is significantly different from the expected one. Instead of the note being played twice for a very short period of time, the note is played continuously. Besides,

the same problem of the note being played after the event up has occurred, still applies.

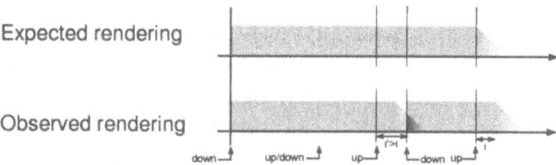

Fig. 15: A problem (c) with a short temporal parameter t

Another problem is related to the client-server architecture of the X Window system. This client-server architecture may dissociate the synthetic (Up, Down) events produced if the user holds the key pressed. If the delay between the two events is longer than t, then the system will interpret these events as user's events thus stopping the note and starting it again. The observed behaviour of such a misinterpretation is described in the second part of Fig. 15.

4.5 Discussion and design options

The problems identified in the previous section are related to the to the parameter t. Designers must take into account this parameter in order to improve the quality of the application. However, the first two options of
Fig. 14 recommend to have a short delay associated to t while the last option of Fig. 15 recommend to have a long delay associated to t
This means that the probability of having disturbance in the rendering of the piano application will never be null. The maximum disturbance for the rendering is produced by the problem a) thus we should have a very short t. However, using an heavily loaded network the problem c) will occur each time the user holds the key thus resulting in an unusable application.
These three problems are the result of the X Window transducer presented in Fig. 11 because there is a loss of information when the transducer is in the pipeline an can be characterised in a generic way by the properties presented in section 2.
The first information that is lost is the number of keys that have been pressed by the user. Indeed as the transducer produces the same Down and Up events when the user has pressed a key or is holding it, it is no more possible to know how many times the user has pressed a given key. This can be overcome using the information that the Down event is emitted immediately after the Up one, but due to the client-server architecture of X Window they may be received significantly separated (problem C).
It can be easily proved that the X Window transducer of Fig. 11 is not *regular* and more precisely is *chatty* as it produces Up and Down events when no such events are received (the user is only holding the key).

5. Conclusion

The building of reliable interactive systems featuring a direct manipulation interface requires a clear understanding of all the input devices used by the user to drive the application.
In this paper we have discussed this thesis and proposed a transducer-based model in

order to cope with the problem of the design of such interactive systems. We have considered here keyboard-like input devices, but the approach can be directly generalised to graphical input devices such as mouse or track-ball from the work presented in [1]. We have characterised necessary properties for transducers that have been highlighted by the effective development of a piano application.

This work is part of a more ambitious project aiming at developing a toolkit for direct manipulation interfaces based on a formal description of all the basic bricks to be at the basis of the applications. Indeed, most of the applications currently developed for the management of Air Traffic Control present a direct manipulation interface and there is a need for both reliability and efficiency.

6. References

1. J. Accot, S. Chatty, P. Palanque. A Formal Description of Low Level Interaction and its Application to Multimodal Interactive Systems, In [18], pp. 92-104.

2. A. Albert. The effect of graphic input devices on performance in a cursor positioning task. In proceedings of the 26th Annual meeting of the Human Factor Society., 1982, pp. 54-58.

3. Ajmone-Marsan et al. Generalised Stochastic Petri nets, Wiley, 1996.

4. M. Beaudouin-Lafon, Y. Berteaud, S. Chatty. Creating direct manipulation interfaces with XTV. EX'90. European conference on the X Window System. London 1990.

5. A. Beck, C. Janssen, A. Weisbecker, J. Ziegler. Integrating object-oriented analysis and graphical user interface design. In Coutaz J. & Taylor R. (Eds) LNCS Springer Verlag 1995.

6. G. Booch & J. Rumbaugh Unified Method for Object-Oriented Development, Documentation Set Version 0.8, October 1995. Available by http at www.rational.com

7. W. Buxton. Lexical and Pragmatic Considerations of Input Structures. Computer Graphics, 17 (1), 31-37, 1983.

8. W. Buxton. There's more to interaction than meet the eye: Some issues in manual input. In Norman and Draper Eds. User Centered System Design: New Perspectives on Human-Computer Interaction, Hillsdale, NJ, Lawrence Erlbaum Publ. Pp. 319-337.

9. W. Buxton. A three state model of graphical input. In proceedings of the Interact'90 conference, p.449-456, North Holland 1990.

10. S. Card, J. Mackinlay, G. Robertson. The design space of input devices. In proceedings of ACM conference on Computer Human Interaction (CHI'90) pp.117-124.

11. L. Cardelli, R. Pike. Squeak: a Language for Communicating with Mice. In proceedings of the ACM conference on Graphics (SIGGRAPH'95), pp. 199-204.

12. S. Chatty. Defining the behaviour of animated interfaces. Engineering for Human Computer Interfaces conference 1992. p. 95-109. North-Holland.

13. S. Chatty. Extending a graphical toolkit for two-handed interaction. In ACM UIST'94, pages 195-204. ACM Press, 1994.

14. A. Dix. Formal Methods for Interactive Systems. Academic Press, 1991.

15. D. Duke, M. Harrison. Interaction and Tasks Requirements, in [17], pp. 54-76

16. Proceedings of the First Eurographics workshop on Design, Specification and Verification of Interactive Systems, F. Paternó Ed. Springer Verlag 1995.

17. Proceedings of the Second Eurographics workshop on Design, Specification and Verification of Interactive Systems, P. Palanque & R. Bastide Eds. Springer Verlag 1995.

18. Proceedings of the Third Eurographics workshop on Design, Specification and Verification of Interactive Systems,F. Bodard & J. Vanderdonckt Eds. Springer Verlag 1996.

19.   B. Epps, H. Snyder, W. Mutol. Comparison of six cursor devices on a target acquisition task. In proceedings of the Society for Information Display, 1986, pp. 302-305.

20.   O. Esteban, S. Chatty, P. Palanque. Whizz'Ed: a visual environment for building highly interactive interfaces. Proceedings of the Interact'95 conference, p. 121-126.

21.   G. Faconti, A. Fornari, N. Zani. Visual representation of formal specifications: an application to hierarchical logical input devices. In [16] pp. 349-367.

22.   G. Faconti, D. Duke. Device Models. In [18] pp. 73-91.

23.   F. Feldbrudge. Petri net tool overview 1992. Advances in Petri nets 1993. In G. Rozenberg (Ed.), Lecture Notes in Computer Science n° 674, p. 169-209. Springer Verlag 1993.

24.   K. Jensen. Coloured Petri nets. Vol. 1 (Basic concepts) and Vol. 2 (Analysis methods and practical use) Springer Verlag, 1995.

25.   C.W. Johnson. Literate Specifications. Software Engineering Journal, July 1996, pp. 225-237

26.   C.W. Johnson, S. Jones. Human Computer Interaction and Requirements Engineering, SIGCHI Bulletin, Editorial For Special Edition On HCI and Requirements, vol. 29, n°1, pp.31-32, 1997

27.   Lautenbach K. Linear algebraic techniques for Place/Transition Nets. Application and Theory of Petri nets, LNCS 254 & 255, Springer Verlag. 1986.

28.   J. McCarthy, P. Wright, M. Harrison. A requirements Space for Group-Work Systems. In Proceedings of Interact'95, pp. 283-288, Chapman & Hall.

29.   B. Meyer. Object-Oriented Software Construction. Prentice Hall 1988.

30.   P. Palanque & R. Bastide. Petri net based design of user-driven interfaces using the interactive cooperative object formalism. In [16], p. 383-401.

31.   P. Palanque & R. Bastide. Time modelling in Petri nets for the design of Interactive Systems. GIST workshop on Time in Interactive Systems. Glasgow, July 1995, and also SIGCHI bulletin vol 28 n°2, p. 43-46.

32.   P. Palanque, F. Paterno, R. Bastide, M. Mezzanotte Towards an integrated proposal for interactive systems design based on TLIM and MICO. In [18] pp 162-187.

33.   C. Ramstein et al. Touching and Hearing GUI's: Design issues for the PC-Access System. In ACM/ASSETS'96, ACM Press, pp. 2-10, 1996.

34.   W. Van Biljon. Extending Petri nets for specifying man-machine dialogues. Int. J. Man-Machine Studies (1988) 28, p. 437-455.

35.   A. Wasserman. Extending state transition diagrams for the specification of human-computer interaction. IEEE Transactions on Software Engineering, 11(8), August 1985.

From text to Petri Nets: the difficulties of describing accident scenarios formally

J. C. Hill and P. C. Wright

The Human Computer Interaction Group, Department of Computing Science,
University of York, Heslington, YO1 5DD, UK
{julia, pcw}@cs.york.ac.uk

Keywords: Authoring, Natural language, Petri Nets, Accident Reports, Safety Critical Systems

Much work has been carried out on using Petri Nets to describe interaction and the design of interactive systems. In this paper we are concerned with the use of Petri Nets to help describe accident scenarios. The issue here is that Petri Nets or some other formal notation might help eliminate ambiguities and imprecision that are characteristic of natural language descriptions in accident reports. We present a case study in which an attempt was made to describe a fragment of an aircraft accident report using a Petri Net description and identify four problems associated with this process. We argue that these problems can be overcome by the use of multiple renderings of the accident data. But this solution has its own problems of how to coordinate information from multiple renderings. A hypertext tool is outlined, which provides support for information coordination across multiple representations.

1. Introduction

Johnson, McCarthy and Wright (1995) argue that the information represented in accident reports was often unclear and ambiguous. The major reason for this, they said, was the reliance on natural language descriptions. For instance, it was argued that it was difficult to recover the temporal sequencing of events leading up to an accident from such narrative. Johnson et al. (op. cit.) suggested that formal notations in general, in particular the Petri Net notation (Reisig 1982), would be a useful utility as a means of supporting accident reports by providing a high level model of the accident in addition to the original textual presentation. This is because Petri Nets allow precision and unambiguity in causal and temporal sequencing. As an example, the Johnson et al. paper focuses on an aircraft accident report published by the UK Air Accident Investigation Branch (AAIB 1990), and in particular the first section entitled, *History of the flight* which is common to all AAIB reports. Johnson et al. demonstrated how the process of constructing a Petri Net description of the *History of the flight*, highlighted a number of ambiguities and causal relations in the text.

The aim of this paper is to identify more specifically, some of the imprecisions and ambiguities that may be encountered in the process of Petri Net construction from natural language texts and explores how these are resolved in the construction process. The core then of the paper is an examination of the difficulties that occur when information is abstracted from a natural language to create a formal model of the accident. During the research, four main areas of difficulties were found: (1) the need to force fit text to formalism; (2) the need to go beyond the information given in the accident description; (3) the need to aggregate information from multiple sources; and (4) the need to resolve structural ambiguity. We further argue, however, that such resolution leads to information loss and potential misrepresentation of the accident scenario, and that these problems are not just problems associated with the Petri Net notation, rather, they are problems general to many formalisation processes. We argue that the existence of ambiguities or vagueness in the natural language descriptions is a useful source of information to the reader alongside the exactness of formal models. In order to guide the development of a safety critical system, such as aircraft, the positive attributes of both these types of representations, we argue, could be made to work well together within a hypertext environment.

Following Johnson et al (op. cit.), this paper uses an aircraft accident report,[1] as a case study and basis for its research. The focus is on re-describing an aircraft accident report's *History of the flight* using Petri Net notation. Section 2 highlights the most important events identified in the text and are presented in the same order as the original report. Note that throughout this paper verbatim quotes from the AAIB report are enclosed in double quotation marks. Sections 3 and 4 examine and describe the difficulties of authoring Petri Net descriptions. Section 5 outlines a hypertext tool to resolve these difficulties.

2 Résumé of the Cowly incident, near Oxford [1]

On the 11th August 1991, a British Aerospace ATP (G-BMYK) took off from East Midlands airport on a scheduled flight to Jersey, Channel Islands and return; *"at 1423 hours with two pilots, two cabin crew and 59 passengers. [...] The commander set the propeller revolution per minute (rpm) to 85% after take-off and to 82.5% on passing FL80 in the climb to the assigned level of FL160. [...] The aircraft entered cloud just below FL130 at 160knots (kt) and a rate of climb of around 500 feet per minute (ft/min). [...] During the period that the aircraft entered cloud, the crew observed sleet and rain. At FL154, the commander requested Air Traffic Control (ATC) for a reduction in his cleared cruise level to FL140 but the controller was unable to approve the lower level immediately because it had already been allocated to another aircraft. In the event the maximum level achieved by the Advanced Turbo Prop (ATP) was FL156."*

"The engine and propeller ice protection systems had remained switched on from take-off and both pilots had been looking for signs of airframe ice, in order to determine if operation of the airframe de-icing boots was necessary. The only indication of ice was rime ice on the leading edges of the wings and three eighths of an inch of rime ice on the windscreen wiper arm. The outside air temperature (OAT) was between -2°C and -5°C and the total air temperature (TAT) was calculated to have fallen to -2°C. The aircraft was being flown by the autopilot in the heading mode with the attitude being controlled by the autopilot pitch wheel."

---

[1] The résumé is taken from: AAIB (1992), *Report on the incident to British Aerospace ATP, G-BMYK, 10 miles north of COWLY, near Oxford, on 11 August 1991*, Aircraft Accident Report 4/92, Air Accidents Investigation Branch, Department of Transport, HMSO, pp.1-4.

"At 1444 hrs, when the aircraft was at FL156, it began to experience vibration which rapidly increased in severity. The vibration was thought by the cabin attendants to be more severe in the rear of the aircraft than at the front. Both pilots had experienced propeller icing and associated vibration on an ATP before but on this occasion they thought it to be much more extreme [...] while the severe vibration lasted" the electronic flight instruments became partially unreadable (Synopsis, p. 1).

"Shortly after the onset of the vibration the left wing dropped and the aircraft began to descend, the aircraft initially pitched down approximately 15° and began a rolling oscillation. The commander said that at the point of initial wing drop he disengaged autopilot and flew the aircraft manually. He felt that the aircraft was slow to respond to aileron control inputs and large bank angles were reached, particularly to the left, where a single peak 68° of bank was recorded."

"During the period of roll oscillation and rapid descent the first officer transmitted a 'PAN' call and altered the transponder to the emergency code 7700. He also switched the airframe de-icing to ON."

"The aircraft descended below the cloud base at FL130 at about that time the vibration subsided[...]." Control was fully regained by FL120. *"[...] The crew reported that at no time during the incident were they aware of a warning from the pre-stall warning system (PSW). [...] Now clear of icing conditions, the commander continued to Jersey clear of cloud, and the remainder of the flight was uneventful to its destination."* Injuries were either minor or none. (Injuries to persons, p. 4) (AAIB 4/92, p. 3-4).

3. Petri Nets and applying them to accident reports

Petri Nets (Reisig 1982), a form of directed graph, are used to model and explore certain properties of concurrent systems, statically and/or dynamically. In particular Petri Nets focus on the transfer of information and synchronous properties. This information can be represented using formal, mathematically-based notation, or represented pictorially using symbology (Oxford Reference 1990). In accordance with Johnson et al. (op. cit.), this paper focuses solely on the pictorial representation of Petri Nets. This is because graphical representations of graphs are accessible to a wider variety of people than is a formal mathematical notation.

Petri Nets formally consist of a set of *places* P , *transitions* T, *edges* E and *tokens* M; this is symbolised by PN = (P, T, E, M) (Johnson et al. op. cit.). *Edges* connect together two types of nodes: *places* (depicted as clear circles) and *transitions* (depicted as bars). Places may only be connected to transitions, and transitions may only be connected to places (Biljon 1988, p. 440) and are linked together using edges (arrows). Figures 1 and 2 are extracts from the Petri Net in figure 4 which is created mainly from the Cowly report's *History of the flight.* The supporting text contains summarised versions of events from the subsection's text.

An instance of a place is known as a condition, and likewise, a transition is known as an event. In natural language and logic, *conditions* and *events* can be compared to "only if X then Y" clauses. Before an event can occur, its conditions must hold. To help signify the difference between conditions and events, a *condition* can be thought of as occurring over a *period of time*, whereas an *event* represents

164

logically a *point in time*, or an instantaneous occurrence, although in real time this can never be the case. For example, the first condition in figure 1 says, *the aircraft is ready to take off with engine and ice propeller switched on*, and the following event is, *the aircraft takes off at 1423 hours*; meaning, the aircraft can take off if it is ready.

Fig. 1   Fig. 2

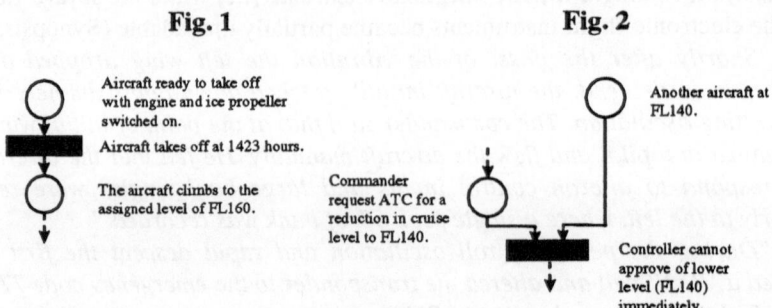

In an accident scenario, according to Johnson et al. (op. cit.), edges can be used to connect together the conditions and events that lead up to a specific action occurring or the accident itself. Places signify conditions acting as preconditions to the events in the accident scenario; in particular, they can signify preconditions for disaster (Johnson et al. op.cit.). Transitions signify events initiated by an operator or the aircraft system. For instance, in the *History of the flight* of the *Cowly* report (figure 2), it states that the Air Traffic Controller does not allow the aircraft to cruise at a lower level because it has been allocated to another aircraft. The event here is that the controller does not allow the aircraft to cruise at the lower level. The preconditions to this event are: a) the G-BMYK Commander requests permission for the aircraft to cruise at the lower level of FL140; and b) another aircraft is already at this level. Alternatively, places can represent the behaviour of a particular system (Johnson et al. op. cit.), for example, the partially unreadable electronic flight instruments (figure 4).

Since the information structures within the text of the *History of the flight* are sequential and concurrent in their nature, Petri Nets are extremely suitable to represent these structures pictorially. Figure 4 shows how concurrent and sequential structures fit together. The Petri Net allows the linear sequencing of logical time to be shown in conjunction with sequential and concurrent events. The events are displayed clearly by the definite pictorial representation of transitions, giving the reader's eyes focus points on the page and in so doing, aiding the reader in their comprehension of the accident.

4. Problems of constructing Petri Nets from accident texts

In response to the Johnson et al. (op. cit.) paper, we constructed the Petri Net in Figure 4 re-describing what happened based on the information in the *History of the flight* from the Cowly report (AAIB 1992). The process of constructing this Petri Net from the natural language text of the accident report, led us to identify a number potential difficulties that face the Petri Net author involved in accident re-description.

The four most significant of these problems are described below; they are: (1) forcing a fit between text and the Petri Net; (2) the need to go beyond the information given in the text of the accident description; (3) the need to aggregate information from multiple sources; and (4) the problem of resolving structural ambiguity.

Fig. 4

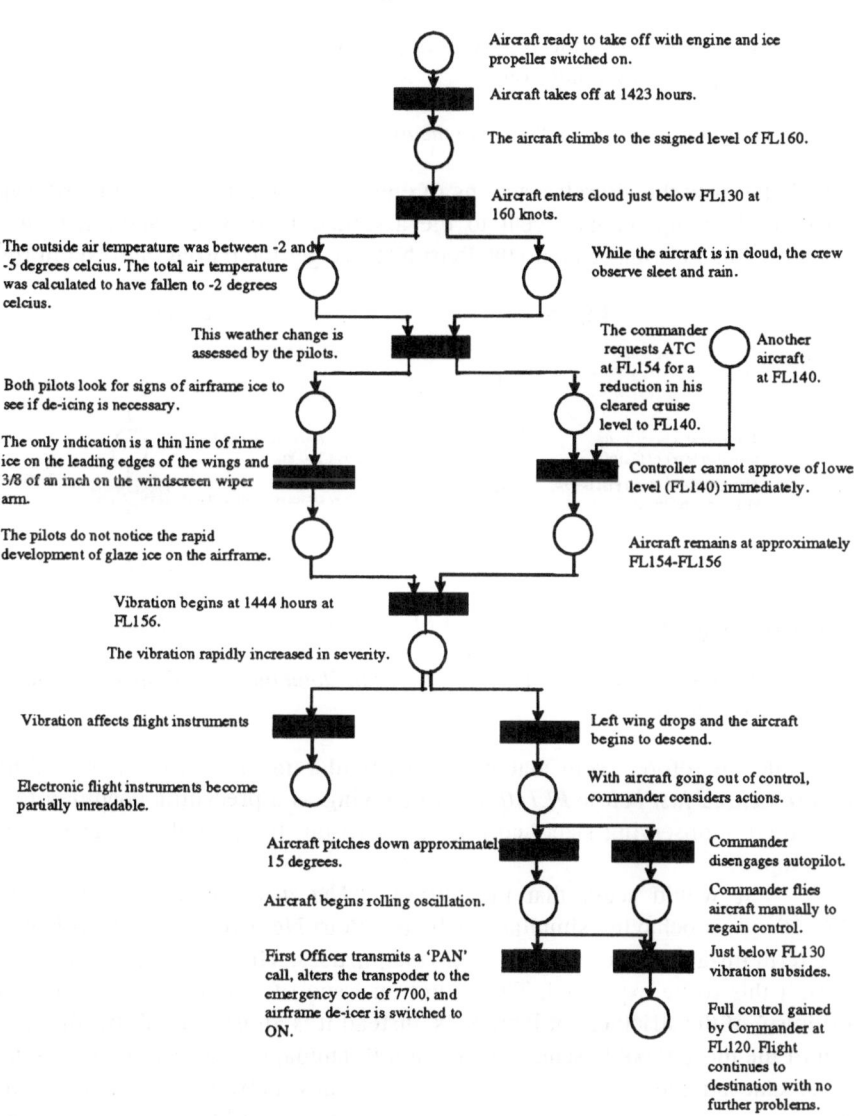

Aircraft ready to take off with engine and ice propeller switched on.

Aircraft takes off at 1423 hours.

The aircraft climbs to the ssigned level of FL160.

Aircraft enters cloud just below FL130 at 160 knots.

The outside air temperature was between -2 and -5 degrees celcius. The total air temperature was calculated to have fallen to -2 degrees celcius.

While the aircraft is in cloud, the crew observe sleet and rain.

This weather change is assessed by the pilots.

The commander requests ATC at FL154 for a reduction in his cleared cruise level to FL140.

Another aircraft at FL140.

Both pilots look for signs of airframe ice to see if de-icing is necessary.

The only indication is a thin line of rime ice on the leading edges of the wings and 3/8 of an inch on the windscreen wiper arm.

Controller cannot approve of lower level (FL140) immediately.

The pilots do not notice the rapid development of glaze ice on the airframe.

Aircraft remains at approximately FL154-FL156

Vibration begins at 1444 hours at FL156.

The vibration rapidly increased in severity.

Vibration affects flight instruments

Left wing drops and the aircraft begins to descend.

Electronic flight instruments become partially unreadable.

With aircraft going out of control, commander considers actions.

Aircraft pitches down approximatel 15 degrees.

Commander disengages autopilot.

Aircraft begins rolling oscillation.

Commander flies aircraft manually to regain control.

First Officer transmits a 'PAN' call, alters the transpoder to the emergency code of 7700, and airframe de-icer is switched to ON.

Just below FL130 vibration subsides.

Full control gained by Commander at FL120. Flight continues to destination with no further problems.

4.1 Forcing a fit: dual-role phrases

The issue in this first section is one that highlights the difference between the semantic structures of natural language and that of petri nets. Take the phrase:

> *"The aircraft entered cloud just below FL130 at 160 knots (kt) and at a rate of climb of around 500 feet per minute" (p.3).*

Read sequentially from the report, this phrase at first appears to act as a Petri Net event to the preceding condition,

> The aircraft was on its *"climb to the assigned level of FL160"* (p. 3).

This is because the aircraft's actions of entering cloud just below FL130 was a direct result of it being on its ascent to the assigned level after take-off. Consequently, mapping this information onto the Petri Net, we get the partial Petri Net in figure 5.

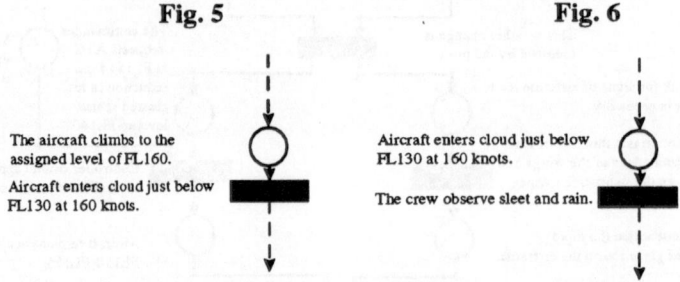

However, reading on through the text of *the History of the flight,* it is seen that:

> *"During the period that the aircraft was in cloud the crew observed sleet and rain."* (p.3)

It would, therefore, seem that in this particular instance the phrase, *"The aircraft entered cloud just below FL130..."* is behaving as a preceding condition to the event of the crew observing sleet and rain. As a result, the partial Petri Net in figure 6 is developed.

It would seem that the phrase, *"The aircraft entered cloud just below FL130..."* is behaving simultaneously as a Petri Net event and a Petri Net condition. We term instances likes these as *dual-role phrases*. The semantics of Petri Nets do not permit this to be expressed. This is not an issue of ambiguity in the text nor is it a criticism of the strictness of Petri Nets, instead it is an issue of abstracting information out of the more flexible semantics of natural language to the stricter semantics of petri nets. One simple way to solve this discrepancy between two diverse information structures is to decide which role a dual-role phrase will play. It can be seen in figure 4 that the authors chose this particular dual-role phrase to behave as an event.

4.2 Going beyond the information in the text

The issue here is that the author of the Petri Net may have to make inferences beyond that which is explicitly stated in the text of the *History of the flight* in order to map successfully onto the condition-event syntax of Petri Net notation. Consider the following example:

> *"During the period that the aircraft was in cloud* [from FL130 upwards] *the crew observed sleet and rain. At FL154 the commander requested Air Traffic Control (ATC) for a reduction in his cleared cruise level to FL140 but the controller was unable to approve the lower level immediately because it had already been allocated to another aircraft".* (p.3)

In attempting to map the above text to the Petri Net structure we began by representing the phrase, *"...but the controller was unable to approve the lower level immediately because it had already been allocated to another aircraft",* as a Petri Net event. This seemed relatively intuitive and non-controversial. The syntactic constraints of the notation thus lead to the following partial Petri Net (figure 7).

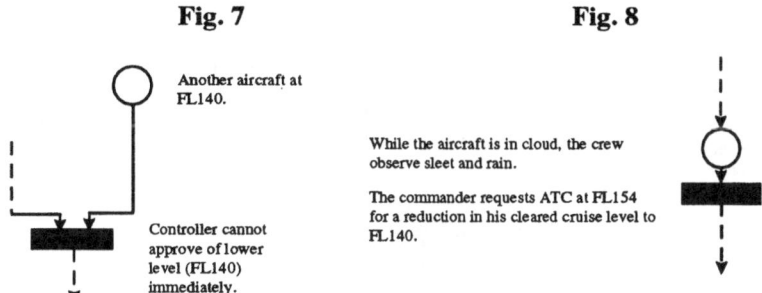

Fig. 7   **Fig. 8**

Another aircraft at FL140.

Controller cannot approve of lower level (FL140) immediately.

While the aircraft is in cloud, the crew observe sleet and rain.

The commander requests ATC at FL154 for a reduction in his cleared cruise level to FL140.

In addition, we analysed the phrase, *"During the period that the aircraft was in cloud* [from FL130 upwards] *the crew observed sleet and rain",* as a Petri Net condition and the phrase, *"At FL154 the commander requested Air Traffic Control (ATC) for a reduction in his cleared cruise level to FL140...",* as a Petri Net event which again seemed intuitively obvious. The result is shown in the partial Petri Net in figure 8. It was found that when the two partial Petri Nets (figures 7 and 8) were brought together, a structural problem occurred, this being the placement of two events adjacent to one another (figure 9).

One solution to this problem is realising that the phrase, *"At FL154 the commander requested Air Traffic Control (ATC) for a reduction in his cleared cruise level to FL140...",* is actually a dual-role phrase. It can be reinterpreted as the preceding condition to the event, Air Traffic Control being unable to approve of a lower cruise level.

Unfortunately, on closer examination, this seems to do violence to the underlying semantics of the scenario because the causal connection between *"During the period that the aircraft was in cloud* [from FL130 upwards] *the crew observed sleet and rain"* and *"At FL154 the commander requested Air Traffic Control (ATC) for a reduction in his cleared cruise level to FL140..."* is misrepresented.

Fig. 9

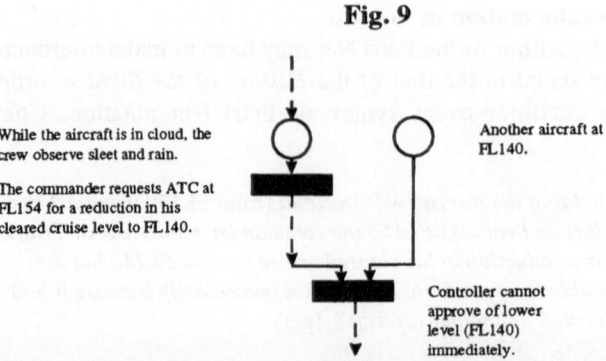

There are now two conditions together sequentially which brings us back to the same problem of structural clashing represented in figure 9. Figure 10 illustrates this.

Fig. 10

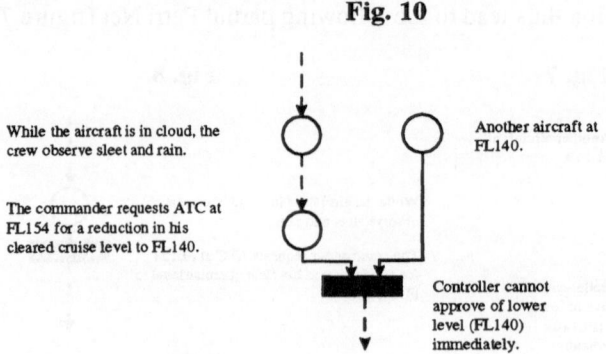

There is, however, a solution to the two sequential events in figure 9. This is to infer an additional condition between the event, *"At FL154 the commander*

Fig. 11

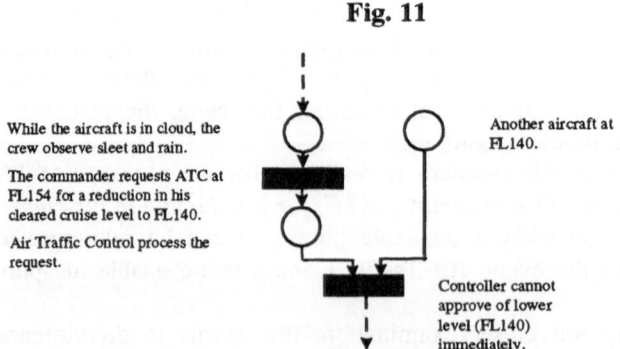

requested Air Traffic Control (ATC) for a reduction in his cleared cruise level to FL140...", and the event, *"...but the controller was unable to approve the lower level immediately because it had already been allocated to another aircraft".* For example, if the condition, *Air Traffic Control process the request,* is inferred from the text and our world knowledge, it is possible to complete the partial Petri Net as presented in figure 11. However, there is no evidence in the text to support this inference.

4.3 The need to aggregate information to build petri nets

The third issue is that the Petri Net author may have to aggregate information which, although is explicitly stated in the text of the report, is not part of the *History of the flight* itself. By doing so, the Petri Net author can map the events of the accident onto the condition-event sequence more successfully. Consider the following example:

> *"...both pilots had been looking for signs of airframe ice, in order to determine if operation of the airframe de-icing boots was necessary. The only indication was a thin line of what they described as rime ice on the leading edges of the wings and three eighths of an inch of rime ice on the windscreen wiper arm...At 1444 hrs, when the aircraft was at FL156, it began to experience vibration which rapidly increased in severity."* (p. 3)

When considered in isolation, this phrase can be taken at face value to lead to the partial Petri Net in figure 12. However, it can be seen that there is a gap in this partial Petri Net between the two events. This is because there seems to be no other information in the text of the *History of the flight* that could be behave as the preceding condition to the event, Vibration begins at 1444 hours at FL156.

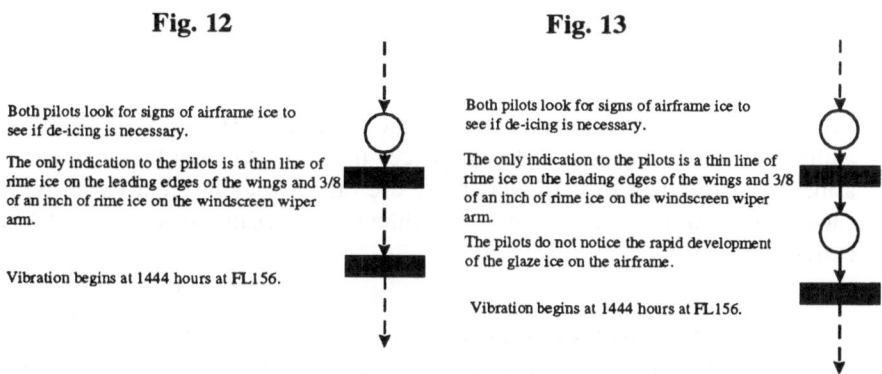

Fig. 12

Both pilots look for signs of airframe ice to see if de-icing is necessary.

The only indication to the pilots is a thin line of rime ice on the leading edges of the wings and 3/8 of an inch of rime ice on the windscreen wiper arm.

Vibration begins at 1444 hours at FL156.

Fig. 13

Both pilots look for signs of airframe ice to see if de-icing is necessary.

The only indication to the pilots is a thin line of rime ice on the leading edges of the wings and 3/8 of an inch of rime ice on the windscreen wiper arm.

The pilots do not notice the rapid development of the glaze ice on the airframe.

Vibration begins at 1444 hours at FL156.

Consequently, we found that it was necessary to search the rest of the report for the answer in order to fill in the gap. The information,

> *"The rapid accumulation of glaze ice, which was not evident to the crew, but which produced significant aerodynamic degradation",* (p. 1, p. 40)

found in the *Synopsis* and *Conclusions* shows us that the pilots had not seen the glaze ice on the airframe when they had been looking. The phrase, *"The only indication* [to the pilots] *was...",* in the *History of the flight,* however, does lend the author a clue that there was more ice developing out of sight of the pilots' visual range. This piece of additional information allows us to modify the Petri Net seen in figure 13.

It is clear then from this illustration of the importance of information distributed elsewhere in the text of the report other than the *History of the flight* itself in order to build a Petri Net model of the accident. With respect to this example, this extra information has permitted us to know that other types of ice were also developing. The phrase, *"the only indication..."*, therefore, carries more weight than first realised. If they had seen any signs of glaze ice, they probably would have operated the de-icing boots and the outcome of the flight would have most likely been different (see Analysis 2.2.3, p. 30).

Not only can information in the text of the report change the structure of the Petri Net, it can also change the relevance of other events and conditions. Consider as an example the following extract from the BMA's ATP Operations Manual in section 1.6.3.4, *Anti-ice and de-ice operating procedures*, of the report:

> *"The first in-flight indication of airframe ice build-up is apparent on the windscreen wipers and this is used to alert the crew to the need for wing leading edge inspection. When approximately ½ inch of ice has accumulated the airframe de-icing system is selected ON at the required level. The broken ice from the wing leading edges is removed by the airflow" (Volume 8, page 8.13.1).* [p. 9]

Having knowledge of this extra piece of information has relevance to the information that there was three eighths of an inch of rime ice on the windscreen wiper arm. This relevance cannot be seen easily in the text of the report since it is located in another part of the accident report.

4.4 Structural ambiguity

In sections 4.1 and 4.2 we saw how the Petri Net author was forced to collect additional information and make inferences from the accident text in order to execute a mapping from text to Petri Net. There are other cases in the accident report where such a resolution is not possible to achieve. For example, consider the following extract:

> *"The engine and propeller ice protection systems had remained switched on from take-off and both pilots had been looking for signs of airframe ice, in order to determine if operation of the airframe de-icing boots was necessary".* (p. 3)

In the text of the *History of the flight*, this extract is at the beginning of paragraph 2 breaking up the temporal sequence of the flight's history which flows linearly from the first paragraph to the third paragraph. The latter half of paragraph 1 mentions that the aircraft was in cloud, sleet and rain and that the commander had been refused permission to fly the aircraft at a lower level, and it finished stating that:

> *"In the event the maximum level achieved by the Advanced Turbo Prop (ATP) was FL156"* (p. 3)

Paragraph 3 picks up the temporal sequence by first stating that:

"At 1444 hrs, when the aircraft was at FL156, it began to experience vibration which rapidly increased in severity" (p. 3)

Consequently, there is confusion about when the pilots did begin looking for signs for airframe ice. If the extract from the beginning of paragraph 2 is read by itself, it seems that the pilots started to look for signs of airframe ice from the beginning of the flight; this is the first interpretation. Conversely, when paragraph 2 is read in linear sequence, it can be interpreted in this second way: the pilots' had started to look for signs of airframe icing from when the aircraft entered cloud. These two possible interpretations of the pilots' actions conflict and as a result can cause different Petri Nets to be created.

Figures 14 and 15 show the two partial Petri Nets depicting these different structures. The first partial Petri Net (figure 14) is a representation of the first interpretation. The second partial Petri Net (figure 15) and extracted from figure 4, is a representation of the second interpretation of paragraph 2. The appropriate text on both the Petri Nets are highlighted by the rectangle.

Since it is not clear from the text when the pilots actually did start looking for signs of airframe ice, the issue here is whether the analysts should provide all possible Petri Net interpretations in order to maintain the readers awareness of ambiguity or whether they should opt for one representation of the accident. The latter solution, of course effectively leads to information loss on the part of the reader which is the problem discussed in section 5.

Fig. 14   **Fig.15**

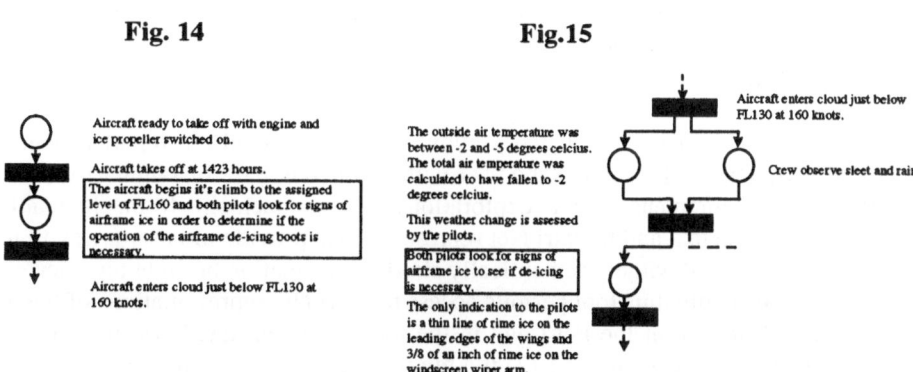

5. Coordinating information structures

Our description of the process of constructing Petri Nets models of the accident from the report's textual descriptions and the difficulties we encountered can be taken to imply a number of different things. The first is that besides providing a high level model of an accident, Petri Nets are indeed very useful tools for highlighting weaknesses in the textual descriptions. This is certainly true in some cases, for example, the need to aggregate information from different parts of the accident report can be seen as highlighting a flaw in the design of the texts. A second interpretation is that Petri Nets are not sufficiently rich as a formalism to be of use in accident analysis. The problems we encountered with dual phrases and the need to make inferences beyond the information given, are examples of the 'poor fit'.

Both of these interpretations are premised on the idea that Petri Nets might be used to refine or even replace the existing textual description of the accident. Such an interpretation would be consistent with the idea that all ambiguities and vagueness should be expunged from accident description.

From a linguistic perspective, however, it is often argued that the unique value of natural language description is to support the reader viewing the description from a number of different perspectives and to emphasise the uncertainty there may be on what is actually the case. For example, ambiguity of meaning in an accident report may indicate an area where the report authors themselves were not sure about a piece of evidence. In this view, natural language provides a valuable representational format that might stand alongside a more formal description.

This leads us to a final interpretation of our analysis. Which is, there is a role for both textual and formal representations. This has a number of practical advantages concerning the use of accident reports by a non-formalist audience, but more importantly it resolves what we have termed the dilemma of abstraction.

5.1 Coordinating information structures through a hypertext tool

At this point, we have two types of information structures that are used to represent accidents, accident reports and Petri Nets. Both have advantages and disadvantages but we feel that both are necessary in order to communicate different levels of information to the reader. We argue that a hypertext tool is required to bring these two types of communication modes together in order for the reader to appreciate both types of information structures. A working prototype of this tool is currently available.

This hypertext tool firstly allows the user to read the report as it is seen in hard copy format. It provides the user with a concrete base of familiarity from which they could commence their explorations of the accident from. Semantic links throughout the text and to Petri Net representations provide the user a way to navigate the document and witness semantically similar information brought together.

Secondly, this tool permits access to Petri Net representations of the accident scenario. The role of the Petri Net in the tool has been developed to provide (1) an overview of the accident, and (2) the temporal and causal sequences of the accident, both of which Johnson et al (op. cit.) indicated. Point (1) is concerned with letting the user see a brief representation of the accident having been rid of the extraneous material in the text. In so doing it allows the user to view the accident removed from the complexities of the text. Point (2) is concerned with letting the user see clearly one interpretation of how the incident flight developed.

Most importantly, however, this hypertext tool allows there to be semantic (electronic) links between items in the original text and on the Petri Net, thus drawing together the two types of information structures. These links allow the user to witness at some degree the decisions taken by the Petri Net author with respect to the ambiguities in the text and the process of moving between two diverse representations. Furthermore, these links allow semantically similar information to be collated together through a series of electronic links. In turn, this prevents the dangers of information loss and misrepresentation that accompany abstraction, and at the same time, the user has access to a representation that has attempted to rid the accident scenario of all its ambiguities and imprecisions. As a result, this tool through a series of electronic links gives the user all the semantic advantages of both types of information structures giving them a more heuristic picture of flight's history.

Fig. 16

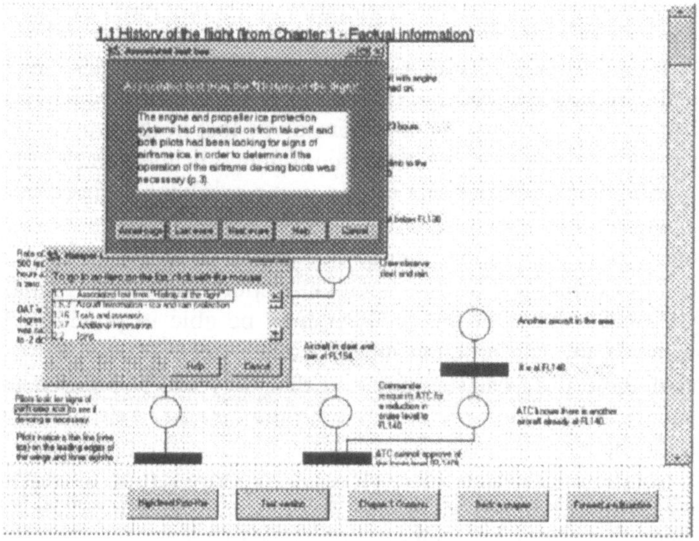

Figure 16 shows an example screen dump from the prototype. This screen shows a window of standard design with a title bar, menu bar and scroll bar functions. The display itself is of a Petri Net of which the user is navigating in order to see where in the original text the condition, *Pilots look for airframe ice to see if de-icing is necessary,* was extracted from. The user from here has a number of options open. They can navigate up and down the Petri Net using the command buttons, *Next event, Last event, Next condition* and *Last conditions,* on the *Associated text box* to observe the original text from where the various conditions and events were extracted. Another option is to navigate from the pop-up menu below the *Associated text box.* From here users can move easily to other parts of the document to which the aircraft condition, airframe ice, has semantic relations.

Conclusions

In this paper we identified a number of problems with the process of constructing Petri Net descriptions from textual accident reports. From a purely formal perspective the problems encountered were not surprising ones. It may be that in one guise or another they are an inevitable consequence of trying to map natural language semantics and discourse styles onto a much sparser formal semantics. Indeed it could argued that the identification of these problems is precisely the reason for attempting such a formalisation.

However, our interpretation of the results is that there is a need for providing the users of accident reports with a number of different representations. We adopt this interpretation for various reasons. Perhaps the most fundamental is a concern that by introducing formalism as a means of capturing accident information in an unambiguous way, a number of inherent dangers arise. A key concern, for instance, is the fact that if the author is required to resolve ambiguities or go beyond the information given in the formal notation, there is no guidance within the notation itself as to how to do this. Different authors may resolve ambiguities in different ways. Furthermore, from a readers point of view the notation alone provides no indication of this resolution process. This includes the decisions made by the author which result in information loss that are themselves lost in the process. For example, the fact that formalism tends to instill overconfidence in the veracity of results may lead to undue confidence per se being placed in the resultant formal description of an accident's history.

Despite these reservations, we do accept the conclusion that there is a need for multiple representations of the accident report, and that graphical models representing various aspects of the accident may be able to provide a new way at analysing the accident. The problem then becomes one of how do we support the coordination of these different structures so that they might be used together in a synergetic way, to help readers see clearly both the detail and the abstraction and the relation between them?

Our solution has been to explore a hypertext tool to support multiple representations. This solution is more than just throwing new interface technology at a problem. It is a solution that allows the user to see drawn together, different information structures of the same accident. By doing this, the user receives the best of both the worlds of textual descriptions and formalisms. Having the original text accessible together with a Petri Net representation connected by a semantically rich set of electronic links, there is no fear of information loss and misrepresentation that is inherent in formalisms. At the same time, the ambiguities in the text are highlighted using formal graphical notations. Therefore, by having direct access in the tool to both representations, the move to a formal notation allows the user to review an abstraction which is not bound up in the danger associated with self-standing formal notation representations. Furthermore, having access to the original text from where conditions and events are taken from enables the user to hopefully recreate in their own minds of the decision process that the author of the Petri Net underwent themselves. By having this facility, a deeper understanding of the complexities of the accident and the process of moving from a textual notation to a formal notation may be achieved.

At the moment our research has been purely theoretical. We hope to in future research to test some of the ideas outlined in this paper. Firstly we intend to request a number of formalists and non-formalist to create Petri Nets of the accident to examine how different their interpretations of the accident are. Secondly we intend to research empirically how having a formal high level model of the accident assists with the process of accident analysis and test this data against people using only the original text. Finally, we hope to test this hypertext prototype to analyse the benefits it would draw in for accident analysis.

References

1. AAIB (1990), *Report on the accident to Boeing 737-400G-OBME near Kegworth, Leicestershire on 8 January 1989.* Aircraft Accident Report 4/90. Air Accidents Investigation Branch, Department of Transport, HMSO.

2. AAIB (1992), *Report on the incident to British Aerospace ATP, G-BMYK, 10 miles north of COWLY, near Oxford on 11 August 1991*, Aircraft Accident Report 4/92, Air Accident Investigation Branch Department of Transport, HMSO.

3. Bignell, V and Fortune, J. (1984), *Understanding systems failures,* Manchester University Press.

4. Biljon, W. R. van (1988), *Extending Petri Nets for specifying man-machine dialogues*, Man-Machine Studies, **28**, p. 437.

5. Johnson, C. W., (1993), *The Application of Petri Nets to Represent and Reason About Human Factors Problems During Accident Analysis*, Department of Computer Science, University of York.

6. Johnson, C. W., McCarthy, J. C., Wright, P. C. (1995), *Using a formal language to support natural language in accident reports*, Ergonomics Vol. **38.6**, pp. 1265-1283.

7. McKnight, C., Dillon, A., Richardson, J. (1991), *Hypertext in Context*, CUP.

8. Meziane, F. and Vadera, S. (1993), *From English to Formal Specifications*, Technical Report MCS-93-06, Department of Mathematics and Computer Science, University of Salford.

9. Nielson, J. (1990), *Hypertext and Hypermedia*, Academic Press, Inc.

10. Oxford Reference (1990), *Dictionary of Computing*, 3rd edition, OUP.

11. Palanque, P. and Bastide, R. (1996), *Time Modelling in Petri Nets for the Design of Interactive Systems*, SIGCHI, **28.2**, p. 43.

12. Peterson, J. L. (1977), *Petri Nets*, Computing Surveys, **9**, p. 223.

13. Preece, J., Rogers, Y., Sharp, H., Benyon, D., Holland, S., Carey, T. (1994), *Human-Computer Interaction*, Addison-Wesley.

14. Reisig, W. (1982), *Petri Nets, An Introduction*, Springer-Verlag (1982).

15. Shneiderman, B. and Kearsley, G. (1989), *Hypertext Hands-On!: An Introduction to a New way of Organizing and Accessing Information*, Addison-Wesley .

Unifying Toolkit Programming Layers:
a Multi-purpose Toolkit Integration Module

Anthony Savidis, Constantine Stephanidis and Demosthenes Akoumianakis

Institute of Computer Science,
Foundation for Research and Technology-Hellas (FORTH),
Science and Technology Park of Crete,
P.O. Box 1385, GR 711 10, Heraklion, Crete, Greece,
Tel: +30-81-391741, Fax: +30-81-391740
E-mails: {as, cs, demosthe}@ics.forth.gr

Abstract Learning to program with interface toolkits requires a considerable amount of time, while programmers familiar with one toolkit require considerable additional training before being able to effectively use another toolkit. Even though virtual toolkits have contributed positively in this context, users of virtual toolkits are not enabled: (i) to locally incorporate a new toolkit, or (ii) to extend or modify the supplied programming layer. A tool has been developed, called PIM, through which interface developers may establish the desired programming layers on top of toolkits, with reduced development effort. The PIM tool provides: (a) a language for the specification of the desired programming layers for toolkits; (b) a compiler to translate such a specification to a C++ software library (i.e. generated programming layer); and (c) an asynchronous communication library, called generic toolkit interfacing protocol, for "connecting" the generated programming layer with the original target toolkit.

1 Introduction

Interface toolkits [10] require a considerable learning time before effective programming with the supplied interaction elements can be practically achieved. Programmers that already utilise a particular toolkit, will normally have to spend a significant amount of time, in order to reach the same level of programming knowledge and ability for another toolkit. Virtual toolkits [10], also called cross-platform or multi-platform toolkits, provide a single fixed programming layer over specific number of target toolkits (i.e. platforms). Through virtual toolkits, client programs can be built which are re-targetable [4] to the supported (by the virtual toolkit) platforms. Consider the following situations: (a) a new toolkit needs to be incorporated; (b) new interaction facilities are added within one of the target toolkits; (c) development experimentation is required for purposely designed sets of generic interaction primitives, particularly suited to relatively new domains (e.g. Virtual Reality applications, non-visual auditory / tactile interaction, interfaces for motor-impaired users); (d) some aspects of the programming layer need to be changed (e.g. naming conventions, changing the programming layer for a GKS-like component, from an OO model to a traditional procedural model) due to the needs of the target programmers (some programmers have been used to manipulate entities with specific names and used to program graphics for a long time with function calls, instead of managing object instantiations); and (e) there is a need to provide a simple and primitive set of programming interaction elements for teaching purposes. The first three situations concern technical needs, while the last two are related to human-programmer needs; virtual toolkits currently fail to support these needs.

1.1 Related work

Throughout this paper, we will use the term programming interface as a synonym to programming layer; both terms will concern the non-interactive programming picture of a software library for end-programmers. Apart from virtual toolkits, significant previous work can be identified, potentially related to the issue of programming interfaces for toolkits. Interaction tasks [6] captured various input behavioural aspects in direct manipulation graphical interfaces, while Interactors [9] provided a generic set of highly parameterized primitives through which complex interactions can be assembled in a modular manner. Both approaches practically provided alternative structural and behavioural views for the lexical level of interaction, which can be also faced as powerful and highly expressive programming models. The issue of platform integration is addressed in the SERPENT language-based UIMS [3], which introduced the concept of lexical technology integration [5] and lexical technology interface specification. In SERPENT, only object-based toolkits can be integrated. The HOMER language-based UIMS [13] also supported integration of toolkits, by providing a toolkit integration model that allowed virtually any type of interaction element to be imported (apart from object-based items).

In both previous platform integration approaches (i.e. of SERPENT and HOMER) the manipulation of the imported toolkit elements is possible only in the context of their respective dialogue specification languages. As a result, the five situation scenarios that we have previously identified, practically still remain today without any solution, when widely used programming languages are employed for interactive software development. Approaches such as SUIT [11] have been proved valuable and enabled support for quick-learning of interface programming. SUIT offered a simple, though powerful programming model, for assembling interfaces with objects. However, apart from the required simplicity of a programming model, it is important to also support incremental complexity of the supplied set of interaction elements for teaching purposes; for instance, an initial small set of common interaction objects with a specifically chosen set of attributes, could be transformed to a rich set of comprehensive elements (even naming conventions may be different from the initial simple versions).

1.2 The PIM tool

A tool has been developed, called PIM (Platform Integration Module) which, seen from a functionality point of view, automates the process of establishing desirable C++ programming layers on top of toolkits. The exploitation opportunities of such a technical capability for different types of relevant problems will be shown, and it will be demonstrated how the advantages are beyond the low-level technical, and enable enhancement of the overall development process. In the context of the PIM tool, a toolkit is considered to be any software library (independently of the way its implementation is structured) which provides to software developers a collection of elements for building interactions. It should be noted that we will use the term "specification" to designate source text compliant to a particular 4GL (as in UIMSs), and not to imply "formal specification" which has a clearly different meaning.

The process of building a programming layer (on top of a particular toolkit) via the PIM tool, is realized via the following three stages: (i) specification of the desired programming layer through the PIM language; (ii) translation of the supplied specification to a corresponding C++ software programming layer by the PIM compiler; and (iii) implementation of a toolkit server (or servers) which will "connect" a generated programming layer (GPL) with the target toolkit or toolkits. A toolkit server (TS) will play the role of a run-time "translator", while the generic toolkit interface protocol (GTIP) library of the PIM tool must be utilised for implementing the asynchronous communication between the TS and the GPL components. The interfaces developed with PIM programming interfaces realize the native "look & feel" of the underlying toolkits.

1.3   Overall contributions of this work

In the course of developing the PIM tool, a number of technical milestones have been produced which may be directly employed and used in the context of User Interface tool development. These outcomes are not tight to a specific metaphor of interaction, like graphical windowing-based interaction; indeed, they have already been applied for alternative interaction approaches (i.e. non-visual auditory tactile interaction, augmented windowing-based interaction for motor-impaired users), as it will be discussed later on. These milestones are:

(a)   the *generic toolkit meta-model*, which can be employed in all situations where a generally applicable physical level representation method is needed (e.g. UIMSs, design-based tools, user modelling tools encompassing knowledge on the physical level of interaction);

(b)   the *toolkit interface specification language* (i.e. the PIM language), which can be used in all situations where the functional aspects of an interface toolkit (which does not include the behavioural aspects of its elements), need to be represented within another appropriate meta-layer (e.g. UIMSs, design-based tools);

(c)   the *generic toolkit interface protocol*, which may be employed in all cases where the dialogue control logic (i.e. interactive application client) must be physically separated (and possibly running remotely) from the real toolkit implementation (i.e. toolkit server); and

(d)   the *task-based attribute defaults' method*, which introduces an approach of bridging low-level external attribute defaults' specification, with the real interface design structure (user task hierarchy), that can be implemented as part of any category of interface development tools.

2   Generic programming meta-model for toolkit elements

This model constituted the basis for the design of the PIM language, which facilitates the specification of the desired programming layer structure. According to this model, toolkits are considered to support three fundamental categories of elements: *objects*, *input events* and *output events*. Description of each such category follows:

2.1   Objects

Objects have an arbitrary number of typed *attributes* (like "x","font","text", etc) and an arbitrary number of *methods* (like "Selected","Pressed","FocusIn", etc). Methods typically characterize what the user is able to do with an object (e.g selecting an option, pressing the button). Apart from conventional interaction objects (e.g. "Buttons", "Textfields"), objects can represent graphic interaction elements (e.g. "Lines", "Circles"). In this case, the attributes of an object will correspond to the parameters of the particular graphic element (e.g. "x", "y", "radius"), while methods will characterize the interactive manipulation facilities (e.g. "Picked", "Moved", "Rotated", "Stretched"). The model does not restrict the physical nature and target metaphor for interaction objects; for instance a "Room" object [14] can be modelled, with its various attributes (e.g. "soundOnEnter", "soundOnLeave", "tactileOn") and methods (e.g. "Entered", "Exited") directly expressed.

2.2   Input events

Input events have an arbitrary number of typed *parameters*, carrying event-specific data, and asynchronously occur in the context of objects. Events may concern: device-oriented input (e.g. key presses, mouse moves), notifications for window management events (e.g. exposure / Xlib, repainting / WINDOWS, window destruction / WINDOWS) or navigation-specific events for alternative metaphors (e.g. "glove pos", "glove obj", "ring left voice command", etc, for a 3D auditory ring navigation space supporting 3D hand pointing [15], client specific processing (i.e. user events for WINDOWS / Xlib) that may generate high-level events (e.g. a gesture recognizer generating gesture events [20]), etc.

2.3   Output events

Output events have an arbitrary number of *output parameters* (necessary for the toolkit to perform an output event) and an arbitrary number of *input parameters* (values possibly returned from the toolkit to the caller, after an output event has been served). Output events are practically functions of the form $y^n=f(x^m)$, where x^m is the list of output parameters, while y^n is the list of input parameters. Output events may concern: procedural graphics primitives and drawing facilities (e.g. "POINT_ABS_2" , "VIEWPORT_2", "LINE_REL_2" - [7]), toolkit functions for managing interaction objects (e.g. "RealizeWidget" / Xt, moving / hiding / re-displaying / destroying objects), toolkit resource management (e.g. "CreateGC" /

Xlib, font management, bitmap manipulation), window management or navigation functions (e.g. changing listener window / Xlib, "ring turn left" / "ring turn right" - [15]), etc.

3   Specification of the programming layer structure

The specification of the programming layer (PL) structure is the definition, through the PIM language, of the desired set of object classes, input events and output events. In Example 3.1, such a simple specification is illustrated. In Example 3.1, the name of the toolkit is defined to be *W95* (corresponding to WINDOWS 95), while the desired programming layer to be established on top of WINDOWS 95 is specified as: one object class (i.e. *Button*), one input event type (i.e. *MouseMoved*) and one output event (i.e. *GetBitmap*); every such item is also associated with the defined toolkit name.

```
toolkit W95;                         outputevent GetBitmap(W95) [
object Button(W95) [                     out:
      method Pressed;                    objectid obj;
      int x,y;                           int x, y;
      int width, height;                 int width, height;
      string label;                      in:
]                                        int bitmapid;
inputevent MouseMoved(W95) [     ]
      int x,y;
]
```

Example 3.1: Simple programming layer structure specification.

From the specifications in Example 3.1, it is observed that: (i) some naming conventions (as originally supplied in WINDOWS 95) have been changed (e.g. event name for mouse motion, attributes for label on buttons); and (ii) the *GetBitmap* output event does not have a directly corresponding function of this form in WINDOWS 95 (some lower-level "operators", such as "BitBlt" are provided). Such allowed deviations from the original structure of the target toolkit functionality are primarily supported by the PIM tool; as it will be discussed in Section 4, such "transformations" on the original programming interfaces of target toolkits, need to be realized via programming in the context of toolkit server development.

3.1   Specification approaches for the *PL* structure

Each specification of the programming layer structure via the PIM language, realizes a different "view" of the original target toolkit functionality. From the "distance" between the specified PL structure and the original toolkit, the following specification approaches, inherently defining alternative strategies for establishment of programming layers on top of toolkits, are distinguished (a combination of the following strategies is also possible):

(i)   *Mapping*. The original naming conventions, as well as the number and structure of elements, is preserved within the specification of the desired PL structure. The resulting programming layer practically provides the original toolkit facilities, though via the PIM toolkit programming model. Mapping is appropriate for quickly creating an initial programming layer on top of a toolkit, from which preferable modifications (following approaches to be discussed below) can be subsequently applied.

(ii)   *Renaming*. Within PL specification, the original toolkit naming conventions for interaction elements can change. Even with such simple modifications, there are a number of practical advantages like: (i) toolkit elements and their attributes / parameters may become more understandable; or (ii) naming conventions from toolkits already known by end-programmers may be employed.

(iii)   *Simplification*. This is a combined application of mapping and renaming, where the number of specified elements and also their associated attributes / parameters, is purposely reduced. Emphasis is put on the ease of use (i.e. programming) of the resulting GPLs.

(iv)   *Transformation*. This is the general case, in which virtually all aspects of toolkit elements (i.e. naming conventions, number and structure of elements) can be changed during specification. By applying transformation, the distance between the toolkit elements and the resulting GPL may be considerably increased, and in some cases (as it will be discussed in the Section 4) the toolkit server development task (for connecting the GPL with the original toolkit) can become more complicated.

(v)   *Generalization*. This approach concerns the specification of PL structures targeted towards multiple toolkits. It is a special case of transformation, and each resulting GPL will realize a virtual toolkit (it will have to be connected to multiple target toolkits, via the implementation of multiple toolkit servers).

```
toolkit Xaw;                          toolkit W95;
enum ShapeStyle = [                   object Button (W95) [
Rect,Oval,Ellipse,RoundedRect               method Pressed;
];                                           string title;
                                      ]
object Command (Xaw) [
      int x, y;
      int width,height;               object Textfield (W95) [
      string font, fg, bg;                  string text;
      bool sensitive;                       method textChanged;
      ShapeStyle shapeStyle;          ]
      method Activated;
]
```

Example 3.2.1: (i) application of Mapping, Renaming and Simplification (left column, Xaw); and (ii) application of Simplification (right column, W95).

3.2 Examples for the various *PL* specification approaches

Examples for each of the previous specification approaches will be provided and discussed; the target toolkits considered are Xlib, Xaw/Athena widget set and WINDOWS 95 basic object library. The toolkit server development requirements for some of the examples are discussed in Section 4.

In Example 3.2.1 - left column, the target toolkit is Xaw \ Athena widget set, and a combination of mapping, renaming and simplification is applied. The name of the object class (i.e. *Command*), and the names & types of attributes *x*, *y*, *width*, *height, sensitive, label, shapeStyle*, are preserved from the original Xaw\Athena class. Some callback classes like *XtNdestroy* and *XtNcreate* have been ignored (i.e. simplification). The *Activated* method corresponds to the *XtNselected* callback class in Xaw\Athena (i.e. renaming).

```
object ListBox (W95) [
      method Selected;
      method Unselected;
      string whichItem;
      int itemIndex;
      string* items;
      bool* selectStatus;
]
```

Example 3.2.2: Applying Transformation and Simplification (W95).

In Example 3.2.1 - right column, simplification is applied for two classes of WINDOWS 95 object library. The specified *Button* object class has the same name in WINDOWS 95, while the *Textfield* object class corresponds to the *EditControl* object class (in WINDOWS 95). One attribute and one method have been specified for each class; considerable reduction of attributes, and also renaming for the remaining attributes and methods has been applied.

In Example 3.2.2, a typical example of transformation is shown. In WINDOWS 95, a list box supports the selection of multiple items by the user (as opposed to the *List* widget of Xaw/Athena library, where a single selection is only possible). The original programming interface for the *ListBox* class has been transformed and simplified, as defined in Example 3.2.2: *items* concerns the list of string items initially supplied, *Selected* and *Unselected* indicate the callback lists for selection and "un-selection" (i.e. pressing an already selected list item), while *whichItem* and *itemIndex* return the content and the index of the selected / unselected item respectively. The attribute *selectStatus* is an array of flags holding the selection status for each of the list items. In the context of the ACCESS project, programmers have found much easier [18] this programming interface for multiple-choice list boxes, than the original one in WINDOWS 95. In Example 3.2.3, the generalization strategy is illustrated. The virtual GPL toolkit to be established is named *Vlib* (the name can be arbitrary). One object class is specified, called *Button* (i.e. *Button* for WINDOWS 95, *Command* for Xaw/Athena), which has one method named *Pressed* (WINDOWS 95 and Xaw/Athena methods have been renamed). The *AllocateGraphics* output event "unifies" the *CreateGC* Xlib call, and the *GetDC* WINDOWS 95 call).

```
toolkit Vlib;                         inputevent KeyPress (Vlib) [
                                        int pressCount;
object Button (Vlib) [                  string key;
    method Pressed;                   ]
    string label;
    int x,y,width,height;             outputevent AllocateGraphics
    s t r i n g    f g , b g ,        (Vlib) [
    bordColor;                            out: objectid obj;
    int bordWidth;                        in: int gid;
]                                     ]
```

Example 3.2.3: Applying Generalization (W95, Xaw).

A key issue during the design and specification of the structure for a programming layer, is to ensure the feasibility of translating the specified elements to the particular elements of the target toolkit (or of the target toolkits, in the case of virtual GPLs). Otherwise, various problems may emerge during the development of the corresponding toolkit server(-s), due to implementation limitations on realizing particular "translations". Performing such initial implementation studies, as part the toolkit server development stage, is crucial and is likely to provide valuable feedback to the programming layer design- and specification- process.

3.3   Unified Programming Layers (UPLs): Merging Toolkits

The PIM tool supports the specification of a programming layer in which: (i) an arbitrary number of toolkits are issued; and (ii) interaction elements belonging to any of the issued toolkits are defined. As it will be discussed in the next Section, one toolkit server will have to be developed for every different issued toolkit, each handling the interaction elements associated with it in the context of the PL specification. This supports development of interface clients by combining elements from the various toolkits (via the resulting GPL which is called a *unified programming layer*).

This method provides a modular approach for organizing various independent collections of building blocks for constructing interactive applications (i.e. different toolkits), in order to provide a common programming layer for utilising these sets of building blocks be means of a unified toolkit. More specifically, apart from conventional toolkits of interaction objects (like WINDOWS object library, OSF / Motif, Xaw / Athena), the following are some typical lasses of software libraries which are considered as very appropriate candidates for unification:

o   libraries of graphic primitives (e.g. GKS, PHIGS);
o   audio I/O interaction facilities;
o   re-usable interactive navigation components (like a 3D auditory ring [15];
o   video display control libraries;
o   animation engines;
o   non-visual interaction toolkits (like Rooms - [14]).

The integration of such diverse libraries into a single programming layer, apart from the significant advantage of providing to programmers a single programming model and the "single toolkit illusion", may enable them to overcome practical difficulties such as: (i) *language conflicts*, since not all libraries are made available through the same programming language; (ii) *compile conflicts* (even variables, constants or data types may collide), in the case of the same or compatible language; (iii) *linking conflicts* (it is not allowed to build an interface utilising elements from more than one X WINDOWING SYSTEM toolkits like OSF / Motif, Xaw / Athena or InterViews); and (iv) *execution conflicts*, in which necessary library calls made at one toolkit will always exclude / conflict with calls from other toolkits (e.g. toolkit initialization calls, main loops).

In Example 3.3.1, an excerpt from a unified specification is illustrated. The overhead of building a toolkit server for each such toolkit is minimal (that of a mapping of function calls and object instantiations for the original toolkit), assuming that the programming method is preserved. More specifically, if a procedural / OO programming element is provided within the original toolkit, then a corresponding output event / interaction object must be supplied as part of the unified toolkit; this strategy is necessary in order to avoid the *procedural / OOP model conflict*, which will be defined and discussed under Section 4.

```
toolkit GKS;                          toolkit AudioLib;

outputevent OpenDevice(GKS) [         object Playback(AudioLib) [
    out:                                  string file;
    int WinId;                            bool notifyOnEnd;
    int x1,y1,x2,y2;                      method Ended;
    in:                                   real sampleRate;
    int deviceHandle;                 ]
]
```

Example 3.3.1: Excerpt of a unified specification.

4   Building a toolkit server

The toolkit server plays the role of the intermediate "translator" between the GPL and the target toolkit. The toolkit server has a twofold role: (i) it receives requests from the GPL, corresponding to object instantiations, attribute modifications, and output events, that the client program will normally perform, and it serves such requests by calling the original toolkit functionality; the "physical" interface is created and maintained locally within the toolkit server; and (ii) it sends messages to the GPL regarding input events, method notification, and attribute modification, as a result of user interaction with the physical interface locally managed by the toolkit server; also, returned values from the execution of output events are also sent to the GPL. The communication between the GPL and the toolkit server is transparent to programmers of GPL clients (i.e. developed interfaces). The run-time architecture of a client interface program built with a GPL is shown in Figure 4.1. The GTIP (Generic Toolkit Interfacing Protocol) component is the protocol library for realizing the asynchronous communication between the GPL and the toolkit servers (the GTIP is discussed in Section 5). The GPL client program and the toolkit servers are independent local / remote processes. In order to run an interface developed via a GPL, the following default steps are taken (these are managed automatically and are transparent to GPL client users): (a) an instance (i.e. process) of the GPL client is created locally; and (b) the various toolkit servers, associated with the particular GPL, which has been utilised for the client implementation, are also locally executed.

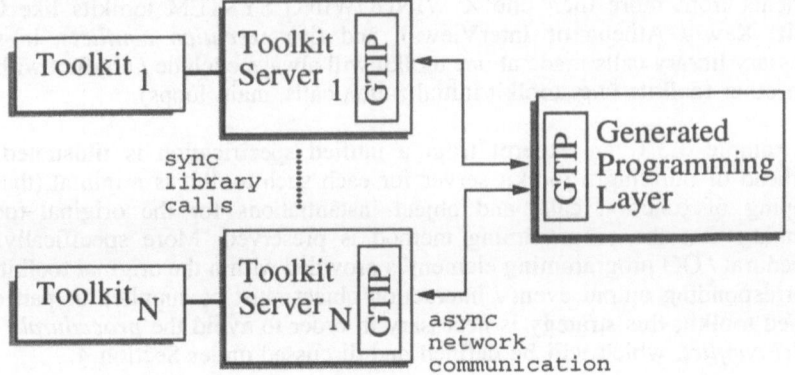

Fig 4.1: The run-time architecture of interfaces programmed through a GPL.

4.1 Server development complexity for specific *PL* specification scenarios

There are certain cases in which the introduction of particular features within the programming layer structure specification (reflecting functionality that needs to be provided by the resulting GPL) results into more complex toolkit servers. Such typical cases are discussed below:

(i)   *Toolkit resource management.* In this case, the PL specification includes output events for manipulating toolkit-specific resources such as: fonts, bitmaps, graphics contexts, etc. When programming with the original toolkit, these resources are managed by toolkit functionality through local specialized types (e.g. *XFontStruct** in Xlib for fonts, *HBITMAP* for bitmaps in WINDOWS 95) and are not visible within the GPL (which supports only the types defined within PL specification).

```
outputevent GetFont(Xaw) [        outputevent TextWidth(Xaw) [
    out:                              out:
    string font;                      string text;
    in:                               int font;
    int fontid;                       in:
]                                     int width;
                                  ]
```

Example 4.1.1: Output events for toolkit resource management.

In order to support such resource management (see Example 4.1.1, managing font resources) alternative reference types, mainly integers, are used within the PL specification (e.g. *int fontid*, Example 4.1.1); the toolkit server should allocate local resources, generate unique integer identifiers per resource, maintain locally mapping tables between such identifiers and local resources, and return to the GPL the integer identifier (e.g. *out:* parameter in *GetFont* output event) to be used subsequently by the GPL programmer as a parameter to the output events for manipulating that particular resource (e.g *int font* in the set of *out:* parameters for *TextWidth* output event).

(ii)   *New presentation / behaviour attributes for objects*. In this case, the specified interaction objects reflect an augmented presentation / behaviour structure, with respect to the corresponding original toolkit object classes. The realization of such augmented characteristics must be explicitly programmed as part of the toolkit server implementation. For instance, the necessary drawing statements must be programmed for additional presentation attributes (e.g. supporting background bitmaps for object classes which originally do not posses such visual attributes), while code for the extra dialogue facilities emerging from the new behaviour attributes must be appropriately realized (e.g. supporting keyboard manipulation of list boxes for Xaw).

(iii)   *Procedural vs OO programming model conflict*. One typical case in which such conflicts may emerge concerns the introduction of graphic primitives within PL specification. This type of conflict appears in either of the following cases: (i) having an Object Oriented (OO) PL specification for a procedural graphics package implementation, or (ii) having a procedural PL specification for an OO graphics package implementation. The toolkit server is required to perform model translation, which introduces considerable complexity; the same issue of model difference has been raised in the context of a GKS library integration within the SERPENT UIMS, since SERPENT supports only object-oriented entities for the integration process [5].

(iv)   *Importing libraries which need to be linked together*. It concerns the situation where for the toolkits to be integrated (under a common programming layer), in order to allow interoperation and data exchange, linking of their respective libraries and object files is required. Moreover, communication and data exchange at the library-call level is needed in certain cases. This scenario cannot be managed via two separate servers, since such library-connections must be established at the same memory space. In this case, a merged server is built; upon start-up (of the merged server), the GPL will be informed of the toolkit names served by the merged server.

5   GTIP: generic toolkit interfacing protocol

The Generic Toolkit Interfacing Protocol has been designed to support the asynchronous communication between GPLs and toolkit servers. The first version of the protocol has been realized in the context of HOMER [13], where it supported the communication between the dialogue control and the incorporated toolkits. GTIP reflects the toolkit programming model which has been defined in Section 2, and is well suited for connecting toolkit-independent software layers with target toolkits. Such a separation is analogous to the case of X WINDOW SYSTEM, where the X server runs locally, handling all screen and device management details, while the client program may run remotely; X client programs

188

are actually linked with the programming interface library for accessing X server facilities. The GTIP is split in two parts: (i) structure of messages that are sent to toolkit servers (GPL->TS part, see Figure 5), and (ii) structure of messages that are sent from toolkit servers (GPL<-TS part, see Figure 5). Each message packet has a standard header indicating the type of *request* (GPL->TS part), or the type of *notification* (GPL<-TS part).

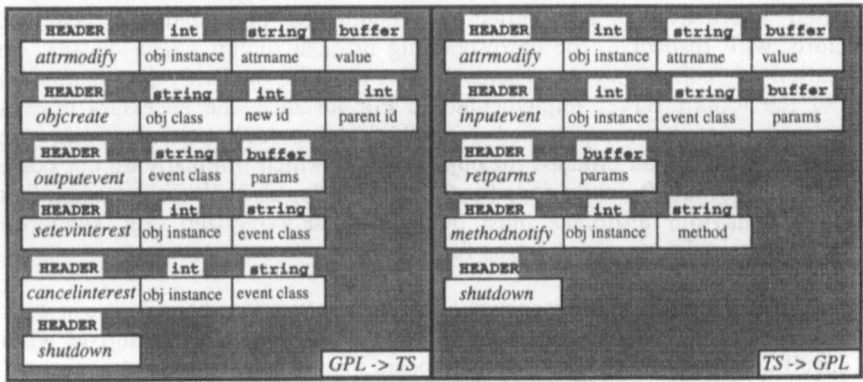

Fig 5.1: GTIP message structure.

6   Task-based attribute default method for PIM GPLs

All PIM generated programming layers support a specific type of initialization files for passing attribute default values to interaction objects. Attribute default values are given by means of attribute default tuples. These tuples have the syntax *<object class, task context, attribute name, attribute value>*. The *task context* is a string-type entry and, as it will be explained later on, it has a significant role: it defines the user tasks for which an attribute default tuple is active during use-computer interaction. An example of an attribute default tuple is *<Button KillProcess bitmap shoot.bmp>*, which indicates that all objects belonging to the *Button* class, and having as task context *KillProcess*, will have the *bitmap* attribute with value *shoot.bmp*.

```
Label Confirm font 8x16romankana
Label Comfirm borderWidth 0
Command Confirm borderWidth 4
Command Confirm font lucidasans-bold-18
Label FileManagement borderWidth 1
Label FileManagement font helvetica-oblique
Toggle FileManagement bitmap doc.bmp
```

Example 6.1: Attribute default tupples for the file manager- and confirm box- dialogues.

The connection between the user tasks defined within the interface design process, and the task contexts given to object instances used for the real implementation of the interface is accomplished as follows: All object classes of PIM GPLs have an extra (optional) constructor attribute *char* task_context*. The programmer may pass a task context name for any object instance, which will then be matched with the task context names provided within the attribute default tupples. If no value is given, the default value "*" (i.e. any task) is given to the task context name of an object instance. During this programming process, the interface programmer should cooperate with the interface designer in order to pass the correct task context names for each object instance. Since interaction objects are combined to construct interface components with which the user will preform specific tasks, the objects belonging to any component may be given the name of the task that the user will perform via this particular component.

In Example 6.1, a list of such task-based attribute defaults is provided for a real application example. This example shows how differentiation of object appearance attributes can be easily achieved without requiring direct programming of those attribute values. The interface components concerning the two tasks (*Confirm* and *FileManagement*) are shown in Figure 6.1. The attribute default mechanism is fully controllable by the programmer. A dedicated member function is provided for all generated interaction object classes called *Adapt()*, which can be called at any time. The default values are applied only to attributes which have not been given values by the interface programmer at the time of call (i.e. programmer's values to attributes have higher priority). As previously mentioned, if no task context is given to an object instance, the value "*" is passed, which is matched to any task context. If the value "-" is passed, then the task context of the parent object is inherited. For instance, at the confirm box implementation of Figure 6.1, it suffices to pass "Confirm" as the task context of the parent window, and define "-" as the task context of all child objects.

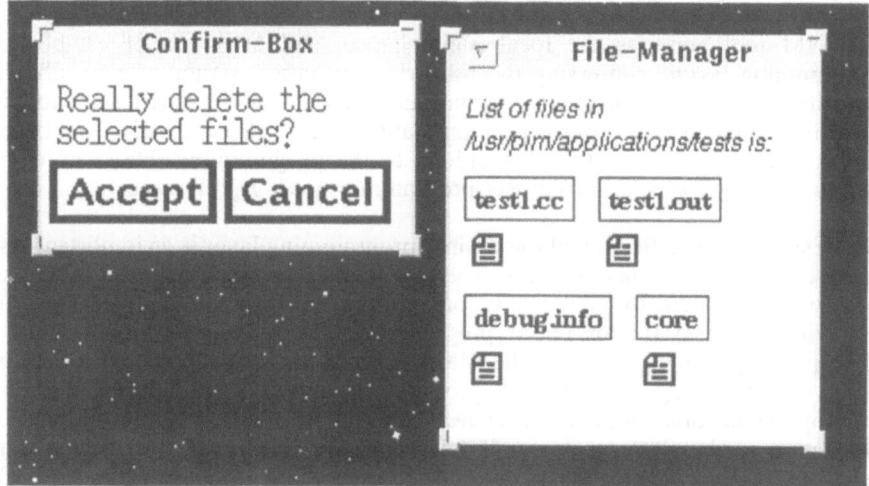

Fig. 6.1: Confirm box and file manager tests for attribute defaults.

From our initial tests with this approach, it quickly became evident that since the attribute default tupples are practically design decisions, they can be re-used. For instance, in the context of a *Confirm* task, the defaults of Example 6.1 can be chosen. This, not only promotes re-usability, but also cross-application consistency.

In existing attribute default methods, the task variable is missing, leaving a list of defaults with no syntactic context; it is this simple inadequacy which further excludes re-usability.

7   Summary and discussion

A tool has been developed, called PIM, to automate the process of establishing desirable, locally maintained, programming layers on top of toolkits. The tool supplies the PIM language to specify the structure of the desired programming layers; the PIM language reflects our generic programming model for toolkit elements. Specified programming layers are translated to C++ programming libraries via the PIM compiler. The process of "connecting" a generated programming layer (GPL) to target toolkits is realized by the development of toolkit servers. Communication between toolkit servers and a GPL must be implemented by the communication library of the PIM tool, i.e. the Generic Toolkit Interfacing Protocol (GTIP) library.

The PIM tool enables the establishment of programming layers such as: (a) generalized programming layers for multiple toolkits, realizing virtual toolkits; (b) simplified programming interfaces, providing reduced functionality and simple properties of interaction elements (e.g. for teaching purposes); (c) transformed programming interfaces on top of a particular toolkit A, to approach naming conventions, as well as number and structure of elements, of another toolkit B (providing a programming layer for A toolkit, resembling the original B toolkit, targeted to programmers familiar with the B toolkit).

The PIM tool supports the local maintenance, and evolution of established programming layers, addressing the following scenarios: (i) the target toolkit is expanded (new interaction objects / techniques, new devices, etc); (ii) a new toolkit to be incorporated (i.e. provide programmable access via an already established programming layer); and (iii) adaptations to the programming interfaces to be locally applied (e.g. specialized user-programmer needs / preferences).

The design and specification of the desired programming layer is an important task in the overall development process. The PIM tool facilitates quick *prototyping* of programming layers for toolkits, before building a toolkit server, through the following process: (a) an initial programming layer design is mapped to a corresponding specification; (b) the PIM compiler translates such a specification to the corresponding GPL; and (c) programmers are called to utilise the library and implement some predefined selected scenarios (resulting programs will not be interactive on the absence of a toolkit server). The purpose of this process is to quickly test the usability of a programming layer, in order to provide early feedback for necessary modifications. The toolkit server development is initiated at an appropriate later stage.

Acknowledgements

The work reported in this paper has been partially funded by the TIDE Programme of the European Commission (DG XIII), under the project ACCESS TP1001 (*Development Platform for Unified Access to Enabling Environments*). The partners of the ACCESS consortium are: IROE-CNR, Italy; Institute of Computer Science-FORTH, Greece; University of Athens, Greece; RNIB, UK; University of Hertfordshire, UK; SELECO, Italy; MA Systems & Control, UK; Hereward College, UK; National R&D Centre for Welfare and Health, Finland; VTT, Finland; Pikomed, Finland.

References

1.   Akoumianakis, D., Savidis, A., Stephanidis, C. Design assistance for user-adapted interaction. In the proceedings of the *3rd International Eurographics Workshop on Design, Specification and Verification of Interactive Systems*, DSV-IS'96, Namur (Belgium), 5-7 June 1996, Springer-Verlag.

2.   Akoumianakis, D., Savidis, A., Stephanidis, C. An Expert User Interface Design Assistant for Deriving Maximally Preferred Lexical Adaptability Rules. In *Proceedings of the 3rd World Congress on Expert Systems*, Seoul (Korea), 5-9 February 1996, 1298-1315.

3.   Bass, L., Hardy, E., Little, R., Seacord, R. Incremental development of User Interfaces. In *Engineering for Human-Computer Interaction*. G. Cockton, Ed. North-Holland, 1990, 155-173.

4.   Cowan, D. D., Durance, C. M., Giguere, E., Pianosi, G. M. CIRL/PIWI: A GUI Toolkit Supporting Retargetability. Software-Practice and Experience, *Vol 23 (5)*, May 1993, 511-527.

5.   CMU/SEI. CMU/SEI-91-UG-8. *Guide to Adding Toolkits*. Serpent User's Guide, May 1991.

6.   Foley, J. D., Wallace, V. L., Chan, P. The human factors of computer graphics interaction techniques. *IEEE Computer Gr. & Appl, 4, 11* (November 1984), 13-48.

7.   Foley, J., Van Dam, A. Fundamentals fo interactive computer graphics. Addison-Wesley Publishing, 1983 (1st edition), 137-179.

8.   Krell, M., Cubranic, D. V-Lynx: Bringing the World Wide Web to Sighted Impaired Users. In proceedings of the *ACM ASSETS'96 conference*, Vancouver, Canada, April 11-12, 23-26.

9.   Myers, B. A. A New Model for Handling Input. *ACM Trans. Inform. Syst.* 8, 3 (July 1990), 289-320.

10.   Myers, B. User Interface Software Tools. In *ACM Transactions on Human-Computer Interaction, Vol 2, No. 1*, March 1995, 64-103.

11.   Pausch, R., Conway, M.,DeLine, R. Lessons learned from SUIT, the Simple User Interface Toolkit. *ACM Trans. Inform. Syst.* 10, 4 (October 1992), 320-344.

12.   Petrie, H., Morley, S., Mcnally, P., Graziani, P., Stephanidis, C., Savidis, A., Majoe, D. An interface to hypermedia systems for blind people. In the proceedings of the *ACM Hypertext'96* (demonstration).

13.   Savidis, A., Stephanidis, C. Developing Dual Interfaces for Integrating Blind and Sighted Users: the HOMER UIMS. In proceedings of the *CHI'95 conference in Human Factors in Computing Systems*, Denver, Colorado, May 7-11, 106-113.

14.   Savidis, A., Stephanidis, C. Building non-visual interaction through the development of the Rooms metaphor. In companion of the *CHI'95 conference in Human Factors in Computing Systems*, Denver, Colorado, May 7-11, 244-245.

15.   Savidis, A., Stephanidis, C., Korte, A., Crispien, K., Fellbaum, K. A Generic Direct-Manipulation 3D-Auditory Environment for Hierarchical Navigation in Non-visual Interaction. In proceedings of the *ACM ASSETS'96 conference*, Vancouver, Canada, April 11-12, 1996, 117-123.

16.   Savidis, A., Vernardos, G., Stephanidis, C. Embedding Scanning Techniques Accessible to Motor-Impaired Users in the WINDOWS Object Library. In proceedings of the *HCI International'97* conference, San Francisco, USA, August 24-29, 1997.

17.   Savidis, A., Stergiou, A., Stephanidis, C. Generic Containers for Metaphor-Fusion in Non-Visual Interaction: the HAWK Interface Tooolkit. In proceedings of the *Interfaces'97* conference, Montpellier, France, May 28-30, 1997.

18.   Savidis, A., Petrie, H., McNally, P., Ahonen, J., Koskinnen, M. Stamatis, C. Internal report on the evaluation of the PIM toolkits. ACCESS Consortium (c). January 1997.

19.   Sun Microsystems. The Java™ Language: A White Paper. 1994-1995.

20.   Zhao, R. Incremental recognition in gesture-based and syntax-directed diagram editors. In *Proceedings of the INTERCHI'93 Conference on Human Factors in Computing Systems* (Nederlands, Amsterdam, April 24-29, 1993), ACM, New York, 1993, 95-100.

Editing MAD* task descriptions for specifying user interfaces, at both semantic and presentation levels

F. Gamboa Rodríguez[1] and D. L. Scapin

Institut National de Recherche en Informatique et en Automatique
Domaine de Voluceau - Rocquencourt - B.P. 105, 78153 Le Chesnay Cedex, France
Fernando.Gamboa_Rodriguez@inria.fr   Dominique.Scapin@inria.fr

Abstract

This paper presents an approach to interactive system design known as task-based design. The approach is centered on the task-oriented formalism (MAD*), and consists in the translation of a formal task description into an intermediary semantic interface (SSI), which can be linked to an actual interface. Various characteristics of the approach are described : the MAD* model and notation, the SSI model, and the different implementations (IMAD*, ISSI, and the links with the actual interface). The tools that support the process are then described. The conclusion identifies the limits of the approach, the relationships with similar approaches and further research work.

Keywords : Human-computer interaction, tasks models, task-based design, user interface specification, model-based tools.

1. Introduction

A user-oriented perspective for the design of user interfaces, especially at early design stages, is now almost on everyone's wish list. When such an approach is adopted, ergonomists, whose specialty includes strong skills in job, task and activity analyses, perform through various techniques (observation, interviews, experiments, etc.) analyses of a work situation, usually documented in plain text, resulting in some form of user as well as task requirements. These requirements are further translated by the designers into high level interface specifications, then actual interface specifications. The early stages of this process are often informal; the cooperation between ergonomists and designers is concentrated on exchanging requirements (free-form or mock-ups for the first ones; models, notations and prototypes for the latter), and sometimes on cooperating in early evaluations.

While the strong point of ergonomic analyses can be the precision and accuracy in the analysis of existing situations, one draw back is the lack of usable formal models to transmit what is know about users and tasks that would be useful to consider for the design. In other words, the degree of formalization of the models exchanged may vary. Also, for both ergonomists and designers, the link between task requirements and

---

[1] this work was partly supported by a grant from the Mexican Minister of Science and Technology (CONACYT)

194

design is not explicit, when formalized. A number of approaches do offer methods, notations for such task issues, but not many do offer tools supporting that process, MUSE [8], DIANE+[16], etc.

The general research perspective is the following. The ultimate goal is to supply methods and tools contributing to the design and evaluation of ergonomic interfaces [10 ; 11]. Concerning design, one area of research has been to incorporate task issues in the design process. To do so, a first step has been to design a notation MAD (*Méthode Analytique de Description des tâches*) [13]. The expected benefits are :
- to improve the quality of task descriptions, i.e., to maximize completeness as well as coherence and to reduce inter-analyst variability
- to improve the collaboration between ergonomists and designers by using a common formal language

That notation has been associated with a data gathering technique, through semi-directed interviews [14], and observation techniques for validating the descriptions.

Further work has been to validate the MAD model on real tasks (air-traffic control and fire situation management on merchant ships, [1 ; 3], to improve the model and to built tools to help the analysis. Such tools appear quite necessary when considering how tedious it is to describe tree structures and formal notations with paper/pencil. However, the additional purpose of the tool approach is to allow the editing and manipulation of the task model in order to translate this information in terms of interface semantics (dialogue control, application main functions, synchronization, etc.) and presentation aspects (choice of input options, positions, coding, etc.).

Our approach is quite parallel to the traditional user-oriented approach (field analysis, task requirements, high level specification, interface specification) except that it is based on a formal model and that tools are provided for that whole process. It can be characterized as starting from actual users and their tasks and establishing an incremental path that permits the translation of the collected information into a formal application architecture inherently coherent with the user's point of view at a semantic level as well as at the presentation level.

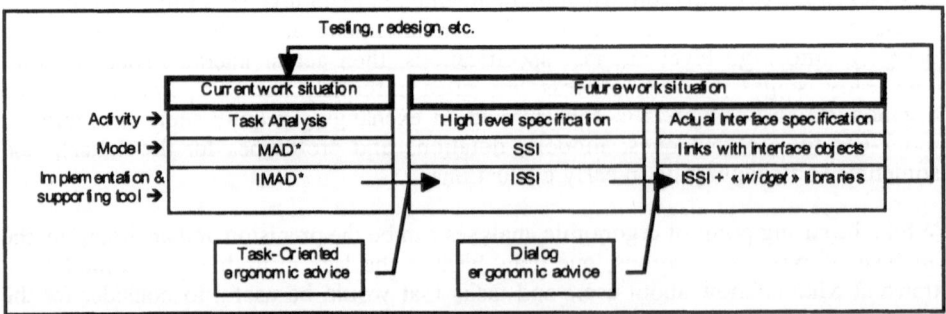

Fig. 1 Design process, models and tools

The approach is based on four basic concepts : a model of user's tasks (MAD*), a set of high-level ergonomics rules independent of any specific dialogue technique, a semantic model of the interface (SSI), and a set of design rules. The design process and associated models and tools are shown Fig. 1. The process starts with a task analysis carried out in the user's context, using semi-directed interviews. For this analysis, we use the MAD* task model, with the IMAD*-tool. The design process proceeds with the translation of the task's information into an intermediary conceptual interface, called SSI, using the ISSI-tool. This translation will be later directed by a set of high level rules which aim to help organize the application as well as the interface dynamics in an ergonomic way. The SSI elements are then translated into visual "widgets", with the help of a set of design rules.

At this stage, the ergonomic help and advice have not been yet incorporated; however some ideas can be found for task level in [15] and for both the task and presentation levels in [12]. This paper deals mainly with the design process up to the definition of the SSI and the actual interface. It describes the modifications made to the original MAD formalism and the characteristics of the resultant model called MAD*, second, the model of the intermediary interface SSI is explained as well as the procedures that direct the path from one model to the other. Later sections explains the tools that supports the methodology. The conclusion identifies the limits of the approach, the relationships with similar approaches and further research work.

2. Models: MAD*, SSI

2.1 Modelling user's tasks : The MAD* Model

The first version of the model for task descriptions [13] as well as further versions, uses the hierarchical planning paradigm [9], expanding the notion of hierarchical planning, and including synchronization aspects. In MAD, each item is characterized by a group of descriptors, distinguishing between procedural aspects (the structural subdivision of tasks in sub-tasks or actions), and declarative aspects (the objects needed to execute the task, and their features). It allows the description of well-structured tasks as well as weakly-structured ones, and proposes a graphical syntax.

Nevertheless, while using MAD to describe complex tasks, two mayor kind of problems appeared [18]: some of the tasks attributes were incorrectly used (misunderstandings, confusions) ; the existing constructors could not describe some of the situations which came up. In order to correct these deficiencies, an effort was made to formalize and reorganize the model. MAD* or MAD-STAR (Analytical Model for Tasks Description Oriented towards Interface Specification) [5] incorporates such modifications. These can be grouped into three main categories : formal definition of all tasks attributes, of pre- and post- conditions, of the objects used by tasks.

In MAD* the basic element is the *Task Unit*. This element is a uniform and unitary structure which comprehends both concepts of elementary and composed task. To each Task Unit corresponds a goal; it is composed by two main descriptors : the *Task Unit Body*, and the *Task Components*. The *Task Unit Body* is subdivided in two different structures : the *Task body*, including the task's name, identification number, goal, priority, etc. and the *Tasks conditions*, i.e., the input and output parameters describing the context allowing first, the execution of the task, and later the end of it. The *Task Components* defines the different operators that allows the hierarchical subdivision of one task into simpler ones. Two categories of decomposition operators are defined : *Synchronization operators* (SEQuential, PARallel, SIMultaneous), and *Ordering operators* (AND, OR, ALT).

Further elements concerning the MAD* syntax are provided in the section « MAD* implementation (IMAD*) ».

2.2 Modelling the semantic interface: the SSI model

The SSI model (Semantic Specification of the Interface) is an intermediate generic model of the interface. Strongly inspired from the work of [5], SSI allows the specification of interfaces based on the information collected in the user's task description. Four main elements constitute the semantic interface : the Schema of Procedures (SP), the Procedures (P), the Functional Objects (FO) and the Display (D):

- *Schema of procedures* (SP), constitute the logical representation of future functions in the application. It is a component grouping and delimiting the necessary elements for the accomplishment of a specific function, and it is composed of a set of procedures. From the MAD* tasks, the SP inherits the control of interruptions, priorities, etc. In other words, it takes the control of one part of the tree, establishing the strategies for the control and the synchronization of the involved elements.
- *Procedures* (P), sub-element of the *schema of procedures*, can be considered as a structure equivalent to the *Task*. Just as tasks are subdivided in sub-tasks in MAD*, procedures are subdivided into simpler ones ; an special case of P is the *Action* in the sense that it uses the same data structure, but it is not subdivided further.
- *Functional objects(FO),* are the SSI representation of the objects used in the task description. All the objects used by tasks pre- and post- conditions are joined to the list of *functional object*, so they can be initialized, used and modified during the execution of the *Procedure*.
- *Display* (D), constitutes a support to the physical implementation. It represents the space where the visual objects will be placed (e.g., windows).

This model (further described in the implementation section) has facets: other than the equivalence with task's description, or the synchronization aspects attached to each one of the stated elements, we have added a *Presentation facet*, which will allow representing elements in terms of visual widgets. This organization attempts first, to facilitate the translation of a MAD* description into the model of the semantic interface linking both models with a common concept : the task, formalizing in this form its role in the interface's architecture. On the other hand, the elements of the presentation facet are defined according to the semantic characteristics of each element, ensuring the coherence between the physical interface and the tasks characteristics.

3. Implementation of MAD* (IMAD*) and SSI (ISSI)

3.1 IMAD* : an object oriented implementation of the MAD* task-unit

In order to establish a compatible and easy-to-translate data structure between the two models, an object oriented implementation of the task unit was performed : IMAD* (Fig. 2). This implementation has been influenced by the perspective of facilitating the realization and formalization of mechanisms capable to determine the coherence and the completeness of task descriptions : information querying and re-structuration of the task tree, identification of the objects used by a task, the objects structure, etc.

The implementation uses C++ and specifies the generic elements that set up a MAD* task, particularly the *intra-tasks* relations expressed in the pre- and post- conditions, and the *inter-tasks* relations expressed by the temporal structures. One feature of this approach is the attempt to model the procedural aspects of the task as a sequence of actions (the functional model), and the objects used in these procedures in an explicit form. In that way, one can build the data model at the same time one defines the procedures. Besides, representing two data structures on the same model has many advantages in terms of implementation (e.g., algorithms for the navigation between the elements of both structures, the verification of links, coherence and completeness, the identification and categorization of tasks using the same type of object, etc.) The elements included in IMAD*, their organization and characteristics are listed below.

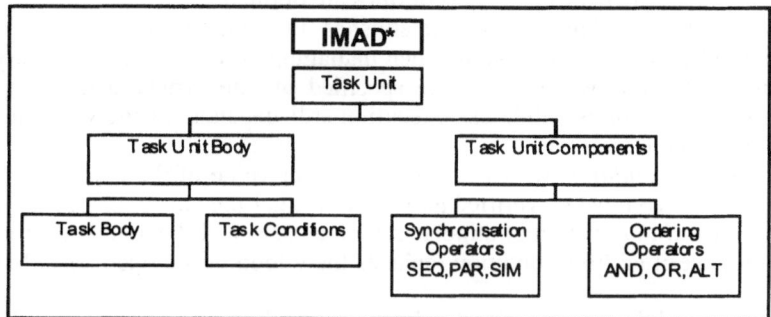

Fig. 2 General structure of the MAD* Model *(modified from [5])*

As shown in Fig. 2, the *Task Unit Body* is divided into two different structures : the *task body* and the *task conditions*. For these two structures, the body is the main part, and the conditions are the input and output parameters. For the *Task Components* operators, only the « Synchronization » part has been implemented.

Task's body

Attribute name	Values
Identification Number	alphanumeric
Name	alphanumeric
Goal	alphanumeric
Comments	alphanumeric (free-form)
Degree of freedom	{ optional, mandatory}
Priority	integer
Interruptibility	{True, False}
Upper Task	Pointer to the upper task (IMAD*)
Modality	{manual, automatic, interactive}
Type	{sensori-motor, cognitive}
Centrality	{important, not important}
Frequency	{high, medium, low}
Important entities	{among the task's objects}
Experience	{user = novice, occasional, expert}
State	{waiting for execution, inaccessible, in execution, interrupted, finished, ignored}
Mandatory sub-tasks finished	integer

Task's conditions

IMAD* conditions are based on : 1) the *State of the World*, which includes the objects used by the tasks on which the validation rules are applied ; 2) the « Conditional Structure » which states the formal grammar of the rules. These rules express constraints over objects attributes values, i.e., they evaluate the state of objects. Two kinds of evaluations are possible : the first one implies the notion of logical predicates or first order logic ; the second one implies arithmetic conditions.

Both the pre- and the post- conditions use the grammar as shown on Figure 3. For the pre-conditions, three different types of rules are defined :
- *triggering pre-condition*, which establishes the conditions for triggering the execution of the task. This is useful when managing system events or to execute the tasks in a different order than the one specified by the synchronization operators. Even if this condition is valid, task execution still depends on the validation of the *execution pre-condition* ;
- *execution pre-condition*, which verifies the proper value of the objects of the task. This pre-condition must be verified in order to trigger the execution of the task ;
- *stop pre-condition*, rule that stipulates that a task will be re-executed until the condition is verified (this condition replaces the « loop -@- » operator in MAD).

For the post-conditions, only one kind of rule is defined : end post-condition ; it specifies the values of the objects involved at the end of the execution of the task.

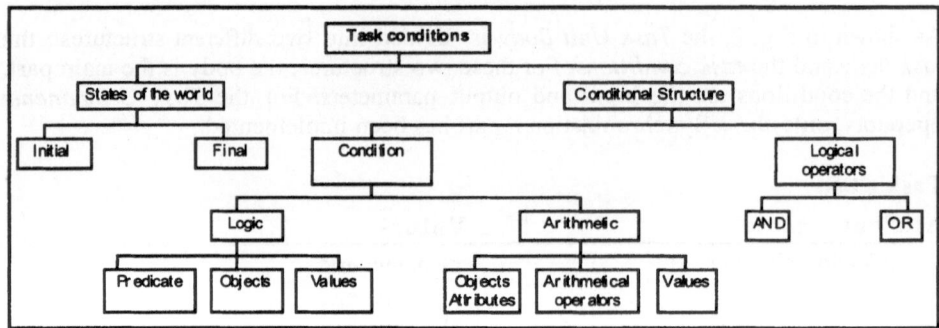

Fig. 3 Task Conditions *(modified from [5])*

Tasks Conditions

Attribute name		Values
Conditional structure		
< CS >	➔	< CS > < Op > < CS >
< CS >	➔	Condition
< Op >	➔	AND I OR I XOR Condition :
Predicate (Objects, [values]) : {True, False}		
Input conditions		
Initial state of the World....................		{C++ objects}
Kinds of input conditions		triggering, execution, stop
Output conditions		
Final state of the world		{C++ objects}

Kinds of output conditions...............end

Execution result............................{C++ objects}

Task Components

In order to describe the way the tasks are structured and subdivided into simpler ones, four different constructors have been defined : SEQuential (sub-tasks are executed in sequence), PARallel (sub-tasks are executed in any order), SIMultaneous (*n* tasks are executed at the same time by *n* different operators), and ALTernative (only one of the subtasks is executed). When the task is not subdivided further, it is considered as an ELEMentary task. Finally, a *provisional* option allows the designer to continue with the description, even if a task body is temporally unknown, or only partially defined.

Task Components

Attribute name	Values
Component Structure (CS) ....integer	
CS = 0 ➔ PROV (i.e., provisional)	
CS = 1 ➔SEQ	
CS = 2 ➔PAR	
CS = 3 ➔ALT	
CS = 4 ➔SIM	
CS = 5 ➔ELEM	
sub-tasks list......................................list of IMAD* tasks	

3.2 ISSI : The object oriented implementation of SSI

While the MAD* model has been used as the starting point of the design process, the ISSI model is the final point where all the elements created before should find an equivalent component. The main contributions of the ISSI implementation are :

1) the formal translation of each one of the task elements into *Schema of Procedures, Procedures*, or *Actions* ;

2) total compatibility between the two models, giving a consistent framework to designers all along the process. All the ISSI elements have a structure coherent with the IMAD* components (e.g., they share the same kind of constructors, synchronisation strategies, interruptions and syntax), the *functional objects* are calculated directly from tasks pre- and post- conditions, etc. ;

3) finally, the *Presentation facet*, allows to present these elements as visual *widgets*.

ISSI has been implemented using the « *graphic attribute* » and « *variable* » from ILOG Views libraries. These libraries not only offer a powerful way to automatically modify the visual aspects of an object by changing their logical value, but they also offer a mechanism to propagate the objects values to other objects. These two characteristics allows to create objects capable to auto-control their visual aspects, and to communicate their logical changes to other objects.

Three different objects have been implemented with the characteristics just described above : SSI_SP for the *schema of procedure*, SSI_P for the *Procedures*, and SSI_Window for the *Display*. The *Action* element is included in the *Procedure* structure, as it has an identical data structure but it includes no further subdivisions.

The SSI_SP (SSI *Schema of Procedures*)

The attributes forming a *schema of procedure* relate to three description categories: identification, control and presentation. The identification category regroups the data necessary to differentiate a SP : name and title (both normally taken directly from the task body). The control category includes the number of procedures concerned, their list as well as their component structure, and a counter indicating which state is actually been executed. The presentation category is established automatically for the SSI-SP object. As it is supposed to regroup all the concerned *Procedures*, *Actions* and *Functional Objects*, this element is directly translated as a new window where all the stated elements will be displayed.

Schema of Procedures

Identification

Attribute name	Values
Title	alphanumeric
Name	alphanumeric
Number	integer

Control

Attribute name	Values
Number of Procedures	integer
Component Structure	integer
List of procedures	*SS_P*
Sequence	integer

Presentation

Attribute name	Values
Window	SSI_window

The SSI_P (SSI Procedure)

As the equivalent element of the task object, the *Procedure* object is divided in a very similar way : Procedure body, Procedure Conditions, and Procedure Components. Furthermore, it adds a new facet expressed in terms of presentation attributes which permits to give a viewable representation of the objects on the screen.

Each *Procedure* object is able to take a physical representation depending on its semantic characteristics. Seven different generic forms of presentation were defined : button, menu, selector, notebook, screen-zone, edition fields, not-presented. The possibilities of taking one of the potential forms depends on two factors : 1) the actual representation of the *Mother-Procedure* (if it exists), and 2) the type of component structure established for the *Mother-Procedure* (e.g., no menu for a sequential procedure). Another presentation attribute for the SSI_P objects is the possibility to pop-up a new window when the procedure is triggered. This is particularly useful for dialog or messages boxes displayed after a system event while executing the application. When a new window is declared, the system asks for its moment of display: from the beginning of the application, when called by the *Upper procedure*, or when the triggering preconditions are satisfied.

Procedures body

Attribute name	Values
Title	alphanumeric
Name	alphanumeric
Degree of freedom	{ optional, mandatory}
Priority	integer
Interruptibility	{True, False}
Upper procedure	SSI_P
Modality	{manual, automatic, interactive}
Component Structure	integer
State	integer
Mandatory sub-procedures finished	integer

Procedure conditions (see Task conditions)

Procedure components (see Task components)

Procedure Presentation

Attribute name	Values
Detached Window	{True, False}
Pop-Up window at	integer
Visual presentation	IlvGraphic (button, menu, etc.)
Window	SSI_Window

The SSI_Window

This object is in charge of the physical presentation of all the selected widgets. It is organized in two different structures : Identification and Edition. The main feature of this object is its « Widgets container », capable to react in two different ways, depending on the selected interaction mode. If the « *modifications mode* » is selected, the designer can move the graphical objects all over the window, in order to organize the information. If the « *interaction mode* » is selected, each object reacts in a normal way (e.g., a button pressed executes an action, etc.), empowering designers to test immediately the different elaborated designs.

Identification

Attribute name	Values
Number	integer
Name	alphanumeric
Title	alphanumeric

Edition

Attribute name	Values
Edition Zone	gadgets container
Modification mode	button
Test mode	button

3.3. Implementation of the paths from IMAD* to ISSI

As explained by [7], systems are not generally designed to support or replicate work as it currently exists, rather they are designed to satisfy specific requirements for changes to the work.

Designing a system usually requires changes in existing tasks at least in two cases:
- in the case of manual tasks, the definition of a new system modifies the analyzed tasks, in the sense that new functions can replace manual tasks.
- in the case of tasks already computer-supported, the future tools (e.g., new interaction technologies) may not correspond exactly to requirements, as they provide new functions and new tools.

In our case, this design process is viewed as an opportunistic, iterative and incremental process, where the appropriate aspects of the tasks are progressively translated and organized in terms of ISSI elements. This process is assisted by specialized tools, allowing a rapid visualization of current choices, their impact on the overall design, construction of different versions of the interface, etc.

The approach is divided in two stages :
1. division of the IMAD* tree into one or more *selected tasks* which will be translated into *schema of procedures;*
2. refinement and re-organization (when needed), of the semantic elements (*procedures*), belonging to the *schema of procedures*. Selection of the appropriate visual representations for the semantic elements.

These stages do not have to be sequential, which means that one can work with a *procedure*, without knowing in advance the *schema of procedures* it will be attached to. In this case, in order to guarantee the coherence between the procedures involved in the *schema of procedure* and their constraints, a set of dedicated tools is needed.

Stage 1: Definition of *selected tasks* : the MAD* model used as a database

The specification of the *selected task* is equivalent to dividing and separating the whole task description into various *logical* blocks. This is done based on the information obtained from the description, the designer's experience, and the specific design requirements. It is undoubtedly the main step during the design process, in the sense that it will define the organization of the future application. Once the *selected tasks* are defined, it is then possible to generate most of the attributes and the synchronization methods of the SSI components.

The tree splitting is basically done in a manual way by the designer, helped by a set of tools designed to support the process. The decisions can be based on some of the following strategies :
- a *selected task* normally starts from tasks at the highest level of abstraction in the description, but it can be subdivided in simpler ones at any level,
- *selected tasks* can be grouped for an specific operator,
- *selected tasks* can be defined based on the used domain objects,
- *selected tasks* can be defined based on the information treated
- *selected tasks* can be defined based on the tasks centrality,
- etc.

In order to assist the designer in this process, some basic rules related to tasks have been included :
- A *selected task* cannot include two different human operators
- Manual tasks are not considered (unless "transformed" into an automatic or interactive task)
- The cut up of the task tree determines the choice between one or more windows
- The sequence of transactions is based on the existing synchronization operators
- Objects and functions are grouped in terms of their semantic relationship
- Different display zones are assigned to different *Schema of Procedure* or *Procedures*
- A menu only has the options necessary to a *Procedure* element

While specific ergonomic advice has not yet been integrated in the current tools, a set of re-structuring algorithms and coherence verifiers are offered to the designer : the designer can hide or put apart all the unwanted tasks in the description, while the resultant tasks can be re-organized, modified, set together or divided. In this way, several different versions of the application's interface can be produced, based on a single task description.

Stage 2: Refinement of semantic elements : defining the characteristics of the elements.

Once the *schema of procedures* are defined, different attributes have to be established for each one of their elements : semantic attributes, logical attributes, visual attributes, etc. This refinement process consists of three main steps : 1) definition of the element as a procedure, an action, or a new schema of procedures (subdividing the original one); 2) selection of its visual representation (if any); 3) decision on whether the attached sub-procedures (if they exist), will be presented on a new window or not. In order to facilitate these changes of structures, the reorganization tools offered to the designer were complemented with a « *virtual procedure* ». A *virtual procedure* is a procedure not existing in the original task's description, i.e., artificially created by the designer while defining the structure of the current *schema of procedures*, in order to put together elements originally placed on different parts of the description.

This refinement process is also assisted by semi-automated tools, allowing :
- the verification of the defined *schema of procedures*, *procedure* and *action* elements,
- the determination of the visual representation depending on the mother's component structure, mother's representation, etc.,
- construction and management of the different created windows,
- construction and verification of different interface versions according to given values, their modification, reuse, etc.

4. ALACIE : an integrated software environment

ALACIE (for *Atelier Logiciel d'Aide à la Conception d'Interface Ergonomiques/ Software Workbench for the Design of Ergonomic Interfaces*) is an integrated software bench that incorporates IMAD* and ISSI, as well as tools supporting respectively the path between IMAD* and ISSI; and the path between ISSI and the Actual Interface.

4.1 IMAD*-tool : a dedicated tool supporting MAD* descriptions

IMAD*-tool has been designed to address the main shortcomings of describing tasks by hand. Its main interest lies in the implementation of the formal task model MAD* under the form of the IMAD object, as well as in the design of authoring and validating tools. A screen dump of the actual tool is shown in Fig. 5 (a & b).

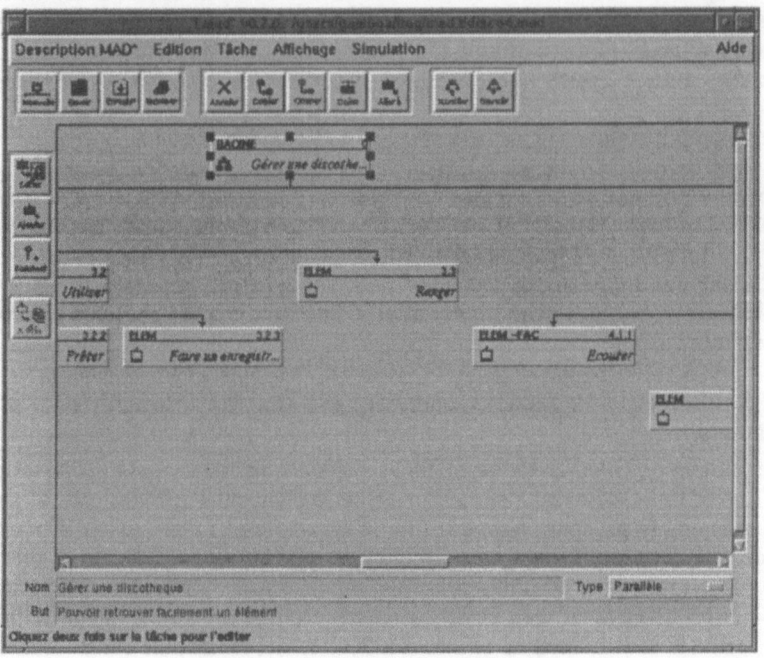

Fig. 4a The IMAD* tool Tree Editor

Considering that the task description will be the basis for interface design, a rigorous validation is fundamental for the rest of the design process. In IMAD* are included a set of functions for such purpose, making the tool go beyond simple tasks trees editors. The specification of the tool has been made in close cooperation with ergonomics and computer science people. The goal was to design a tool that would allow an opportunistic development of the task description, while including functions allowing : the authoring and the simulation of the description ; the verification of the description completeness ; the management and the supervising of the involved objects ; and the syntactical validation of pre- and post- conditions.

The tool supervises every change in the description and checks automatically all the logical and visual structures to be up-dated. It also tests the coherence at every level of the specification, verifying the existence of objects, the syntax of the procedures (conflicts between task attributes, conditions, illegal constraints, etc.), the syntax of pre- and post- conditions, etc.

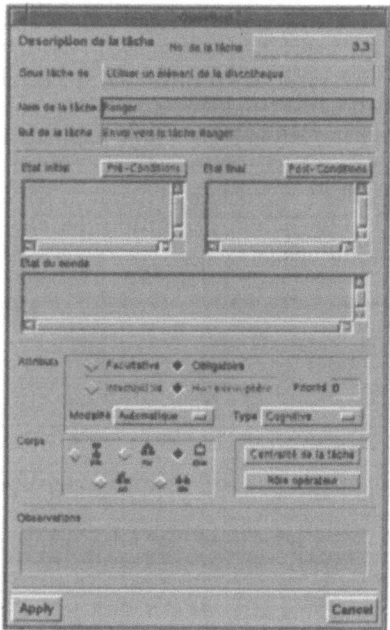

Fig. 5b The IMAD* tool Task Editor

4.2 ISSI-tool : translating tasks into interface elements

The process of translating an IMAD* description into the ISSI model manages a lot of different information difficult to organize. In order to help designers, a specialized tool was designed to support the process. At first, ISSI shows the original IMAD* description to the designer, and asks to define the tasks as being *schema of procedure, procedures* or *actions*. In order to support these decisions, visualization tools are offered, so the designer can hide or view different parts or representations of the description according to various parameters such as : involved human operator, domain objects used, task's priorities, etc. At this stage, very little supervision is done by the tool. The different restrictions imposed to the designer are based on the rules suggested in section 3.3.

With this tool, top-down design is not mandatory. It is not necessary to specify a *procedure* as being a sub-element of a *schema of procedure*, to define its characteristics. When the attachment to the *schema of procedure* will be later established, the tool will verify the links, and will point out to the designer the identified lack of consistency.

For ISSI, each task declared as *schema of procedures* will create a new window. However, the designer has to specify the moment of display for the new window : from the start, when called by an other task, when called by the user, when the triggering precondition if verified, etc.

When the designer selects a *procedure* or an *action*, the system suggests a visual representation depending on its semantic characteristics. This automatic pre-selection is based on the work from [17]. The designer is free to accept this selection or to change it for an other valid representation. The list of valid representations is automatically updated by ISSI. Each time that a visual representation is assigned to an element, a physical representation is shown, so the designer can follow the consequences of design choices and be able to validate or modify them.

Finally, the tool allows the construction of as-many-as-wanted versions of the interface based on a single task description, permitting the comparison between versions, or the reuse of previous solutions.

IMAD*
description

ISSI
translation

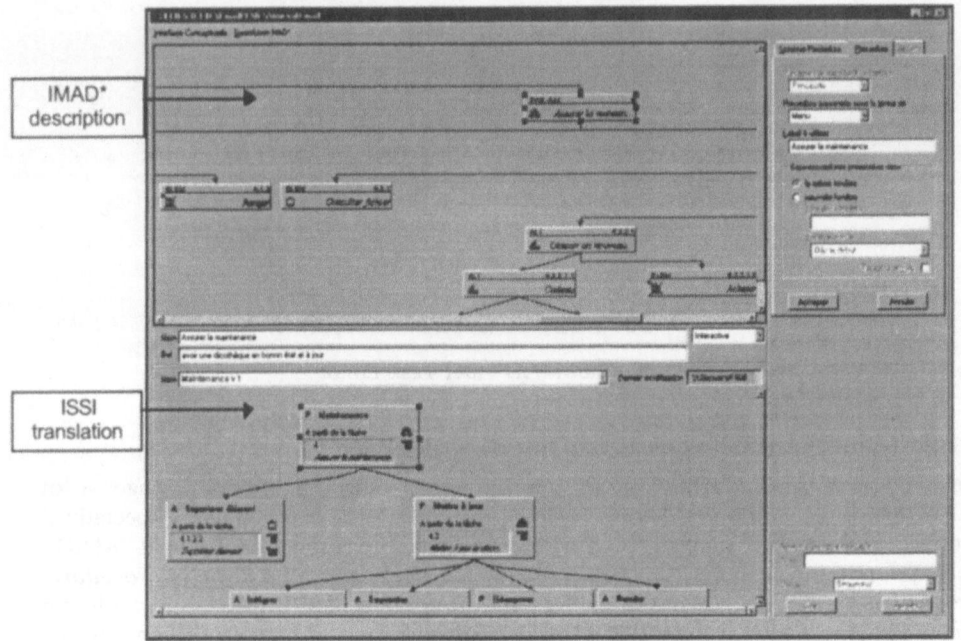

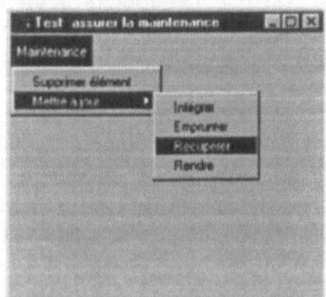

Fig. 6 The ISSI tool with one of the actual interface possible versions

5 Conclusion

In this paper, we have described an interface design approach based on a user task model. The underlying models and tools have been presented. The tools have been developed to a certain extent, but more work is required.

Of course, the tools have to be extended in the area of task ordering; some refinements should be done, for instance, in terms of synchronization (e.g., [6]). A large effort in validating the existing tools on real tasks description is needed : from the models implementation point of view, in order to assess the completeness of the notation, but also from a usability point of view (can designers use the tool ?).

On this point, it will be quite interesting to study experimentally designers while extracting task knowledge and building actual interfaces (how do they proceed, what do they select, how many versions are built, how different are they, etc.)

Another important issue is to further incorporate some kind of ergonomic advice for designers, both at the task and presentation levels. On this issue, there are at least two research questions: one is to be able to extract and use explicit task-oriented recommendations, the other is to be able to assign lower level recommendations, such as the ones used for automatic evaluation [4]. Concerning the first problem, unfortunately task-oriented ergonomic recommendations are not very explicitly defined in ergonomic guides (Smith, 1986; Vandedonckt, 1993). Concerning the second problem, automatic evaluation tends to incorporate as much style guides considerations as it does genuine ergonomic rules.

Other research issues are also worth mentioning: how to compare descriptions, how to assign weights to description items (to define metrics), how to evaluate using task descriptions, e.g., [2].

One should also state some of the limitations of the approach : it is not fully linked to traditional software design processes and methods, it does not incorporate organizational characteristics, nor software requirements (e.g., in terms of platforms, tools, etc.); and finally, it is only based on existing situations : only cases of computerization of manual tasks and "re-engineering" of computerized tasks are considered. But, are these « design from scratch » situations so frequent ?

6 References

1. Alonso, B. (1996) *Analyse des tâches mono et multi-opérateurs du contrôle aérien par le formalisme MAD pour la spécification ergonomique de l'interface*. Thèse, Université Paris 5, France.

2. Balbo, S. (1994) *Évaluation ergonomique des interfaces utilisateur: un pas vers l'automatisation*. Thèse, Université Joseph Fourier, Grenoble, France.

3. Fallah, D. (1997). *Evaluation empirique d'une maquette d'aide à la résolution de situation d'incendie à bord de navires* (Technical Report No.200). Rocquencourt, France: INRIA, Rocquencourt.

4. Farenc, A. (1997) *ERGOVAL: une méthode de structuration des règles ergonomiques permettant l'évaluation automatique d'interfaces graphiques*. Thèse, Université de Toulouse I, France.

5. Hammouche, H. (1995) *De la modélisation des tâches utilisateurs à la spécification conceptuelle d'interfaces Homme-Machine*. Thèse, Paris VI, France.

6. Jambon, F. (1996) *Erreurs et Interruptions du Point de vue de L'Ingenierie de l'Interaction Homme-Machine*. Thèse, Joseph Fourier- Grenoble I, France.

7. Johnson, P., Wilson, S., Markopoulos, P., & Pycock, J. (1993). ADEPT – Advanced Environment for Prototyping with Task Models. In *Proceedings of ACM INTERCHI'93 Conference on Human Factors in Computing Systems* (p. 56).

8. Lim, K. Y. (1996). Structured task analysis: an instantiation of the MUSE method for usability engineering. *Interacting with Computers, 8*, 31-50.

9. Sacerdoti, E. D. (1977). *A structure for Plans and behavior*. Amsterdam: Elseiver Computer Science Library.

10. Scapin, D. L. (1990). Aiding mechanisms for the design of user interfaces : some research issues. In *The First International Conference on Automation Technology* (July 4-6)(pp. 587-593). Taipei, Taiwan.

11. Scapin, D. L. (1993). Situation et perspectives en ergonomie du logiciel. In J.-C. Sperandio (Ed.) *L'Ergonomie dans la conception des projets informatiques* (pp. 7-68). Toulouse, France: Octares.

12. Scapin, D. L., & Bastien, J. M. C. (1997). Ergonomic Criteria for Evaluating the Ergonomic Quality of Interactive Systems. *Special Issue of Behavior and Information Technology on Usability Methods (in press)*.

13. Scapin, D. L., & Pierret-Golbreich, C. (1990). Towards a method for task description: MAD. In L. Berlinguet & D. Berthelette (Eds.), *Work with Display Unit '89* (pp. 371-380). Amsterdam, The Netherlands: Elsevier Science Publishers.

14. Sebillotte, S. (1991). Décrire des tâches selon les objectifs des opérateurs. De l'interview à la formalisation. *Le Travail Humain, 54*, 193-223.

15. Sebillotte, S. (1995). Methodology guide to task analysis with the goal of extracting relevant characteristics for human-computer interfaces. *International Journal of Human-Computer Interaction, 7*, 341-363.

16. Tarby, J. C. (1993) *Gestion Automatique di Dialogue Homme-Machine à partir des Spécification Conceptuelles*. Thèse, Université de Toulouse I, France.

17. Vanderdonckt, J. M., & Bodart, F. (1993). Encapsulating knowledge for intelligent automatic interaction objects selection. In S. Ashlund, K. Mullet, A. Henderson, E. Hollnagel, & T. White (Eds.), *Proceedings of ACM INTERCHI'93 Conference on Human Factors in Computing Systems* (April 27-May 2)(pp. 424-429). Amsterdam, The Netherlands: ACM.

[18] Värnild, E. (1993). *Etude sur le formalisme de description de tâches MAD* Mémoire de DESS d'Ergonomie Cognitive, Paris: Université de Paris 8.

Formal aspects of task based design

Panos Markopoulos, Peter Johnson and Jon Rowson

Department of Computer Science
Queen Mary and Westfield College, University of London
London E1 4NS, U.K.

Abstract The paper discusses the formalisation of some intuitions which underlie the task based design of user interfaces. Some aspects of user task knowledge are modelled formally and the user interface is represented using a formal interactor model. A conceptual framework is introduced which relates the two representations and helps formalise their relationship as a conformance relationship. The discussion gives rise to a practical scheme for verifying and testing user interfaces and their specifications with respect to task models.

1   Introduction

Task based design emphasises the importance of understanding users' tasks, the requirements for changing those tasks and the consequences that a design can have on a task [22]. Task models provide the focus for generating designs and help ensure that novel design ideas are motivated by a user-task perspective. This paper discusses a formal representation of user task knowledge in conjunction with a formal model of user interface software to express, explicitly and formally, some intuitions underlying this family of design approaches.

A generalised description of task based design can be found in section 2. The formal representation of the user interface software used is the Abstraction-Display-Controller (ADC) interactor model [12], which is summarised in section 3. Section 4 discusses how aspects of user task knowledge are represented in a formal model based on the Task Knowledge Structures (TKS) theory [8]. Section 5 proposes a conceptual framework for relating the two models and section 6 proposes a formal expression of the required relationship between them. A scheme for using the formal representation to guide the evaluation of user interfaces by testing is proposed. Section 7 compares the approach introduced with related research in using formal models of tasks to inform user interface design.

2   Task conformance and task based design

The requirement that an interactive system should be designed with due consideration of user tasks has been called *task conformance*. Abowd et al. [1] define *task conformance* in terms of the notion of *task completeness* (whether a system supports all tasks of interest) and *task adequacy* (whether a system support user tasks as the

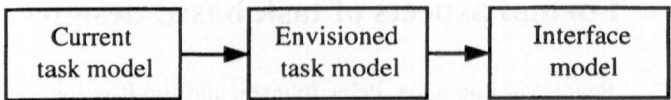

Fig. 1. Overview of task based design.

user understands them). While there are several theories as to how users understand their tasks there has not yet been a clear and widely accepted statement of principles concerning the mapping of task models to interface models [22].

Task based design prescribes the process and the heuristics to progress from a task model to an interface model (see figure 1). A task analysis of user task knowledge prior to the creation of the system design produces a model called the *current task model*. This model is the starting point of the design process. In task based design the task is redesigned and the result of this design activity is called the *envisioned task model*. This model describes how work tasks could be achieved with the introduction of the designed system. Thus it constitutes a user-task oriented requirement for a system. The design proceeds with the design of the interface to support these tasks, the *interface model*.

This is a very simplistic description of task based design which does not portray the structure of the models, their evaluation or the iterative nature of interface design. However, it helps describe some of the issues involved in task based design. Current task based design approaches, e.g. Adept [9], MUSE[10], etc., can be seen as refinements of this process, although not all distinguish so clearly between current and envisioned tasks. Wilson and Johnson [22] discuss ways of using three types of knowledge represented in a task model to progress from the current task model to the interface model. These are the structural properties of user task knowledge, knowledge of task actions and objects, and the task sequencing knowledge. Their main recommendations are summarised below.

The structural knowledge of the user, i.e. the decomposition of higher level tasks to lower level task components must be reflected in the structure of the user interface. The structure of the user interface pertains to 'groupings' of interactive objects. Components of the interface model that correspond to closely related components of the task model (goals, subgoals, actions, objects) should be grouped together in the user interface display.

Actions in the task model should be mapped to commands that the user will issue to the system. Additionally, objects suggest the types of information that may be manipulated by the commands. Complex objects may be supported by groups of interactive objects. The user interface design should support objects and actions at an abstraction level determined by the task model.

The interface model should not violate task sequencing knowledge, i.e. it should not force the users to perform their tasks in a different order than that of the task model. This sequencing may be relaxed but the grouping of the interface components should still reflect the task model. In other words, users should be able to perform their tasks

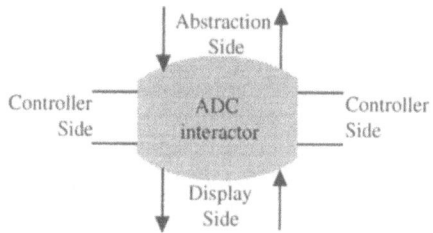

Fig. 2 Illustration of the Abstraction-Display-Controller interactor model.

as they are currently performed or they should be allowed to develop alternative strategies for achieving their task goals, without being forced to do so.

3   Modelling the user interface system

The Abstraction-Display-Controller (ADC) formal interactor model [20, 23] supports the constructive specification of user interface software. The user interface system can be modelled as a single ADC interactor or as a composition of many smaller scale ADC interactors, modelling individual interactive objects. An ADC interactor interacts with its environment through a set of *gates*. Interactions are modelled by their effect on the state parameters of the interactor, which describe its *Abstraction* and its *Display*. The temporal ordering of interactions is described in a process specification called the *Controller Unit*.

Figure 2 illustrates an ADC interactor as a barrel-shaped node. Arrows indicate *gates* which are associated with the communication of data. Gates destined for simple synchronisation interactions are drawn as lines. The gates are drawn on different sides of the barrel to indicate their different purpose or *role*. Gates for graphical input and output are attached to the bottom arch of the interactor, which is called the *display side*. Non graphical input and output interactions are attached to the *abstraction side* of the interactor. The vertical sides of the barrel, its *controller sides*, are associated with interactions that have no effect on the abstraction and display data but which are important for specifying the temporal ordering of interactions (alias its dialogue).

Interactors can be composed together into 'groups' of interactors that synchronise with each other. This grouping is described using the LOTOS parallel composition operator. For example, figure 3 illustrates how a scrolling list of elements is modelled as a composition of a list interactor and a scroll bar interactor. The two interactors start, suspend, resume, restart and abort (SSRRA for short) synchronously, since they serve the same interaction task. Also they synchronise on a gate which supports the communication of data from the scrollbar interactor to the list interactor. The scrollbar computes a natural number value as its result, when the user scrolls up and down with the mouse. The list interactor receives this input from the scroll bar and uses it to compute the index of the element which is displayed on the top of the window. Clearly this is a very simple model of scrolling but it demonstrates the use of composition.

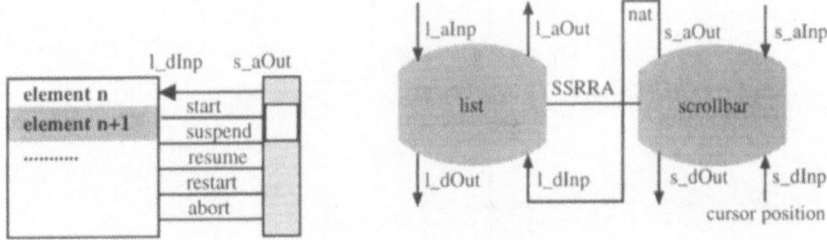

Fig. 3 Interactors can be combined to describe composite interface objects.

The concepts discussed in this section are given discussed in a more formal manner in [12], which documents a template which can help read and write formal specifications of user interface software. Also, [12] discusses various ways of composing interactor specifications to specify more complex interfaces. In the discussion that follows, distinguishing the role of a gate is important in determining which aspects of the behaviour of the user interface need to be related to the task specification.

4   A formal representation of some aspects of task knowledge

The TKS theory [8] suggests that the knowledge a person has about a task is structured and stored in the person's memory as a *Task Knowledge Structure*. This knowledge is activated and processed during task execution and its structure is reflected in the behaviour of the person during task performance. A model of this knowledge structure may be constructed by means of a task analysis. A TKS model consists in a *goal structure*, a *procedure set* and an *object structure*. The formal model discussed in this section focusses on the goal structure and the temporal ordering of task activity which it describes, and a brief introduction to these concepts is given below. The reader is referred to [8] for a more comprehensive account of the the TKS model.

Consider a person engaged in a purposeful activity within a given domain. This domain is characterised by a state and the person is aware of a state to be achieved which constitutes that person's *goal*. In the process of achieving a goal there may be identifiable, meaningful intermediate states that constitute *subgoals*. This decomposition of goals is structured into what is called the *goal structure*. The most basic element of activity identified in task performance is a single *action*. Actions are atomic and they can be combined into subgoals. Procedures encode well-rehearsed chunks of activity which are executed under appropriate conditions of the task domain. Actions can apply to *objects*. Objects reflect knowledge of the task domain and are described in terms of their attributes and relationships to other objects. The goal structure also describes logical and temporal relations between task components, e.g. the user has to perform either of two sub-tasks or both, an action may be optional, the tasks have to be performed in sequence, or in any order, etc.

LOTOS processes are used to model goals and subgoals and LOTOS actions to model

Table 1. The meaning of LOTOS operators in the context of task modelling.

Operator	Meaning in terms of the task model
\<action>;B	perform \<action> then perform task B
[b]→ B	if the Boolean expression b is true then perform B
A [] B	perform A or B
A ||| B	tasks A and B are multi-threaded
A >> B	perform A then B
A [> B	perform A until its termination, unless B interrupts A

task actions. Temporal relations between these task components can be described by the standard LOTOS process algebra operators. The LOTOS operators used and their meaning in the context of task specification are summarised in table 1. This use of LOTOS was introduced in [11] and some limitations of using LOTOS for the specifications of task knowledge were noted. LOTOS is obscure to the untrained and so difficulties arise regarding the validation of the model by users. However, LOTOS is a powerful and standard notation with a well defined theoretical framework for reasoning about specifications and has good tool support, e.g. [4]. Using LOTOS to specify both interface and task models allows a natural path to formalising the relation between the two models although they are concerned with entirely different domains. The following section outlines a conceptual framework which relates the two models.

5   Relating task and interface representations

The general idea of relating tasks to interface models is illustrated in figure 5. Tasks and interfaces may be modelled at a range of abstraction levels. Abstraction levels for interactors range over the presentation, the dialogue and the conceptual levels. Tasks which model the intentions of the user are characterised as *external tasks*. *Internal tasks* describe how external tasks are achieved by using the system. There does not need to be a one-to-one correspondence between the abstraction levels indicated for tasks and interactors. At the lowest abstraction level task actions describing physical interaction, perception and elementary motor movements by the user can be related directly to interactions with physical input devices. At the highest level of abstraction for the user interface, individual actions refer to abstractions of application functionality. Task descriptions may extend to tasks of the *work domain*, i.e. the world in which work originates, is performed and has its consequences [22].

Task actions determine an abstraction level at which the task can be related directly to the interface model, which must abstract away from entities and behaviours related to lower levels of abstraction. In the framework of the ADC interactor model, this is achieved by studying interactors of the appropriate levels of abstraction, i.e. whose input and output actions correspond directly to task actions. For example, the actions of an interactor modelling the cursor of a text editing program are too low a level to

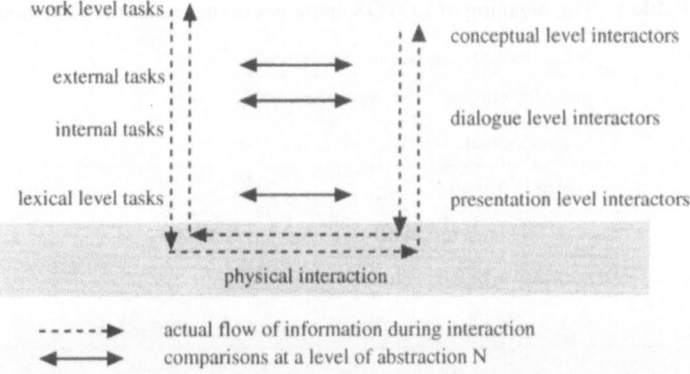

work level tasks

external tasks

internal tasks

lexical level tasks

conceptual level interactors

dialogue level interactors

presentation level interactors

physical interaction

- - - - ▶ actual flow of information during interaction

◀——▶ comparisons at a level of abstraction N

Fig. 5 Illustration of the framework for relating task and interface representations.
Comparisons between task and interface models at a given level of abstraction
implicitly assume the operation of lower level entities.

correspond to actions of the task of writing an article. In contrast, the task action of
moving to the end of a document can be mapped to dragging a scroll bar.

Figure 5 does not imply a particular design strategy nor does it prescribe a standard set
of abstraction levels through which the design should proceed. A similarly 'coupled'
view of user and system model is proposed by Barnard and Harrison in [2]. Contrary
to their 'interaction framework', the framework of figure 5 does not aim to predict the
course of interaction or the psychological phenomena taking place as it unfolds. It
simply helps to map an expression of task related requirements to the interface
specification.

By identifying the appropriate level of abstraction for the interface model, a subset of
the interactors (only those of a higher level of abstraction) and a subset of the
interaction gates (only those that support input/output and synchronisation with
interactors of lower levels) are considered. Interactions on other gates can be
considered as 'internal detail' which is not directly of concern for the comparison with
the task. If the interface is described as a composition of interactors only interactors at
a level of abstraction higher than of the selected set of gates need to be considered.
Let G be the set of gates over which the interactions with the interface are observed.
The behaviour of the interface which is related to the task representation is described
by the following expression:

$$IM_G := \text{hide all but G in IM}$$

Let A be all task actions that have a direct correspondence to interface actions. The
correspondence of task actions to the actions of the interface model can be represented
by a mapping $R: A \mapsto G$. Some task actions may not correspond directly to an
interaction. For example, they may represent user decisions or simply task actions
which are not supported by the interface, e.g. telephone communications, etc. The
interface model should not support corresponding interactions but these actions are
significant in describing task sequencing.

There may be gates in G that are not the image of any task action. Interactions on these gates correspond to task actions introduced in order to control the user interface. A different task requirement results if these interactions are modelled explicitly or not. At one level they may be abstracted away from, encouraging the current and the envisioned task models to be described independent of the tools that support the task. The corresponding gates can then be considered internal detail of the interface model for the comparison with the task. In this case, conformance pertains to whether task sequencing is preserved without respect to intermediary interactions, e.g. changing modes, navigating through screens, etc., which are crucial to describe the interaction tasks. When such interactions are explicitly modelled in the task model the conformance relationship reveals differences in the way the interaction dialogue hinders or supports the task sequencing described in the task model.

In the discussion that follows, it is assumed that the envisioned task model incorporates internal tasks necessary to interact with the interface modelled by IM_G, so the mapping R is surjective. The task model is renamed according to the mapping R, so it is represented as $TM_R=TM[R(A)]$. IM_G and TM_R are both LOTOS processes so the next question that arises is how to compare them formally.

6   A formal definition of task conformance

The choice of any mathematical relationship established between the two models should reflect how a human observes a computer system during task performance and how the human compares observed behaviours. Defining what an observation is and how its outcome may help distinguish or identify systems is a hard problem. Paternó [19] compares user interface specifications with respect to observational equivalence [13]. However, for reasons discussed extensively in [15], observational equivalence is too strong a requirement for comparing user interface systems. It discriminates systems which can not be distinguished on the basis of their visible actions and the way their reaction to external stimuli. A weaker comparison is to compare just the traces of a process. In the context of comparing two interfaces, this means that two interfaces that offer the same sequences of actions from their initial state, but which offer different options as the interaction unfolds, will be considered equivalent. Clearly, the comparison of interfaces requires some relationship that lies between these two equivalences

A comprehensive review of the various proposals for comparing system behaviours and a cognitive theory of how users perceive and compare interface behaviours are outside the scope of this paper. In this paper, interfaces are compared to task models using the notion of *conformance* [3]. Following [3] the conformance relation is introduced in terms of labelled transition systems which are a simple relational model underlying many languages for describing concurrent systems, (including LOTOS).

Labelled Transition Systems (LTS). A LTS is a quadruple $(Q, A, \xrightarrow{\mu}, q_0)$, where Q is a set of states, A is a set of *labels* (or *actions*), $\xrightarrow{\mu}$ is a binary relation between states representing *transitions,* with $\mu \in A \cup \{\tau\}$ where τ represents an

Table 2. Some notation for describing LTS.

Notation	Meaning
$q \xrightarrow{\mu_1 \cdots \mu_n} r$	$\exists q_1 \cdots q_{n-1} \in Q \mid q \xrightarrow{\mu_1} q_1 \xrightarrow{\mu_2} q_2 \cdots q_{n-1} \xrightarrow{\mu_n} r$
$q \Rightarrow^{\varepsilon} r$	$q \equiv r \vee \exists n \geq 1 \mid q \xrightarrow{\tau^n} r$
$q \Rightarrow^{\mu} r$	$\exists q_1, q_2 \in Q \mid q \Rightarrow^{\varepsilon} q_1 \xrightarrow{\mu} q_2 \Rightarrow^{\varepsilon} r$
$q \Rightarrow^{\mu_1 \cdots \mu_n} r$	$\exists q_1 \cdots q_{n-1} \in Q \mid q \Rightarrow^{\mu_1} q_1 \Rightarrow^{\mu_2} \cdots q_{n-1} \Rightarrow^{\mu_n} r$
$q \not\Rightarrow^{\alpha}$	$\not\exists r \in Q \mid q \Rightarrow^{\alpha} r$
$Tr(q)$	$\{\sigma \in A^* \mid \exists r \in Q \bullet q \Rightarrow^{\sigma} r\}$

unobservable internal action used to model non-determinism and q_0 is the initial state of the LTS. Table 2 summarises some notation used below.

Conformance of behaviour expressions. Let Q_1 and Q_2 be processes and let $\mathcal{L}$ be the set of all possible labels for all LTS. Q_1 conf Q_2 if

$$\forall \sigma \in Tr(Q_2) \wedge \forall A \subseteq \mathcal{L} \bullet$$

$$\text{if } \exists Q_1' \mid \forall \alpha \in A \bullet Q_1 \Rightarrow^{\sigma} Q_1' \not\Rightarrow^{\alpha} \text{ then } \exists Q_2' \mid \forall \alpha \in A \bullet Q_2 \Rightarrow^{\sigma} Q_2' \not\Rightarrow^{\alpha}$$

If Q_1 can perform some trace σ and then behave like a process Q_1' and if Q_2 can perform the same trace σ and then behave like Q_2', then the following conditions are required: whenever Q_1' refuses to perform an action α from a set A then Q_2' must also refuse every action in A. In other words, Q_1 conf Q_2 means that testing the traces of Q_2 against the process Q_1 will not lead to deadlocks that could not occur with the same test performed with Q_2 itself.

A formal expression for task conformance can now be written as follows:

$$IM_G \text{ conf } TM_R$$

This expression means that a user interacting with an interface, that behaves as IM_G, will not reach an impasse when performing a task, as described in TM, when it is possible to support a mapping of task actions A to interactions on gates G of the interface, as defined in the previous section. IM_G may specify behaviours which are not specified in TM_R, in other words, the task model is a partial specification of requirements for the interface model. Conformance is not symmetrical and is sensitive to the non-determinism that results from hiding the internal behaviour of the user interface. Primarily it requires from the interface model that all tasks specified in the task model are possible. Therefore the interface should conform to the behaviour specified by the task model and the mapping R. However, it is not required that an interface model be limited to the tasks described by the task model.

Conformance can be verified through a comprehensive deadlock analysis, but perhaps more interestingly it can be tested [3]. Testing compares systems with respect to their response to a set of finite sequences of interactions with the environment, the tests. A formal definition of conformance, due to Brinksma [3], which is based on testing is summarised below:

- A *test suite* is a set of processes which are called *test cases*.

- Let $\sigma \in A^*$ and T be a test case. A derivation $T\|Q \Rightarrow^\sigma T'\|Q'$ is a *test run* of T and Q. A test run is *completed* when $T'\|Q' \sim stop$.

- A completed test run is *successful* if its last event prior to terminating is a *success* event. A completed test run *fails* if it is not successful.

- A test case T is successful, denoted as Succ(T,Q), if all test runs of T and Q are successful. A test suite is successful if all its test cases are successful.

- Let S be a process and Q be the set of all possible processes. The *canonical tester* of S is a process T(S) such that

$$\mathrm{Tr}(T(S))=\mathrm{Tr}(S) \wedge \forall Q \in Q \mid Q \text{ conf } S \text{ iff } \mathrm{Succ}(T(S),Q)$$

It has been shown in [3] that for all LOTOS process specifications there exists a canonical tester. The details of the generation of the canonical tester are not given here. The generation of the canonical tester is supported by LOTOS general purpose tools, for example the COOPER component of the LITE toolset [4].

6.1 Verifying task conformance

An interesting property of the canonical tester is that it relates testing and verification. In [3] it is shown that by the definition of the canonical testers it follows that Q_1 conf Q_2 iff every deadlock of $T(Q_2) \parallel Q_1$ can be explained by $T(Q_2)$ having reached a terminal state, i.e. Q_1 conf Q_2 if

$$\forall \sigma \in \mathrm{Tr}(Q_2), \ \forall \alpha \in A \bullet \text{ if } T(Q_2)\|Q_1 \Rightarrow^\sigma T(Q_2')\|Q_1' \not\Rightarrow^\alpha \text{ then } T(Q_2) \Rightarrow^\sigma T(Q_2') \not\Rightarrow^\alpha$$

Thus task conformance can be verified by a deadlock analysis on the parallel behaviour expression $T(TM_R) \parallel IM_G$. If there is a trace leading to a deadlock of this expression, but not for $T(TM_R)$ on its own then the interface model is not conformant to the task model. If all deadlocks of the synchronous composition $T(TM_R) \parallel IM_G$ are also deadlocks for TM_R alone, then the interface model conforms to the task model.

6.2 A practical method for testing task conformance

An alternative to comprehensive deadlock analysis is to generate a finite set of tests which can be tested against the interface specification on a specification test bed. A practical method of testing the task conformance of an interface model can now be outlined:

1. Select a level of abstraction for studying the task in question and define the interface model as the composition expression involving interactors of a higher abstraction level. Determine the set of gates G through which lower level interactors communicate with the selected interactors. Define the correspondence of task actions to interface actions as a mapping $R:A \mapsto G$.

2.   Produce the 'canonical tester' $T(TM_R)$, for the modified task model TM_R. Let $CT = T(TM_R)$. Hide all gates of the task model which do not correspond to interactions with the user interface.

3.   From CT produce a set of finite tests T_i, with i:1..n, that the interface specification will be tested against.

4.   Compare the results of testing of one model and the other. Testing may be performed on a test bed tool, like the LOLA component of the TOPO toolset [20]. A full exploration of the synchronous composition of a test t_i against the interface model should give a 'may' outcome after a full exploration of all behaviours. A successful test run is an indication (only) that the system is conformant. A failed test run means that the system is not conformant to the task.

Testing is promising as a practical framework for the validation of an interactive system with respect to task requirements. A test suite can be expanded and refined with implementation constructs during the development of an interactive system. A realisation of a formally specified test suite may be used to test the realisation of the system, possibly with the involvement of users. Testing can thus link the formal specification of interfaces and tasks with other stages of the development of the user interface. A small set of tests of finite size may reveal interesting problems with an interface design and can focus the attention of the designer on the behaviours required by the task model. In comparison, model checking requires the generation and manipulation of quite sizeable models even when very small specifications are concerned. A practical question that arises is how to choose an effective set of tests that provides a good coverage of the task behaviour and is economical as well. This issue is a subject of future work and is not addressed here.

6.3   Example

The remainder of this section demonstrates how a model of a task may help assess two interface designs. The task is fabricated for the purposes of the discussion. It is envisaged that this type of assessment should follow a task analysis. The exemplar task is to produce a small text, e.g., a party invitation, which has already been composed with a word processor. The imaginary user experiments with the typesetting, i.e. changing the fonts, letter sizes, column layouts, margins, etc. The task is performed with the Microsoft Word application on the Macintosh computer. The example compares how versions 5.1 and 6.0 of Microsoft Word fare with respect to the particular task. Both versions have the same functionality as far as this task is concerned but their interfaces are different. In reality, the two versions are distinct applications whose functional core offers different functionality. However, this is overlooked in this example since the functionality accessed through the two interfaces is the same.

For brevity, the task description is restricted to changing the orientation of the page, which is effected through the 'page set-up' dialogue box of Word, and changing the margins, which is effected through the 'document layout' dialogue box or by direct

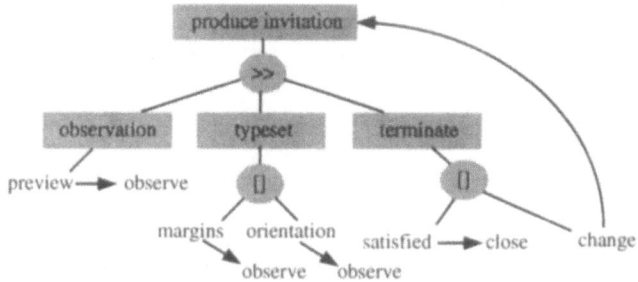

Fig. 6 Diagrammatic illustration of the task 'produce invitation'.

manipulation on the 'print preview'. Print preview is an operating mode for the word processor in which the text is displayed to resemble its appearance in printed form. In this mode the user cannot modify the text content of the document, as is possible in the standard mode of a word processor, i.e. the 'Normal View' or 'Page Layout View' of Microsoft Word. Unlike Word 5, Word 6 lets the user set the margins and the orientation of the document in the preview mode as well as in the standard mode.

Figure 6 illustrates the goal structure of this simple task as a hierarchical representation, which denotes the decomposition of goals and subgoals. This structure is annotated with special nodes indicating the temporal ordering between the subgoals and actions of the task, giving a simple graphical notation for the task specification. A variant of this notation is supported by the Adept toolset [9]. The task *produceInvitation* is defined with three subtasks *observation*, *typeset* and *terminate*, which are performed in sequence (operator >>). Observation involves the interaction *preview* and the task action *observe* performed in sequence (the arrow between the two actions stands for the action prefix operator). Typesetting is described here as a choice of two actions: setting the margins and setting the orientation. The subtask *termination* is where the user decides whether to make more changes, in which case the task is repeated. If the user decides that the result is satisfactory then the task terminates.

For both versions, the interface was modelled as the parallel composition of two ADC interactors (see figure 7). Interactor *word5* (res. *word6*) models the standard interface to the word processor during editing operations. In both versions, the final result can be inspected through the preview facility, which is modelled by the preview interactor. The difference between the two versions is that in Word 6 the document layout and page orientation dialogue boxes can also be accessed through the preview interactor, along with other editing operations which apply to the whole document.

The interactor labelled word5 in figure 7 may invoke the preview interactor. This is achieved via a control gate that is connected to the *start* and *resume* gates for the latter. *Word5* also sends data to *preview* through gate *w5ToPrv*. Changes to the document effected via the *preview* interactor, are communicated to word5 through the gate *prvToW5*. The suspend gate of the *preview* interactor is connected to a control gate of *word5*. The specifications of *word6* and *prv6* are very similar. The only

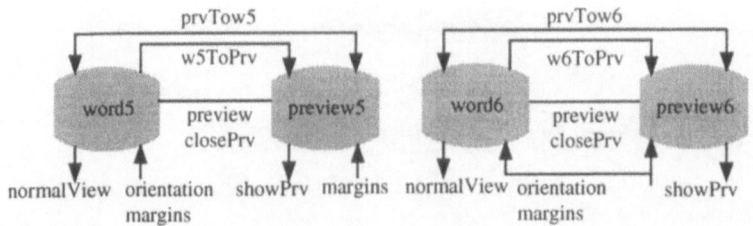

Fig. 7 The specification architecture for Word 5 and Word 6. Word 6 supports interaction to set the margins and the orientation, even through the preview interactor.

difference is that *prv6* also receives orientation information from the 'page set up' dialogue box. Relevant changes will appear in the data type specifications of *prv6* and the controller component.

The task is defined recursively, so possibly infinite cycles of activity follow from the above description. The task action *observe* is mapped to interactions on gate *showPrv*. The actions *satisfied* and *change* represent user decisions and have no image on the interface model (however hiding must be applied after the generation of the canonical tester for reasons that have to do with the meaning of non-determinism for conformance testing). A set of finite tests were derived (manually) with the process described in the previous paragraph. Each is a finite sequence of steps ending with a success event, to signify the successful termination of a test. For example, the tests t1 and t2 below are produced from the canonical tester.

```
process t1[preview, observe, margins satisfied, close, success]: exit :=
    preview; observe; margins; observe; satisfied; close; success; exit
endproc
process t2[preview, observe, orientation, satisfied, close, success]: exit :=
    preview; observe; orientation; observe; satisfied; close; success; exit
endproc
```

The test t1 describes a task action sequence where the user observes the preview display, sets the margins in any of the two ways supported, checks the result of this action, is satisfied by it and terminates the task. The task action satisfied must hidden so the actual test for the interface model is:

hide satisfied in t1

Testing t1 against *version5* shows that it may succeed while t2 is rejected, indicating that it does not conform to the task *produceInvitation*. The result is 'may succeed' for both tests with version 6. This is a positive indication for task conformance, although not definitive, given that the test suite is only of a finite size. Note, that test generation activity (here done by hand) may evolve in parallel with testing, using its results to select an efficient set of tests.

7   Related work

The 'syndetic' model of [6] models both system and users by interactors, providing a formal framework for analysing the cognitive component of interaction in terms of the mental resources needed to use a device for a specific task. In contrast to this analytical and theoretically motivated approach [16] draws parallels between TLIM and MICO, two formal approaches to design which relate representations of user tasks with system behaviour. TLIM uses a formal specification of the user's tasks in the LOTOS formal specification language. The task model specifies the temporal relationships between component tasks in a very similar fashion to the formal representation of TKS described previously. TLIM generates an interactor based system description from a task specification so the task model may be seen as a very abstract system specification. The MICO design method models tasks and systems using the Interactive Communicating Objects formalism ICO which is based on Petri-Nets. MICO does not prescribe how the system and the user model are derived, but it suggests that the design of the system involves the iterative re-design of both system behaviour and user tasks. MICO supports this iterative design process, by providing a framework for specifying formally the user interface and the user tasks. The two models are merged into a single representation, which is analysed to determine whether the system conforms to the task. The 'semantic consistency' of task and interface model is verified in the MICO method [17] by a deadlock analysis of the combined task and interface representations. This is the same as performing a deadlock analysis on the expression $TM_R \parallel IM_G$, which verifies the feasibility of completing the task rather than that all task ordering can be supported by the interface model.

The formal framework proposed in this paper shares some characteristics with the related approaches mentioned. The ADC interactor model is similar to that of the [18], so the method discussed in this paper could extend also to that interactor model. Like the syndetic model of [6] it adopts a psychologically informed method for describing aspects of user cognition. However, it does not do so with the aim to provide a model of the interaction of system and user, nor does it use the task model as an abstract specification of the system as the TLIM method does. Rather, as is the case with the MICO method, the two models are developed independently. The formal framework enables their combined analysis to ensure the conformance of the user interface design to a given task model. The method presented in this paper places its emphasis on defining this notion of conformance. This definition is informed by the consideration of task based design methods which prescribe heuristics rules for mapping aspects of the task model to an interface model.

The definition of task conformance has given rise to a framework for mapping task requirements to a formal architectural model of user interface software. This helps use the task model to generate systematically test cases for the assessment of the user interface design. Test cases can themselves be refined along with the interface design and they can be enriched with information regarding the context of the envisioned task performance. Thus, task and interface models can be used throughout the design and the development of the interactive system.

8   Discussion

The work presented here has provided a partial but precise definition of the notion of task conformance. In particular, it has focused on the correspondence of the sequencing information of the task model and the temporal structure of interaction. The definition of the task conformance requirement is determined by two main hypotheses:

1. That the formal notion of conformance captures the required relationship between task and interface models. Few attempts have been made to define this relationship explicitly. A rare example, is the MICO method [17, 18] which seeks to establish deadlock freedom for the combined task and interface behaviours.

2. The task and the interface models are compared at the level of abstraction of the task model, which in turn is determined by the task analysis. Interactors of lower abstraction levels are ignored and behaviours internal to the interface model are abstracted away. Some task actions are mapped directly to interface actions. The remaining task actions are a source of non-determinism as far as the system is concerned, e.g. the user makes a commitment to a particular course of action which is not 'known' to the interface.

In theory, it is possible to verify the conformance relationship. In practice it may be unwieldy to compare all deadlocks of the two processes as discussed in section 6.1. A more practical approach is to test the interface specification against test cases derived from the task model, using a testing tool like LOLA [20]. This can give feedback quickly and easily as to the appropriateness of a user interface design with respect to a particular task.

The set of tests produced from the task model may be used to test different interface designs and at varying levels of abstraction. Testing in this sense may be associated with techniques from the domain of human computer interaction. A suite of tests derived from a task model may benefit the evaluation of user interface designs, in combination with systematic evaluation techniques, e.g. user testing [21], cooperative evaluation [14], etc., which rely on either users or designers working through a predefined set of tasks. The method described in this paper could help generate systematically the required suite of task action sequences from the task model. The addition of concrete detail to test cases is an interesting aspect of testing, e.g. specifying data exchanged with interaction, the information to be extracted from the display, upper limits on the response time, etc.

The approach presented has put a lot of emphasis on the use of tools to support the construction and validation of the models. Tools support the generation of tests only in part, mainly because from the canonical tester it is possible to derive an infinitely large set of tests. An important practical problem is how to select the most interesting tests, and having performed some tests how to use their results to determine which further tests to perform. From the point of view of task based design it is most important to establish principles to help determine the mapping between task and interface actions, and to determine how the envisioned task model is designed from the current task model.

9 Acknowledgements

This research is funded by EPSRC grant number GR/K79796. Acknowledgement is due to INRIA for providing the MiniLite toolset, and to UPM for the TOPO toolset.

10 References

[1]   Abowd GD, Coutaz J & Nigay L (1992) Structuring the Space of Interactive system Properties, In Larson J & Unger C (Eds.) Engineering for Human Computer Interaction, Proc. IFIP TC2/WG2.7 working conference, Elsevier (North-Holland), pp. 113-129.

[2]   Barnard PJ & Harrison MD (1992) Towards a Framework for Modelling Human-Computer Interactions. In Gornostaev J (Ed.) Proc. East-West International Conference on Human-Computer Interaction EWHCI'92, St. Petersburg, Russia, ICSTI(Moscow), pp. 189-197.

[3]   Brinksma E (1989) A theory for the derivation of tests. In van Eijk PHJ, Vissers CA & Diaz M (Eds.) The Formal Description Technique Lotos, Elsevier (North-Holland), pp. 235-247.

[4]   Caneve M & Salvatori E (1992) LITE user manual. LOTOSPHERE Project Technical Report, Lo/WP2/N0034/Vo8.

[5]   Duke DJ & Harrison MD (1993) Abstract Interaction Objects, in Hubbold RJ & Juan R (Eds.) EUROGRAPHICS'93, Computer Graphics Forum, Vol. 12, No.3, pp. 26-36.

[6]   Faconti GP & Duke DJ (1996) Device Models. In Bodart F & Vanderdonckt J (Eds.) Interactive Systems '96, Proc. DSV-IS '96, Springer (Wien), pp.73 -91.

[7]   ISO (1989) Information Processing Systems - Open Systems Interconnection - LOTOS - A Formal Description Technique based on the Temporal Ordering of Observational Behaviour, ISO/IEC 8807, International Organisation for Standardisation, Geneva.

[8]   Johnson H & Johnson P (1991) Task knowledge structures: Psychological basis and integration into systems design. Acta Psychologica, Vol. 78, pp. 3-26.

[9]   Johnson P, Wilson S, Markopoulos P & Pycock J (1993) ADEPT - Advanced design environment for prototyping with task models, Demonstration abstract. In Aschlund S et al. (Eds.) Bridges Between Worlds - INTERCHI '93, Addison-Wesley, pp. 56.

[10] Lim KY & Long J (1994) The MUSE method for usability engineering. Cambridge University Press, Glasgow.

[11] Markopoulos P, Wilson S & Johnson P (1994) Representation and Use of Task Knowledge in a User Interface Design Environment. IEE Proceedings~E, Computers and Digital Techniques, Vol. 141, No. 2, pp. 79-84.

[12]   Markopoulos P (1997) A compositional model for the formal specification of user interfaces. PhD Thesis, Queen Mary and Westfield College, University of London, March 1997.

[13]   Milner R (1989) Communication and Concurrency. Prentice Hall, UK.

[14]   Monk A, Wright P, Haber J & Davenport (1993) Improving your human computer interface: a practical technique. Prentice-Hall (Hemel-Hempstead).

[15]   De Nicola R (1989)   Extensional equivalences for transition systems, Acta Informatica, Vol. 24, 211-237.

[16]   Palanque P, Paternó F, Bastide R & Mezzanotte M (1996)   Towards an integrated proposal for interactive systems design based in TLIM and ICO. In Bodart F & Vanderdonckt J (Eds.) Interactive Systems '96, Proc. DSV-IS '96, Springer (Wien), pp. 162-187.

[17]   Palanque P & Bastide R (1996) A design life-cylce for the formal design of user interface.   In Roast C & Siddiqi J (Eds.) Formal Aspects of the Human Computer Interface, BCS-FACS workshop, Springer, eWiC series.

[18]   Paternó F & Faconti G (1992) On the use of LOTOS to describe graphical interaction. In Monk A, Diaper D & Harrison MD, People and Computers VII, Proc. HCI'92, Cambridge University Press, pp. 155-173.

[19]   Paternó F (1993) A formal approach to the evaluation of interactive systems. SIGCHI Bulletin, Vol. 26, No. 2, pp. 69 -73.

[20]   Pavón S & Larrabeiti D (1993) LOLA (LOtos LAboratory) User Manual v.3.4, http://www.dcs.upm.es/~lotos.

[21]   Whiteside J, Bennet J & Holtzblatt J (1988)   Usability Engineering: Our experience and evolution. In Helander M (Ed.) Handbook of Human Computer Interaction, Elsevier (North-Holland), pp. 791-817.

[22]   Wilson S & Johnson P (1996) Bridging the generation gap: From work tasks to user interface designs. In Vanderdonckt J (Ed.) 2nd International Workshop on Computer-Aided Design of User Interfaces, CADUI'96, Presses Universitaires de Namur, pp. 77-94.

Reusable Structures in Task Models

I.M. Breedvelt-Schouten[+], F.D. Paternò[*], C.A. Severijns[+]

(+)Baan Research, Baan Company
N.V.
P.O. Box 250
6710 BG, Ede, The Netherlands
{ibreedvelt@research.baan.nl,
cseverijns@research.baan.nl}

(*)CNUCE - C.N.R.
Via Santa Maria 36
56126 Pisa, Italy
f.paterno@cnuce.cnr.it

Abstract

Task Analysis is a well-known approach that has been used to analyse usability of existing applications. Recently there is an increasing interest to apply this type of technique to the design and development of new applications, too. However if user interface designers want to apply task modelling on a larger scale, to industrial size case studies, the possibility of reuse is useful for saving time and effort. In this paper we present an approach for designing reusable structures in task models that allows designers to focus more clearly on the needs of the user and that speeds up the application design.

Keywords: Task Models, Reuse, Industrial Applications of Formal Methods

Introduction

In this paper we present the first results of a co-operation between the User-centred Design Group at CNUCE and Baan Company on new methods for the design of user interfaces. In this research we have considered ConcurTaskTrees [11], a diagrammatic notation to describe hierarchical task models, which allows designers to enrich the traditional functional specification by including the user's view of system functionality. And we have investigated its use for new applications of interest for Baan Company.

There are various reasons for choosing a task-based approach. This type of approach allows designers to focus on high-level semantic oriented aspects and developers to obtain system functionalities, which reflect the user's view of these. Thus, while interacting with the user interface of an application designed with a task-based approach, the user will easily understand how to use the system. This is because: i) the user interface provides actions which can be immediately mapped to logical actions, ii) the temporal relationships between the actions in the user interface reflect those defined in the task models, and iii) all implementation aspects which are less comprehensible for the user are hidden. Another aspect is that task modifications can be more easily implemented. In Interactive Systems designed by task-driven approaches it is easy to locate which part of the system should be changed, when support of some tasks is removed, added or modified, because it is possible to create a direct correspondence between tasks and the software components used to perform them.

Baan Company is one of the major vendors of solutions for Enterprise Resource Planning. These solutions are implemented by customising a large generic software package, that is developed by Baan Company itself and consists of approximately 5×10^3 applications ranging in functionality from simple editing of data to complicated planning tools. In order to manage this complexity it became soon important to achieve a relevant issue in the design and development of user interfaces: the possibility to reuse good design solutions of recurrent problems in dialogue specifications to save time and effort.

ConcurTaskTrees is a notation for specifying task models which has been developed to overcome limitations of notations previously used to design user interfaces, such as UAN [8]. Its main purpose is to be an easy-to-use notation that can support the design of real industrial applications, which usually means applications with medium-large dimensions. It can solve the problem of many notations, such as Interface Object Graph [5], which, while they are effective for simple limited examples, show low scalability for specifications of real case studies, thus soon becoming difficult to interpret.

The ConcurTaskTrees notation provides a graphical representation in a tree-like form of a hierarchical decomposition of tasks. A set of operators, mainly taken from the LOTOS [9] notation, is used to indicate the temporal relationships among tasks such as iteration, sequentiality, concurrency, disabling, and recursion. We used it to design various solutions for different problems. After performing several exercises we have realised that an interesting element is the possibility to identify specific task patterns in the tree-like structures describing task models which can be reused across different applications which, in some points, raise the same requirements.

One further possible advantage of task-driven user interface development, where a direct correspondence is created between software components and tasks to support, is that this correspondence can be exploited for software reuse purposes as well. This possibility has not yet been investigated in current task-driven proposals. In this paper we do not discuss this aspect since we want to focus on the possibility of reusable structures in task models for design purposes. We leave the topic of reusable task structures for supporting the implementation phase for a further paper because it requires different considerations.

In this paper, after a short discussion of related work, we introduce the ConcurTask-Trees notation, which we use for building task models and we introduce the concepts of reusability relevant to the approach presented. Then we introduce examples of possible reusable task structures and one application designed with the support of a task template. We conclude with some remarks and indications for future work.

Related Works

A different task-oriented approach is proposed by Wilson et al. with Adept [17]. In their proposal they address the design of a task model, an abstract architectural model, and a related implementation. However, this is obtained mainly by the skill of the designer with limited support from predefined rules incorporated in an automatic tool.

In model-based approaches to user interface design and development there are some proposals (such as Trident [2] and Mastermind [15] which consider task specification as an abstract model. However these proposals usually do not consider an explicit abstract architectural level moving directly from the task level to the implementation level. Similarly they do not consider reuse aspects in their approach.

UAN supports hierarchical specifications and has operators to express temporal relationships among tasks. However we found it has some limitations: first, it has a textual specification, which makes it difficult to read and interpret (for example to find cross-references among tasks). It also provides limited support for deriving a software architecture, as its main purpose is to specify only the externally perceivable behaviour of the user interface by associating tables indicating above all user actions and system responses. As a consequence, it is oriented to provide low-level specifications with many details and is not very well suited for applying reuse.

In the field of formal methods for human-computer interaction there are approaches which consider task abstraction aspects [6, 13]. In these approaches the goal is usually oriented to analyse the dialogue of existing systems rather than giving the possibility to build an architectural specification which can be used for prototyping purposes as well. Other approaches to task-driven design are in [18, 19], but they mainly focus on presentation-related aspects rather than analysing the dialogue of Interactive Systems.

The analysis of current task-oriented approaches highlights the lack of proposals supporting design reuse. This is a relevant issue given the increasing complexity of Interactive Systems. Reuse has already been recognised as such in other areas of application design, for example, in object-orientation [7].

ConcurTaskTrees

It is becoming increasingly common for the various specialists (developers, designers, psychologists, and application domain experts) involved in the design process to discuss the tasks that the system should support. To this end it is very important to have notations to develop task specifications so that:

- they are easy to understand and use, thus improving communication among people discussing the design;
- they are able to structure the large sized specifications which are developed in industrial applications;
- their semantics are precisely defined to avoid ambiguities in the communication.

When choosing the notation we found that some important features have to be supported:

- hierarchical logical structures which were introduced by GOMS have proved to be a useful way to represent task models because they allow designers to reason about the design at different abstraction levels and they support the refinement design process better;
- to be able to express a wide variety of temporal relationships since modern user interfaces are characterised by highly interactive behaviours in multimedia environments;
- to handle the complexity of task models for industrial applications, it is thus important to be able to express relevant relationships precisely and to have information on more detailed aspects in an interactive way.

A task defines how the user can reach a goal in a specific application domain. The goal is a desired modification of the state of a system or a query to it.

We can identify four types of tasks depending on their performance allocation:

- *User tasks* are completely performed by the user, they require cognitive or physical activities without interacting with the system. One example is when the user reads a list of flights satisfying some constraints and decides to select one of them for his/her journey. Another one is a video conference application, that allows the user to analyse the contents of some information generated in a remote site. More generally, we say that user tasks are associated with some processing performed by the user on information received from the environment.
- *Application tasks* are completely executed by the application. They receive information from the functional core and they can supply information to the user. They are activated by the application itself. For example, compiling a program and sending messages when some errors are detected, or receiving network messages and displaying them.
- *Interaction tasks* are performed by user interactions with the application. The user activates these interactions. Examples are editing a diagram or formulating a query to a database.
- *Abstract tasks* are tasks that require complex actions, though how to allocate their performance has not yet been decided.

In the task specification the types of tasks are presented either by different icons or different geometric shapes as in Figure 1.

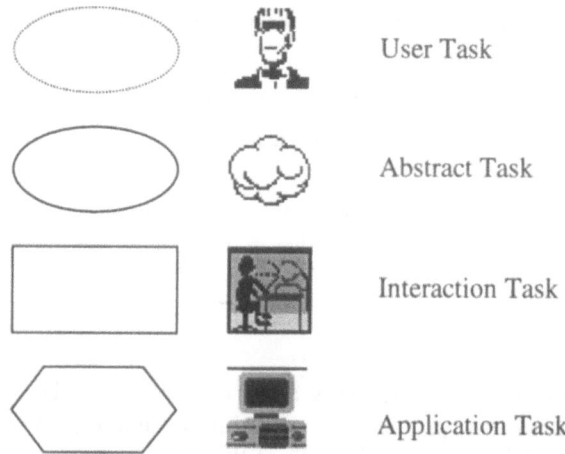

Figure 1: The two possible presentations of Task types.

The temporal relationships among tasks are expressed by extending the operators of LOTOS, which is a concurrent notation. This allows us to describe concurrent tasks, unlike the GOMS proposal, which uses hierarchical task decomposition only consisting of sequential tasks. It is possible to specify both synchronous and asynchronous communication among tasks. Tree-like structures combined with operators to indicate temporal relationships among tasks at the same level allow designers to specify more complex behaviours than those associated with basic LOTOS operators.

The operators that we use to describe the temporal relationships are:

T1 ||| T2 *interleaving*: the actions of the two tasks can be performed in any order;

T1 |[]| T2 *synchronisation*: the two tasks have to synchronise on some actions in order to exchange information;

T1 >> T2 *enabling*: when the first task is terminated then the second task is activated;

T1 []>> T2 *enabling with information passing*: when task T1 terminates it provides some value for task T2 besides activating it;

T1 [] T2 *choice*: when it is possible to choose between two tasks to perform;

T1 [> T2 *disabling/deactivation*: when one action from the second task occurs the first task is deactivated;

T1 [][> T2 *disabling/deactivation with information passing*: when one action from the second task occurs the first task is deactivated while passing some value;

T1*	*iteration*: the task can be iterated many times;
T1(n)	*finite iteration*: the task is performed n times.
[T1]	*optional task*: the performance of this task is optional. It is not mandatory to perform this task

Recursion is obtained by allowing the use of a task within its own specification. This means that in the task subtree, which defines a given task, we can find again its occurence.

Reusability

Reusability is an important issue in every stage of application development. Object-orientation is a well-known approach for analysing, designing and implementing applications which simplifies the reuse in each of these three phases of the software development process, [1, 14]. Many reusable structures or *patterns* that occur in object-oriented systems, have been documented [7, 3]. By using these patterns developers can build more easily upon the work of others. If similar structures are available for task models, this would enhance the development of task models, too.

We distinguish two possible types of reuse: design reuse and software reuse. While software reuse indicates the possibility to use the same pieces of implementation in different contexts, design reuse means that we can identify pieces of task specifications which can be used in various applications. Thus, whenever designers realise that the problem they are considering is similar to one, which has already been found, and solved, then they can immediately reuse the solution previously developed. This can be done by applying the related task specification which is represented by a task pattern in a ConcurTaskTrees specification.

The hierarchical structure of this specification has two advantages:

i)   it provides a large range of granularity allowing large and small task structures to be reused,

ii) it enables reusable task structures to be defined at both a low and a high semantic level.

Furthermore, it is possible to associate the tasks defining the template with a set of interactors, which define the architecture of the application [12]. This correspondence can be used to ease and speed-up the development process.

An additional advantage of using task patterns is that they help to make the task specification easier to read and interpret since it is possible to indicate their names if they occur in the lowest part of the task tree rather than specifying them completely. This makes the specification more compact and legible since some repetitive small specifications, which do not add new conceptual aspects, can be indicated very briefly. Examples are the modal dialogues controlling the printing of information or the closing of a session with the optional possibility of applying the modifications performed.

However, defining templates is not an easy task. There are at least two basic problems:

i) to identify the characteristic situations which can occur in different applications,

ii) to identify the information that should be used to define instances of these dialogues patterns.

Reusable Structures in Task Models

While analysing and (re-)designing parts of the Baan software, we found several templates in our models. In this section we will discuss four of the most common templates that we found.

i) A *Multi-values Input Task* appears in every application in which the user edits various values until (s)he decides to submit them. For this behaviour we found that the recurring structure is the one shown in Figure 2. We first have a distinction between the Edit values task and the Submit task. The second task must be able to disable the editing activities. Editing is performed by the interleaving of the editing of the various attributes. Each attribute editing is iterative because the user can decide to change the value before submitting it. As a result, all sub-tasks can be performed any number of times.

An example of an instance of the *Multi-value Input* task is the description of an input to a database which allows the user to provide, for example, name, surname and telephone number of each element.

We can note that this task template is independent of the number of attributes to be edited because this element does not change its global behaviour.

ii) A *Search Task* is a very common task template, because it allows a user to search

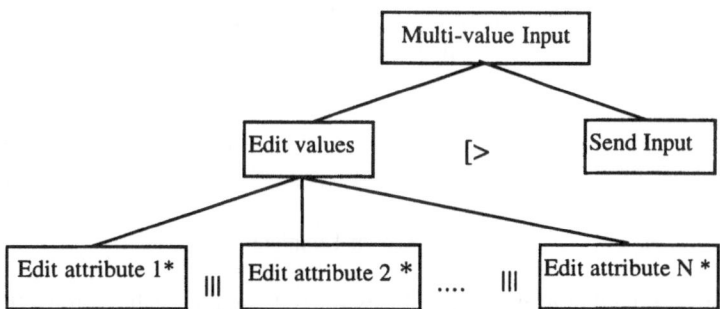

Figure 2: A Multi-value Input template

for specific information. Searching is not only "locating" data by using one query statement, it is also a navigational way of searching in which the next query is based upon the results of the previous one; this is called refinement. The only aspect that changes during refinement is the information used by the user to decide how to specify the next query.

The basic semantics of this task (see Figure 3) are: i) the user indicates what data to search for via a query statement entry, ii) the query manager is activated via submitting the query to search for the matching data, iii) the results are shown and iv) the user is able to refine his/her query results. These results will be used as new input for the next search. More specifically, the user can decide, depending on the result of the previous query, to enter a new formulation of a query, which probably will provide the desired information without additional disturbing elements. To describe this activity we introduced explicitly an additional user task (*Decide refinement*) which receives information from an application task (*Show data set ...*) and produces input for the next interaction task (*Refine query*) which requires the same user interactions as the *Define Query* task. As you can note the application tasks used are the same to provide both the result of an initial query and the query result deriving from a user refinement.

This search task can be applied in many applications where searching is needed, like search engines, database query applications and file managers.

iii) An *Evaluation Task* is a more complicated template (see Figure 4). It consists of

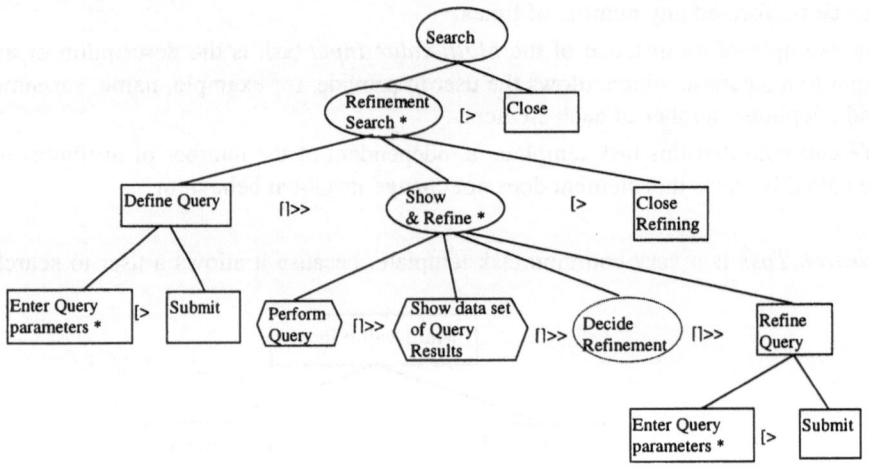

Figure 3: A Search Template

two activities, selection of the data to be evaluated and the evaluation itself, which can be repeated until the user decides to stop. The evaluation consists of five subtasks: first the user selects the evaluation type. Next the required data structures for this type of evaluation are created by the application. Then the user can edit the parameters that are needed during the evaluation until (s)he decides to start the calculations required for the evaluation. Finally, the results of the evaluation are shown. Note, that the tasks Select Data and Evaluate Data are synchronised, because the selection is directly influencing the types of evaluation that can be applied. An example is an information system, which gives the user the possibility to get information about houses and evaluations about them (pricing, history, mortgage, sizes, etc.). The user can select a set of houses and concurrently the

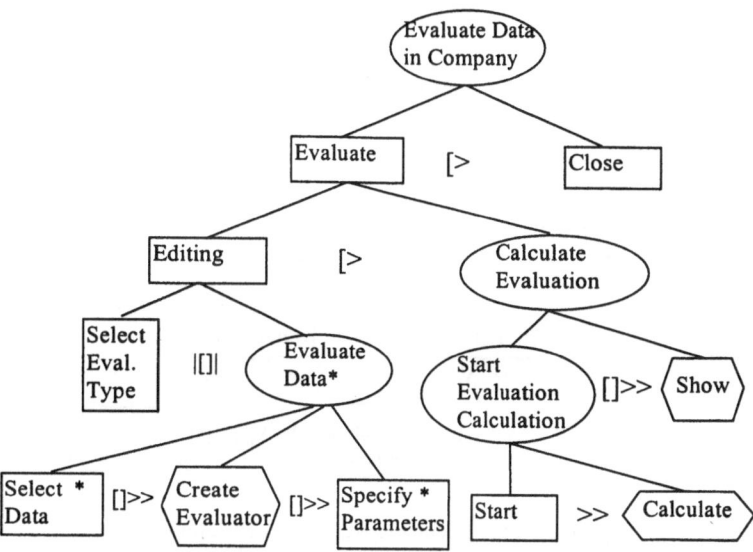

Figure 4: An Evaluation Task template

that can be applied. An example is an information system, which gives the user the possibility to get information about houses and evaluations about them (pricing, history, mortgage, sizes, etc.). The user can select a set of houses and concurrently the evaluation type. After selecting the evaluation type, it is possible to specify the parameters, like mortgage-rates, room-sizes, and taxes. Finally, results are shown. In some cases, depending on the type of evaluation requested, some houses cannot be selected, because the related information is not available.

iv) A *Recursive Activation Task* template captures the recurrent situation in many dynamic modern user interfaces which makes available an initial task whose main purpose is to allow the user to activate new instances of another task. An example can be a word processor which, whenever a specific interaction technique is selected, allows the editing of a new file other than maintaining the possibility to edit files previously opened. A generic example of use of this template is shown in Figure 5, where the double occurrence of the abstract Handle set of Objects task indicates this type of recursion. In the example we have an application for handling a set of objects. If it is not closed, it allows the user to select and/or delete various objects until the Start Object task is performed, which means that the presentation for editing the selected Object is activated. The recursion ensures that the Handle Objects task is available again. As a result of this recursion, the user can create several instances of the Handle One Object task by performing the Handle Objects task.

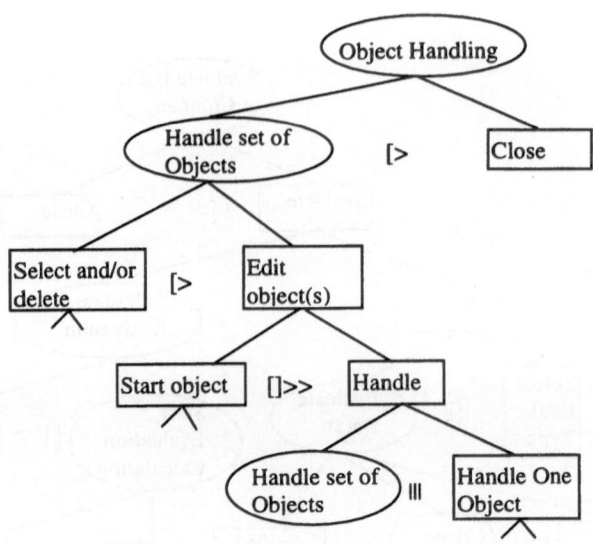

Figure 5: A Recursive Activation Task template

As illustrated by these examples, these templates are similar to patterns in object-oriented analysis and design [7]: they give a problem definition, describe a solution to this problem, and they can occur regularly in many applications.

Using Templates to Design an Application

The goal of most commercial companies is to sell as many products as possible. The activities of many departments within a company are aimed at achieving this goal. For example, the main activity of the sales department is to accept orders from customers and to provide other departments with the information required to deliver the products. Nowadays many companies support their activities, including those of their sales department, with an automated system for Enterprise Resource Planning (ERP). Amongst others, such an ERP system maintains information on the sales orders that have been and are being processed by the company. Sales employees have the task to start the processing of an order by entering new sales order information into the ERP system. They can also change existing sales order information when needed. In this section we will show how we can obtain an application for this task using templates, in this case the Recursive Activation Task and the Multi-Value Input templates.

The starting-point of the edit sales order task is the set of sales orders. The employee can add a new sales order, or delete or open an existing one. Once a sales order has been created (opened), the following data can be entered (modified): the order-specific data, the data related to the customer and the products, each product on its own order line. Regularly, a sales employee needs to access information on several sales orders simultaneously, e.g. while the sales employee is entering a sales order for customer A, customer B calls and wants a change in his/her sales order. This implies that a sales employee should be allowed to activate multiple instances of the sales order entry task. Therefore, we conclude that we can use the Recursive Activation Task Template as a starting point to construct our "Order Handling" task model. By replacing the word "Object" in the template by "Order" we obtain the part of the task model of

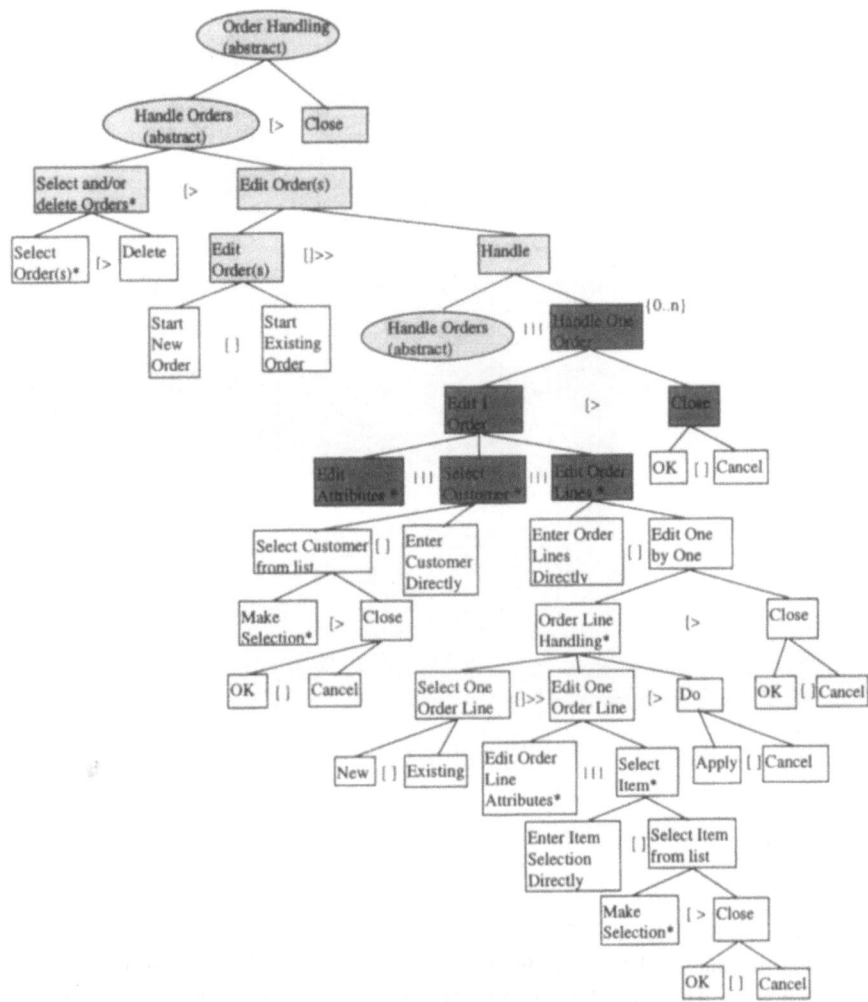

Figure 6: The task model that results from applying the Recursive Activation Task
template to Orders and extending it with application specific tasks.

Figure 6 shown in grey. The left part of the task model implies that the user can select
orders until s/he decides to interrupt this selection by deleting or starting the selected
orders or by starting a total new order.

We still need to extend this model for specific actions on a sales order: entering order
specific information (e.g. an order date), selecting the customer, entering the order
lines and selecting the products for the order lines. For this purpose we can use the
Multi-value Input task template.

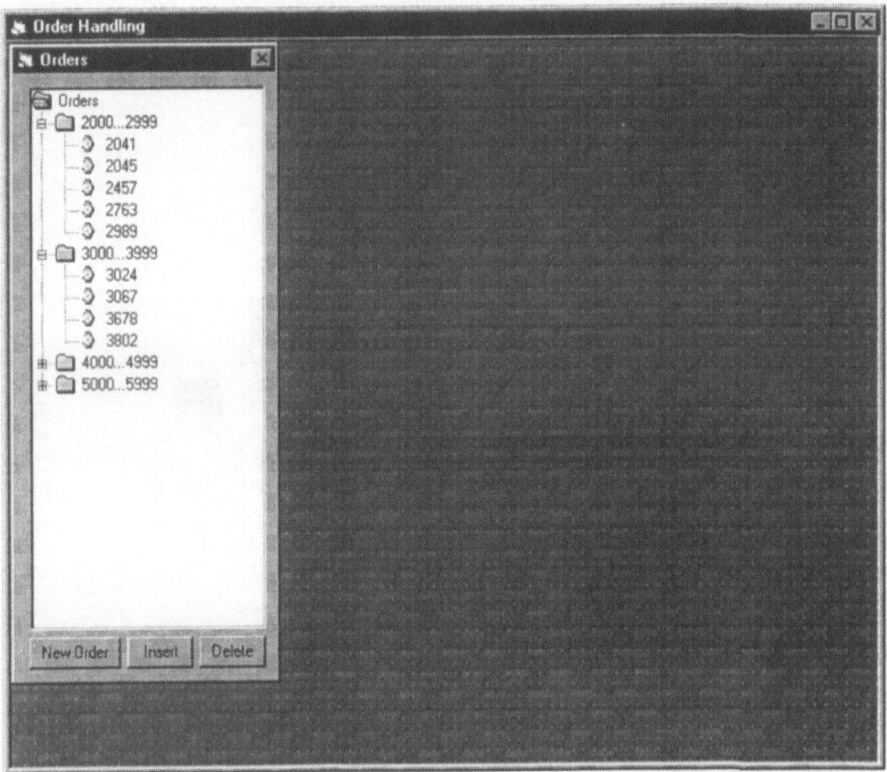

Figure 7: The set of orders, from which a user can select the orders.

The activation of the Edit One Order task is envisioned in the user interface by Figure 7. (Note that the sales orders are indicated via numbers, which is a common practice in many companies). The order lines can be edited directly in the table of the Order window as shown in Figure 8., or the user can open another dialogue to edit the order lines in a separate dialogue for order lines (see Figure 9). The difference between 'enter selection directly' and 'select from list' is introduced to indicate that the user respectively knows the data to select by heart or needs extra support by selecting correct data from an existing list/set.

As a concluding remark we note that we can use the Recursive Activation Task Template in a similar manner to manage some other data types, such as editing production orders, customers, and inventories.

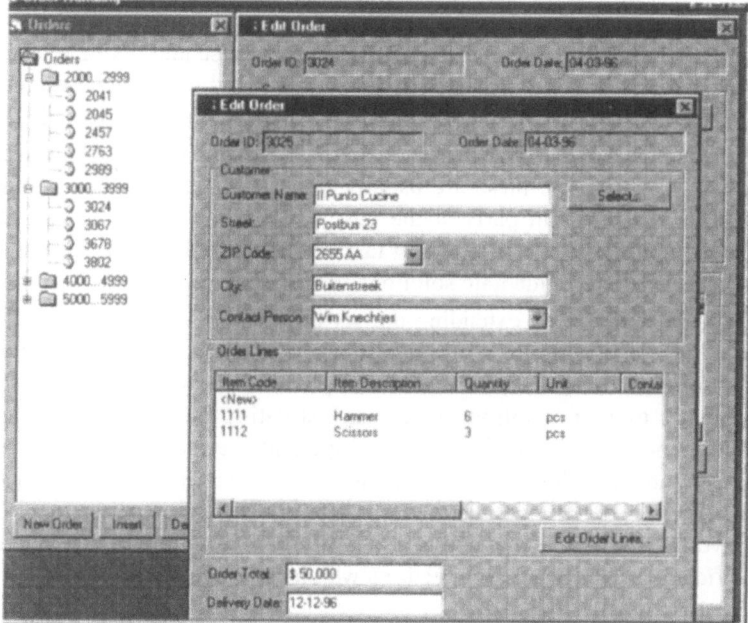

Figure 8: Two Edit Order tasks are open.

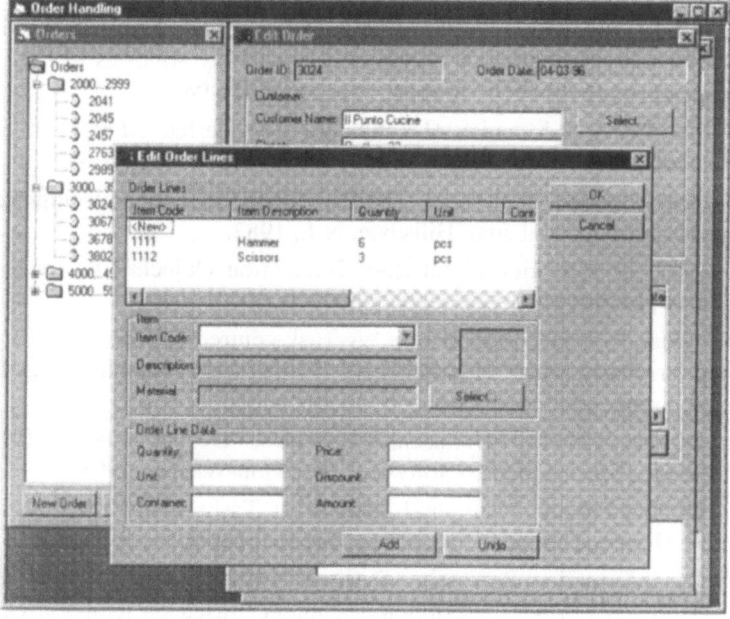

Figure 9: The Edit Order Lines dialogue in an Edit Order Task.

Conclusions

In this paper we have shown how it is possible to recognise and define reusable structures in task models. These reusable structures enable and encourage designers to focus more on the needs of users by providing high-level, semantics-oriented elements.

The need for them was raised by work on using task models to design industrial applications in the business area: these are usually large applications where similar problems occur often in different parts of the design. We found reusable task structures useful to speed-up the process of building task models for discussing design solutions because they incorporate immediate solutions for recurrent problems.

Currently we are working on extending the set of reusable structures in task models. We consider the set of templates presented here as a good starting-point for further investigation of reusability in task models. We plan to support the use of templates in a semi-automatic tool. In addition, we are investigating the possibility of obtaining reusable interactor networks: the software components, associated with the specification of tasks templates which can be used to describe similar situations in different contexts, in order to directly include them in different software applications. Thus, the software developer has the advantage of using a high-level, more immediate to understand, specification of software architectures which can be reused.

References

1. G.Booch, "Object-oriented Analysis and Design", Benjamin/Cummings Publ. Comp., 2nd ed., 1991, pg. 327.

2. F.Bodart, A.Hennerbert, J.Leheureux, J.Vanderdonckt, "A Model-based approach to Presentation: A Continuum from Task Analysis to Prototype", in Proceedings DSV-IS'94, Springer Verlag, pp.77-94.

3. F.Buschmann, R.Meunier, H.Rohnert, P.Sommerlad, M.Stal, "A System of Patterns: Pattern-oriented Software Architecture", Wiley, 1996.

4. S.Card, T.Moran, A.Newell. "The Psychology of Human-Computer Interaction", Lawrence Erlbaum, Hillsdale, N.J., 1983.

5. D.Carr, "Specification of Interface Interaction Objects", Proceedings ACM CHI'94, pp.372-377.

6. R.Fields, P.Wright, M.Harrison, "A Task-centred approach to analysing human error tolerance requirements". Proceedings Requirements Engineering'95, pp.18-26.

7. E.Gamma, R.Helm, R.Johnson, J.Vlissides, "Design Patterns: Elements of Reusable Object-Oriented Software", Addison-Wesley, 1995.

8. R.Hartson, P.Gray, "Temporal Aspects of Tasks in the User Action Notation", Human Computer Interaction, Vol.7, pp.1-45.

9. ISO - Information Processing Systems - Open Systems Interconnection - LOTOS - A Formal Description Technique Based on temporal Ordering of Observational Behaviour. ISO/IS 8807, ISO Central Secretariat.

10. I.Jacobson, "Object-oriented Software Engineering - A use case driven approach", Addison Wesley, 1992.

11. F.Paterno', C.Mancini, S.Meniconi, "ConcurTaskTrees: A Diagrammatic Notation for Specifying Task Models", Proceedings Interact'97, Chapmann&Hall, Sydney.

12. F.Paterno', C.Mancini, S.Meniconi, "Understanding Tasks and Software Architecture Relationships", CNUCE Internal Report, December 1996.

13. P.Palanque, R.Bastide, Verification of an Interactive Software by Analysis of its Formal Specification, Proceedings INTERACT'95, Lillehammer, June'95.

14. J.Rumbaugh, M.Blaha, W.Premerlani, F. Eddy, W. Lorensen, "Object-oriented Modeling and Design", Prentice-Hall, 1991, pg. 282.

15. P.Szekely, P.Sukaviriya, P.Castells, J.Muthukumarasamy, E.Salcher, "Declarative Interface Models for User Interface Construction Tools: the Mastermind Project", Proceedings EHCI'95, Chapmann&Hall, August '95.

16. D.Schmidt, M.Fayad, R.Johnson, "Software Patterns", Communications of ACM, October 1996, pp.36-40.

17. S.Wilson, P.Johnson, C.Kelly, J.Cunningham, P.Markopoulos, "Beyond Hacking: a Model-based Approach to User Interface Design, Proceedings HCI'93, Cambridge University Press.

18. A.Sutcliffe, P.Faraday, "Designing Presentation in Multimedia Interfaces", Proceedings CHI'94, pp.92-98.

19. A.Sears, AIDE: A step toward metric-based user interface development tools. Proceedings of UIST'95. ACM Press, pp.101-110.

The Interaction Specification Workspace: Specifying and Designing the Interaction Issues of Virtual Reality Training Environments From Within

C. N. Diplas[1,2], A. D. Kameas[1], P. E. Pintelas[1,2]

[1] Educational Software Development Laboratory, Department of Mathematics, University of Patras, Greece.
[2] Division of Computational Mathematics and Informatics, Department of Mathematics, University of Patras, Greece.

Abstract Advances in Virtual Reality (VR) systems, Intelligent Tutoring Systems and Agent Technology make it possible to design and develop Virtual Training Environments (VTEs), where the trainees can immerse themselves and interact directly with the learning domain. This paper presents the Interaction Specification Workspace (ISW) architecture for the specification and design of virtual environments for training purposes. ISW architecture provides the interaction designer with the capability to specify the training interaction with the virtual environment using the Virtual Reality Multi Flow Graph (VR-MFG) as the underlying interaction specification model. ISW implements a design space, where the processes of interaction specification and design of VTEs take place inside a three-dimensional virtual environment, the objects of which are tools by themselves. Inside this workspace, the designer can associate the abstract objects (the components of the VR-MFG) with "actual" objects of the target virtual environment (kept in a "world" database) and apply a number of agent templates with training capabilities.

1 Introduction

In Graphical User Interfaces (GUIs) of conventional programs the user "feeds" the application program with data or acts on some data via standard input devices such as keyboard and mouse, and perceives the information through the screen display. In order to do this, a number of interface components (e.g. buttons, list-boxes, etc.) have been invented, that behave as "handles" allowing the end-user to manipulate the data and information processed by the application program. These user interface components receive the events caused by the user, and display the information produced by the program, serving both the user interface designer, who chooses among a limited number of these standard components to construct the user interface of the application program, and the end-user who learns how to operate on these specific user interface components. Things would be complicated for the end-users if user interface designers used custom-made "controls", which did not fall within the known categories. In addition, every contemporary application program, (e.g. word processing packages, spreadsheets, multimedia tools and authoring systems for educational programs) uses the desktop metaphor as the underlying interaction model through a WIMP (windows-icons-menus-and-pointing) type user interface. In these programs, the *interface* point of view has the leading-role, with the creation of ease-to-use and functional controls and widgets. The *interactivity* point of view follows as a consequence, due to the limited capabilities provided by the standard user interface components which are restrictive for the user-computer dialogue representation. Virtual Reality (VR) applications tend to unify the application program and its user interface: the user interface becomes transparent and can not be distinguished from the "pure" application. VR uses techniques for immersing the user into a computer simulated environment where natural behavior is the interaction paradigm. In a virtual environment (VE) the application functionality and the application interface are not visually or physically separated, but only conceptually. The user interfaces of conventional application programs (even those with Graphical User Interfaces) serve as a representation of that functionality, and are constructed in a way which conveys to the user what the program can do. In the case of VR applications, the term functionality needs to be redefined as what a person can do with the computer program rather than what a computer program has the capacity to do [9]. According to this, the user interface of a VR application must *tell the user what he can do* inside the virtual environment, as well as, *indicate the correct way* in which he must interact with the application program itself in order to accomplish the desired tasks or to achieve the desired goals. To construct user interfaces which satisfy these requirements, the specification and design practices must concentrate more on the *interactivity* issues, rather than on the *interface* issues, since the latter are embedded into the VR applications. Of course, in VR (as well as any other) applications the user does not interact with the entire application, but with specific components of the VE. Thus, in a VR application which is composed mostly of computer-generated three dimensional models, the user is able to navigate, push, move, manipulate or even construct new objects inside the VE. Not all VE objects are interactive but every interactive object needs to be equipped with a number of "controls" which serve as the interface components for a VR application. However, like the physical objects that exist into our surrounding real environment, their virtual counterparts have their own "knobs". For example, all the members that belong to a specific class of objects (e.g. all the doors) can be handled using these common fundamental control "knobs", inside the corresponding virtual environment. This is analogous to the conventional WIMP interfaces: if a window class with one *system-menu*, one *minimize-restore* and one *close button* is specified, then all the windows (members of the same class) are expected to be equipped with at least these controls. In any case, the existence of these "controls" or "knobs" is not restrictive for the representation of the user-computer dialogue, as it happens in conventional application programs, since these "knobs" refer to the handlers of the objects, and not to the UI widgets. So, the user interface embodied into a VR application ought to be depended on the application domain, rather than the platform used to implement the application. However, during design and development of VR applications the problem arises when conceptual and "abstract" information objects must be visualized.

The problem of bridging the gap between a user's goals and intentions, and the low-level commands and mechanisms required by any application program in order to realize those goals and intentions still exists, despite of the many attempts that have been made, through the creation of effective UIs. The VE designer may find the solution to this problem if he takes advantage of the VR applications' special nature. In general, application programs provide a user interface (even a GUI) as a medium to help both user and system bridge the above mentioned gap. This gap can be expressed in two ways: as the common medium where user and system border on (optimistic view), or as the separating line between the user and the system (pessimistic view). VR applications introduce themselves as a *user interspace* (rather than a *user interface*), a concept which is closer to the optimistic view. This *user interspace* realizes the concept of the interface not simply as a means where a user and a computer system represent themselves to each other, but as a shared context for action where both are agents [21].

Every user's goal and intention in an application program (e.g. modify a database, delete a document, access a site on the web) is being accompanied by the problem: *how this goal can be achieved?* In conventional application programs the solution is provided by the user interface, which must guide the user to accomplish the desired tasks. It is obvious that the user interface has to provide the appropriate widgets and components that must be used by the user in order to accomplish the desired tasks. Concerning VEs, the solution to the same problem is embodied inside the virtual environment itself. The nature of the virtual environment objects shows the user the correct way of interaction, in the sense that the user must perform almost physical actions in order to interact with the VE objects. But, the friendlier the user interface is, the more difficult it is to design it. So, the designers of VEs have to establish unambiguous and robust interaction techniques, providing the user with obvious ways of interaction so that he does not worry about specific controls that exist in the virtual environment but concentrates solely on his specific goals. Moreover, the purpose of VR applications is to provide the user with the capability to perceive with more natural ways the information produced by an application program and interact with complex data. This means that the user's goals and intentions are translated not to abstract actions (e.g. click a button, roll up/down a slider, etc.) but to physical movements, often directly onto the objects of the VE. This forces the VE developers to provide the user with clearly defined goals. As shown and statistically measured in [24], most users focus on what there is to do, and what is already done, inside the virtual environment and not only on how to do it.

So, the VE designer deals with the *interaction design* rather than the *interface design*. Consequently, the specification and design tools for VR applications must provide ways to express interaction, rather than to "build" the interface; this is the major goal to the achievement of which our work attempts to contribute.

1.1 Related Work

The prime effort for the establishment of VR as a new technology and the development of virtual environments was on the high quality graphics that should be supported, the construction of three-dimensional objects and virtual scenes and the development of new hardware devices that could be used for interacting with the constructed VEs [13]. Architectures and systems for virtual world building, VE modeling for various application domains and object manipulation led to systems which combine easy object modeling, creation and manipulation along with (sometimes intelligent) object behavior [11, 30]. Also, approaches which focus on the visualization of physical systems in virtual environments and on the graphical representation of the information retrieval process make use of VE technology as presented in [23, 10].

Recently, interaction design was recognized as an important issue for the implementation of highly interactive VR systems, that exceed a simple 3-D interface, and many attempts have been made in this direction. MR (Minimal Reality) Toolkit [27] is a set of software tools for the production of virtual reality systems and other forms of three dimensional user interfaces. It consists of subroutine libraries, device drivers, support programs and a geometry and behavior description language. Immersive Metaphors project [25], focuses on the design and development of a consistent collection of the immersive techniques and metaphors which would be as powerful and ubiquitous as techniques which are used to build present day 2D Graphical User Interfaces. It is claimed that interface designers could use these techniques and guidelines to build 3D immersive user interfaces quickly and with high quality of interaction. Virtual Reality Interface Toolkit project [5] aims to develop a 3D user interface software toolkit which would provide all necessary 3D widgets, interaction techniques and tools for programmers to design and implement 3D user interfaces for various application domains. A developer can use the provided widgets and techniques or construct custom interface elements by inheriting attributes from existing objects. For the user, the applications built with the toolkit will have a consistent generic 3D user interface, based on a single paradigm that has been evaluated by theoretical and experimental studies. The focus of the Interface Toolkit is to design and evaluate software architectures which allow seamless integration of the 3D interaction techniques and widgets with VR world building functionality. VB2 [14] architecture for the construction of three-dimensional interactive applications proposed that the system's state and behavior are uniformly represented as a network of interrelated objects. The interaction techniques used in this architecture, among others (direct manipulation, gestural input, etc.) included three-dimensional virtual tools, which offered an interaction metaphor to control the VE models' information. Moreover, the evolution of VB2, the AVIARY [29] architecture proposes that everything that lies inside a Virtual Environment is treated as an *object*. Then each single object which is presented to the user is an *artifact,* and objects that cause the artifacts are called *demons* [28]. Conceptual Design Space [7], attempts to provide virtual tools and 3D interface elements for the construction of VEs. 3D menu systems, widgets, dialog boxes, tool palettes, etc., are used in order to provide a new interaction design metaphor, where users can be able to create virtual worlds, while immersed in one themselves.

The architectures and systems mentioned above are general purpose systems and have not being specifically designed for the development of VEs for training. This application area can exhibit theoretical frameworks and working prototypes [35, 8, 22, 17, 18]. Moreover, almost all of the above mentioned architectures, systems and tools, and most commercial VR development platforms [33, 36] use diverse metaphors for the design and implementation of virtual environments. The designer uses tools with conventional user interface and produces applications with three-dimensional and immersive interfaces. So, the problem which arises is twofold: how to provide the authors-designers with appropriate tools to design the interaction and instructional aspects of the desired Virtual Training Environment, and how to bridge the consequent semantic gap between designers and users of Virtual Training Environments.

The proposed solution is composed of the establishment of a *Petri-Net based graphical formal model for interaction specification with capabilities to represent the instructional aspects of the final application*, and an *architecture which implements a virtual reality tool for interaction specification, proposing the "virtual programming" metaphor, as the natural evolution of contemporary visual programming*. The ISW architecture, along with the underlying graphical formal model is presented in the next section. An example showing the model capabilities is presented in section 3 and the paper concludes with discussion and future work in section 4.

2 The Interaction Specification Workspace (ISW)

The basic components of the Interaction Specification Workspace are the Virtual Reality Multi Flow Graphs (VR-MFG) graphical model and the ISW Architecture.

2.1 The ISW underlying Interaction Specification Model (VR-MFG)

VR-MFG is a graphical formal model that can be used for the specification and design of Virtual Reality Agent-based Training Applications. The model is defined as an extension of IMFG [19, 20], a model used for the specification and design of conventional interactive applications, and incorporates the cognitive features and the powerful analysis techniques of Petri Nets.

Virtual environments due to the three-dimensional graphics they provide, are the ideal platform for representing the elements used by VR-MFG (cubes, spheres, cones, etc.) and the visualization of the concepts these graphical elements reflect. On the other hand, the graphical notation of VR-MFG (mostly adopted from IMFG) makes the specific model one of the most suitable, among other similar approaches [16] for interaction specification in VEs. Moreover, since VR-MFG is a Petri-Net based model, there is the capability for another similar Petri-Net model to be used for the interaction specification of the hardware devices that will be used in the final training application [1]. The usage of a 3D environment as a workspace provides:

- *Reduction of the space* needed for the entire specification due to the capability of the three-dimensional graphical objects to "include" other objects.
- *Supervision* over the specification [34].
- *Definition of different views* and *data abstraction* due to the "depth" provided by the third dimension.
- *Uniformity* between the design space and the executable one.
- *Establishment of a common context* (the 3D visual representation) for both the author-designer and the user-trainee, enabling the designer to think in user terms.

As a virtual environment consists of *interactive* (active) and *non-interactive* (passive) virtual elements (e.g. objects, concepts, abstractions, information), the VR-MFG which models this VE consists of active (actors) and passive (links) components. Although there is a close relation between the VE's elements and the VR-MFG components, there is an indirect correspondence between them. An active VR-MFG component does not refer directly to an *interactive element* of the VE, but to the task, goal or high and lower level action into which this element is involved. The correspondence between a passive VR-MFG component and a *non-interactive* VE's element, is analogous, since a passive VR-MFG component refers to the visualization of the different information flows that occur in a Virtual Reality interactive application.

Analytically, the components of Virtual Reality-MFG model are:

- *actors* (that correspond to the actions, tasks or goals of the VE's elements), which model the interactive responses that must be performed by the agents that participate in a VE, as a consequence of the occurrence of an event. Events may be caused by other agents, since the user, the objects of the VE and the VE itself, are all agents that act inside a common space. Actors are always preceded and followed by

- *links* (that correspond to the non-interactive VE's elements), which describe the situation that precedes and that results from a user action, through the storage of

- *tokens* (that correspond to the data or/and control information that exist into the VE), which represent abstract data or control structures that are produced or consumed by the VR-MFG components.

All the actors that are ready-to-fire (that is, which may fire after the next event) are maintained in the *actor-ready list* . Moreover, an actor can be viewed as an integral goal, which can be achieved by the satisfaction of a number of sub-goals.

Actors are described by: a *name*, a *set of input* and a *set of output links*, which precede and follow the actor, a *set of firing rules*, which represent the actor's behavior, since the left hand side forms the pre-conditions (that are kept in its input links) and the right hand side includes the post-conditions (that are kept in its output links), a *method*, which represents the lower level actor's functionality, that is, how the actor handles its input data and produces its output ones, and a *type*.

There are four types of actors, namely:

- *Action actors*: they represent a single response which is performed by a VE agent. These actors do not have any VR-MFG represented internal structure. The rules part of each action actor defines how this single task is implemented. VR-MFG does not give a clear description of the task to be done, but specifies the goal decomposition (or the task analysis) in order for the goal to be achieved (or the task to be completed). Action actors define the way the VE's agents interface with the domain-dependent functional core of the application, via single interactive responses.

- *Context actors*: their internal structure represents the task or goal decomposition into sub-tasks or sub-goals, via a number of other context or action actors.

- *Guide actors*: similar to Library IMFG actors, are used to represent the way the task or goal decomposition is achieved. AND and OR decomposition are provided, since these two fundamental actions can model any task or goal decomposition. These two decomposition styles represent a minimal functionality; also, serve the formality and facilitate the conversion of the VR-MFG graphs to a corresponding petri-net. For complex task representation (e.g. task interleaving, task interruption etc.), VR-MFG model provides the *actor-ready list*, the *condition links* and the link *usage properties* (*read-only*, *debit*, *OK*). Of course there is the capability to add more guide actors in the future.

- *Virtual actors*: used for a graphical grouping of actors, without any other significance, but may serve as reusable components during design process.

Links are described by: a *name*, a *set of input* and a *set of output actors* that produce and consume the tokens stored in this link, a *method*, which is performed upon the link's tokens, and a *type*. The definition of link types distinguishes among the type of tokens they store. Each link type stores a specific kind of tokens. This allows the designer to model the different types of information (e.g. data, control) that exist inside a VR Application, and permits system design from alternative perspectives. VR-MFG links are typed so that the different information flows that occur in a VR application are distinguished and each information flow can have its own visualization. The seven types of links, are:

Event links: describe the events that are caused by the agents that participate in the VR application. Users are also treated as agents in VR-MFG, so event links can be used in order to describe any *external* or *internal* communication of events. In VEs, events may be composite, having their own existence, unlike applications that use a 2D GUI, where events can be caused by simple actions (e.g. click, scroll, key-press, etc.). For example, event generation process in numerous cases [6] (e.g. where gesture interaction methods are used), includes an internal structure. Moreover, this is recommended by a number of diverse interaction methods which have already proposed in [4, 31].

VR-MFG provides *event links decomposition*, so the designer can explicitly specify how events can be caused, representing the internal structure of event links.

Perception links: a special kind of event links, which are used in order to represent system responses that are directed to the input-output devices, in order to provide the user of the VR application with the capability to perceive with natural ways special VE responses (e.g. haptic feedback, position orientation feedback activities etc.). These are event links with internal structure, that represent any cognitive perceptual state of the user agent and the tokens they contain are produced and consumed exclusively by the user (or the user agent). *Perception links* are designed in order to make VR-MFG model adaptive to any kind of interaction technique (e.g. direct or indirect manipulation of VR objects, immersion techniques where input is entered via sensors and output is processed by advanced hardware interface devices) and permit platform-independent interaction specification.

Condition links: represent the global or local conditions that precede and result from any agent action that takes place into the VE. Consequently they represent priority of execution and availability of actors. Moreover condition links describe whether any of the VE agents is ready to process another agent's action, that will lead to the achievement of a subgoal, or to the completion of a specific task, into the VE.

Data links: represent the data or control flow, into the VR application. Moreover, they represent the content of messages that pass between the participating agents.

Context links: represent the context, into which a number of interactions are performed. Consequently, context links describe the context to which a specific goal or task belongs and indicate whether a major goal is decomposed into sub-goals, so that a new "session" starts for the accomplishment of each sub-goal. Moreover, context links contribute to the representation of the system's *memory* and *knowledge* issues which are of major importance for any VR agent-based Application. Every actor that belongs to a specific context *knows* the goal of all the other actors that belong in the same context and the VR-MFG can model long-term memory by maintaining the actor ready list and the content of context-out links, since the short-term memory is represented directly inside the current context.

Communication links: model the effects that the separate micro-worlds existing inside the entire VR application may have on one another, since there exists a separate VR-MFG for each virtual micro-world.

Learning Links: represent the learning issues which rule the training interactions and the student-trainee dialogue. These links are founded upon alternative instructional strategies and provide representation of autonomous agents with instructional capabilities [26].

VR-MFG, being graphical tool, has its special symbolism which is shown in Figure1.

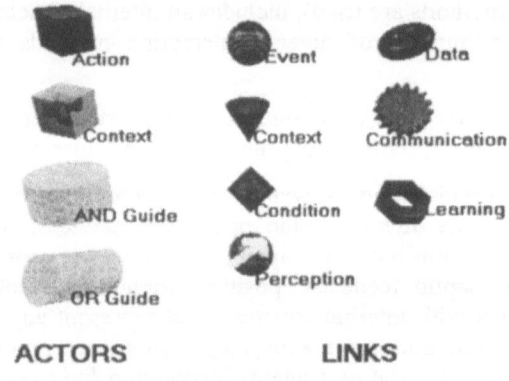

Fig. 1 VR-MFG symbolism

2.2 ISW architecture

The Interaction Specification Workspace is a software architecture for the specification and design of 3D virtual training environments. The overall system structure includes three major modules: The Prototype Interaction Editor (Practor), The Analysis and Evaluation module and the Prototyping facility; the application content, is an external entity which belongs partially to ISW since the pure content (objects, lights, real-time graphics etc.) can be produced by a third party VR development tool. The system structure is presented in Figure 2.

ISW provides the interaction designer with the capability to use the Prototype Interaction Editor in order to construct the graphs that represent the interactive and training sessions of the application. The workspace of the Prototype Interaction Editor is an abstraction of the virtual tutoring environment which is constructed. The actual objects contained into the final virtual environment have their own abstract representation into the workspace, enabling the designer to think and design in user terms.

VR-MFG, described in the previous section, is used as the underlying ISW model. The translator processes the interaction graphs at a low-level of lexical and syntactical detail. The analyzer evaluates the correctness of the produced graphs and the integrity of the interaction sessions, and produces and updates the interaction data structure. The analyzer can also be used as a wizard, which can guide the designer during the authoring process.

The prototyping facility enables the user to swap between the 3D graphical Prototype Interaction Editor and the virtual environment which is under construction. This enables the designer to take the place of the user-trainee and check if the application meets its initial interaction and learning specification [15]. At this point, the designer is able to evaluate the results which are related with the interaction and instructional design rather than the results related with the functionality of the entire application.

The tools of ISW can be used as "add-ins" utilities for a third-party VR development environment, extending the capabilities of this environment. The author-designer uses this VR development tool in order to construct the "pure" application content. According to the methodology the ISW proposes, he is able to use the *3D Graphical Prototype Interaction Editor*, in order to specify the interaction aspects of the final virtual environment. The *Analysis and Evaluation module* checks the graphs for correctness and the specification is recorded in the *Interaction Data Structure*. This data structure contains the interactivity and behavioral characteristics of the objects (e.g. data about the types of the objects, the tasks that are performed by these objects, the context, the user goals and intentions, the driver intelligent agents that are associated with specific objects, etc.). The *Interaction Data Structure* along with the *Dialogue and Presentation Managers* "tie up" the ISW and the VR development environment, in order to form a loosely coupled system. The interaction specifications of Interaction Data Structure are applied on the objects of the *World Information Database* which is updated via the VR development environment.

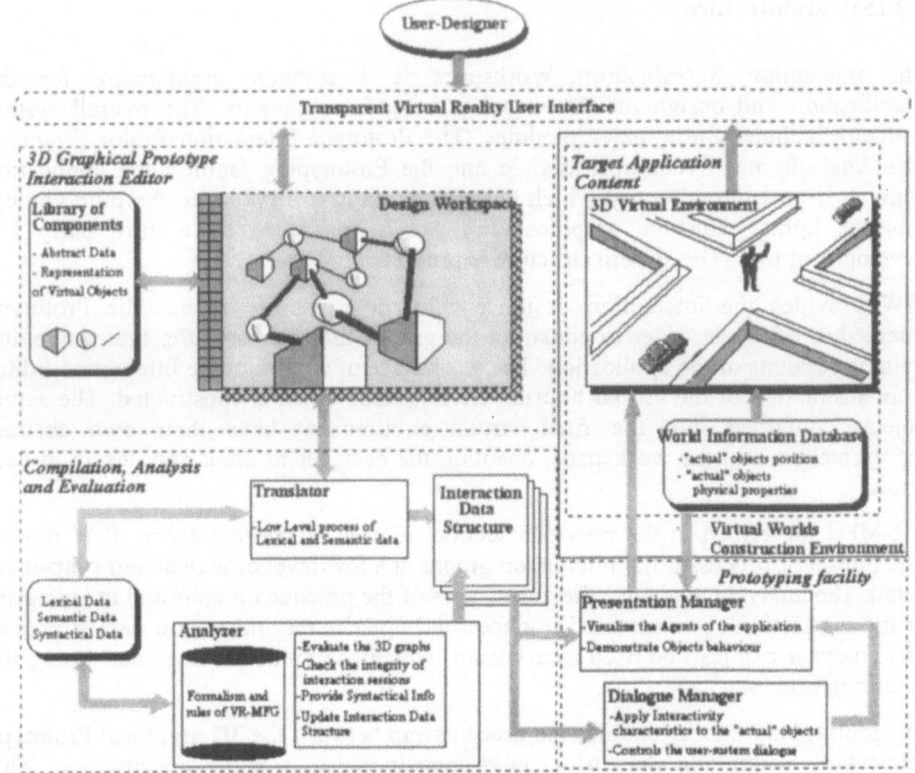

Fig. 2 Overall structure of ISW

3 An example application

Any VR Application can be viewed as a collection of different VEs (micro-worlds) that constitute the entire application. These multiple worlds may be concurrently active, just like a conventional GUI application, where several windows are open and running different applications, but only one can have the user focus. The aim of ISW, is not to specify the concurrency for the entire application, but to split the design effort for concurrency, among these multiple worlds, via the use of VR-MFG. The designer is provided with the capability to associate the abstract objects (the components of the VR-MFG) with "actual" objects of the target virtual environment kept in the object database, and apply a number of agent templates, inside a common virtual workspace (Figure 3).

DrIVE [12] is a virtual training environment intended to train novice car-drivers in common driving situations. It is based on desktop VR, with a minimum of requirements in processing power and data storage. DrIVE is a medium scale application and consists of three main parts: *driving lessons*, *tests for the trainee*, and *free driving* with on-line guidance.

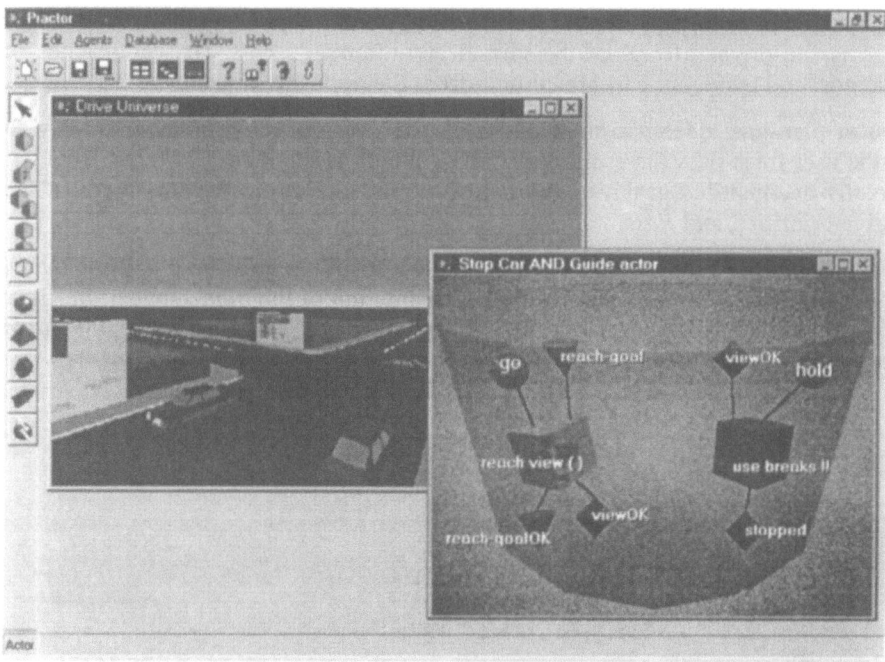

Fig. 3 Snapshot of the common virtual workspace where abstract objects (the components of the VR-MFG) are associated with "actual" objects of the target virtual environment and appropriate agent templates with instructional capabilities are applied.

The aim of the application is to transfer experience on the domain of driving behavior, which can be done using the synthetic experience that virtual environments are able to provide rather than actual practicing which involves obvious dangers. DrIVE has been developed with Superscape VRT software. The physical properties were attached to the objects which constitute the DrIVE environment using the appropriate editors. In the first system version the interactive properties were extracted informally and code was assigned incrementally and directly into the objects using SCL (a C-like programming language with event driven code execution) in order to implement these properties. In the second system version, the third part of *free driving* has been designed afresh, using VR-MFG for the interaction design, in the framework of ISW, before any code was assigned to the objects. Then, the implementation of this part was realized, using this formal specification. The benefit was twofold: evaluation of VR-MFG and a substantiated system. Moreover, a temporal comparison shows that for the implementation of the *free driving part* with the classical method three person-months were needed, and only two person-months using VR-MFG in the interaction specification phase. The design team designed the VR-MFG graphs by hand instead of the 3D Graphical Interaction Editor and typed the intermediate code which constitutes the *Interaction Data Structure* in text files the same way, because the editor and the analysis modules were under development.

The Crossroads example refers to the third part of the application where the user-trainee is the driver of one of the virtual environment's cars. His car reaches the crossroads, and two other cars are coming from the opposite directions.

The user plan-goal decomposition approach will be applied in order to specify the way the user must pass the crossroads safely, which is the main user-goal. This goal is directly decomposed in three sub-goals: *Stop* the car before the crossroads, *Check* and give priorities, and *Pass*.

Two representative graphs will be presented, one for the representation of the overall goal (*Cross-Goal*), and the other for the representation of the *Stop*-subgoal. In Figure 4 the overall goal is decomposed into the three sub-goals, using the *AND guide actor* (represented with a cylinder which includes all the other VR-MFG components).

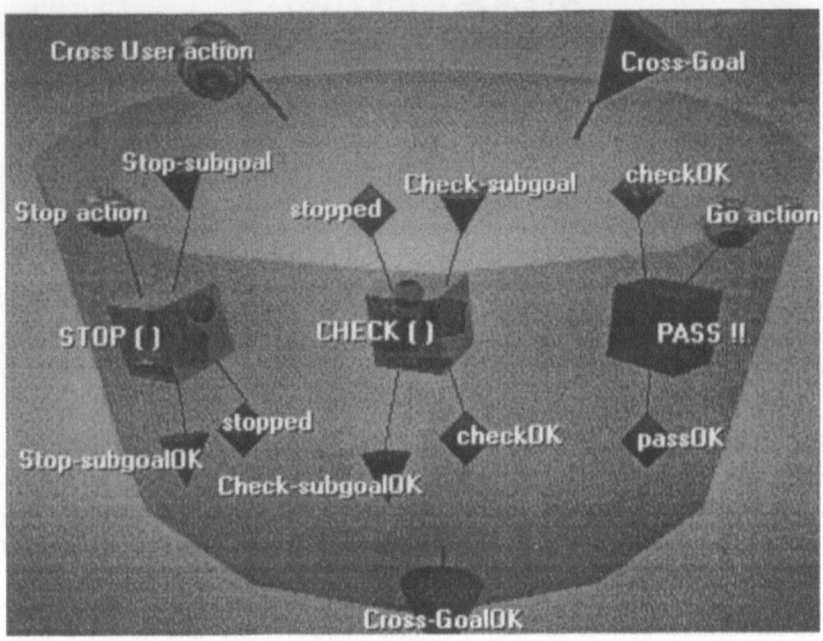

Fig. 4 The *Cross-Goal* represents the user-intention, and the *Cross User* action the actions he must perform to achieve this goal. Inside this *AND Guide actor,* there exist the *STOP ( )* and the *CHECK ( )* context actors, and the *PASS !!* action actor.

The *Stop action* event link (represents the user actions in order to stop the car) and the *Stop-subgoal* context input link (shows that the user intents to stop the car) form the *STOP ( )* context actor set of input links. Also, the *stopped* logical condition link (shows that the car actually stopped) and *Stop-subgoalOK* context link (the existence of a token indicates that the *stop the car* subgoal is being satisfied) form its set of output links. The *stopped* condition is then checked by the *CHECK ( )* context actor which can be further decomposed in order to fulfill the *checkOK* condition, permitting (along with Go action) the *PASS !!* action actor to fire.

In Figure 5 the *STOP ( )* context actor is decomposed. *STOP ( )* context actor includes the *REACH VIEW ( )* context actor and the *USE BRAKES !!* action actor. The user actions in order to drive the car in a position that gives him an appropriate view of the crossroads, are represented by the *Go* event link. The actor *REACH VIEW ( )* fires and a token is produced in the *viewOK* condition. This token is consumed by the *USE BRAKES !!* action actor, if there is a token in the *Hold action* event link, also. Then a token is produced in the *shakeFeedback* perception link (which can be used in order to provide the user with real feedback through an advanced hardware interface device, e.g. a data-glove or a cyber-data-chair), the *stopped* condition link and in the *Stop-subgoalOK* context link. Five more graphs, with almost the same complexity with those presented, are enough in order to complete the entire interaction specification and design for the *Crossroads* example.

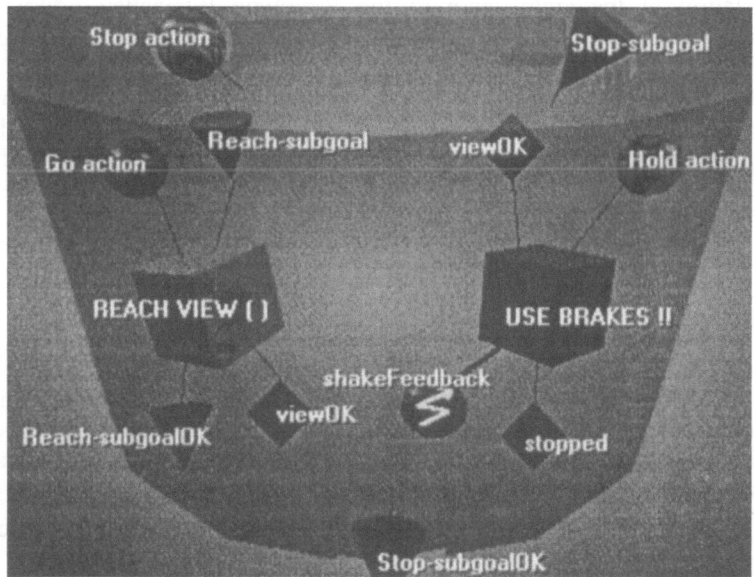

Fig. 5 The *STOP ( )* context actor set of input and output links are the same with these presented inside the AND Guide actor of the previous figure. *STOP ( )* includes the *REACH VIEW ( )* context actor and the *USE BRAKES !!* action actor. The condition *viewOK* that exist as an output link of *REACH ( )* actor and as an input link of *USE BRAKES !!* is responsible for the preservation of the correct interaction sequence.

4 Conclusions - Future Directions

In this paper, the Interaction Specification Workspace for the specification and design of virtual environments for training purposes, along with the VR-MFG graphical model and the architecture components were presented. A first working prototype of the system and two training VR applications are currently under development, one of them presented as an example application showing the model capabilities.

ISW architecture provides the author of highly-interactive VR training applications with the capability to specify the interactive dialogue between the trainee and the final virtual training environment. ISW implements the "virtual programming" concept, suggesting the use of virtual environments as 3D workspaces and authoring tools rather than as simple 3D interactive application programs.

Further research will investigate the integration of intelligent agents' behavior models [2, 32] into the basic VR-MFG formalism, and the ISW structure will be extended in the same direction and new guide actors will be added, too. Also, the specification of tutor-learner interaction sessions points to the need of establishing techniques for specifying models of instruction (for example: tutor models the desired task, then student practices on this, teacher coaches him and lets him accomplish the task alone as he gains proficiency). Moreover, network features, formally substantiated will be included [3], providing multi-user (or/and multi-agent) capabilities. The implementation of the architecture of the Prototype Interaction Editor and the Prototyping Mechanism which relies on the model's formalism, will be integrated along with a third-party VR development platform and a prototype system will be constructed. Providing the designer with the capability to switch between the design and prototype process, the complete ISW architecture could serve as the basic platform for the interaction specification and design, for the design of tutorial interactions and for the rapid prototyping of the complete Virtual Training Environments in any application domain.

References

1. Accot, J., Chatty, S., Maury, S., Palanque, P., "Formal transducers: models of devices and building bricks for highly interactive systems". In (informal) Proceedings of 4th Eurographics Workshop on Design, Specification and Verification of Interactive Systems, June 4-6, 1997, Spain, pp.155-168.

2. Beale, R., Wood, A., "Agent-Based Interaction", in People and Computers IX:Proceedings of HCI '94, Glaskow, UK, August 1994, pp.239-245.

3. Bell, G., Parisi, A. and Pesce, M., "Virtual Reality Modeling Language: Version 1.0 Specification", May 26, 1995.

4. Benford, S. et al., "From Rooms to Cyberspace: Models of Interaction in Large Virtual Computer Spaces", in Interacting with Computers (Butterworth-Heinmann), 1993.

5. Billinghurst, M. & Savage, J. (1996). Adding Intelligence to the Interface. In Proceedings of the IEEE 1996 Virtual Reality Annual International Symposium (pp. 168-176). Piscataway, NJ: IEEE Press.

6. Bolzoni, M. L. G., "Eliciting a Context for Rules of Interaction: A Taxonomy of Metaphors for Human-Objects Communication in Virtual and Synthetic

Environments", Proceedings of the 2nd UK VR-SIG and Contributors, December, 1, 1994, Reading, UK, pp. 78-87.

7.   Bowman, D. A., and Hodges, L. F. "User interface constraints for immersive virtual environment applications", TR GIT-GVU-95-26, Graphics, Visualisation and Usability Center, Georgia Institute of Technology, USA, 1995.

8.   Bricken, M. and Byrne, C. M., Summer Students In Virtual Reality: A Pilot Study On Educational Applications Of Virtual Reality Technology. (unpublished paper) Human Interface Technology Laboratory (HITL) of the Washington Technology Center (WTC) at the University of Washington (UW), 1992.

9.   Burks, L., "Information Architecture: The Representation of Virtual Environments", Harvard University Graduate School of Design, Thesis Document, May 1996.

10.   Card S., K., Robertson, G., G., Mackinley, J., D., Information Visualizer, An Information Workspace, Proceedings of SIGCHI 1991, pp. 181-188.

11.   Deering, M., The HoloScetch VR sketching system, Communications of the ACM, Vol 39, No 5, May 1996, pp.54-61.

12.   Diplas C., Giakovis D., Pintelas P., "DrIVE: A Virtual Training Environment For Driving Behaviour", in Proceedings of the First International Conference on Computers and Advanced Technologies in Education (CATE 96), pp.191-200, March 18-20, 1996, Cairo, Egypt.

13.   Fuchs, J., and Bishop, G., "Research Directions in Virtual Environments. An Invitational Workshop on the Future of Virtual Environments". TR92-027, March 1992, The University of North Carolina at Chapel Hill, Department of Computer Science.

14.   Gobbetti, E., Balaguer, J., F., VB2 An Architecture for Interaction in Synthetic Worlds, Proceedings of UIST'93, November 3-5, Atlanta, Georgia, 1993, pp.167-178.

15.   Hall, A., "Do interactive systems need specifications?", In (informal) Proceedings of 4th Eurographics Workshop on Design, Specification and Verification of Interactive Systems, June 4-6, 1997, Spain, pp.3-14.

16.   Harrison, M., D., and Duke, D., J., "A Review of Formalisms for Describing Interactive Behavior", Amodeus Project Document: System Modelling/WP28, January 1994.

17.   Hill, R.W., Johnson, W.L., "Situated Plan Attribution", Journal of Artificial Intelligence in Education, (6)1, pp. 35-67, 1995.

18.   Johnson, W.L., "Pedagogical Agents for Virtual Learning Environments", Proceedings of the International Conference on Computers in Education, pages 41-48, Singapore, 1995.

19.   Kameas, A., "A Formal Model for the Specification of Interaction and the Design of Interactive Applications". Ph.D. Thesis, Department of Computer Engineering, University of Patras, Greece, 1995.

20.   Kameas, A., Diplas, C., Gerogiannis, V. and Pintelas, P., "Encapsulating multiple perspectives in interaction specification". Proceedings of 20th EUROMICRO Conference, Liverpool, England, September 5-10, 1994.

21. Laurel, B., Computers as Theatre, Addison-Wesley Publishing Company, Inc., Reading, Massachusetts, 1993, p.32.

22. Mikropoulos, A., Diplas C., Giakovis, D., Halkidis, A., Pintelas, P., "Virtual Reality & Education: New Tool or New Methodology?", Proceedings of 2nd Conference on Informatics in Education, pp.57-67, November, 11-13, 1994, Athens, Hellas.

23. Opdenbosch, A., and Rodriguez, W., " Interactive Visualizer: Object and View Manipulation Algorithms", Journal of Theoretical Graphics and Computing, STCG, Vol 6 (in press)

24. Pausch, R., et al, "Disney's Aladdin: First Steps Toward Storytelling in Virtual Reality", Proceedings of Computer Graphics, Annual Conference Series, pp. 193-203, 1996.

25. Poupyrev, I., Billinghurst, M., Weghorst, S., & Ichikawa, T. (1996). The Go-Go Interaction Technique: Non-linear Mapping for Direct Manipulation in VR. In Proceedings of UIST '96 (pp. 79-80). New York, NY: ACM

26. Rickel, J., and Johnson, W., L., "Integrating Pedagogical Capabilities in a Virtual Environment Agent", to be presented in First International Conference on Autonomous Agents, February 1997.

27. Shaw, C, Green, M. , Liang J. and Sun, Y., Decoupled Simulation in Virtual Reality with the MRToolkit. ACM Trans. On Information Systems (11-3), July 1993, p. 287.

28. Snowdon, D. N., West, A. J. and Howard T. L. J., "Towards the next generation of Human-Computer Interface", Proceedings of Informatique '93: Interface to Real & Virtual Worlds, 26-26th March 1993, Montpellier, France, pp. 399-408.

29. Snowdon, D., West, A., "The AVIARY Distibuted Virtual Environment", Proceedings of the 2nd UK VR-SIG and Contributors, December, 1, 1994, Reading, UK, pp. 39-54.

30. Stoakley, R., Conway, M., J., Pausch, R.. Virtual Reality on a WIM: Interactive Worlds in Miniature. In Proceedings of ACM CHI95, Denver-USA, May 7-11 1995.

31. Sturman, J. and Zeltzer, D., A Design Method for "Whole-Hand" Human-Computer Interaction. ACM Trans. On Information Systems (11-3), July 1993, pp. 219-238.

32. Tambe, M., et al, "Intelligent Agents for interactive simulation environments". AI Magazine, 16(1), pp. 15-39, Spring 1995.

33. VRT 3.60, Superscape Ltd., Reference Manual.

34. Ware, C., Franck, G., "Viewing a graph in a Virtual Reality Display is Three Times as Good as a 2D Diagram", Proceedings of 1994 IEEE Conference on Visual Languages, S. Louis, Missouri, USA, October, 1994, pp. 182-183.

35. Whitelock, D., Brna, P., Holland, S., What is the value of virtual reality for conceptual learning? Towards a theoretical framework. In Proceedings of European Conference on AI in Education (in press), 1996, Lisbon, Portugal.

36. World Up, Sense8 Corporation., User & Reference Manual, 1996.

The Notion of Trajectory
in Graphical User Interfaces

Dorian Gorgan[1] and David A. Duce[2]

[1] Technical University of Cluj-Napoca, 26 G. Baritiu, RO-3400 Cluj-Napoca, Romania
[2] Rutherford Appleton Laboratory, Chilton, Didcot, Oxon OX11 0QX, United Kingdom

Abstract. The Active Objects Model (AOM) as a model-based user interface development environment is presented. The paper highlights the convenience of the trajectory notion in the description of the structure and functionality of graphical user interfaces. The AOM model consists of a set of active agents with private rule based behaviours. Model entities involve topological information which defines the behaviour of active objects, parallel and cooperative evolution of agents, time controlling, event oriented or supervised behaviour, interactive techniques, visual programming constructs, rapid prototyping, and intelligent user interfaces. All model entities may be defined by direct manipulation techniques.

1   Introduction

Over recent years development of user interface construction tools has emphasized a set of concepts, methodologies and techniques which support the process of designing of interfaces with good performance. These user interface construction tools have to support applications from new domains such as: distributed and cooperative functionality, animation and dynamic graphics, multimedia platforms [3], visual programming, navigation within virtual spaces, network communication, and courseware authoring [8].

There are a set of concepts that characterize the design of user interfaces: dialogue independence, structural modelling, interface representation, interactive tools, rapid prototyping, designing methodology, and control structures [9]. The most important design concept seems to be dialogue independence (or interface independence). The first tools for constructing user interfaces were interface builders (interface generators, procedural libraries). These were then replaced by user interface management systems (UIMS), a term introduced for the first time by Kasik in 1982. UIMSs introduced the idea that the design of the user interface is an integral part of the overall design process of interactive applications [9], and provide for the dialogue independence. UIMS focus on dialogue specification and use various representations: metalanguages (BNF, grammars [14]), state transition diagrams [18], Petri nets [5], script based representation, example based representation [13], or event based representation [15]. The next stage involves model-based interface development environments (MB-IDE), which generate more sophisticated interfaces [17]. MB-IDEs are based around the notion of specification of the tasks that are to be achieved through the interface. They encompass features such as data models, specifications of the presentation and dialogue, user models, and so on. A few experimental model based systems can be mentioned: Garnet [13], HUMANOID [11], UIDE [16], Mastermind [17], ITS [19], TRIDENT [1], etc.

There are a few interactive systems such as RIDES [12], DIGIS [2] which focus on the description of object behaviour for virtual worlds. In these approaches the system structure and functionality is built around a model that defines tasks, objects, attributes, constraints, and graphical presentations.

The last few years highlight a new direction in functionality modelling: parallel and cooperative multi agent based models. Also, the direct manipulation technique has been expanded to three dimensions and virtual space. All of these developments are based on a technology involving high performance graphics, multimedia platforms, multiprocessing, distributed resources, etc.

A user interface construction tool has to provide more natural manipulation approaches for manipulating both interface and application objects. The user interface has to be enriched to support the requirements of new applications. The notion of trajectory introduced in this paper attempts to respond to these requirements.

This paper explores the use of the notion of trajectory in model based user interface environments. It starts with a short presentation of the AOM model, and then continues with the presentation of the notion of trajectory. A few examples are used to emphasize the features achieved by using the trajectory concept: rule based behaviour definition using direct manipulation, supervised and event oriented behaviour modelling, navigation inside the space of characteristics, visual programming constructs, time control, graphical presentation control and modelling interaction techniques in graphical user interfaces. The components of the AOM model are described in more detail in sections 3 and 4.

2   Background to the Active Objects Model

Figure 1 shows an example application defined in the Active Object Model.

The key features of the AOM model are:
- the use of active objects (agents) to model the behaviour of application entities. Active objects in AOM are fundamentally distributed objects.
- the notion of trajectory which captures the idea that the agent is evolving along a path in some abstract space.
- the use of rule sets to describe the behaviour of active objects. Rule sets may contain references to attributes of other objects which is basis for the description of cooperative behaviour.
- the use of direct manipulation to define active objects and their behaviour.
- visual programming paradigms for interface development.

The fundamental notion of trajectory is explained in the next section.

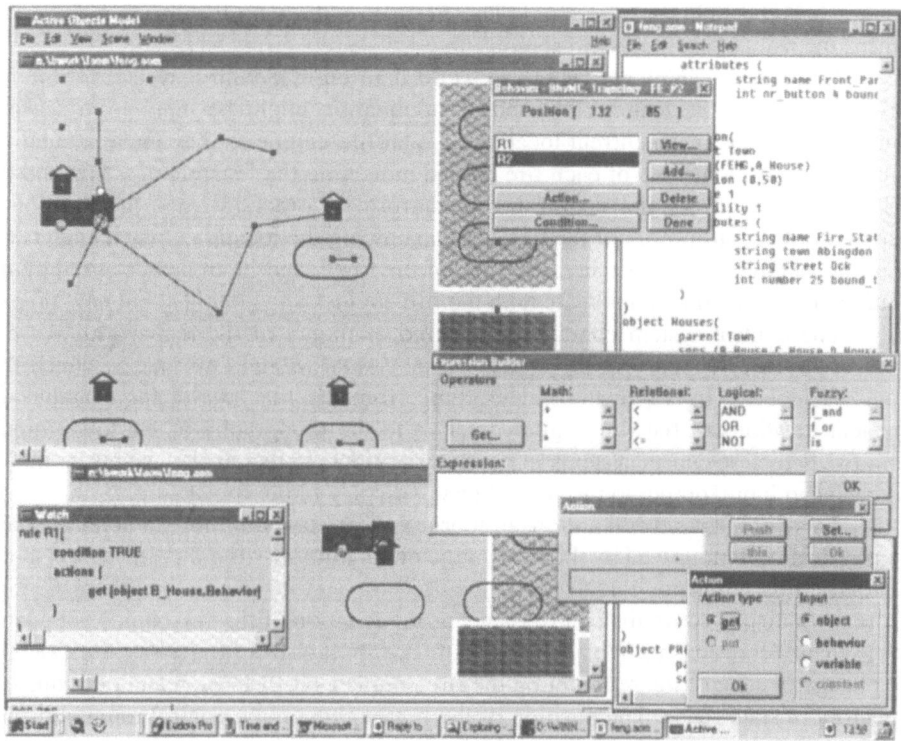

Fig. 1. The AOM implementation of the fire service example.

3 The Trajectory Notion

3.1 Motivation

To motivate the key concepts in AOM we present an application scenarios, a simple example in the real world: a fire service for a small town.

Suppose we have a fire station A, and three houses in the town B, C and D. The fire station consists of a building, a phone and a fire engine. The fire engine is equipped with siren, flashing light and driving controls.

A mission starts when the fire station is notified about a new fire. The phone operator receives the message at the fire station that there is a fire at one of the houses and informs the fire engine. A message informing the fire crew of the location of the fire is displayed on a control panel in the cab of the fire engine. The driver of the fire engine accomplishes the following sequence of actions: (a) turns on the flashing light by pressing a light button, (b) turns on the siren by a siren button, and finally (c) starts the engine by pressing the start-engine button. The fire engine is driven to the burning house along a specific route. On reaching the destination the driver turns off the engine, flashing light and the siren. The firemen extinguish the fire and the driver returns the fire engine to the fire station.

One way in which we could use AOM is to build a control system for the fire service. Some of the features of such an application might be input from sensors/transducers to report the current location of each fire engine as they move around the town, a display in the cab of each fire engine indicating the location of a fire, and the tasks the driver of the fire engine has to perform in order to reach the location, a display in the control room of the fire station showing the location of each engine, the locations of fires, etc. on a schematic map of the town, and input devices used by the control room staff to communicate with the fire engines and be told about new fires.

The control system contains some kind of model of the real world. We can think of AOM as supporting the concept of a Virtual Model Universe in which this model is located. Inputs to the model come from the real world, for example the physical locations of the fire engines relative to the topography of the town, inputs from fire detection/ alarm systems in buildings, outputs to the display panels in the fire engines, and input/ output to the control panel/ display in the fire station.

There are also several notions of journey or trajectory in this example. We have the physical route followed by the fire engine on its journey from the fire station to the scene of a fire, corresponding to this is the trajectory traced out on the schematic map of the town displayed on the control panel as the location of the fire engine is updated from sensors/ transducers. We also have more abstract forms of trajectory, for example the change in state of the red light on the fire engine as it flashes on and off - this is a trajectory in state space. The position of the fire engine on the control room's display panel might be indicated by an icon which is moving when a fire engine is on its way to a fire. Here again there is a trajectory in the state space of the representation of the icon.

The notion of journey in the real world and its representation in its Virtual Model Universe and the notion of trajectory in state space are captured in the single AOM notion of trajectory.

AOM in this example provides for a rapid prototyping, interaction techniques, and a metaphorical presentation (where we use metaphorical in a sense exemplified by the desk-top metaphor, and we apply the term to presentations in media other than visual media, for example audio). The user develops the model through an incremental approach.

The AOM model is a virtual component between real application and model developer, or finally user. Let us describe the notions which are involved in AOM modelling with reference to this example.

3.2   Real Application Universe

A real application consists of a set of objects which have associated behaviours and presentations. The real objects evolve in time according to the application's algorithms. Formally, the real application is a tuple: RM = (RO, RB, RP), where the real application RM involves RO which is the space of characteristics of the *real objects*, RB as the space of characteristics of the associated *behaviours*, and RP as the space of characteristics of the *presentation* of the objects. For example, RO is described as RO = RAttr x RState x RVis x ... , where RAttr is the space of real attributes (e.g. position, name, components, age, etc.), RState is the space of real states, etc.

The application has an evolution in *real space* (S^R) and *real time* (T^R) which define the *real universe*. The real space is generally three dimensional space (S^3).

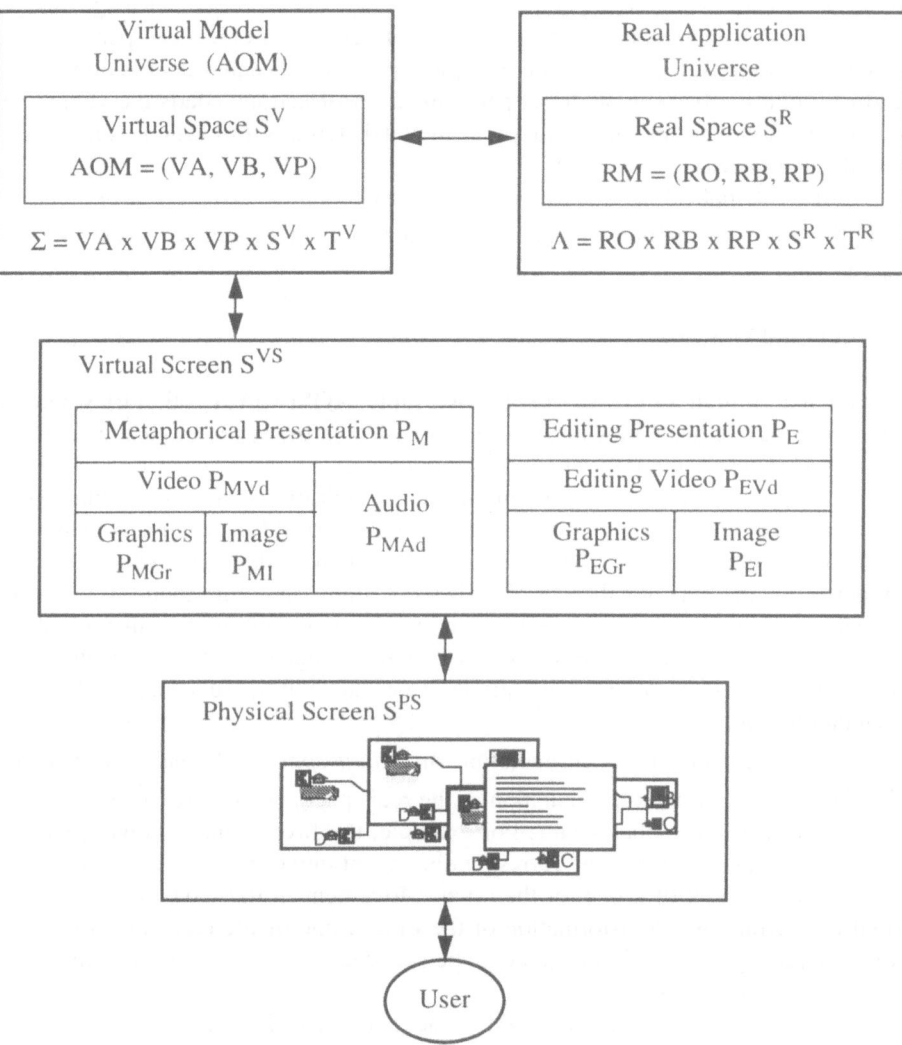

Fig. 2. The representation of the application in real universe, virtual universe, virtual screen and physical screen. The user interface is achieved through the physical screen which involves a set of metaphorical and editing windows.

There are applications defined also in two (plane), or one dimensional space (line). The *state space* of the application is: $\Lambda = RO \times RB \times RP \times S^R \times T^R$

The characteristics define the application objects, behaviours, presentations, and evolution in space and time. These characteristics are the basic coordinates of the application's state space. For example, a characteristic is the visual presentation of the flashing light of the fire engine. That presentation could have one value from a discrete set of graphical presentations: FL_PRES1, ..., FL_PRES4. A characteristic can be a coordinate in three dimensional space, (e.g. x coordinate of the position of the fire engine within the town), or application oriented attributes (e.g. name, age, weight, etc.). Another characteristic could be the type of actions an object can performs. For every value of the type characteristic the object performs a sequence of actions, e.g. at the fire station the fire engine driver performs a set of actions (starts the vehicle, the siren, etc.), and at burning house are performed a different set of actions (turns off the siren, the engine, etc.).

The real application is represented in a virtual universe by an AOM model. The model describes the application and its evolution in virtual space (S^V), and in virtual time (T^V).

3.3   Virtual Universe

The formal definition for the AOM *model* is a tuple: AOM = (VA, VB, VP), where VA is the space of characteristics of *virtual agents*, VB is the space of characteristics of *virtual behaviours*, and VP the space of characteristics of *virtual presentations*.

An application object can be modelled through one or a set of virtual agents. For example, the flashing light object could be represented by a complex agent which has another component agent. The component is a non visible agent which describes and performs the functionality of the flashing light, and the complex agent has associated the metaphorical presentation, i.e. graphical animation. It is also possible to have application objects that have no corresponding agent, and new agents can be defined for different application entities (e.g. attributes, functions, behaviours, presentations, etc.).

The AOM model has an evolution in *virtual space* (S^V) and in *virtual time* (T^V). Virtual space is the representation of the real space, and defines the position and the movement of the virtual agents. For example, the fire engine is moving within a three dimensional space, and the corresponding agent moves within a two dimensional space that is a model of a map of the town. Movement in the model is described in virtual time which is a transformation of the time frame of the real application. This allows the passage of time in the model to be speeded up or slowed down compared to time in the real application.

The *space of states* for the AOM model is described as: $\Sigma = VA \times VB \times VP \times S^V \times T^V$ which includes the characteristics which define the modelled application. Typical characteristics are the attribute of an agent (e.g. nominal current), the agent's visibility in the metaphorical presentation, and the agent's position within a virtual screen (section 3.6).

The characteristics of the virtual state space can include the real application characteristics. For example, three attributes of an agent can be the real space coordinates x, y and z, of the application space. That feature provides for instance, for a synchronised movement of the metaphorical presentation and the real fire engine within the town.

3.4   Trajectory

A *trajectory* is a sequence of positions within the state space of the model: $T^\Sigma_i = <P^\Sigma_{1i}$, $P^\Sigma_{2i}, \ldots, P^\Sigma_{qi} >$. There is a trajectory $T^S_i = < P^S_{1i}, P^S_{2i}, \ldots, P^S_{qi} >$, in the virtual space S^V corresponding to the trajectory T^Σ_i. Progression along a trajectory T^S in virtual space implies progression along the corresponding trajectory T^Σ in state space. Thus navigation in display space provides a basis for navigation in state space. For example, the application object named flashing light has a specific functionality. The light changes its presentation with a given period of time, e.g. FL_PRES1, ..., FL_PRES4. That means the state of the corresponding virtual agent changes its state. This can be modelled as a movement along a cyclic trajectory with four positions inside the state space. The projection of this trajectory into the virtual space for instance, is a sequence of four positions: $P_1(x_{v1}, y_{v1}), \ldots, P_4(x_{v4}, y_{v4})$.

This means that abstract notions such as successive moments, or movements in time are transposed onto distinct positions inside the S^V space. Therefore the time intervals may be expanded and refined. The trajectory concept enables navigation through the time dimension in both directions (i.e. forward and backward).

3.5   Trajectory Positions

A trajectory $T^S = < P^S_1, P^S_2, \ldots, P^S_q >$ is a sequence of explicit positions called *explicit trajectory positions* (ETP). An active agent evolves in state space from a state corresponding to the current ETP to a state corresponding to the next ETP. The space between two ETPs is covered through a sequence of *computed trajectory positions* (CTP). The next CTP is computed relative to the current CTP, previous and next ETP and behaviour parameters. In section 3.6 the evolution of the agent is represented in the virtual screen space by progression along the line joining the two ETPs.

The projection of the state space Σ into S^V provides the possibility to associate to an ETP a current agent with a set of specific actions and an appropriate presentation. If we consider a generic agent then a generic trajectory with associated specific actions may be defined. For example, if we define a generic trajectory that describes the flashing presentation through four ETPs, all agents which have that trajectory associated with them will have a flashing evolution of their presentation.

The formal and conceptual structure [7] of an ETP is: ETP = (n, p, t, E, RS), where n is the ETP *name*. It is a unique identifier among all ETPs from the current AOM. p is the *position* inside the virtual space S^V. The *type* t and *expression* E define the semantics (e.g. repetition, iteration, branches) associated to the ETP.

The behaviour of the agent at a given ETP is defined by an attached *set of rules* (RS). The rules describe a set of actions the current agent performs on itself or on other objects if a given condition is true. Depending on the kind of trajectory position, an active object performs the following activities:

- at a CTP position the current object performs only the actions requested by a remote agent, e.g. modifies the value of an attribute within its structure.
- at an ETP position the current object performs the previously mentioned activities and also delegates other agents to execute actions involved in its own private behaviour. For example, responds to another object that inquires an attribute value, or inquires from a remote object the name of its parent object.

The trajectory positions as a sequence of rules can control some subtasks. More complex tasks can be built through the call action (e.g. nested tasks), jump action (e.g. sequence of tasks), complex agents (e.g. hierarchical tasks), and binding mechanism (e.g. event oriented tasks).

Trajectory in AOM is used to describe movement in a very general state space of the virtual model. The power of the notion comes from the very abstract form this state space may take and from the use of the trajectory notion in prototyping functionality in AOM. The key ideas here are associating behaviour of agents with specified positions in the virtual space. The AOM system provides a virtual programming interface to trajectories state space and a behaviour definition which is a highly convenient and flexible way to prototype functionality.

3.6 Virtual Screen

The user interacts with the AOM model in two phases. One is the model development phase which constructs and incrementally modifies the prototype model structure and functionality, and the other is the runtime phase. Both phases use interaction through visual techniques which are embodied in a visual user interface (e.g. graphical user interface, menus, dialogue boxes, animation, direct manipulation, etc.). The user interface has to provide for access to all of the model's entities and characteristics. Likewise at runtime the model prototypes its functionality through a metaphorical presentation. In the majority of graphical environments in which direct manipulation is used the user operates on entities in a two dimensional space (S^2 - display screen).

Visual interaction is achieved through the *virtual screen* (S^{VS}) that is a projection of the state space Σ into a two dimensional virtual space, S^{2V}. For example, the virtual screen can be a projection of the virtual three dimensional space onto a specific plane.

The transformation of the state space into the virtual screen involves the presentation of the model's entities and their elements. The AOM model embodies both types of presentation: for the editing and runtime phases. The concept of presentation has been enriched with audio presentation too.

The model's virtual presentation has two components: $VP = (VP_E, VP_M)$. VP_E is projected onto the *editing presentation*, P_E and VP_M onto the *metaphorical presentation* P_M, on the virtual screen S^{VS} (see figure 2). P_M and P_E are then mapped onto a physical display screen, typically on a collection of windows (see figure 1). VP_E provides presentations for all the model's entities and their elements, i.e. attributes, presentation entities, etc. In the AOM model there are default graphical presentations for model's entities (agent, behaviour, trajectory, ETP, action, rule, expression, presentation), and interaction techniques (dialogue boxes, radio buttons, etc.) for entity's elements (name, attributes, parameters, etc.). The user interface is based on direct manipulation approaches. The visualization in the editing phase associates to a model's entity a presentation (P_E) into the virtual screen. For example, in the editing phase the agent named flashing light functionality (FL_FUNC) has a default presentation as a specific icon and an editing browser (such as the window "watch" in figure 1). It has a position inside the virtual screen computed from the position of the virtual agent within the virtual space.

VP_M provides a presentation only for the model's agents: active objects and variables. The visualization in the runtime phase associates to a model's entity a metaphorical presentation (P_M) into the virtual screen. For example, in the runtime phase the FL_FUNC agent is not visible, but its parent agent named flashing light (FL) has a metaphorical presentation as a circle with a set of four alternating coloured patterns.

The virtual screen provides for visualization and access of the same state space through different projecting directions in order to highlight specific elements of the model (e.g. in figure 1 the trajectory of the fire engine through the town is on the same screen as the trajectory of the flashing light through its state space).

4   The Active Objects Model

AOM embodies two types of entities: active and passive [7]. Active entities are agents each having associated an expression or a rule based behaviour. The passive entities are behaviours, processors, trajectories, explicit trajectory positions, rules, expressions, and actions. They are global resources and all AOM agents can access them to build appropriate tasks.

The model has two equivalent states: a *runtime model* form, and a *high-level specification language* form (AGML) [6]. Both forms provide consistent information for critique of the design of an application model, and for assisting the user interface designer, during the model validation phase.

4.1   Agents

There are two types of virtual agents (VA): *active objects* and *variables*. An active object $O \in VA$ (section 3.2) has a formal conceptual structure $O = (S, PO, SO, B, P, PR)$, where $S = (n, p, sf, pf, A)$ is the state of the object O. The object has a *name* (n), and a *position* $p \in S^V$ that locates the object in the virtual space, and in the virtual screen too. The *state flag* (sf) controls the evolution of the object [7] on the attached trajectory. *Attributes* A are application oriented characteristics, e.g. cost, nominal electric current, propagation time, and so on. An attribute may have a type as in RIDES, e.g. integer, real, boolean, and text (in version [6, 8]).

The *presentation* P ∈ VP defines the video, graphics or audio presentation of the object. Visibility in the virtual screen is controlled through the *presentation flag* (pf). The *parent object* PO ∈ VA and the *child object* SO ∈ VA provide the aggregate object construction, similar to that of Garnet. *The behaviour* B ∈ VB identifies an attached behaviour. It describes the evolution of the object within the virtual space. The notion of behaviour implements the concept of goal similar to that of Mastermind.

There are four types of associated processors PR: *behaviour, server, player*, and *interactor*. The behaviour processor moves the object along its trajectory and interprets the set of rules specified at ETP positions. The server processor executes delegated actions ordered by the object itself or by a remote agent. The player performs the presentation of active objects, and interactors [4, 10] are run-time connections between agent attributes and interface connectors (e.g. external modules connections, mouse, keyboard, timers, sensors and transducers for real time processes, network channels, other software modules, etc.). It will be assumed that an interactor updates or reads an agent's attribute value and the AOM model operates on those attributes only.

A *variable* is an agent with a simple behaviour. It has an attached *expression* that is defined in terms of model elements. A variable implements constraints as in RIDES and the concept of condition similar to that in Mastermind.

4.2   Behaviour, Trajectory and Trajectory Positions

The *behaviour* is a passive model entity which describes the object evolution along an attached *trajectory* (section 3.3). The behaviour structure contains a set of parameters that define the evolution. A trajectory is a set of ETPs processed in an implicit sequence. The control flow can be changed through explicit actions (e.g. actions call and jump).

4.3   Rules, Expressions and Actions

AOM uses a *rule based* description of agent behaviour on an ETP position. The formal conceptual structure of a rule is: R = (n, c, AS), where the rule has a *name* n, an optional *condition* c and a set of *actions* AS.

The *conditions* and the *expressions* are defined in terms of model entity elements [6], such as names, positions, behaviours, presentations, and so on. For reasons of efficiency at execution time the internal form of expressions and conditions is *directly executable* rather than a textual form as in AGML.

A basic set of actions has been defined: *create, delete, instantiate, append, get, set, assign, call* and *jump*. The first four actions control the creation and destruction of model entities. Get and set actions inquire and modify respectively, the content of model entities. The action assign is a pair consisting of a get action and a set action. The call action provides for complex task and modular based behaviour. The jump action controls the sequence of trajectory positions (i.e. subtasks).

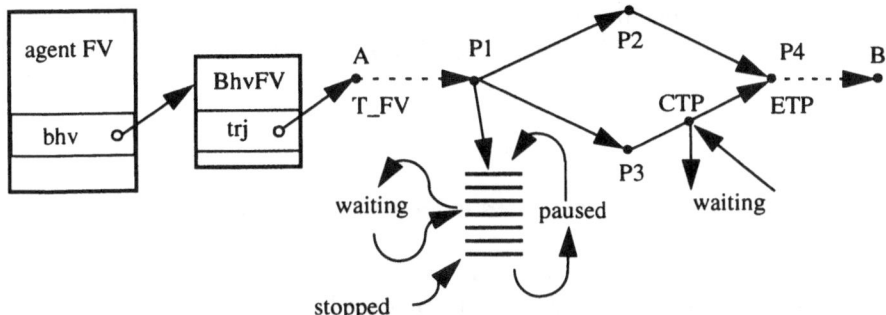

Fig. 3. The agent FV has an associated behaviour BhvFV and trajectory T_FV. At position P1 the agent FV performs a set of attached rules.

5 Trajectory Based Modelling

The previous section has defined the notion of trajectory in order to emphasize in this section a few features provided by trajectory based interfaces:

- rule based behaviour definition using direct manipulation
- supervised and event oriented behaviour modelling
- graphics animation modelling
- functionality modelling through state transition diagram
- task oriented modelling: complex tasks, sequential and parallel tasks
- visual programming constructs: repetition, iteration, branches, procedure calls
- interaction techniques: button, menu, dialogue box

5.1 Rule Based Behaviour Definition

The trajectory attached to a behaviour consists of a set of explicit trajectory positions. Each ETP is a sequence of rules which embody a conditional set of actions (Fig. 3). The execution of an ETP may be in one of the states play, paused, stopped, and waiting [3, 7]. For example, the agent Vehicle (FV) moves along the trajectory T_FV from the fire station A to the house B. At position P1 the agent selects the next ETP according to information about traffic, inquiring from another agent Traffic_Controller. The set of rules associated to position P1 could be for example:

```
trjposition P1 {
        . . .
        rule Ri {
                assign (agent(Control_Traffic).attribute(nod)),P2;
        };
        . . .
        rule Rj {
```

```
                    condition (!(agent(Control_Traffic).attribute(traffic)));
                    append (trajectory(T_FV).trjposition(P1)),(trjposition(P2));
            };
                ...
        };
```

5.2   Supervised and Event Oriented Behaviour Modelling

In the AOM model there are two ways to access the element of an entity: the *supervising* mechanism and the *binding* mechanism. The first mechanism is achieved by an agent's behaviour, mainly by performing a set of actions. The second mechanism implements the event oriented behaviour concept [7]. An agent is notified about an event which it has to process, through the "bound_to" mechanism. The second binding mechanism, named "bound_from" *is* provided to update an entity's element only when it is inquired by an agent.

For example, the y coordinate in the virtual screen of the next ETP position P2 can be updated automatically through the bound_to mechanism by a variable named Semaphore (Fig. 4). The variable computes the y coordinate according to a specific expression.

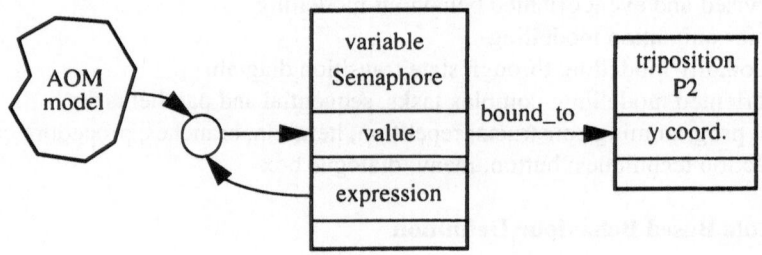

Fig. 4. The y coordinate of the P2 trajectory position is updated through the bound_to mechanism by the Semaphore agent. Its value is computed related with the state of the AOM model.

5.3   Graphics Animation Modelling

An active object has an implicit movement along its trajectory in virtual space. If the agent is visible the agent's play processor achieves the attached presentation. A graphical presentation is animated along the trajectory in the virtual screen. The behaviour's parameters define the movement in the sense of speed (e.g. number of CTPs between two successive ETPs, delay at each CTP), sense of movement (e.g. forward, backward), type of trajectory (e.g. cycle, polyline, etc.). For example, the movement of the fire engine is prototyped as an animated image of a vehicle around the map of the town (Fig. 1).

The presentation of an agent can be controlled through the behaviour of another agent. For example, the presentation of the flashing light agent FL, is controlled by the child agent named FL_FUNC. The last agent is not visible and its behaviour is defined by a trajectory with four ETPs. At each ETP the FL_FUNC agent changes the presentation of its parent FL.

```
agent FL {                                  agent FL_FUNC {
        . . .                                       . . .
        child FL_FUNC;                              behavior BFL_FUNC {
        presentation FL_PRES3;                              . . .
        visibility TRUE;                                    trajectory T_FL;
        . . .                                       };
};                                          };

trajectory T_FL
        P1{
                rule R11{
                        assign (agent($).parent.presentation),FL_PRES1;
                };
        }, P2{...}, P3{...}, P4{...};
```

5.4   State Transition Diagram Based Modelling

A *controller* agent may be built as an autonomous finite state machine (FSM). The FSM is defined by the four-tuple (S, C, I, R), where, e.g. S = {S0, S1, S2, S3, ...} is a set of states, I = {i1, i2, ...} is a set of inputs, C = {c1, c2, c3, c4, ...} is a set of outputs, and R is a set of rules which define the transitions from the current state to the next state.

The set of states can be represented through a set of trajectory positions: $T_S=\{P_{S0}, P_{S1}, P_{S2}, P_{S3}, ...\}$, which are covered by an agent, e.g. the agent FL_FUNC without a visible presentation. The evolution of the agent along the trajectory mirrors the control flow trace whilst the FSM is running. The initial state is S0, i.e. the position P_{S0}. The outputs C have the significance of actions that the agent performs on other agents, e.g. c1 sets the presentation of agent FL to the value FL_PRES1. Also, the inputs are attributes of other agents in the AOM model.

For example the rules which the controller agent performs at position P_{S0} are:

P_{S0}: . . .
if (agent(AG2).attribute(message) == "Fire at House B") then jmp P_{S2}
jmp P_{S1}

5.5   Task Oriented Modelling

In AOM a task is described by the behaviour associated with an agent. A complex task can be accomplished through sequential, parallel and nested subtasks. Sequential subtasks can be successive ETPs of the same trajectory associated with an agent. For example, the flashing light agent's presentation is a sequence of four presentations set at four successive positions: P1 (set FL_PRES1),..., P4(set FL_PRES4). By controlling the sequence of ETPs the model controls the sequence of the subtasks. The parallel subtasks are achieved through the behaviours associated with different agents, e.g. the child agents. For example, the evolution of the fire engines around the town are parallel subtasks of the fire station agent's task. The nested tasks are implemented through the call action. At an ETP the current agent can insert a subtask described by another ETP, trajectory or behaviour. Then the evolution continues with the next action of the caller ETP. For example, the fire engine executes a subtask that starts the engine:

```
if (agent(FENG).attribute(get_msg))
    then call (trjposition(Start_FENG))
```

5.6   Visual Programming Constructs

The trajectory concept also implements the semantics of programming control structures such as: *repetition, iteration, branching*, and *procedure call*. Through a visual programming technique the notion of trajectory can provide the definition and manipulation of elements involved in the semantics and syntax of these constructs. Repetition provides for semantics similar to the *while_do* and *repeat_until* constructs. Iteration implements the semantics of the instruction *for_do*, and branching involves semantics similar to *if_then_else*, and *switch_case* constructs. The call instruction provides for procedure call semantics. For example, the analysis of the pressed button may be implemented through a trajectory based switch case semantics. The switch element is a Buttons agent's attribute (e.g. pressed_button), and the cases are successive ETPs of the same trajectory (P_Light, P_Siren, P_Engine):

```
trjposition P_Siren{
        type COND;  //the agent executes the ETP only if the expression is true.
        expression (agent(Buttons).attribute(pressed_button)=="Siren");
        rule R1_1, R1_2,...;
};
```

5.7   User Interface Presentation

The AOM entities provide for interface objects modelling. The objects have associated virtual agents which perform both the corresponding functionality and presentation. For example the fire engine has a front panel which consists of three buttons (e.g. Light_Button, Siren_Button, and Engine_Button) and a message screen (Msg_Screen) (Fig. 1). The presentation of each button can be controlled by a child agent which sets the presentation of the parent button according to its state (e.g. attribute press is true or false).

Simple and complex interaction techniques (buttons, menus, dialogue boxes, drag and drop, palettes, etc.) can be described as agents with attached behaviours (i.e. trajectory).

6   Current Status and Future Work

The AOM model has been developed in an experimental form at the University of Cluj-Napoca (Borland C++ version), and an extended version is being developed at the Rutherford Appleton Laboratory, UK (Visual C++, multi-threads version). The current version concentrates mainly on functionality specification and less on graphical, visual or audio presentation, and internal and external dialogue [9].

The model will be extended with connection tools to different application components (e.g. multimedia systems, simulation processes, graphical based applications, network communication, etc.). We also intend to extend the model with more interactive techniques facilities (e.g. through a library of interaction tools).

7   Conclusions

There is a continuing need to generate new and improved user interface construction tools to support new application domains such as: distributed and cooperative functionality, animation and dynamic graphics, multimedia, visual programming, navigation within virtual space, network communication, courseware authoring, etc.

These areas all have notions of navigation in abstract spaces, time dependent presentation (animation, audio, etc.), and object orientation. The AOM model, being based on the concept of trajectory, is offered as an approach to addressing these requirements.

Acknowledgment

Part of the work described in this paper was carried out whilst Dorian Gorgan was an ERCIM Fellow at Rutherford Appleton Laboratory. Financial support from ERCIM is gratefully acknowledged.

References

1.   F. Bodart, A. Hennebert, I. Provot, J. Leheureux, J. Vanderdonckt: A Model-Based Approach to Presentation: A Continuum from Task Analysis to Prototype. In the Proceedings for the Eurographics Workshop on Design, Specification, and Verification of Interactive Systems. Bocca di Magra, Italy, June 8-10, 1994.
2.   H. de Bruin, P. Bouwman, J. van den Bos: A Graphical User Interface Design Environment for Non-Programmers. In Computer Graphics Forum, 12(3), 1993, pp. C13-24.
3.   D.A. Duce, D.J. Duke, P.J.W. ten Hagen, I. Herman, G.J. Reynolds: Formal methods in the development of PREMO, in: Computer Standards and Interfaces (17) 1995, pp. 491-509.
4.   D.J. Duke, M.D. Harrison: Abstract Interaction Objects, Computer Graphics Forum, 12(3), 1993, pp. 25 - 36.
5.   T. Elwert, E. Schlungbaum: Modelling and Generation of Graphical User

Interfaces in the TADEUS Approach. In the Proceedings for the Eurographics Workshop on Design, Specification, and Verification of Interactive Systems, pp. 193-208. Toulouse, France, June 7-9, 1994.

6. D. Gorgan: Dynamic Model Functionality, in: Research Report, Rutherford Appleton Laboratory, UK, August 1995, pp. 1-27.

7. D. Gorgan, D. A. Duce: Multimedia Synchronization Through Interactive Active Objects, in: EUROGRAPHICS97 UK Chapter Conference, pp. 131-155. University of East Anglia, 24-26 March 1997.

8. D. Gorgan, D. Rusu: Lesson Generating by Direct Manipulation, in: Proceedings of the International Conference on Computer Aided Engineering Education - CAEE'93, Vol.1, pp. 223-228, September 22-24, Bucharest, 1993.

9. H.R. Hartson, D. Hix: Human-Computer Interface Development: Concepts and Systems for its Management. ACM Computing Surveys, Vol. 21(1), pp. 5-92, March 1989.

10. A. Lie and N. Correia: Cineloop Synchronization in the MADE Environment, in: Proceedings of the IS&T/SPIE Symposium on Electronic Imaging, Conference on Multimedia Computing and Networking, San Jose, 1995.

11. P. Luo, P. Szekely, and R. Neches: Management of Interface Design in HUMANOID. Proceedings of the INTERCHI'93 Conference, pp. 107-114, Amsterdam, 1993.

12. A. Munro, M.C. Johnson, D.S. Surmon, J.A. Wogulis: Specifying Interactive Graphical Behaviours in RIDES. Research Report. Behavioral Technology Laboratories - University of Southern California. 1996.

13. B.A. Myers, B.V. Zanden, R.B. Dannenberg: Creating Graphical Interactive Application Objects by Demonstration. The Garnet Compendium: Collected Papers, 1989-1990, pp.95-114, Carnegie-Mellon Univ., Aug. 1990.

14. D.R. Olsen, E.P. Dempsey: "SYNGRAPH: A Graphical User Interface Generator". Computer Graphics, Vol. 23(3), pp.43-50, 1983.

15. G. Singh, M. Green: Automating the Lexical and Syntactic Design of Graphical User Interfaces: The UofA UIMS. ACM Transactions on Graphics, Vol. 10(3), pp.213-254, 1991.

16. P. "Noi" Sukaviriya, J.D. Foley, T. Griffith: A Second Generation User Interface Design Environment: The Model and the Runtime Architecture. Proceedings of the INTERCHI'93 Conference, pp. 375-382, Amsterdam, 1993.

17. P. Szekely, P. Sukaviriya, P. Castells, J. Muthukumarasamy, E. Salcher: Declarative interface models for user interface construction tools: the Mastermind approach. In L. Bass and C. Unger (eds.): Engineering for Human-Computer Interaction, Proceedings of EHCI'95. London: Chapman & Hall 1995, pp. 120-150.

18. A.I. Wasserman, D.T. Shewmake: The Role of Prototypes in the User Software Engineering Methodology. Advances in Human-Computer Interaction, Vol. 1. H.R. Hartson (Ed.) Ablex, Norwood, N.J., pp.191-210, 1985

19. C. Wiecha, W. Bennett, S. Boies, J. Gould, S. Greene: ITS: A Tool For Rapidly Developing Interactive Applications. ACM Transactions on Information Systems 8(3), July 1990, pp. 204-236.

A Representational Approach to the Specification of Presentations

Gavin Doherty & Michael D. Harrison

Human-Computer Interaction Group
Department of Computer Science, University of York
Heslington, York YO1 5DD, U.K.

Abstract. The principled design approach improves the quality of user interfaces by ensuring conformance to certain carefully chosen design principles. This involves reasoning about the properties of an interactive system specification. Such specifications usually concentrate on interactive system state and behaviour, and pay little attention to the presentation. We show that arguments about the properties of an interactive system **cannot** be relied upon without placing requirements on the presentation mapping. We consider in detail these requirements, and the manner in which we can verify their satisfaction. Taking this approach, we can prove that a presentation is valid with respect to a given property, and thus extend our reasoning into the perceptual domain of the presentation.

1 Introduction

In recent years, the approach of *principled design* [DFAB93] has become more widespread in the area of interactive system design. In the principled development process, we improve the quality of the system by ensuring conformance to certain carefully chosen design principles, such as reactivity, predictability and support for the user's task. This is done through the use of *formal specifications*, which we analyse with respect to the desired principles.

Interactive systems rely on concepts concerned with the presentation, and therefore interactive system specifications must include such concepts. In the interactor model for example, attributes may be tagged as *visible* to indicate that they are made visible to the user by the presentation mapping. Such tagging is important in relating properties of the system to the user's behaviour.

The problem is that presentations rarely display all data exactly, even in the simplest cases. Real world interfaces contain truncated text fields, approximate representations of numerical data, long lists of items of which only a subset is visible at one time and many other imperfect presentations. Given that such approximation is common, and in many cases desirable, *it is important that the approximation preserves the desired properties of the system*. For example, if the desired principle is that the system support the user in carrying out a proposed task, then we must ensure that information is presented in such a way that the user can make decisions and gather information as required by the task. We refer to these operations which refer to the presentation as *perceptual operations*. If the perceptual operations used in performing a task are not taken into account during development, then we can have no confidence in the ability of the system to support the user's task.

Consider other properties such as reactivity - that something is seen to happen when the user invokes an action. Proving this property to be true at an abstract level would involve showing that some subset of the attributes change when the action is invoked. For this to hold true on the presentation we must have the property that a change to this subset results in a visible change in the presentation. Thus our abstract requirements generate presentation requirements. Consider now a property such as predictability - that it is possible for the user to predict the outcome of his next action by using information displayed in the presentation. If the user needs to compare two quantities, it might be assumed that this activity is supported if both quantities are tagged as visible in the specification. However if the quantities are represented in a graphical display (eg. by bars on a histogram) then rounding will occur unless the quantity is guaranteed to be from a small discrete range, so proportionately small (but perhaps significant) differences between the quantities will not be visible. The result is that the user may not be able to reliably compare the quantities, and thus the interface is not predictable.

1.1 The Development Process

To put forward arguments about properties that depend upon the visibility of certain attributes, one must be confident that these attributes are presented in such a way that the properties are preserved (eg. that the user has enough information to carry out the task). This involves input from both the human factors analysis (eg. a task analysis [Dia89] in the case of the task support property) and the behavioural specification. A certain degree of decoupling of specification of presentation requirements and the interactive system specification is still possible, since we are only interested in the presented attributes from the behavioural specification. The human factors analysis provides conjectures about how these attributes are to be used.

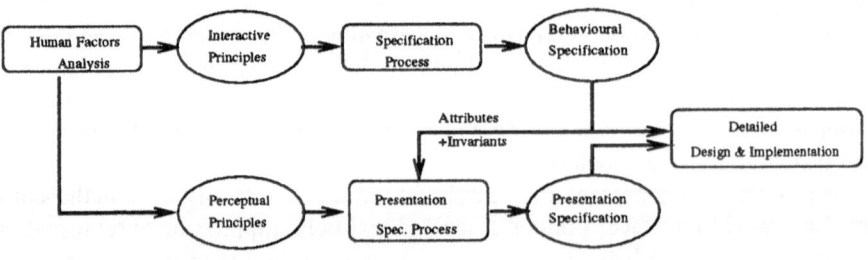

Fig. 1. Partial view of the development process

This approach leads us to put forward a new model of development, where a presentation specification is necessary before we can progress from the principled specification to detailed design and implementation (see figure 1). By following the approach of **a.** generating requirements which interactive system properties place upon the presentation and **b.** proving a particular presentation meets these requirements, we will have addressed the problem of specifying valid presentations.

1.2 The Interactor Model

In this paper, we use the interactor model [DH93] to structure our specifications. The interactor is a concept developed for the specification of interactive systems. Interactors are independent communicating agents (the interactor model is a refinement of the agent model of Abowd [Abo91]), which may participate in events caused by the user, the functional core, or by other interactors. The state of an interactor is made visible to the user by a presentation mapping. An interactive system will typically be specified as a number of cooperating but independent interactors. To summarise, an interactor has three components:

- some internal state
- a set of operations on this state, which may participate in events
- a presentation mapping, which makes some portion of the state perceivable to the user.

The model itself is independent of notation; interactor specifications have been written in a wide variety of notations. In this document we use a VDM [Jon86] based notation since it is probably the most widely used of the model based notations, and has a well developed proof theory and theory of refinement.

1.3 Document Overview

Our concern in the next section is the modelling of the presentation mapping and the manner in which we place requirements on the presentation - the first component of our presentation development process. We use the notion of logical and perceptual operators as the basis of these requirements. The section following uses an example to explore the means by which we can prove conformance to the requirements considered in the previous section, and proposes a method for doing this. Once this has been done we can have confidence that the presentation preserves the desired properties and the detailed design and development of the interactive system can begin. The final section summarises the work, and sets an agenda for future work.

2 A Model of the Presentation Mapping

2.1 Logical and Perceptual Operators

Recent research on graphical presentations has produced a number of interesting and useful results, concerned with the role of external representations in easing the cognitive load on users for certain types of task. Theories of *distributed cognition* postulate that an important role is played by such artifacts in the cognitive process. These theories and related issues, such as representation, have recently been receiving much attention in HCI [ZN94]. One interesting viewpoint adopted by Casner [Cas91] is to guide the development of graphic presentations by replacing logical operators in the task specification with perceptual operators on a graphic presentation. This determines what representations are *valid* for a given task. Various heuristic rules are then used to determine which of the valid representations is the most appropriate. Here we are concerned with *specification* and the *validity* of a representation, rather than *design* and *appropriateness*.

Perceptual operators are used as the basis of our treatment of the properties of the presentation entities (which we will refer to as percepts [DH94][1]) and hence help us develop requirements involving what is actually perceivable by the user. We restate the problem being addressed for the specific example of task support as follows (see figure 2):

> *the presentation is valid only if the logical operators necessary to perform the task have equivalents composed of perceptual operators in the presentation.*

The information in the presentation is extracted by the user's perceptual subsystem, so it is desirable that our model of perceptual operators bears some similarity to the way in which the perceptual subsystem is thought to work. In our examples we shall use a small number of simple concepts closely tied to the visual medium such as determining containment and adjacency, which we assume can be performed by the user.

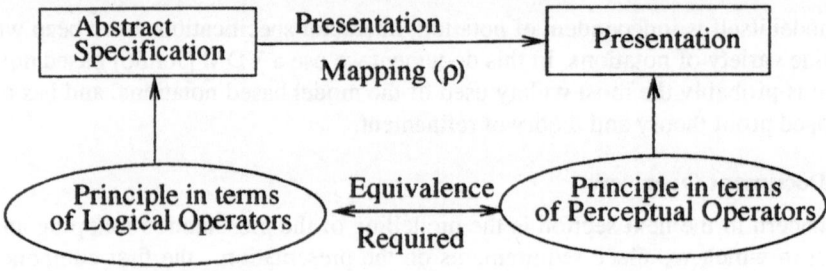

Fig. 2. Required equivalence of logical and perceptual operators

2.2 Perceptual Operators for Graphical Displays

To make the concept of perceptual operator more concrete, we introduce here some perceptual operators for graphical displays, which will be used in our examples. We make no claims that these operators are the most psychologically valid, but this does not affect the validity of the analysis. Our only assumption is that the perceptual operations can be performed by the user. Also, one must remember that different modalities will require a different set of perceptual operators, since from the human perspective the operators define the essential characteristics of the modality. For example, the operators below are spatial since they deal with a graphical display; were we dealing with an auditory interface, then the operators would be primarily temporal [DH94]. Analysis of the operators themselves can be useful; for example, Zhang [Zha96] applies the scale types of Stevens [Ste46] in the analysis of relational information displays. The operators below will suffice for the purposes of our examples, where we will use them to formulate perceptual equivalents of the interactive system properties.

Equivalence Identifying equivalences such as colour or shading is an important class of operator. Simple equivalences will be implicit in the data of the percept. More complex equivalences may involve some combination of the simple equivalences. For brevity, we

---

[1] Note that this differs from the usual use of the word in psychological literature.

will often denote equivalence by "=", though strictly speaking, the perceptual operator differs with each representation.

Comparison Comparing the magnitudes of two objects is likewise very common. Perceptually, magnitude may be defined in a number of ways - the length of a line or bar, the approximate area of a complex shape, comparison of two decimal strings (which we denote by "$<_s$") or the lexicographic comparison of two strings (which we denote by "$<_l$").

Location For graphical displays, location is obviously an important aspect of objects in the display. In our examples, we use operators for determining adjacency, containment, and relative positioning, eg.

$$adjacent: \quad \mathrm{Obj} \times \mathrm{Obj} \rightarrow \mathbb{B}$$

Special Purpose Operators It will sometimes be useful to define special purpose operators for a single application. In one of the examples we will make use of such an operator, *text-field*, which extracts fields from a text string. *text-field* takes three parameters: the string, the token delimiting the start of the field (START if this is the start of the string), and the token delimiting the end of the field (END if this is the end of the string).

Composite Operators Operators may be combined to form new perceptual operators. For example, we can define an operator *immediately-above* in terms of the *adjacent* and *above* operators.

$$\text{immediately-above} : \mathrm{Object} \times \mathrm{Object} \rightarrow \mathbb{B}$$
$$\text{immediately-above}(\mathrm{obj}_1, \mathrm{obj}_2) \triangleq$$
$$\quad \text{above}(\mathrm{obj}_1, \mathrm{obj}_2) \wedge \text{adjacent}(\mathrm{obj}_1, \mathrm{obj}_2)$$

Perceptual operators may also be combined using existential and universal quantifiers; for example if i is an item on a display, and *iset* is the set of all such items, then we can construct a predicate which returns whether i is the lowest item.

$$\text{is-lowest} : \mathrm{Object} \times \mathrm{Object}\text{-set} \rightarrow \mathbb{B}$$
$$\text{is-lowest}(\mathrm{i}, \mathrm{iset}) \triangleq$$
$$\quad \mathrm{i} \in \mathrm{iset} \wedge \forall \mathrm{x} \in \mathrm{iset} \cdot \text{below}(\mathrm{i}, \mathrm{x}) \vee \mathrm{x} = \mathrm{i}$$

Now that we have established a basis for our requirements (in terms of logical and perceptual operators), we go on to look at how they can be specified.

2.3 Specification of Presentation Requirements

We now introduce a simple functional model of the presentation. The presentation (ρ) takes a number of attributes, mapping them to a number of percepts.

$$\rho : \mathrm{Attribute}\text{-set} \rightarrow \mathrm{Percept}\text{-set}$$

278

These percepts are more representative of what the user actually sees because unlike the abstract state, the information in the percepts is fully visible to the user, with no approximation or information loss. The user can in theory perceive *exactly* the information contained by the percept. If we are considering height of a histogram bar, then the percept will contain the height in pixels of the bar, which can be perceived in terms of magnitude by the user, rather than some higher level representation to be passed to a graphics toolkit. There is obviously a balance between faithfulness and pragmatism here - in considering a 3D graphics toolkit we probably do not want to consider things at the pixel level.

We are interested in whether the presentation mapping supports perceptual operators equivalent to the logical operators over the abstract state. The question is how to formalise these imprecise definitions of conformance whilst incorporating some model of the perceptual capabilities of the user, as motivated by the previous section. With such a specification of presentation requirements, itself generated by the properties we wish the system to embody, we know that our reasoning about properties is valid for any presentation that meets these requirements.

2.4   A Model of Verification for Presentations

Taking the abstract model as the initial model and the perceptual model as the reified model, we can view the presentation mapping as a reification [BJ82]. The traditional approach to proving the correctness of this reification is to prove that state changing operations on the target model are equivalent to state changing operations on the initial model, for example, through the use of a retrieve function (see figure 3). This approach does not address the aspect of the problem with which we are concerned however, since it tells us nothing about how the presentation supports the principles.

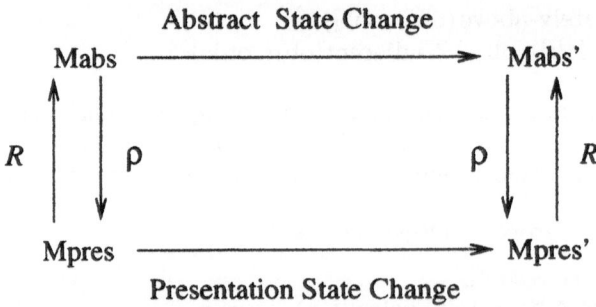

Fig. 3. Traditional approach to verification

To have confidence in this reification, we need to incorporate the notion that the reification is *valid*; that if the principle holds on the abstract specification, then it also holds on the presentation. We do this by relating both the abstract and perceptual models to a common model, in which the principle can be expressed. Thus for the task support property, we formulate both abstract and perceptual definitions of the decision making and information gathering operations in the task. Proving the validity of the presentation mapping then becomes a matter of showing that both the abstract model and the representation of the abstract model map onto the same result (via the abstract and perceptual operators respectively) in the task model. A diagram illustrating this approach is given in figure 4.

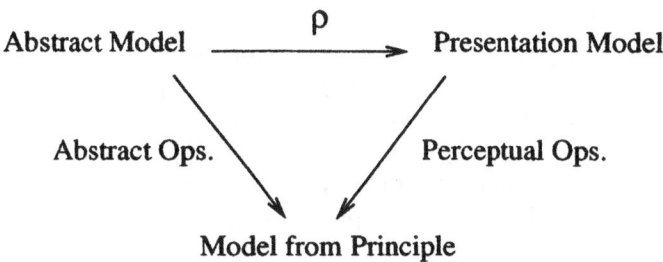

Fig. 4. Alternative approach to verification

Taking this approach, our requirements on the presentation mapping take the form:

$$\text{Abstract-op}(\text{Attribute-set}) = \text{Perceptual-op}(\rho(\text{Attribute-set}))$$

For example, consider a list of prioritised jobs from which the user must extract the highest priority job; the requirement that this operation be supported by the presentation might be expressed as:

$$\exists \Lambda \cdot \text{HighestPriority}(\text{jobs}) = \Lambda(\rho(\text{jobs}))$$

That is, there is some Λ, expressed in terms of perceptual operators such that when it is applied to the presentation of the system, it gives the same result as the logical operator *HighestPriority* applied to the abstract state.

This can be contrasted with the *expressiveness* model of Mackinlay[Mac87], which shows only that a set of facts can be encoded in a graphical language (such as horizontal position language), without reference to approximation or perception.

To recap then, conformance to interactive properties is dependent upon requirements on the presentation being met. These requirements may be defined in terms of the existence of perceptual equivalents of the logical operators used by the property. In the next section, we will consider how we can prove such equivalences to be true.

3 Property Proof and Presentation Refinement

Having produced a model the next step is to demonstrate how to verify whether requirements of the type discussed in the previous section hold for a specific presentation. We will conduct our exploration primarily through the use of examples. We focus particularly on the problem of task support, that is, whether the user has the information necessary to carry out a specific task. Verifying other properties will be very similar, but we feel this example to be both representative of properties concerned with system output and accessible to those not familiar with principled design.

3.1 Method

Working from the basis of our new development model and our logical and perceptual operator model of requirements on the presentation, we propose a simple procedure for determining the validity of a presentation.

identify the logical operators used in the reasoning about the principle (eg. in the logical operators in the task description for the task support principle).

formalise the descriptions of these operators, in terms of the abstract system model.

specify the presentation mapping. From this specification we formulate the equivalents of the logical operators in terms of perceptual operators over the percepts.

transform the perceptual operator descriptions by replacing perceptual operators with their simple logical equivalents.

show equivalence of the logical and perceptual operations
ie. logical ops = perceptual ops $\circ \rho$.

The first step - identifying the logical operators, is a crucial one, and it is worth considering how this may be done for a number of different properties. For the task support property, we must identify the decision making predicates and information gathering procedures in the task specification. For the predictability property, our formal reasoning depends on the visibility of certain attributes from which the effect of an action can be computed. In this case, the logical operators are the operations applied to the state in computing the effect of an action. For reactivity, we require that the equivalence operator over the *state* which we wish to be reactive is preserved with respect to the state change *operations* which we wish to be reactive. If we know this, then we know that changes by *reactive operations* to *reactive state* will cause a visible state change.

If we follow this procedure, we can be confident that the user can perform perceptual operations on the percepts which are equivalent to the logical operators in the abstract description, and thus that the presentation is valid with respect to the interactive property. Let us consider a simple property defined over a single interactor. Given an operation defined over the abstract state, we must prove that this operation has an equivalent on the presentation.

3.2 Progress Indicator

Consider the progress indicator on a WWW browser such as Netscape or Mosaic. The purpose of such an indicator is to let the user know how the down-loading of a document is progressing. Formally, we can express this as a requirement that the *less than* relation over the number of units of work done (*CurUnits*), in this case measured in bytes or kilobytes, is preserved by the presentation. We also know that the current number of units is monotonically increasing. So the *less than* relation between the new and old values of *CurUnits* is telling us either:

– more units have been done (and roughly what proportion more), or
– no units have been done.

That is, our requirement for supporting the *download document* task is that the user can distinguish between the above two cases. In this case, we envisage the entities being compared over time rather than space. Abstractly, we have two attributes - the current and total number of units of work.[2]

$$\text{ProgressIndicator} :: \text{TotalUnits} : \mathbb{N}_1$$
$$\text{CurUnits} : \mathbb{N}$$

inv pi $\triangleq$ pi.CurUnits $\leq$ pi.TotalUnits

We can specify the logical operator to support the task quite simply:

Compare-Progress : ProgressIndicator $\times$ ProgressIndicator $\rightarrow \mathbb{B}$

Compare-Progress (p_1, p_2) $\triangleq$
  p_1.CurUnits $< p_2$.CurUnits
pre p_1.TotalUnits $= p_2$.TotalUnits — To determine when the comparison is valid.

By this means we have specified our **abstract model** and **logical operators**. The progress indicator is represented by a horizontal bar, a certain proportion of which is "filled". Due to the limitations of graphic displays, an arbitrary sized indicator is not possible, so the usual approach is to perform a scaling and rounding operation, so our **presentation specification** is:

types

  HorizBar :: Filled : $\mathbb{N}$
  Total : $\mathbb{N}$

functions

  ρ-ProgressIndicator : ProgressIndicator $\rightarrow$ HorizBar

  ρ-ProgressIndicator (p) $\triangleq$
    mk-HorizBar(round($\frac{p.\text{CurUnits}*\text{BarSize}}{p.\text{TotalUnits}}$), BarSize)

We define the **perceptual operator** to support the task as follows:

Compare-Bar : HorizBar $\times$ HorizBar $\rightarrow \mathbb{B}$

Compare-Bar (b_1, b_2) $\triangleq$
  b_1.Filled $< b_2$.Filled
pre b_1.Total $= b_2$.Total — As above, we specify when the comparison is valid.

Where $<$ and $=$ can be viewed as perceptual operators such as those defined in §2.2, or as their transformed equivalents. If we attempt to prove the **equivalence** (see figure 5)

Compare-Progress(x, y) = Compare-Bar (ρ-ProgressIndicator(x), ρ-ProgressIndicator(y))

---

[2] For brevity, in this and following specifications, declarations of constants such as *BarSize*, *MaxDesc*, etc. are omitted

we find that the rounding operation does not preserve the *less than* relation (ie. Compare-Bar is *not* equivalent to Compare-Progress); the best we can achieve is the *less than or equal to* relation. Thus a simple bar progress indicator does not support the user's task, and so we must enhance or change the presentation of this attribute.

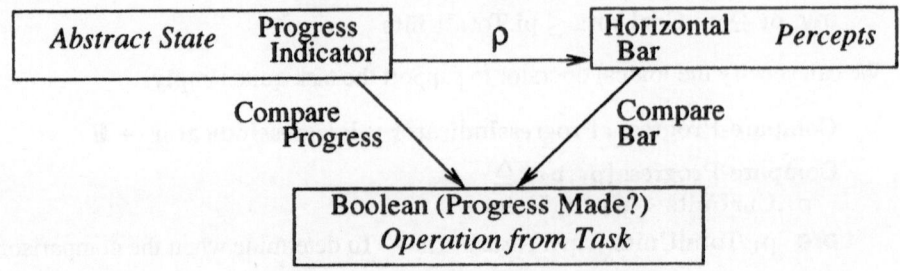

Fig. 5. Progress Indicator Requirement

3.3 File Handling System Example

We take as our second example an interactive system which provides a number of file handling facilities. The interactive system must support a number of tasks, one of which is the deletion of large, unnecessary files. By applying the method proposed above, we shall analyse the system with respect to support for this specific task.

Abstract File Model In specifying the functionality and behaviour of the interactive system, we have constructed the following model of files:

> **types**
>
>> $\text{FileType} = \text{DIRECTORY} \mid \text{TEXT} \mid \text{LATEX} \mid \text{POSTSCRIPT} \mid \text{BINARY};$
>>
>> $\text{FileName} = \text{char}^*;$
>>
>> $\text{File} :: \text{type} : \text{FileType}$
>> $\qquad\quad \text{name} : \text{FileName}$
>> $\qquad\quad \text{size} : \mathbb{N}$
>> $\qquad\quad \text{version} : \mathbb{N}_1$
>> $\qquad\quad \text{date} : \text{TimeStamp}$
>
> **state** FHSys **of**
>> $\text{FS} : \text{File-set}$
>>
>> **inv** $\text{mk-FHSys(FS)} \triangleq \forall i_1, i_2 \in \text{FS} \cdot i_1.\text{name} = i_2.\text{name}$
>> $\qquad\qquad \Rightarrow (i_1.\text{date}(i_1) < i_2.\text{date} \iff i_1.\text{version} < i_2.\text{version})$
> **end**

That is, files have a name, type, size, version and date. As a simple illustration of how invariants can be useful in the presentation specification, we introduce the invariant that dates and versions are consistent in the sense that higher versions of the same file will have a more recent date. (Note that this formulation precludes files with the same name from having the same timestamp). We assume (from the human factors analysis) a specification of a task which is to be supported. The goal of the task is the deletion of large, unnecessary files. *One* sequence of actions to accomplish this task is as follows:

> for *each object*
>> if *object is a file*
>>> and then *size is larger than some maximum*
>>> and then *file is an old version*
>>> then do
>>>> *delete file*
>>>> *check file is deleted*
>>> end do
>> end if
> end for

We assume here that this is representative of a class of strategies which will use the same logical operators, even if the order and manner of use is different.

Logical Operators Examining the above specification, we separate out the logical operators:

- check that file is not a directory
- check that file is larger than maximum
- check that file is an old version (version test)
- check that file is deleted (existence test)

For brevity, we will consider two of these; the existence test and the version test. Let us first specify these operations in terms of the abstract model of files. This can be viewed as defining a mapping from the abstract model to the task model.

> $\text{version-test} : \text{File} \times \text{File-set} \to \mathbb{B}$
>
> $\text{version-test}\,(f, fd) \;\triangleq$
> $\quad \exists i \in fd \cdot i.name = f.name \land i.version > f.version$
> **pre** $f \in fd$

> $\text{existence-test} : \text{File} \times \text{File-set} \to \mathbb{B}$
>
> $\text{existence-test}\,(f, fd) \;\triangleq$
> $\quad \neg f \in fd$

So we can see that in principle the system should support the task adequately, since there is enough information to allow the various decisions to be made. The next stage is to consider whether the perceptual model also supports these operations.

We define two different presentations, in order to ascertain whether each preserves the above operators, and thereby form a comparison between them. In the first design, we shall represent each file with a fixed length string in a manner similar to the naming convention used on the VMS[3] operating system. In the second we shall use

---

[3] VMS is a trademark of Digital Equipment Corporation.

iconic and other graphical elements along with the text elements. There is substantial evidence [LS87] that graphical presentations may be more "cognitively efficient" than textual presentations in many cases, and thus we might expect to find that the graphical presentation better supports the user's task. We will conduct the analysis in a similar manner to the last example, defining perceptual versions of the operations needed to support the task, as shown in figure 6.

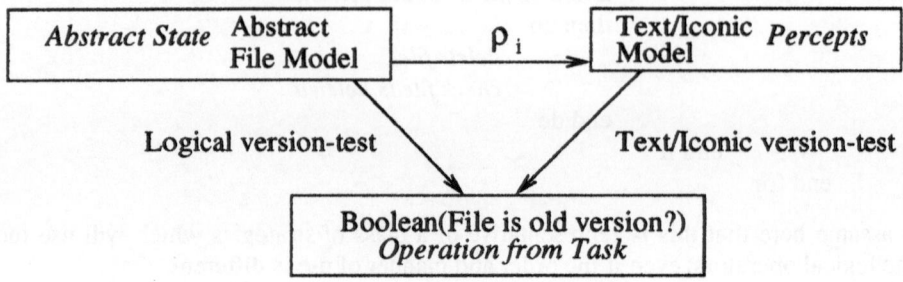

Fig. 6. Equivalence of Logical and Perceptual Models

Textual Representation In the first representation, each file is mapped onto a text string, giving the name, type and version of the file, and a numeric size, which is simply the size in bytes of the file. Within the string, a file name may be up to a fixed limit MaxName in length, followed by a dot and a short extension giving the type of the file. This is followed by a semicolon and a number giving the version of the file. Thus version 3 of a text file called "myfile" would be represented as "myfile.txt;3".

Since our abstract model of files does not impose any restriction on the length of names, we must make a decision on how to shorten file names which are longer than the maximum allowed. For practical reasons we take the simplest option and simply truncate the file name. Thus we can specify the relevant parts of the presentation mapping as follows:

types

$$TextDesc :: text : DescString$$
$$size : NumString ;$$

$$DescString = char^*$$

inv $ds \triangleq len\ ds \leq MaxDesc;$

$$NumString = char^*$$

inv $ns \triangleq len\ ns \leq MaxSize$

functions

ρ_1-File : File $\twoheadrightarrow$ TextDesc

ρ_1-File (f) $\triangleq$
mk-TextDesc (trunc(f.name, MaxName)
$\curvearrowright \rho_1$-type(f.type) $\curvearrowright$ ";" $\curvearrowright \rho_1$-version(f.version),
ρ_1-size(size));

ρ_1-version : $\mathbb{N} \twoheadrightarrow$ char*

ρ_1-version (v) $\triangleq$
trunc(decimal(v), MaxVersion)

We can now consider the perceptual operators for the textual representation.

Perceptual Operators The perceptual operators for this representation rely heavily on the perceptual text-field operation and other text string manipulations.

version-test$_1$: TextDesc $\times$ TextDesc-set $\rightarrow \mathbb{B}$

version-test$_1$ (s, sd) $\triangleq$
$\exists i \in sd \cdot$ text-field(i.text, START, ".") = text-field(s.text, START, ".")
$\wedge$ text-field(i.text, ";", END) > text-field(s.text, ";", END)

Rather than specify the existence test in terms of the *text-field* operator, we write it more concisely as:

existence-test$_1$: TextDesc $\times$ TextDesc-set $\rightarrow \mathbb{B}$

existence-test$_1$ (s, sd) $\triangleq$
$\neg \exists i \in sd \cdot$ i.text = s.text

It is plain that all operations on the presentation rely heavily on text manipulation operations - extracting fields from the strings, comparing decimal representations of numbers and so on. Analysis of the cost of such operations may yield some insight into the relative merits of the representation. Our concern however is with validity, and the biggest problem in this regard is truncation. Names and version numbers must be truncated, and this information loss may affect the faithfulness of the perceptual operations. If file names differ in characters after the first *MaxName* characters then they will be indistinguishable. Similarly version numbers longer than the maximum will cause problems. Both pieces of information are used by the *version-test* operation, and thus we conclude that the presentation is inadequate with respect to this operation and must be altered, or the version test must have a number of preconditions attached to it, ruling out name clashes and version numbers above the maximum.

Graphical Representation Our second representation is more complex and requires a graphical display. The file type is represented by a single icon; for practical reasons (eg. reusing previously written code), the types are different from the model used by the rest of the system, and icons are of type ASCII text, BINary or DIRectory. If the name is too long to fit in the available space then the first and last k characters, separated by an ellipsis, are printed. Given that related filenames often differ only in the last few characters, this is expected to reduce the number of namespace collisions, which was a problem with the textual representation.

The version is not explicitly visible, but files are sorted by date and thus newer versions appear below older ones. The size of a file is represented both textually and graphically. The textual representation is a short decimal string and a letter to denote the unit (Bytes, Kilobytes, Megabytes, etc.). The graphical representation is a horizontal bar, the granularity of which is determined by the largest unit on display. We reuse the definition of HorizBar from the previous example. Part of the specification is given below; since sequencing is important, we define a ρ function which takes the full set of files to be presented. A mockup of the presentation is given in figure 7.

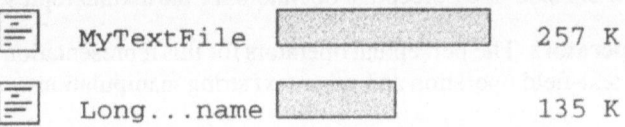

Fig. 7. Mockup of Graphical Presentation

types

    IconType = DIR | ASCII | BIN;

    NameString = char*

    Inv namstr $\triangleq$ len namstr < MaxName;

    SizeUnit = 'B | 'K | 'M | 'G;

    SizeString = char*

    Inv sizestr $\triangleq$ len sizestr < MaxSize;

    Icon :: type : IconType
            name : NameString
            size : SizeString
            unit : SizeUnit
            bar : HorizBar

functions

    ρ_2-FileSet (fs : File-**set**) out : Icon*
    pre $\forall i, j \in$ fs $\cdot$ i.name = j.name $\wedge$ i.date = j.date $\Rightarrow$ i = j

post let $p \in fs$ be st $\forall q \in fs \cdot p.size \geq q.size$ in
$len\ out = \mathbf{card}\ fs$
$\wedge\ \forall i \in fs \cdot (\exists! j \in inds\ out \cdot out(j) = \rho_2\text{-File}(i, p.size))$
$\wedge\ \forall v, w \in inds\ out, x, y \in fs \cdot$
$\quad out(v) = \rho_2\text{-File}(x, p.size) \wedge out(w) = \rho_2\text{-File}(y, p.size)$
$\quad \Rightarrow (v < w \Leftrightarrow (x.name <_1 y.name$
$\quad\quad \vee (x.name = y.name \wedge x.date < y.date)))$

— The invariant over dates and versions in the state definition allows us to
— order the sequence by either date or version.
;

$\rho_2\text{-File} : File \rightarrow Icon$

$\rho_2\text{-File}\ (f, maxs) \triangleq$
$\quad mk\text{-Icon}\ (\rho_2\text{-type}(f.type),$
$\quad\quad\quad\quad \rho_2\text{-name}(f.name),$
$\quad\quad\quad\quad \rho_2\text{-mantissa}(f.size),$
$\quad\quad\quad\quad \rho_2\text{-unit}(f.size),$
$\quad\quad\quad\quad \rho_2\text{-bar}(f.size, maxs));$

$\rho_2\text{-name} : char^* \rightarrow NameString$

$\rho_2\text{-name}\ (n) \triangleq$
$\quad$ if $len\ n \leq 2k + EllipsisLen$ then n
$\quad$ else $n(1, \ldots, k) \frown " \ldots " \frown n(len(n)\text{-}k + 1, \ldots, len(n));$

$\rho_2\text{-bar} : \mathbb{N} \times \mathbb{N} \rightarrow HorizBar$

$\rho_2\text{-bar}\ (s, m) \triangleq$
$\quad mk\text{-HorizBar}(\frac{s*BarSize}{m}, BarSize)$

Perceptual Operators Do these presentations adequately support the user's task? Again, we specify the perceptual operators. The version test relies on a total ordering relation but since files are presented in increasing version order, this is perceptually very simple - we check whether the file is not the last file with the same name in the sequence of icons on the display.

$version\text{-}test_2 : Icon \times Icon\text{-set} \rightarrow \mathbb{B}$

$version\text{-}test_2\ (i, iset) \triangleq$
$\quad$ let $n = \{j \mid j \in iset \cdot name(j) = name(i)\}$
$\quad\quad$ in $\neg\ is\text{-}lowest(i, n)$

This operation is fully supported only if equivalence of file names is perceivable, but even if the problem of truncation is mitigated by a more intelligent truncation scheme, ambiguity can still arise, and thus we must either attach a precondition to the version test to rule out namespace clashes, or modify the presentation. Taking the first option, we would have to establish the precondition through an invariant on the system, or document the failure to meet requirements. Should we decide to take the latter option, one approach suggested by our analysis is to indicate to the user directly whether adjacent files have the same name. For example, we could separate groups of files with the same name with a horizontal line, as illustrated in figure 8, where the first two files have the same name, and the third has a different name.

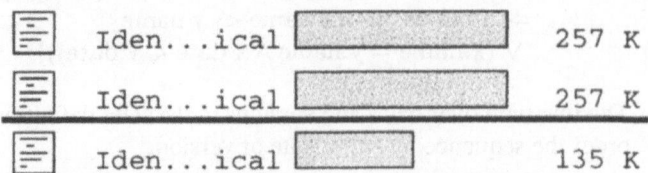

Fig. 8. Enhancement Suggested by Analysis

Again, there is an aid for searching with this representation since files of the same name will be adjacent in the list. The existence test is particularly interesting, as one might expect, since the version is implicit in the ordering of the icons on the display. Thus to determine the success or failure of the deletion action, the user must remember the previous number of files of the same name and compare with the new number. If the user is watching the display when the update takes place, the change to the list of displayed files may be noticeable, but this information is not statically present. From this we must conclude that the existence test is insufficiently supported by this representation.

Summary of example So to summarise the results of our analysis:

- The version test is insufficiently supported by both the textual and graphical representations.
- In spite of a more powerful means of representation in the graphical presentation, the existence test is insufficiently supported.
- The textual representation relies heavily on text manipulation operations which may be cognitively expensive.

So while, as one might have expected, the graphical representation makes use of "cheaper" perceptual operations, both representations had problems! An important point to grasp is that while the same conclusions could have been arrived at by an informal analysis our more formal approach forced these issues out into the open since it is impossible to prove the equivalence of the logical and perceptual operators if the presentation is inadequate.

4 Conclusions

The presentation is a vitally important component of any interactive system, yet it has received little attention in the area of interactive system specification. If we do not specify the presentation requirements generated by the interactive properties, then we can have no confidence in the ability of an implementation to conform to these properties, even if it has been proven to do so at an abstract level. Essentially, our message is this:

interactive system properties are **not** *presentation independent.* Representational issues are too often ignored in reasoning about interactive systems.

The primary concern of our analysis is the *choice of representation*, it is this choice which the analysis can guide, and which we ensure is consistent with the chosen principles. The analysis requires that we know the principles to be supported and the attributes to be presented; knowing the invariants on the attributes is also helpful. We would expect such details to emerge early in the development process, giving us a degree of flexibility in when we choose to apply the analysis. In scoping the analysis, theories of distributed representation may be useful in identifying the critical information resources [WFH96], the representation of which we should give particular attention.

An interesting consideration is the choice of the perceptual operators, since we have made no claims about their psychological validity. If we are reasonably confident that our choice of operators is psychologically justified, then the value of the analysis is enhanced and we can perhaps use the complexity of the mapping from perceptual model to task model as a simple metric of the perceptual demands of the interface. However, this is a complex issue, and some would argue that the abstractions we use for such concepts are determined in part by our own experience [Lak87].

Rather than introducing a new type of property, what we have proposed is a process which allows us to have confidence that reasoning about the usability of the system is valid, despite the *necessary* inexactness of the presentation mapping. Our aim has been to extend the domain of our formal reasoning into that of the percepts of the presentation.

Acknowledgements

This work has been supported by the HCM network for Interactionally Rich Systems, grant no. ERBCHRXCT930099. Many thanks to Bob Fields for his help and and insightful comments on drafts of this paper.

References

[Abo91]   G. D. Abowd. *Formal Aspects of Human-Computer Interaction.* PhD thesis, University of Oxford Computing Laboratory: Programming Research Group, 1991. Available as Technical Monograph PRG-97.

[BJ82]   Dines Bjørner and Cliff B. Jones. *Formal Specification and Software Development.* Prentice-Hall International, Englewood Cliffs, New Jersey, 1982.

[Cas91]   S.M. Casner. A task-analytic approach to the automated design of graphic presentations. *ACM Transactions on Graphics*, 10(2):111–151, April 1991.

[DFAB93]   Alan Dix, Janet Finlay, Gregory Abowd, and Russell Beale. Usability paradigms and principles. In *Human Computer Interaction*, chapter 4. Prentice Hall, 1993.

[DH93]   D. J. Duke and M.D. Harrison. Abstract interaction objects. *Proceedings of Eurographics '93*, Computer Graphics Forum, 12(3), 1993.

[DH94]   D.J. Duke and M.D. Harrison. A Theory of Presentations. In *FME '94: Industrial Benefit of Formal Methods*, volume 873 of *Lecture Notes in Computer Science*, pages 271–290. Springer-Verlag, 1994.

[Dia89]   Dan Diaper, editor. *Task Analysis for Human-Computer Interaction.* Ellis Horwood Books in Information Technology. Ellis Horwood, 1989.

[Jon86]   C. B. Jones. *Systematic Software Development Using VDM.* Prentice-Hall, 1986.

290

[Lak87]   George Lakoff. *Women, fire, and dangerous things: what categories reveal about the mind*. Chicago, 1987.

[LS87]   J. H. Larkin and H. A. Simon. Why a Diagram is (Sometimes) Worth Ten Thousand Words. *Cognitive Science*, 11:65–99, 1987.

[Mac87]   J. Mackinlay. Automating the design of graphical presentations of relational information. *ACM Transactions on Graphics*, 5(2):110–141, April 1987.

[Ste46]   S.S. Stevens. On the theory of scales of measurement. *Science*, 103:677–680, 1946.

[WFH96]   P.C. Wright, B. Fields, and M.D. Harrison. Distributed information resources: An new approach to interaction modelling. In T.R.G. Green, J.J. Canas, and C.P. Warren, editors, *Proceedings of ECCE8: European Conference on Cognitive Ergonomics*, pages 5–10. EACE, 1996.

[Zha96]   J. Zhang. A representational analysis of relational information displays. *International journal of human computer studies*, 45, 1996.

[ZN94]   J. Zhang and D. A. Norman. Representations in distributed cognitive tasks. *Cognitive Science*, 18:87–122, 1994.

On biasing behaviour to the optimal

R. J. Butterworth

D. J. Cooke

School of Computing Science,
Middlesex University, UK

Department of Computer Studies,
Loughborough University, UK

Abstract A formal framework for synthesizing interactive systems is
outlined. A distinction is made between the functional 'behaviour' of a
system, which is a description of everything that the user is permitted to
do, and the 'use' of a system, which is what the user is likely to do. A way
for capturing the use requirements of a system in terms of how 'good'
is a given use is proposed and discussed as well as a way of describing
interface specifications and terms of *what* user interfaces do rather than
how they do it. The two aspects are related so that an analyst can judge
whether changes in the interface model cause required improvements in
the use of the system. Some of the implications of this approach are
discussed and a comparison is made to other formal approaches in HCI.

1 Introduction

This paper reports on a formal approach to modelling and building interactive
systems[1] that has been recently developed at Loughborough University. The
approach is aimed at specifying systems comprising users employing computers
as tools in the achievement of tasks. It should sit comfortably in a software
engineering cycle; we are more interested in the formal *synthesis* of interactive
systems rather than their *post hoc* analysis.

1.1 The ideas behind our approach

The approach is based on a few simple ideas. Namely. . .

- A formal description typically defines a collection of legal activities for a
  system. We call this set the 'behaviour' of the system. In order to more
  comfortably describe what users do in a system one should describe the
  system behaviour not only in terms of what activities are *legal* (which can
  be described by discrete mathematics) but also need what is *likely* (which
  can be described by probabilistic mathematics). This probabilistic aspect
  to what the system does is known as the 'use'[2] of the system.

- A usable interactive system is one which makes activities which are 'optimal' more likely, optimal use being that which we expect the system to
  display if its user population is highly expert.

---

[1] In this paper 'system' refers to *all* of an interactive system — the computerised device *and*
the user population.

[2] Again care should be taken with terminology — 'behaviour' and 'use' are given quite
precise meanings which may be subtly different to their informal meanings.

- The use of an interactive system is biased by the motivations and intentions of the user population and the user-interfaces through which they communicate with the device. Getting the system to be biased to the optimal is a case of playing off the probability distribution of the users' intentions against that caused by the user interface.

The purpose of this paper is to lay down and discuss these ideas. So as not to deluge the reader in mathematics that may obscure the fundamental ideas we illustrate our approach with a simplified model of system behaviour and a simple notation for describing that behaviour

1.2 Formal frameworks and HCI theory

Our approach is an attempt to build a formal framework within which interactive systems can be built. Working within such a structure allows an analyst to pose questions about usability issues within a limited and well defined context. Furthermore the answers to those questions feed back into a design process in a useful way. In the absence of a rigorous and inspectable theory of HCI where those answers come from may be problematic — we may have to resort to heuristics or the craft skill of HCI experts. However, the act of posing questions and receiving answers within a formal structure is a move towards determining HCI theory. If an analyst finds himself repeatedly asking similar questions and getting similar answers then there is a fair possibility of abstracting some HCI 'truth' that underlies these questions and answers.

That said, by necessity parts of HCI are 'woolly' and imprecise. Our structure is intended to be a complement to these areas, it is not intended to be a formal 'straight jacket'.

1.3 Activities, behaviour and a notation for describing them

The 'behaviour' of an interactive systems is the set of all the things it can do. A 'thing a system can do' is an 'activity', which is a full temporal ordering of events and/or state changes that take place. What we call an activity has plenty of pseudonyms in the literature; trace, computation, history and so on.

We model activities as sequences of events. An event is simply something that happens, it is not our intention to get into debates about events and status as discussed by Abowd and Dix [1].

Formally...

$$Event \mathrel{\hat=} \ldots \tag{1}$$

$$Activity \mathrel{\hat=} Event^* \tag{2}$$

$$Behaviour \mathrel{\hat=} \mathcal{P}(Activity) \tag{3}$$

We describe behaviour using a notation based on regular grammars. A formal semantics is given in appendix A.

If A, B and C are events then we describe their sequencing as ABC. $A + B$ describes disjunction; A or B. A^n describes A being repeated n times and A^* describes A being repeated an arbitrary (but finite) number of times.

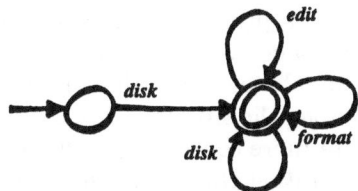

Figure 1 : A finite state machine model of a word processor

1.4 The rest of this paper

In section 2 we briefly look at a very abstract specification of a word processor and discuss how we can model systems that display the behaviour described in the specification.

In section 3 we widen the view of the word processor to think about not only what it can do (its functionality) but how it is actually used. This wider view looks at two aspects...

- the overall use of the word processor and how 'good' that use is, and
- a lower level which considers probabilistic machines which can model interface features. Using these probabilistic models we can capture *what* the interface does rather than *how*.

It is then shown how the two aspects are related so that we can calculate what interface features might cause 'better' use of the word processor.

There are several simplifying assumptions made and they are discussed more fully in section 4. We conclude (section 5) by contrasting our approach to other formal HCI work.

2 Formal system modelling

In this section we briefly look at a very simple formal system synthesis process. Assume that we are synthesizing a word processor. We have been given some requirements for the system and from those requirements we have produced an abstract specification of the system. The user can perform text editing operations, text formating operations and disk operations. The user must first perform a disk operation, in order to load a document for editing and then can perform edits, formats or disk operations in any order. The three operations are characterised by the three events *disk*, *edit* and *format*.

Using the regular grammar-like notation we can describe the possible activities of the word processing system as follows...

$$WP = disk(disk + edit + format)^* \qquad (4)$$

Based on this specification we can make a system model using a finite state machine. Such a machine is shown in figure 1. This machine generates all the legal sequences of the word processor system.

The point of this section is just to briefly show that we can describe and model abstract systems and calculate the behaviour of those models. There are a myriad of techniques available for doing this of which regular grammars and finite state machines are among the simplest. We use them as in illustrative tool in this paper because we are more concerned with what we do with the models and descriptions we produce rather than worrying about more high powered and intricate techniques for describing system models.

However, having said that a finite state machine is a simple modelling technique, it does capture well the important feature of interactive systems that in any situation the user is offered a finite choice of what to do next.

3   The use of systems

The formula WP and the associated finite state machine define a space of legal behaviour for the system. This is the traditional role of formal approaches; describing the legal behaviour of a system and then implementing a working system that displays that legal behaviour.

The system activity...

$$\langle disk, disk, disk, disk, disk, disk \rangle$$

...is just as legal as...

$$\langle disk, edit, edit, edit, format, disk \rangle$$

...despite the fact that we would (presumably) prefer the user to perform more sensible activities such as the latter rather than strange activities such as the former.

Our approach is about capturing what we believe to be 'sensible'[3] and synthesizing systems that make sensible behaviour more likely.

We look at interactive systems from two perspectives; the 'overview' of the system, considering tasks and how well they are performed and the 'interface' perspective which looks at what role the interface plays in influencing the use of the system.

3.1   Describing how 'good' the use of a system is

As well as the specification of everything the system can do (the formula WP) we also produce a specification of what the 'optimal' behaviour of the system is. Such optimal behaviour is heavily dependent on the task of the user. Optimal behaviour is that displayed by systems comprising expert users who perform their task efficiently expending as few resources as possible.

Assume a user employs the word processor specified in equation 4 to open a file with the contents shown in figure 2(a), edit and format that file so it looks like figure 2(b) and save the file.

---

[3] Where 'sensible' implies activities that are in some way useful, efficient or some other criteria we consider to be important.

```
                                              12 The Bladders,
                                             Lower Blodsleigh,
                                                     Quants.
                                                  HP12 TLA.

                              Dear sir,
                                   In reference to our recent conversation,
                              please find enclosed my shoes.

                                                  Yours etc.
```

```
12 The Bladders,
Lower Blodsleigh,
Quants.
HP12 TLA.
Yours etc.
```

(a) The starting file   (b) The required file

Figure 2 : Sample file contents for a word processor

Assuming that *edit* inserts one character at a time and correctly formatting the address, the 'Dear sir,' line, the main body and the 'Yours etc.' line each require one *format* then the optimal behaviour of the task is...

$$WPoptimal = disk \; edit^{83} \; format^4 \; disk \tag{5}$$

Of course, *WPoptimal* is extremely task specific, but we can define more general optimal behaviour if we were considering the word processor in more general use. We may decide that typically the user performs approximately 20 times as many edits as formats when preparing any document. Hence the general case for optimal behaviour with a word processor may be described as...

$$WPgenopt = disk \; edit^n \; format^m \; disk \bullet n \approx 20m \tag{6}$$

The '$\bullet$' reads 'where', hence the general optimal behaviour for a word processor is a disk operations followed by a series of edits, followed by a series of formats, followed by a disk operation, where there are around 20 times as many edits as formats.

This formula shows that a task may have several different optimal activities associated with it. As a rule of thumb we suggest that the more general the task definition, the greater the set of possible equally optimal activities to achieve it.

Given the task of producing the document in figure 2 we assert that the user cannot achieve that task in less than 89 invocations. Therefore an activity that successfully achieves the task with 89 invocations is optimal. The more invocations it takes to achieve the goal, the less optimal is the activity. We can capture a measure of optimality as a ratio of number of erroneous invocations to the number of invocations made. We can simply calculate the number of erroneous invocations by subtracting 89 from the total number of invocations made.

If a user typed 'Dear madam,' then pressed the delete key 6 times and continued with 'sir,' and the rest of the letter successfully then he would take 101

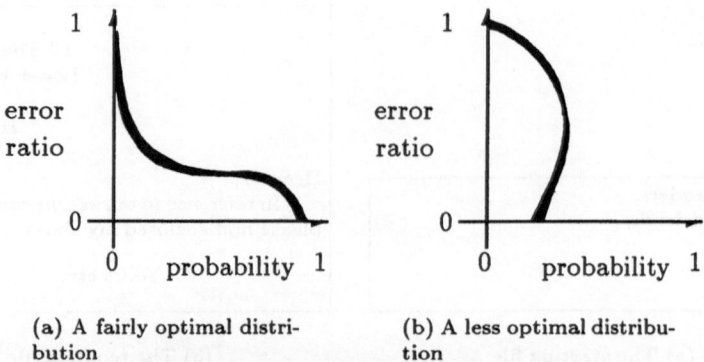

(a) A fairly optimal distribution

(b) A less optimal distribution

Figure 3 : Example usage distributions

events to achieve the task. Hence his error ratio would be...

$$\frac{101 - 89}{101} = \frac{12}{101} \approx 0.119$$

The greater the number of errors the greater the error ratio. An error ratio of 0 is optimal. By this calculation an error ratio of 1 is impossible, but that value can be used to indicate that the user fails to complete the task altogether.

Plotting the error ratio against the normalised frequency of users with that error ratio (again the normalised frequency is a real number between 0 and 1; 0.5 representing 50% of the users and so on) we possibly would obtain graphs that look like those shown on figure 3. We call such graphs 'usage distributions'.

Figure 3(a) shows more optimal use than that in figure 3(b) — more users show more optimal behaviour. The 'better' the system the greater the proportion of its usage distribution falls in the lower error ratios.

We know of no empirical evidence describing the sort of curves we have suggested here. We shall discuss this point later (section 4.4).

Formally a usage distribution is a measurement scheme that takes a given activity to an error ratio and a mapping from error ratio to user ratio. U is the set of all usage distributions.

$$U \mathrel{\hat{=}} (Activity \to [0, 1]) \times ([0, 1] \to [0, 1]) \tag{7}$$

Note that the normalised user ratio is effectively the same as probability, a usage distribution can be thought of as mapping an error ratio (or whatever measurement scheme is used) to the probability of activities with that error ratio occurring.

Usage distributions are a tool for capturing how effective a system is at performing a given task.

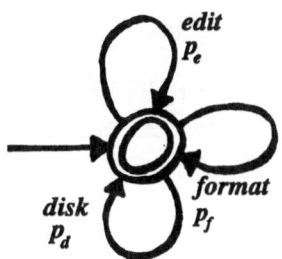

Figure 4 : Modelling the probability of what happens next with a stochastic state machine

3.2 How the user-interface effects use

Consider the finite state machine shown in figure 1. Once the user has started the device and performed a disk operation she is offered a non-deterministic choice of what to do next. By repeatedly observing what choices the users make in this situation we can assign probabilities to each of the transitions. In doing so we are moving the system model out of the realm of discrete mathematics which only describes a set of non-deterministic choices into the realm of probabilistic mathematics where we can describe what the user actually chooses to do in a more expressive way.

In any situation the total probability of what the user can do next is 1. In all likelihood these will not be static, context-free probabilities; what the user does next will be to a large degree determined by what they have already done and what they can see on the screen. Therefore instead of attaching simple probabilities to each transition we attach functions which take the previous event history as an argument and returns the probability of an event occurring next.

In figure 4 we label each transition with the following three probability functions...

$$p_e : Activity \to [0, 1]$$
$$p_f : Activity \to [0, 1]$$
$$p_d : Activity \to [0, 1]$$

...where in any situation the total probability returned by the functions is 1. Formally...

$$\forall \alpha : Activity \bullet p_e(\alpha) + p_f(\alpha) + p_d(\alpha) = 1$$

If *SSM* is the set of all stochastic state machines then we can introduce the function p which takes a stochastic state machine and an activity and returns the probability of that activity occurring.

$$p : SSM \times Activity \to [0, 1]$$

Figure 5 : An example word processor interface

(The set *SSM* and the function *p* are fully defined in the appendix B.)

Interface and user effects Having captured these probabilities the important question is what causes them; why is one choice more or less likely than another? There is no simple answer of course, but we argue that we can separately consider the user interface and the users' intentions, which we refer to as the 'interface effects' and 'user effects' respectively.

The interface effect is what is fundamental about an interface, what biasing effect it has on the use independent of the user population.

The user effect, conversely, captures what is fundamental about the user population; what they will try to do with the device no matter what interface they have to work with. User effect is therefore a blanket term covering all aspects of the user side of a system; their beliefs, motivations, intentions and so on.

Such a separation is contentious and we discuss the arguments surrounding separation in section 4.3.

An example interface effect Consider a user interface to the word processor. The interface is shown in figure 5 and is based on the earlier versions of Word for Windows.

Editing takes place in a prominent window and editing commands are simple and will generally have a one-to-one relationship to device commands; for instance the edit command 'insert(i)' is caused by pressing the key marked 'i'. The interface therefore gives editing a very high probability; 0.95. Formatting is caused by pressing graphical buttons on a tool bar. This requires more effort; moving the mouse or a sequence of command keys. The interface probability of formatting is low; 0.04. The disk operations are in the menu system and therefore require more effort and are therefore even less likely to be invoked; 0.01.

	u	i	E
edit	1	0.95	1
format	0	0.04	0
disk	0	0.01	0

	u	i	E
edit	0	0.95	0
format	0.5	0.04	0.8
disk	0.5	0.01	0.2

(a) A user that only wants to do edits

(b) A user that only wants to do formats or disk operations

	u	i	E
$event_1$	u_1	i_1	$u_1 \times i_1 \times 1/T$
$event_2$	u_2	i_2	$u_2 \times i_2 \times 1/T$
$\vdots$	$\vdots$	$\vdots$	$\vdots$
$event_n$	u_n	i_n	$u_n \times i_n \times 1/T$

$$\text{where } T = \sum_{1 \leq j \leq n} (u_j \times i_j)$$

(c) A general approach to filters

Figure 6 : Modelling probabilistic filters

This is effectively a 'reverse engineering' of the interface. The use of probability measures enables us to capture 'what' the interface does — the biasing it exerts on the user, rather than 'how' the interface causes this biasing. We want to be able to produce an 'interface specification' which describes in probabilistic terms what biasing the interface has on the use. We can then pass this interface specification to a human factors specialist who will 'know' what presentation issues and interface designs will produce this biasing.

User effects The proposing of user effects is a possible point of contact between our approach and user modelling [4, 2, 9]. We would like to be able to use a user modelling technique that could feed predictive results into our approach without having to resort to to expensive user tests to analyse every design decision.

Probabilistic filters We can think of the interface effects and user effects as 'filters' over one another. 'Filtering' is a way of combining the interface and user effects so as make predictions about what the user will do next.

To illustrate this filtering consider two very simple user effects and the interface effect described above. Firstly an extreme user who just wants to perform edits. Editing has a probability of 1, formatting and disk operations have a probability of 0. In this extreme case the interface has no effect; the user will only perform edits no matter what the interface tries to bias her to. See figure 6(a); the column u lists the user effect probabilities, the column i lists the in-

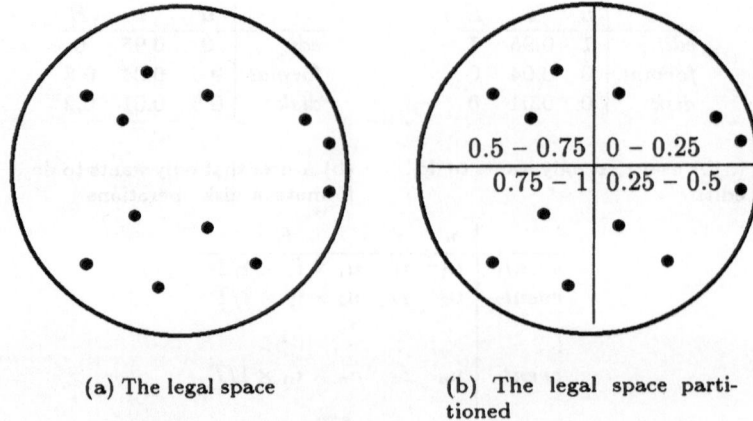

(a) The legal space

(b) The legal space partitioned

Figure 7 : Partitioning the space of legal activities

terface effect probabilities and the column E lists the overall effect of the user effect filtered through the interface effect.

Another user (figure 6(b)) only wants to do formats or disk operations and is not bothered which. The overall effect is that edits have a probability of 0, formats have a probability of 0.8 and disk operations have a probability of 0.2. As the user does not care which of formats or disk operations he does then the biasing is due to the interface; the interface makes formats four times more likely than disk operations.

The filtering is calculated by first multiplying the probabilities of each pair of user and interface effect. These multiplied probabilities are then normalised by multiplying each one by $1/T$ where T is the sum of all the multiplied probabilities. This general case is shown in figure 6(c).

3.3 Relating the interface to the usage distributions

To review what has been done so far in this section; we have proposed usage distributions as a tool for capturing how good the use of a system is and described how stochastic state machines can be used to capture what user interfaces do.

This section shows how the two are related so that it is possible to decide whether a change in the user interface improves (or otherwise) the usability of a system.

A usage distribution is 'consistent' with a stochastic state machine if the machine generates activities with the probabilities implicitly defined in a usage distribution. A usage distribution is effectively an approximation of uses — a distribution implies a collection of uses, the less precise the distribution, the greater the set of uses it describes.

The specification *WP* defines a set of legal activities. Assume it defines the set shown in figure 7(a) where each point represents a possible activity. An error ratio measurement scheme defines a partition of this set. We can divide the set up into (say) activities with a error ratio of 0 to (but not including) 0.25, 0.25 to (but not including) 0.5, 0.5 to (but not including) 0.75 and 0.75 to 1. Such a partition is shown in figure 7(b).

The usage distribution maps an error ratio to the probability of activities with that error ratio occurring. Hence if the probability of error ratios between 0 and 0.25 is 0.5 according to the usage distribution then the total probability of all the activities in the 0 to 0.25 error ratio partition of the legal space must be 0.5. If the summed probability of each activity generated by a stochastic state machine in each partition is equal to that described by a usage distribution then the usage distribution and stochastic machine would be consistent.

Making this more formal, given a usage distribution $(m, u) : U$ (where m is the error ratio measurement scheme and u is the mapping from error ratios to probabilities) and a stochastic state machine ssm the two would be consistent if...

$$\forall erRatio : [0, 1] \bullet$$
$$\exists \alpha s : \mathcal{P}(Activity) \bullet$$
$$\alpha s = \{\alpha : Activity \mid m(\alpha) = erRatio\} \land \tag{8}$$
$$\sum_{\alpha \in \alpha s} p(ssm, \alpha) = u(erRatio)$$

In words; 'for every error ratio *errRatio* there is a set of activities αs with that error ratio. Each of the activities in αs has a probability defined by the stochastic state machine ssm. The total of these probabilities must equal the probability defined for the error ratio in the mapping u.'

Consistency is a very strong relationship. It illustrates that we can relate usage distributions and stochastic state machines. In more realistic analyses it would be preferable to define approximate levels of consistency, or tolerance values on consistency.

3.4 Designing better user interfaces

In user interface terms the crucial question is what effect does a change in the probabilities attached to the stochastic state machine model of the interface have on the usage distributions? The goal of an interface designer is to 'tweak' the values of the probabilities in the stochastic state machine in order to achieve a greater proportion of usages with a low error ratio.

We can now augment the formal development process we outlined in section 2 with some ideas about describing non-functional requirements for how a device is used by the user population.

Requirements for the use of a system are described with a usage distribution. It is possible to define detailed graphs for the requirements, but more likely are more general statements such as 'the users have at least a 0.5 probability of performing their tasks with a error ratio less than 0.05' which we can translate into usage distributions.

We can then make assumptions about the user population by determining their user effect in terms of probabilities attached to stochastic state machines. We can then specify the interface effect, such that when the assumed user effect is filtered through this interface effect we get a stochastic state machine that is consistent with the required usage distribution.

The specified interface effect is then passed to a human factors specialist who will know what interface features to implement in order to achieve the biasing required by the interface effect. Of course it is easy to assume that a human factors expert will 'know' what interface features cause what biasing, but this is rather a utopian assumption. One way of making our approach more practical would be to devise a collection of interface widgets in a toolkit where the biasing effect of each widget is known and documented in the toolkit.

4 Discussion

We have outlined an approach to formally capturing systems with an emphasis on how they are used. There have been several simplifying assumptions made. There are two sources for these simplifications...

- firstly, simplifications we have made to our approach in order to present a simple and clear model of what we are doing in this paper (these are discussed in section 4.1 below), and

- secondly (and more importantly), the simplifications that are inherent in our work, no matter how we present it.

4.1 Simplifications peculiar to this paper

We have used usage distributions and stochastic state machines as a way of expressing the requirements and specifications of the use of systems. Broadly speaking requirements are an approximation of use — there will be a great number of uses that are described by a single usage distribution, whereas specifications are more specific, they are descriptions of machines that generate certain activities at certain probabilities.

Formally we assume there is a set REQ which is the set of all mathematical entities that might be used to express use requirements. (U is a sub-set of REQ.) The function req evaluates members of REQ.

$$req : REQ \rightarrow \mathcal{P}(Activity) \rightarrow [0,1] \qquad (9)$$

req takes an expression of use requirements and returns a function from sets of activities to a measure of probability which is the total probability of all those activities occurring. Therefore it may not be possible to predict the precise probability of a single activity from an expression of requirements.

Similarly assume we have a set $SPEC$ which is the set of all specifications of use (of which SSM is a sub-set) and a function $spec$ which evaluates members of $SPEC$.

$$spec : SPEC \rightarrow Activity \rightarrow [0,1] \qquad (10)$$

Hence $spec$ is more precise than req — it takes single activities to probability measures.

This paper has presented two very simple mathematical entities from REQ and $SPEC$ as illustrations. However it would be very difficult to scale up the notations and modelling techniques we have used here to more complex systems. More advanced specification techniques such as the Temporal Logic of Actions [7] may be more appropriate (see [3]). We are confident that we will be able to comfortably express the models and concepts presented in this paper in the more 'powerful' modelling languages we have investigated.

We have described activities only as being finite because we are primarily interested in the tasks that those activities represent — a task that is infinite is of little interest to anyone. In a more detailed analysis we would present system models that generate infinite activities and then break those activities up into finite tasks to analyse.

4.2   Measurement schemes

We have illustrated our approach with a measurement scheme based on number of errors made. It could be argued that our approach is therefore more about improving performance than about improving usability. We take the stance that the point of making a device usable is to improve the user's performance of their given tasks. Therefore requiring a high level of performance from a system equates to requiring a high level of usability.

Other measurement schemes are possible. For example an analyst might decide that usability is more about how happy users are after having performed a task with a given device. The analyst could observe users performing a task and then apply a psychometric test to determine how happy they are afterwards. Presumably some activities make users happier than others and the analyst could then specify interfaces that make those activities more likely.

We can change the measurements scheme, but this does not change the framework the scheme is in.

4.3   Separation of user and interface effects

In an ideal world there is a function which generates the probability of what happens next parameterised by the user effect u and the interface effect i. By changing u, i.e. by observing what different classes of users do with the system, or by changing i (i.e. by giving different interfaces to the same users) we should theoretically be able to study why certain classes of user work well (or otherwise) with different types of interface.

However it would not be difficult to argue that it is impossible to change i without having an effect on u and *vice versa*. The interface presents the device to the users and colours the users' beliefs and perceptions about the device, so changing the interface will also change the users' beliefs. An interface is not just a simple channel of communication between users and the device, its role is more profound and subtle than that.

However, different users *do* make different uses of interfaces so there must be some level of separation to be made even if it is not the clean, simple separation suggested in this paper. We suggest a move *towards* separation of user and interface effects is beneficial even if a complete separation is impossible.

4.4 Empirical evidence for usage distributions

We are not aware of any empirical work that would allow us to predict the shape of usage distributions. We assume that the curves fall into 'regular' distributions because common sense predicts they should. If such distributions are random then we must fundamentally question HCI as a field. If the use of an interactive system is purely random then there is little point studying it and attempting to propose interfaces that modify the use for the better.

5 Conclusions

We can contrast our approach to interactive systems to the approach we refer to as the 'usability properties approach' typified by [5, 6, 8]. We attempt to characterise behaviour that results from a usable device being used and then design interface effects which will bring about this sort of behaviour.

The usability properties approach considers various properties that are held (with varying levels of confidence) to have relevance to usability, for example, predictability, visibility and so on. Ultimately one would wish to have a set of properties the fulfillment of which guarantees usability. The usability properties approach therefore considers usability to be a composite of sub-properties whereas the approach reported here considers usability in a more 'holistic' way.

The two approaches are complementary. For example an analyst may make the assumption that users are likely to get easily lost. To prevent the users getting lost the analyst may make the decision that a highly visible interface be implemented (based on the definition of visibility given in [6]). The visibility property is then a method guiding the implementation of an interface that biases the users away from getting lost.

Our framework helps in proposing an agenda for further work and therefore how we can add more meat to the bones presented here. For example we suggest that in order to use our framework in a more predictive manner we need to pay more attention to user models, or at least to how we interface the results of existing user models to our approach. Another more practical spin off of our work would be the compilation of a tool kit of interface widgets which have documented interface effects.

Acknowledgments The authors are indebted to Dr Ann Blandford, Prof Harold Thimbleby and the anonymous reviewers for helpful comments on earlier versions of this paper.

References

[1] G. D. Abowd and A. J. Dix. Integrating status and event phenomena in formal specifications of interactive systems. *Softwate Engineering Notices*, 19(5):44–52, 1994.

[2] P. Barnard and J. May. Cognitive modelling for user requirements. In P. F. Byerley, Barnard P. J., and J. May, editors, *Computers, Communications*

and Usability: Design issues, research and methods for integrated service, pages 101–145. Elsevier, 1993.

[3] R. J. Butterworth and D. J. Cooke. Using temporal logic in the specification of reactive and interactive systems. In *Formal Aspects of the Human Computer Interface*. BCS-FACS, Springer Verlag, 1996.

[4] S. Card, T. Moran, and A. Newell. *The Psychology of Human-Computer Interaction*. Lawrence Erlbaum Assoc, 1983.

[5] A. J. Dix. *Formal Methods for Interactive Systems*. Computers and People Series. Academic Press, 1991.

[6] M. D. Harrison and D. J. Duke. A review of formalisms for describing interactive behaviour. In R. N. Taylor and C. Coutaz, editors, *Software engineering and human-computer interaction (Lecture notes in computer science vol. 896)*, pages 49–75. Springer Verlag, 1995.

[7] L. Lamport. The temporal logic of actions. *ACM Transactions on Programming Languages and Systems*, 16(3):872–923, 1994.

[8] B. Sufrin and J. He. Specification, analysis and refinement of interactive processes. In *Formal Methods in Human-Computer Interaction*, Cambridge series on HCI, pages 153–199. Cambridge Uni. Press, 1990.

[9] R. M. Young, T. R. G. Green, and T. Simon. Programmable user models for predictive evaluation of interface design. In K. Bice and C. H. Lewis, editors, *Proceedings of CHI '89: Human Factors in Computing Systems*, pages 15–19. Accociation of computing machinery, 1989.

A A formal description language

In this paper we use a simple regular grammar-like notation. D is the set of all descriptions in this notation. The descriptions are inductively defined. Single events are the base case; *Event* $\subseteq D$. If n is a natural number and d, d_1 and d_2 are descriptions then so are. . .

$$d_1 d_2 \qquad d_1 + d_2 \qquad d^n \qquad d^*$$

The function *sem* holds true if a given description accurately describes a given activity.

$$
\begin{aligned}
&sem : D \to Activity \to \mathbb{B} \\
&sem\,[\![e]\!]\alpha \mathrel{\hat{=}} \alpha = \langle e \rangle \\
&sem\,[\![d_1 d_2]\!]\alpha \mathrel{\hat{=}} \exists \alpha_1, \alpha_2 : Activity \bullet \\
&\qquad\qquad\qquad sem\,[\![d_1]\!]\alpha_1 \wedge sem\,[\![d_2]\!]\alpha_2 \wedge \alpha = \alpha_1 {}^\frown \alpha_2 \\
&sem\,[\![d_1 + d_2]\!]\alpha \mathrel{\hat{=}} sem\,[\![d_1]\!]\alpha \vee sem\,[\![d_2]\!]\alpha \\
&sem\,[\![d^0]\!]\alpha \mathrel{\hat{=}} \alpha = \langle\,\rangle \\
&sem\,[\![d^{n+1}]\!]\alpha \mathrel{\hat{=}} \exists \alpha_1, \alpha_2 : Activity \bullet \\
&\qquad\qquad\qquad sem\,[\![d]\!]\alpha_1 \wedge sem\,[\![d^n]\!]\alpha_2 \wedge \alpha = \alpha_1 {}^\frown \alpha_2 \\
&sem\,[\![d^*]\!]\alpha \mathrel{\hat{=}} \exists n : \mathbb{N} \bullet [\![d^n]\!]\alpha
\end{aligned}
\tag{11}
$$

The behaviour described by a description is the set of all activities that are accurately described.

$$beh : D \rightarrow Behaviour$$
$$beh[\![d]\!] \mathrel{\hat{=}} \{\alpha : Activity \mid sem[\![d]\!]\alpha\} \tag{12}$$

B   Stochastic state machines

We have a set of states Σ. A transition between states is a 4-tuple describing start state, the event and probability function labelled on the transition and the end state. *Tran* is the set of all transitions.

$$Tran \mathrel{\hat{=}} \Sigma \times Event \times (Activity \rightarrow [0,1]) \times \Sigma \tag{13}$$

A stochastic state machine is a 5-tuple consisting a set of states, an alphabet of events, a set of transitions, a start state and a set of final states.

$$SSM \mathrel{\hat{=}} \mathcal{P}(\Sigma) \times \mathcal{P}(Event) \times \mathcal{P}(Tran) \times \Sigma \times \mathcal{P}(\Sigma)$$
$$\textbf{where}\ \ \forall (\sigma, e, \delta, s, F) : SSM \bullet \delta \subseteq \sigma \times e \times (Activity \rightarrow [0,1]) \times \sigma \wedge \tag{14}$$
$$s \in \sigma \wedge F \subseteq \sigma$$

With each activity there is an associated sequence of states σseq that generate that activity and a sequence of probabilities *pseq* generated by each transition. The probability of the activity is the product of all the probabilities in *pseq*.

$$p : SSM \times Activity \rightarrow [0,1]$$
$$p((\sigma, e, \delta, s, F), \langle e_1, \ldots, e_n \rangle) \mathrel{\hat{=}}$$

$$\prod_{1 \leq i \leq n} pseq(i) \tag{15}$$

$$\textbf{where}\ \ \sigma seq = \langle \sigma_1, \ldots, \sigma_{n+1} \rangle \wedge$$
$$\sigma_1 = s \wedge \sigma_{n+1} \in F \wedge pseq = \langle p_1, \ldots, p_n \rangle \wedge$$
$$\forall i : \{1, \ldots, n\} \bullet (\sigma_i, e_i, pf_i, \sigma_{i+1}) \in \delta \wedge p_i = pf_i(\langle e_1, \ldots, e_{i-1} \rangle)$$

Modelling in Action

Reports from the DSVIS '97 working groups

Robert E. Fields   Nicholas A. Merriam

Human-Computer Interaction Group
Department of Computer Science
University of York, York, YO1 5DD, U.K.
nam@cs.york.ac.uk   bob@cs.york.ac.uk

1   Introduction

The present paper is both a description and a discussion of the working group activity at the 1997 International Workshop on Design, Specification and Verification of Interactive Systems, DSVIS '97, in Granada, Spain. In the past, workshop participants have been divided into working groups which discuss and report on subjects nominated by the organisers, during sessions totalling about six hours. However last year at the 1996 meeting in Namur, Belgium, Janet Wesson addressed one of the working groups with a real design problem concerning the interface to software to support doctors' surgeries, see (Wesson 1996). We felt that this focus on a real system and concrete problems contributed to the energy and success of that working group and that similar case studies would benefit the 1997 working groups. Accordingly, we prepared examples of real and imagined software and hardware to provide similar focus for the working group activity.

We hoped to be able to study the modelling and analysis process, very much an open box in the terminology of Latour (1987), by which we mean that there are no widely accepted standard procedures or methods. Research papers tend to present the modelling processes as systematic and orderly. We wondered if the working groups could provide more insight into real modelling activity and its benefits. In addition, it was our intention that the working groups at DSVIS '97 provide clues as to how methods should be selected. It is accepted that different HCI analysis methods deliver their greatest benefits in different ways and at different stages in the development of interactive systems. However relatively little work has been done to determine *which* methods to use *where*.

We invited the working groups to investigate the example systems, looking for usability issues and, furthermore, to reflect on the extent to which various kinds of modelling or specification were employed in such investigation. We were deliberately a little vague in our demands, since we did not want to *prevent* the creative, open-ended discussions of previous years' working groups.

When we chose the examples, we expected that each group would use a variety of models and methods to explore interaction, since individuals might well start off tackling the exercises by applying the method with which they were most familiar. This would mean that within each group several different aspects of the case studies would be worked in several different ways. As the group attempted to integrate these diverse results, we thought that interesting discussions would flourish and that insights would emerge on modelling independent of any particular technique. Our own work, reported in (Fields, Merriam, and Dearden 1997), has observed benefits which accrue to the use of diverse models.

In this report we aim to identify a number of relatively independent strands of thought that include issues touched upon by all of the groups. One disadvantage of reporting on common themes in this way is that the identity of the groups themselves is obscured, and there is no real way of showing how the the very different concerns of each group led to different connections between the streams being made. As a result, Section 2 gives a very brief account of the issues that were of greatest importance to each group. Sections 3, 4, 5, and 6 then describe four sets of issues that were raised in each of the groups: the task and work context, models and modelling, specific artefacts and designs, and criteria and methods of evaluating designs.

2 The Groups

We starting the working group sessions with a short presentation introducing the idea of the case studies. We suggested that all groups initially look at the world-wide web example, which asked the groups to think about the design of navigation buttons at web sites, for example "Previous", "Next" and "Home". Specifically, they were asked to choose a navigation button strategy for a web site given the option of no navigation, only "Home", or all three navigation buttons. However, we encouraged the groups to look beyond this one choice and to explore whatever issues seemed interesting. By ensuring that one case study was worked by all the groups, we would have at least one common reference point in making comparisons between groups. In practice, the groups spent nearly all their time on this one example but some did, additionally, look into others.

Group 1

Working Group 1 was in some ways the most diverse in terms of the range of issues they considered. The diversity of the participants was matched by the range of topics they considered. Discussions covered both web browsers and the design of pages and in-page navigation features and issues of consistency between them. While concentrating on the latter, the group also touched on pages and the context in which they occur, users and tasks they might carry out (such as searching for papers on a hypothetical DSVIS proceedings site).

At one point, the group split up and individuals considered how specific modelling and design techniques (User Action Notation, Formal Specifications, Task models, etc) might have a role to play. In using formal methods, they were unique among the groups. One of the issues raised explicitly by this group (and implicitly by the others) is the importance of understanding context in a number of senses (*e.g.*, both the technical and informational context in which a page occurs, and the social and human context in which a web site is used).

This group also thought about one of the other case studies and considered a number of different scenarios of use as a way of informally understanding the requirements and where problems in them might lie.

Group 2

This group (in common with some of the others) was composed of a variety of "modellers" and "implementers", bringing a range of different perspectives, and it was observed that this may have been one of the reasons that little attention was paid to actually constructing models!

The group concentrated most of its effort on thinking about web site design, turning occasionally to the design of browser technology or the visual layout of individual pages. During several of these detours, a number of interesting points were made about the support that future browsers may give. Examples given were to support users' adaptation of browser behaviour (for example to reduce problems arising from cultural diversity when a web site is accessible globally) and to endow browsers with some degree of "intelligence" (to better support individual preferences and interests).

Group 3

Group 3 adopted a highly systematic approach to their investigation of navigation around a web site. The focus of their activity was to set up a number of thought experiments to test different proposals for navigation schemes against a number of pre-determined criteria.

In doing this, they made a clear distinction between what aspects of their models would remain constant across a number of "experiments" (assumptions about the user, the facilities provided by the browser, the navigation tasks to be carried out) and what was to be altered in each case (the "navigation aids" offered to readers of the web site)

One of the aims of the exercise was to put to the test the hypothesis that successful navigation will be more likely at sites where the navigation mechanism closely matches the web page structure in some way. While this hypothesis was neither falsified nor validated (nor was such an outcome a genuine expectation of the group), a number of interesting observations were made about web site design, and about the value of models and formal notations.

Group 4

The fourth working group reflected in a rather more philosophical way on the kinds of models that are likely to be of use, the notations that may be appropriate for expressing, and what the different kinds of models have to say about web site design.

The starting and finishing point for this group appeared to be the contention that no one modelling approach or paradigm is likely to be sufficient, so several are necessary. A four-layer categorisation of models was suggested, encompassing representations of a range of development artefacts from the "problem space" to the space of design solutions. The four-layer taxonomy is discussed in more detail in Section 4.

Finally, this group looked at a different example (the design of a car radio) and found this a much easier because the context was thought to be better understood and less variable. For design contexts such as this, the human factors model was thought to be particularly useful as it could be used to assess particular aspects of the designed artefact, such as system moding.

The group concluded that the four-layer categorisation of models is a useful way of structuring discussions in HCI. Furthermore, the layering also highlighted the fact that neither mathematics nor natural language is sufficient for modelling in HCI, but that there is a need for both.

3 Tasks and Users

In order to identify requirements for an interactive system, and to assess the usability of a design, it has long been known that understanding how the system will be used is of vital importance. Indeed, a number of papers in this volume discuss techniques and tools for describing aspects of the work context, and in particular, users' tasks, and using these as a basis for design (for example, (Gamboa and Scapin 1997; Markopoulos et al. 1997; Breedvelt-Schouten et al. 1997)). Much of the focus of task-based design has been in the development of "traditional" user interfaces, with less attention paid to world-wide web hypertext design.

However, all of the working groups at DSVIS spent time considering the tasks that web pages are designed to support. An observation was made (in Group 2) that the concept of "task" that is appropriate in the context of world-wide web pages differs slightly from that sometimes used elsewhere. The openness and universal accessibility of the web means that the user population, and the skills, knowledge or goals of those who visit a site are not known in advance by the designers of a site. However, it is still meaningful for designers to design for a particular subset of potential users: tasks and goals therefore have the effect of selecting the desired users form all those who visit the site.

In their consideration of tasks, most working groups found it beneficial to consider particular tasks and scenarios that may be supported on the web. Consider, for example, tasks concerned with finding a particular paper in an online version of a conference proceedings. Group 1 explicitly considered activities surrounding information retrieval from proceedings, and Group 3 considered more general tasks that related to navigating through a group of related pages (presumably with the intention of either reading all of them or searching for a particular item of information). Group 2 considered for a time the different *types* of task a world-wide web site might be intended to support. The categories of tasks range from information acquisition (searching or browsing), through a variety of interactive tasks (such as might be supported by downloaded software, using Java or Javascript), to the kinds of transactions required for electronic commerce (where complex communications between the "reader" and "writer" of the pages may take place).

To all the groups who proceeded in this way it soon became clear, perhaps because of the diversity of potential web page users, that considering tasks and goals were not enough, and that a richer set of assumptions about the expected users must be recorded.

For example, the subset of "web surfers" who decide to look at the proceeding of a conference can be further sub-divided: those who had attended the conference, and those who hadn't. Goals to find specific papers, or to look for papers covering a particular topic may require difference support for the two user groups.

In the documentation provided to working group participants at the beginning of the exercise, nothing was said about tasks to be performed. However, screen-shots showing actual web sites which might have suggested some tasks were provided. This lack of task-related information was mitigated by the fact that most of the working group participants could count themselves as "domain experts" or the web. Most are routine users of web browsers and web pages (either as readers or authors) and were in a position to validate scenarios and generate task models.

4 Models and the Modelling Process

Given the topics of interest and the subjects represented in the talks at the DSVIS workshop, it is natural to ask how the discussion groups saw specification and modelling techniques contributing to their analysis of the case study systems. As suggested in the introduction, it was anticipated that the "WWW navigation problem" would raise a sufficiently focussed collection of issues that modellers could apply their modelling techniques.

An expected outcome, then, was that the groups would have produced models representing various aspects of world-wide web page navigation. In order to achieve a consensus, the case study-based approach would have required that each group attempt to integrate the results of modelling from a number of perspectives. If this had been the case, this report would have been able to describe the successes and failures of the exercise; which models and modelling paradigms worked and were appropriate and which did not; which models delivered analytic power that was useful in this context and which did not; where different modelling paradigms overlapped or came into conflict. One of the reasons for encouraging all the working groups to consider the same case study had been to make possible a comparison of contrast of the approaches used.

In fact, the groups seemed to concern themselves more with "meta-level" questions *about* modelling, rather than actually *doing* modelling and analysis. What this shows is that the original expectations were perhaps founded on a slightly naïve view of how routine and uncontroversial the process and practice of modelling in HCI actually is. The end result was, in any case, very interesting. The evident uncertainty about how to to attack the case study using modelling meant that while several of the groups did discuss and construct actual models, more effort was devoted to considering the types of models that are needed in design and the uses to which they can be put.

Models for Design

At least two of the groups devoted discussion time to a consideration of the types of model that can underlie the design process. In the most ambitious of these, Group 4, presented a hierarchy of models for designing interactive systems, summarised in Table 1.

Table 1. A taxonomy of models in interactive system design

Model	Scope	Appropriate Notations	
Context Models	Organisations, Users	Natural Language	Problem Space
Human Factors Models	Search Strategies	Natural Language / Semi-formal	
Operations models	Link Types	Semi-formal Descriptions	Solution Space
System Models	Information Structures	Formal Notations	

This hierarchy of models in HCI design proved particularly interesting, and is worth a little more comment. At the highest level, *context models* allow users, their work, and the organisational context in which the work is carried out to be described. The group decided that for this kind of model, informal description largely written using natural languages would be most appropriate. The *human factors models*, on the other hand, are concerned with representations of how users carry out their work and, in the context of the world-wide web navigation case study, could include the kinds of search strategies used to find information at a site. Descriptions at this level, it was felt, are best written in a combination of non-formal and semi-formal languages. At the third level, the *operations model* describes the kinds of operations that a system will provide to support the user's tasks, and in the case of web navigation design could include descriptions of link types that a web site will contain. A number of link types were identified, including causal relationships, temporal precedence, spatial containment and contextualisation. At the lowest level, a *system model* will describe the actual system functionality using an appropriate formal language. In the context of this case study, the system model could describe the information structures represented in a collection of pages, as well as the underlying web infrastructure (if appropriate).

Model construction and use

A much simpler taxonomy of models than that devised by Group 4 was proposed, populated and used by Group 3. In their work, the consideration of a "design context" consisted on assumptions about four factors:

- a *user model*, recording assumptions about the type of user and the strategies they have at their disposal for carrying out their tasks;
- a model of the *web structure* on which the task is based;
- *browser controls*, for example, to navigate using the history list;
- a *task model* describing the goals a user will attempt to achieve.

There is clearly a strong correspondence between these information domains and the four levels of Table 1, though the focus here was less on providing a rigorous categorisation of models, and more at looking at how models of this form can be used in evaluating web site designs.

In addition to these four "given" sets of assumptions, the group also considered a fifth domain: a design (in this particular instance, a design of web page navigation scheme) to be evaluated. The four models provide a context in which particular designs (see the next section) can be carried out.

Formality and the function of models

The time spend by most groups in discussions about models, modelling processes and the function of models led naturally to consideration of the languages and notations that are appropriate for expressing models. This in turn led to reflections on the roles that can be played by a model and the effect that notational choices have on the success of the model. Two of the groups expressed a belief that one of the most important roles of formality was in improving the efficacy of models as communicative artefacts. This was considered to be particularly important where the participants to a communication mediated by some form of model are not co-located. It was thought that the formality could function as an arbiter to settle disputes about the meaning of a model or the behaviour of an artefact.

5 Designs and Artefacts

All the groups spent some time looking at the exercise of designing possible products. The progression to the design of a product was partly a reflection of the maturity of the task analysis and modelling processes but also a device for furthering those same processes. It is interesting to note that both of these groups seemed to get very enthusiastic about designing a real product.

When they were tackling the world-wide web case study, group 1 especially considered the particular example of the DSVIS '97 electronic proceedings web site. Having already noted that 'a home page is a well-defined position in a web structure' a statement which we can regard as contributing to the modelling process, and having made the abstract design decision that 'the global picture should be discoverable from any part of the site . . . ', the group proposed that in the designed artefact, every page should have a 'link to the DSVIS home page'. They also proposed that '[the] site should . . . have a navigation mechanism that is orthogonal to the history mechanism.' This was driven by the notion that users are confused by the presence of history buttons, *i.e.* "Back" and "Forward", in conjunction with certain kinds of navigation button that can appear in a web page, *i.e.* "Previous" and "Next".

Fig. 1. A scrollbar navigation device

As the ideas about the product became more refined, group 1 opted to provide 'a single page which offers all ways in which the information at a site can be accessed, for example, through an author index, the programme, . . . ' and to ensure that '[this] page should be reachable from any other page [within the web site].' They elected to name this page 'Workshop Home Page', not only on the basis that this would explain to readers the nature of the page itself but that the references to it from every other page would provide valuable context information at those pages. By thus indicating that the pages were pare of a workshop proceedings readers would be helped to orient themselves when looking at an arbitrary page in the web site.

It was also decided that the interface to the proceedings should be 'recognition-based', rather than asking the user to provide unconstrained search keys. The group thought of the interface as presenting 'a set of observable hints'. Acknowledging that only a limited number of hints can be displayed for the user to recognise, an abstract design decision was made that 'the hints need to be browsable.' The group proposed that 'there is a structure to hints that should be observable.'

Group 3 focussed closely on the design of navigation mechanisms for web sites. Identifying the fact that a reader must use the scroll bar to move through a page but change to using some kind of "Next" button to move through several pages, the group proposed an all-in-one tool, a 'sequential' scroll bar which, as the user moved the handle from left to right, would scroll through a page until reaching the end and then move to the top of the "Next" page. In addition to providing a unified mechanism for progressing through an entire web site, this scroll bar would also provide feedback about where, in an overall, linear structure, the currently displayed text was located.

Since it is not always sensible to impose a linear structure on a web site, the group proposed an alternative tool in a similar vein, for sites to which a tree structure can be attributed. This would take the form of an interactive tree-form map, allowing navigation between pages and providing feedback about location within the overall site's structure. It was also suggested that the scrollbar navigation device could be augmented or replaced by a device that supports easier navigation, like that shown in Figure 2, around tree-like structures.

Fig. 2. Buttons for navigation in tree-structured sites

Group 2 worked on even more generic designs, although they did find this difficult at times when specific tasks or user models might have been useful. They did categorise web sites as information providers and those where there is real interaction, for example for electronic commerce. Looking at interactional web sites they thought about the way that information would flow during a negotiation, considering synchronisation and other temporal aspects, means of acknowledgement, control and adaptivity. Information providing sites supply the reader with large amounts of information in, hopefully, sensibly sized pages. The group observed that the navigational features provided within the web site such as "Previous" and "Next" can interact unfortunately with the browser's history mechanism, so that the "Back" button moves forward through the web site structure and the "Forward" button moves backward. This led directly to suggestions for web sites to, instead, provide a road map like that in Figure 3, using a Java applet for example. They distinguished between 'local' and 'global' links, where 'local' links move to pages within a web site, and 'global' links move to pages outside that site and arrived at the design guideline that pages should present local and non-local links in quite distinct ways. They used the analogy of a road system, where the local roads that allow a driver to navigate within a city are quite different from the trunk routes which connect different cities. However, unlike in a road network, distance is hard to define within the world-wide web, since the semantic connections between information can be highly subjective, reflecting the interests of a particular user or group.

The group recommended that pages within a single web site should have a uniform look and feel, which would be recognised by users and reinforce their perception of the "localness" of the pages. They pointed out that local links should support tasks, and that link placement could be dependent on patterns of usage.

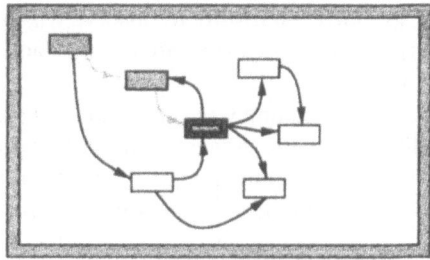

Fig. 3. A map navigation device

Group 2 also looked at how a history mechanism might better be adapted to users' needs. If it is to somehow reflect a user's tasks then these might be determined by a web site's structure, whether hierarchical or linear. Also, different users will have different capabilities.

The process of designing a concrete product also provided a means to make the discussions on tasks and models more concrete and thereby more tractable, and thus fed back into the task analysis and modelling work. Group 1 used the specific example of the DSVIS web proceedings to generate some notion of user models and to extract some tasks from plausible scenarios. Envisaged users were divided into two categories: workshop participants and more general readers interested in the workshop. The more general readers were imagined searching for specific papers by author name, title and keywords. Actual participants might also wish to identify material by the position of the presentation in the workshop programme, or even by diagrams used. These observations lead directly to the suggestion of a form-based interface for searching the proceedings. In this context it was noted that image retrieval based on sketch input was already being developed and could be a real possibility.

This raises an interesting point about what the design process is. Products are intended to meet user requirements but must attempt to fulfil these using proven technology. There is no inherent reason why the result of a requirements elicitation should be implementable at all. The fact that requirements analysis does not usually seem to lead to impossible demands suggests that there are already notions of reasonable solutions embedded in that analysis. One way that this might occur is through low expectations, since modest expectations, especially where they reference existing solutions, will lead to easy to satisfy requirements. It is typically the case that some requirements, whether or not they *could* theoretically be satisfied, will be laid aside in the process of negotiating ease of use, price and time to delivery. All unsatisfiable requirements will need to be removed in this way.

6   The Task-Artefact Cycle

In the previous sections, we have described how some of the group discussions touched upon tasks that web site users may engage in, and artefacts that are constructed to support them. What was especially interesting to observe was how the groups put tasks and artefacts together, to synthesise new tasks and new artefacts — a task-artefact cycle (Carroll and Rosson 1996).

Group 3 spent a lot of time evaluating web sites and browsers, using thought experiments to probe the usability of designs suggested in the case study document and their own, novel designs. They were systematic in their approach to the evaluation, deciding on a user model and a set of assumptions and specifications for the "experiments".

Their user model was 'random behaviour', accessing the information without a particular strategy and in no special order. The goal was set to be 'complete reachability', reaching all the information in the web site. The browser was assumed to provide "Back" and "Forward" history controls. The group agreed on an initial hypothesis that 'successful navigation was more likely if the navigation mechanism closely matched the web page structure in some way.' The loose definition and the limited resources available meant that they did not expect to be able to strongly confirm or refute the hypothesis but it did serve to focus their evaluation.

They initially considered a web site with a sequential structure, where "Next" and "Previous" buttons were provided on the pages. Thinking about this design, they suggested usability problems where individual pages were long. In this situation the reader must scroll through the page to view the required text and then quite possibly scroll up or down to find these navigation buttons before being able to use them. To reduce this informal "distance" between pages, the sequential scroll bar described above was suggested. It was agreed that this would both reduce the distance between different pieces of information and that it would give the reader feedback about where, in an overall, linear structure, the currently displayed text was located. In this respect it was felt that a book metaphor was being exploited, since in a book the reader has an immediate sense of the relative numbers of pages to the left and to the right of the open sides.

Group 3's thought experiments also revealed some potential problems with the sequential scroll bar. If pages are of wildly differing sizes or just very large, then it may be hard to get an accurate idea of location from the scroll bar. With short pages the group pointed out that the device would be unnecessary. Another problem identified was that, even where it is sensible to impose a linear structure on a web site, there may be secondary structure which the user might wish to exploit for efficient reference, dipping into a chapter of a book, for example.

The group next investigated the case where the web site had a tree structure. Considering the use of up and down keys, for moving toward and away from the root note, in conjunction with the sequential scroll bar, for moving within and between sibling nodes, they found no great difficulties. However, when they considered the task of reading text spanning several pages in linear sequence, they found that 'the tree structure makes this impossible.' There is simply no link from one page to its successor; the user must move "up" toward the root of the tree structure and find the appropriate sibling corresponding to linear succession.

Group 3 were very cautious in their conclusions and pointed out that they could not be sure of the ultimate validity of their analyses. Their studies seemed to support the initial hypothesis that a good match between navigation mechanisms and web site structure would be helpful. They qualified this as a design recommendation, however, observing that '[some] designs that attempted to closely represent the web page structure were fiddly and over complex.'

The generic design work presented by group 2 and the more specific design by group 1 indicates that evaluation took place. Unlike group 3, they did not so much present the evaluation as the conclusions of several iterations of the task-artefact cycle. Some of their evaluation was clearly based on the general notion of task conformance, *i.e.* that a user should be able to carry out their typical tasks efficiently. This shows itself in the recommendation that 'local' links should support tasks. Other evaluation, in common with group 1, is based on the user's ability to orient themselves. Group 4 recommended a distinct and uniform look and feel to pages within a site, this was clearly evaluated to assist in orientation. Group 1 designed a DSVIS proceedings web site with home page links on each page, scoring this more highly than other suggestions for the design.

7 Conclusions

The working groups had all displayed considerable energy and enthusiasm, especially considering the length of the timetabled days. We would like to think this is an indication that they enjoyed the case studies and found the working group activity interesting and stimulating. Although we did not see the working groups adopt the kind of strategies we had imagined, we did get to observe a kind of HCI analysis. Whilst the context for the modelling was somewhat contrived, we were at least able to watch the analysis at first hand.

The groups did not work in the way that we had anticipated, in that they did not start by working separately and then comparing their different results. Rather, they started by discussing the problems as groups, trying to make sure that there was common understanding of the issues to be tackled and some possible approaches. Compared with our expectations there was far more discussion and far less work of the form which the participants might undertake in their normal jobs. This can, at least in part, be attributed to difference between working individually and working as a group. We have limited experience of organising such projects and had probably based our expectations on our familiarity with working as individuals.

Several particularly interesting points emerged.

- The *methods described in previous DSVIS proceedings* for analysing interfaces and interaction were almost completely unused by the working groups. It seems to be the case that they are just unsuited to such early stages of analysis with the examples that we presented. It is certainly the case that the groups thought about techniques more than applying them.
- Two groups independently agreed that the primary roles of *formal models* with these examples were to establish agreement and to facilitate communication. These are not typically promoted as the main benefits of formal methods. No proof was performed and no formally defined properties, where proof might have been of value, were investigated. The rigours of formal specification might well have delivered some benefit if the proposed designs were to be taken through to implemented prototypes.
- The *taxonomy of the roles of models* presented by group 4 can be seen as a landmark in the evolution of interaction modelling, in that it is beginning to parcel up "black box" knowledge about where to use what models and what they can be expected to deliver.

We can return to the question of whether there are accepted procedures for analysing and designing interactive systems, whether this process a black box, in the sense of (Latour 1987). Certain patterns emerge from the groups which did substantial design work, *i.e.* 1, 2 and 3. All of these groups seemed to found their investigations on notions about *what* tasks should be supported and then proceeded to think about *how* they could best be supported. They suggested designs and then critiqued them using informally agreed models of the interfaces and plausible scenarios.

However there are large gaps between task models and domain and interface models and the difference in ways of bridging these gaps partially accounts for the difference in the activities of the four groups. Other differences can be attributed to the ways in which the groups perceived their objectives and how they valued diverse usability goals. Group 1 made iterations of the task/model cycle until they were satisfied that they could make hard design recommendations for an example web site. Group 2 underwent a similar process but considered more general web site construction and delivered a set of issues as much as a design. Group 3 modelled two different kinds of web site structure and probed these using thought experiments. Group 4 thought a lot about what they would want to model and why, and particularly what kinds of things would they learn from different kinds of model. Group 4 was perhaps trying to take the most direct route to the discoveries in which we were most interested but this does not necessarily mean that it was the most effective.

In conclusion, we found ourselves opening more black boxes than we were closing. Our expectations about approaches to the problems were challenged by the diverse activities of the different groups and we observed the different ways in which they gravitated toward issues of contribution and validity of models and away from the application of documented techniques. We have thoroughly enjoyed this process of discovery and feel that we have been able to gain real insight into how interface analysis can actually be applied.

A Group Members

We are grateful for the hard work of the working groups and would like to thank all of their members for their contributions.

Group 1

Joëlle Coutaz
Victor Dirda
Gavin Doherty
David Duce *(Reporter)*
Giorgio Faconti
Peter Forbrig
Anthony Hall

Group 2

Ann Blandford *(Reporter)*
Ilse Breedvelt-Schouten
Michael Harrison
Dorian Gorgan
Mieke Massink
Anthony Savidis
Camiel Severijns

Group 3

Richard Butterworth *(Reporter)*
José Campos
Julia Hill
Andreas Homrighausen
Panos Markopoulos
Meurig Sage
Josef Voss

Group 4

Linda Candy
Alan Dix
Ernest Edmonds *(Reporter)*
Michael Freed
Fernando Gamboa Rodriguez
Miguel Gea Megias
Atsumi Imamiya
Bride Mallon
Juan Carlos Torres
Chunbo Zhou

References

Breedvelt-Schouten, I., F. Paternò, and C. Severijns (1997). Reusable structures in task models. See Harrison and Torres (1997).

Carroll, J. M. and M. B. Rosson (1996). Getting around the task artifact cycle: How to make claims and design by scenario. In M. Rudisill, C. Lewis, P. G. Polson, and T. D. McKay (Eds.), *Human computer interface design: success stories, emerging methods and real-world context*. San Francisco: Morgan Kaufmann.

Fields, B., N. Merriam, and A. Dearden (1997). DMVIS: Design, Modelling and Validation of Interactive Systems. See Harrison and Torres (1997).

Gamboa, F. and D. Scapin (1997). Editing MAD task descriptions for specifying user interfaces, at both semantic and presentation levels. See Harrison and Torres (1997).

Harrison, M. and J. Torres (Eds.) (1997). *Proceedings, 4th Eurographics Workshop on Design, Specification, Verification of Interactive Systems*, Springer Computer Science. Springer Wien New York. (This volume).

Latour, B. (1987). *Science in Action: How to Follow Scientists and Engineers Through Society*. Open University Press.

Markopoulos, P., P. Johnson, and J. Rowson (1997). Formal aspects of task based design. See Harrison and Torres (1997).

Wesson, J. L. (1996). User interface evaluation: An empirical study of a primary health-care system in South Africa. In F. Bodart and J. Vanderdonckt (Eds.), *DSVIS Informal Proceedings*, pp. 259–266. University of Namur, Computer Science Department.

Chris Brink, Wolfram Kahl, Gunther Schmidt (eds.)
Relational Methods in Computer Science
1997. 30 figures. XV, 272 pages.
Soft cover DM 69,–, öS 485,–
ISBN 3-211-82971-7

The methods presented in this book include questions of relational databases, applications to program specification, resource-conscious linear logic, semantic and refinement consideration, nonclassical logics for reasoning about programs, tabular methods in software construction, algorithm development, linguistic problems, followed by a comprehensive bibliography. The reader gets an overview of the wide-ranging applicability of relational methods in computer science.

Franc Solina, Walter G. Kropatsch, Reinhard Klette,
Ruzena Bajcsy (eds.)
Advances in Computer Vision
1997. Approx. 50 figures. Approx. 260 pages.
Soft cover DM 69,–, öS 485,–
ISBN 3-211-83022-7
Due: December 1997

Computer vision solutions used to be very specific and difficult to adapt to different or even unforeseen situations. The current development is calling for simple to use yet robust applications that could be employed in various situations. This trend requires the reassessment of some theoretical issues in computer vision. A better general understanding of vision processes, new insights and better theories are needed. The papers selected from the conference staged in Dagstuhl in 1996 to gather scientists from the West and the former eastern-block countries address these goals and cover such fields as 2D images (scale space, morphology, segmentation, neural networks, Hough transform, texture, pyramids), recovery of 3-D structure (shape from shading, optical flow, 3-D object recognition) and how vision is integrated into a larger task-driven framework (hand-eye calibration, navigation, perception-action cycle).

SpringerWienNewYork

Sachsenplatz 4–6, P.O.Box 89, A-1201 Wien, Fax +43-1-330 24 26, e-mail: order@springer.at, Internet: http://www.springer.at
New York, NY 10010, 175 Fifth Avenue • D-14197 Berlin, Heidelberger Platz 3 • Tokyo 113, 3-13 Hongo 3-chome, Bunkyo-ku

SpringerEurographics

Wilfrid Lefer, Michel Grave (eds.)
Visualization in Scientific Computing '97

Proceedings of the Eurographics Workshop in Boulogne-sur-Mer,
France, April 28–30, 1997
1997. 92 partly coloured figures. VII, 187 pages.
Soft cover DM 85,–, öS 595,–
ISBN 3-211-83049-9

Visualization is now recognized as a powerful approach to get insight in large
datasets produced by scientifc experimentations and simulations. The contributions to this book cover technical aspects as well as concrete applications of
visualization in various domains such as finance, physics, astronomy and medi-
cine, providing researchers and engineers with valuable information for setting
up new powerful environments.

Daniel Thalmann, Michiel van de Panne (eds.)
Computer Animation and Simulation '97

Proceedings of the Eurographics Workshop in Budapest,
Hungary, September 1–2, 1997
1997. 121 partly coloured figures. VIII, 203 pages.
Soft cover DM 89,–, öS 625,–
ISBN 3-211-83048-0

The contributions to this book address the problem of synthesizing the realistic
movement and behaviour of human-like characters, simulated animals, fluids,
and other dynamic phenomena. The animation techniques are driven by the
goals of efficiency, as required by real-time interactive animations, and quality,
as demanded by animations used in feature films. This series of workshops provides a high-quality international forum for the exchange of new ideas related
to the themes of character animation, simulation of dynamic natural phenomena, motion capture and analysis, physically-based modeling, behavioral
animation, and visualization.

 SpringerWienNewYork

Sachsenplatz 4-6, P.O.Box 89, A-1201 Wien, Fax +43-1-330 24 26, e-mail: order@springer.at, Internet: http://www.springer.at
New York, NY 10010, 175 Fifth Avenue • D-14197 Berlin, Heidelberger Platz 3 • Tokyo 113, 3-13, Hongo 3-chome, Bunkyo-ku

SpringerEurographics

Julie Dorsey, Philipp Slusallek (eds.)
Rendering Techniques '97
Proceedings of the Eurographics Workshop in St. Etienne, France, June 16–18, 1997
1997. 172 partly coloured figures. IX, 342 pages.
Soft cover DM 118,–, öS 826,–
ISBN 3-211-83001-4

Francois Bodart, Jean Vanderdonckt (eds.)
Design, Specification and Verification of Interactive Systems '96
Proceedings of the Eurographics Workshop in Namur, Belgium, June 5–7, 1996
1996. 114 figures. XI, 383 pages.
Soft cover DM 118,–, öS 826,–
ISBN 3-211-82900-8

Xavier Pueyo, Peter Schröder (eds.)
Rendering Techniques '96
Proceedings of the Eurographics Workshop in Porto, Portugal, June 17–19, 1996
1996. 197 partly coloured figures. IX, 294 pages.
Soft cover DM 118,–, öS 826,–
ISBN 3-211-82883-4

Ronan Boulic, Gerard Hégron (eds.)
Computer Animation and Simulation '96
Proceedings of the Eurographics Workshop in Poitiers,
France, August 31–September 1, 1996
1996. 152 partly coloured figures. X, 225 pages.
Soft cover DM 89,–, öS 625,–
ISBN 3-211-82885-0

SpringerWienNewYork

Sachsenplatz 4-6, P.O.Box 89, A-1201 Wien, Fax +43-1-330 24 26, e-mail: order@springer.at, Internet: http://www.springer.at
New York, NY 10010, 175 Fifth Avenue • D-14197 Berlin, Heidelberger Platz 3 • Tokyo 113, 3-13, Hongo 3-chome, Bunkyo-ku

SpringerEurographics

Martin Göbel, Jacques David, Pavel Slavik, Jarke J. van Wijk (eds.)
Virtual Environments and Scientific Visualization '96
Proceedings of the Eurographics Workshops in Monte Carlo, Monaco,
February 19–20, 1996, and in Prague, Czech Republic, April 23–25, 1996
1996. 169 partly coloured figures. VIII, 324 pages.
Soft cover DM 118,–, öS 826,–
ISBN 3-211-82886-9

Bodo Urban (ed.)
Multimedia '96
Proceedings of the Eurographics Workshop in Rostock,
Federal Republic of Germany, May 28–30, 1996
1996. 71 figures. VII, 178 pages.
Soft cover DM 85,–, öS 595,–
ISBN 3-211-82876-1

Remco C. Veltkamp, Edwin H. Blake (eds.)
Programming Paradigms in Graphics '95
Proceedings of the Eurographics Workshop in Maastricht,
The Netherlands, September 2–3, 1995
1995. 41 partly coloured figures. VIII, 172 pages.
Soft cover DM 94,–, öS 655,–
ISBN 3-211-82788-9

Philippe Palanque, Rémi Bastide (eds.)
Design, Specification and Verification of Interactive Systems '95
Proceedings of the Eurographics Workshop in Toulouse, France, June 7–9, 1995
1995. 153 figures. X, 370 pages.
Soft cover DM 118,–, öS 826,–
ISBN 3-211-82739-0

 SpringerWienNewYork

Sachsenplatz 4-6, P.O.Box 89, A-1201 Wien, Fax +43-1-330 24 26, e-mail: order@springer.at, Internet: http://www.springer.at
New York, NY 10010, 175 Fifth Avenue • D-14197 Berlin, Heidelberger Platz 3 • Tokyo 113, 3-13, Hongo 3-chome, Bunkyo-ku

SpringerEurographics

Martin Göbel (ed.)
Virtual Environments '95
Selected papers of the Eurographics Workshops in Barcelona, Spain, 1993,
and Monte Carlo, Monaco, 1995
1995. 134 partly coloured figures. VII, 307 pages.
Soft cover DM 119,–, öS 832,–
ISBN 3-211-82737-4

Demetri Terzopoulos, Daniel Thalmann (eds.)
Computer Animation and Simulation '95
Proceedings of the Eurographics Workshop in Maastricht, The Netherlands,
September 2–3, 1995
1995. 156 partly coloured figures. VIII, 235 pages.
Soft cover DM 98,–, öS 688,–
ISBN 3-211-82738-2

Riccardo Scateni, Jarke J. van Wijk, Pietro Zanarini (eds.)
Visualization in Scientific Computing '95
Proceedings of the Eurographics Workshop in Chia, Italy, May 3–5, 1995
1995. 110 partly coloured figures. VII, 161 pages.
Soft cover DM 94,–, öS 655,–
ISBN 3-211-82729-3

Patrick M. Hanrahan, Werner Purgathofer (eds.)
Rendering Techniques '95
Proceedings of the Eurographics Workshop in Dublin, Ireland, June 12–14, 1995
1995. 198 partly coloured figures. XI, 372 pages.
Soft cover DM 118,–, öS 826,–
ISBN 3-211-82733-1

Martin Göbel, Heinrich Müller, Bodo Urban (eds.)
Visualization in Scientific Computing
1995. 150 figures. VIII, 238 pages.
Soft cover DM 118,–, öS 826,–
ISBN 3-211-82633-5

 SpringerWienNewYork

Sachsenplatz 4-6, P.O.Box 89, A-1201 Wien, Fax +43-1-330 24 26, e-mail: order@springer.at, Internet: http://www.springer.at
New York, NY 10010, 175 Fifth Avenue • D-14197 Berlin, Heidelberger Platz 3 • Tokyo 113, 3-13, Hongo 3-chome, Bunkyo-ku

Springer-Verlag
and the Environment